The Courage to Be Free

by Charlton Heston

Foreword by Wayne LaPierre

Saudade Press
1-800-697-8844
www.couragetobefree.com

Copyright © 2000 by Saudade Press
All rights reserved, including the right of reproduction in whole or in part in any
form. Saudade Press and colophon are registered trademarks of Saudade Press.

Manufactured in the United States of America.

10   9   8   7   6   5   4   3   2   1

Library of Congress Cataloging-in-Publication Data is available.
ISBN 0-9703688-0-1

Jacket photography by Michael Ives.

All content ©2000 Saudade Press except photography and text which is either
attributed to or reprinted with permission of the copyright owner.

This book, as with what other useful work I may have
done in my life, I dedicate to my wife, Lydia,
whose wisdom, good sense and unwavering love has
carried me throughout our life together.

I must also thank Tim Oden for his crucially valuable pen,
and Carol Lanning, who's long organized just about all I do,
as well as the millions of Americans who've
supported me in this cultural war.

Table of Contents

The Courage of Charlton Heston

By Wayne LaPierre

You, gentle reader, are pages away from feeling inspiration, outrage, pride, insight, humility, perhaps pangs of fear and of hope, and before the curtain falls, the courage to be free.

These things happen when you are in the presence of a legendary actor. Your emotions are awakened. Your life is enriched. Your view is broadened. But this time the actor is a real man, the protagonists are cultural warriors, the stage is your country, and the unfolding plot is yours to write.

In *The Courage to Be Free*, you will witness Charlton Heston, the actor, become Charlton Heston, America's most influential political spokesman who never held an elected political office. Just as he has in film, he has carved out and created an original and powerful interpretation of his role as an American citizen. Except this time, he's writing history.

You will see that Charlton Heston is paying that proverbial price for liberty, eternal vigilance. His vigilance may be mortal, but its spirit is eternal. He sees his beloved country at war within, feasting upon its own heart and consuming its own essence, our personal freedoms. He is not alone.

I know it is almost impossible to think of Charlton Heston as an activist, a sage, or as anything but a reflection of the many men he has played in dozens of – may I say almost fourscore – great American films. He has portrayed many famous men, and a handful of great ones: prophets from the Old and New Testaments, a couple of Christian saints, military generals of various nationalities and different centuries, several kings, a league of statesmen, three American presidents, a French cardinal, and two geniuses, Thomas Jefferson and Michelangelo.

The first films that come to mind are the epics: motion pictures sweeping in scope and often biblical in theme. Films like *Ben Hur* and *The Ten Commandments, The Agony and the Ecstasy* and *El Cid* have been a perfect fit for my friend's craggy good looks and thunderous voice. Charlton Heston may not actually be Moses, but after viewing the man in that deeply touching and spiritually moving role, it is easy to walk away believing that Heston very well could have been an appropriate and capable stand-in, had he been there when the Red Sea parted.

Such is the power and conviction Charlton Heston brings to the wide cinema screen. It's a passion that only the gifted and true believers can claim, displaying a range of emotion that reaches well beyond the camera in Heston's case, most likely because this great spokesman has never been content to rest backstage when America needed a sharp, clear mind and a riveting voice to echo her conscience.

Any Hollywood luminary who has attempted social activism will be quick to affirm that it is much easier, and more lucrative, for actors to remain out of the blistering spotlight of political debate. That's especially true when the brand of politics they espouse doesn't particularly jive with the patently left-of-center line generally adopted by entertainment's elite.

Heston, however, fears no arena and speaks out on behalf of conservative values that have served him well since his boyhood. Charlton Heston grew to manhood in what one can only call an all-American sense, and he has never let go of those middle-class, blue-collar roots that still connect him to the public both as an actor and social commentator.

An Instinct for Courage

To understand Charlton Heston, it helps to understand the lonely, rugged, and uniquely American road that brought him to stardom. His early years were largely cloaked in privacy and, by his own admission, not personally explored until he published his eloquent autobiography, *In the Arena*, in 1995. The story begins in the woods of northern Michigan, where the taciturn young actor-to-be reveled in the rural life, roaming the woods with his dog and gun, bringing home meat for the pot, splitting wood for the cook stove, and battling snowdrifts to walk to the tiny country school where he and a dozen or so fellow students stoked the morning fire to thaw out their inkwells.

Heston recalls those deep, dark woods of his early life as a refuge, a place of dreams and solitude perfectly matched for a shy young man who lived for ideas and the images that danced in his mind. Later he experienced the anguish of a family divorce, and then an unsettling move to the Chicago area during the Depression, where tough times awaited a family now headed by an out-of-work stepfather.

However, it was here that young Charlton learned to work around his shyness through a growing passion for acting. The handsome young thespian of Scottish descent, even then endowed with the voice of a lion, found parts in high school plays, then community theater. He spent those summers sweating through long, tough hours of manual labor in a southside steel mill, earning a much-needed four bits an hour for his toil.

Heston was no stranger to hard work and eventually his dedication paid dividends even greater than his wildest dreams. Charlton was awarded a scholarship to Northwestern University, then and still one of the world's outstanding drama schools. There he met his beloved lifelong wife Lydia, prepared himself for budding stardom on the Broadway stage, and took time out to serve in the military during World War II.

Heston's motion picture career of seventy-nine films and counting has, of course, been sterling. The oft-touted talent carved a niche for himself portraying some of the world's most important historic figures – "far greater men than myself," he is quick to point out. However, I think it may be best to let time be final judge of that statement.

When the Cause Calls

Though I'm now executive vice-president of the National Rifle Association, I first became acquainted with Charlton Heston in the early 1980s when he agreed to appear in the "I'm The NRA" ad campaign.

(You might be interested to know that despite Mr. Heston's gracious warmth, even toward that occasional stranger in a crowd who shouts, "Hey Moses, how about a snapshot with Aunt Jane?" there are unspoken rules of proper address for him. Those who consider him an acquaintance, which includes film crews and most of the civilized world, generally address him as "Mr. Heston." The next layer of colleagues, mostly professional relationships, calls him "C.H." I belong to that very large group. Then there is the small, inner ring of close friends who enjoy use of the more affectionate "Chuck." Finally, there is the exclusive use of "Charlie," reserved for his beloved wife Lydia. And grandson Jack owns sole and absolute worldwide rights to "Ba!")

At that time I was director of the NRA's Institute for Legislative Action and Charlton Heston was, of course, a household name and one of my favorite performers. I knew C.H. was a champion of conservative causes, yet few of us at that time knew that he also had a keen interest in the preservation of the Bill of Rights in general and the Second Amendment in particular.

Heston has championed personal freedoms all of his adult life, even when others found it politically expedient to focus their attention on a more convenient personal and professional course. Few people realize that C.H. was there with Dr. Martin Luther King during the famed Freedom March on Washington in 1963. Heston fought for the civil rights of America's black minority long before the rest of Hollywood jumped on what would later become America's safest, most sacred, and politically correct bandwagon. Even then, Charlton Heston marched to the beat of his conscience and not for headlines or some publicity-generating photo opportunity.

Later, Heston the Democrat watched as his party drifted from its moorings anchored in the basic tenets of the actor's revered Bill of Rights. That's when the Academy Award winner chose to remain steadfast to the values that linked him to his Michigan backwoods childhood, to the hours of backbreaking work in Chicago steel mills that helped finance his education, and to military service for his country during World War II.

Charlton Heston the conservative still marches to his own drum, and the beat remains clear enough to anyone who truly knows him. His is not a party line, but a line connected directly to the old-fashioned brand of constitutional freedom that launched our great American ship of state in 1776. And, as he postulates in these pages, seeing that freedom through now calls upon our personal courage to navigate the stormy seas of cultural warfare.

For example, his outspoken defense of the U.S. Constitution's Second Amendment, the right to keep and bear arms, hasn't exactly been a popular stance among "culturally correct" entertainment and media trendsetters who have been quick to take the world-famous actor to task over his views.

Yet even in the face of powerful peer pressure, Heston has never wavered. He has stood staunch in defense of the Constitution *as it is written*, reluctant to surrender this great document's clear and precise tenets to the vagaries of social fashion or the whim of ever-shifting political wind.

A Lesson in Legends

As a result of C.H.'s proud lead, other famous faces came forward and offered to help NRA with its advertising and public relations efforts. Yet it was Charlton Heston that blazed the trail. He took the first step, endured the ridicule and felt the wrath of anti-gun cultural warmongers. To those of less character, such unwillingness to bend would constitute personal and professional disaster. Charlton Heston, on the other hand, has earned the respect of friends and enemies alike by literally sticking to his guns. Heston's readiness to act in behalf of his convictions carries with it the weight of the celebrity's keen intelligence, quick wit, good humor and above all, fearless candor. Fortunately for the NRA, Charlton Heston had the moral courage to do what he believed was right. Certainly it was a gamble, and a move that easily could have affected his career.

It would have been simpler for an Oscar-winning actor of Heston's stature not to bother with special favors and instead enjoy a comfortable life with his wife and family. After all, it was the NRA that needed Charlton Heston, not the other way around. There was nothing the NRA could give in return except headaches, hassles, demands on his time, and its sincere gratitude when each project was said and done. You can see why it's particularly offensive to C.H. when he is accused of being a paid spokesman for the NRA. He has never asked for, and would never accept, one thin dime from the NRA for his work.

One famous trademark of Charlton Heston is that he comes to the aid of his causes whenever he is needed, despite the inconvenience. At a time in life when most men would be content to enjoy the golden years of their success, Charlton Heston still catches scores of midnight flights, crisscrossing the country, studying complex briefs, and choking down cold sandwiches as he stumps in advocacy of many issues and candidates.

The man's energy remains unbelievable. He can make the 6 A.M. call for a feature film scene on Monday – he'll be there at 5:40 A.M., count on it – appear Tuesday noon on behalf of a political candidate out among the corn and the cows, knock down three newspaper interviews that night, swing through Washington, D.C., for several receptions, address a gathering of the media elite midweek, memorize another ten pages of script and make a film shoot back in L.A. Friday, and then look completely rested for his grandchild's birthday party Saturday morning.

His life teaches us all that being a legend is hard work.

A Model of the Courage to Be Free

It seems fitting that I should end this foreword with a few words about the morality of courage. More than anything else, Charlton Heston believes in values. He sees today's ongoing cultural war against middle class traditions and our long-held heritage of individual liberty as a deepening crack that could wreck more than two centuries of hard-won freedom.

As for a gauge of how much damage has been done, Heston applies the tenets of the Bill of Rights. If new laws, or social or political trends do not sync with the Constitution's Bill of Rights, then Charlton Heston will raise his thunderous voice in protest. That is the theme of this book: Freedom depends on people of courage.

Such fearless conviction is why I and millions more proudly followed him into battle against the forces of cultural war. Like some prophet from the Old Testament, Heston stands tall, stone tablets in hand, to remind us of the black and white of wrong and right. He remains honest as well as eloquent, and continues to rank as one of the most admirable and exemplary men I have ever met.

When Charlton Heston lifted his voice in defense of personal liberty, he made us all better. I thank him for that, just as I'm sure the Founding Fathers look down from heaven and thank him for defending our precious Bill of Rights. They knew that freedom fades among cowards, but thrives among hearts of courage. We are all thankful that such a heart beats within Charlton Heston.

Now in his eighth decade, Charlton Heston retains the powerful voice and talent, the sharp, clear mind, and the strong social conscience that has served as his trademark throughout the years. He remains a devoted husband, loving father, and a grandfather who passionately insists that his grandchildren inherit the same personal freedoms and opportunities available to the generations that came before him.

While others of equal fame bask undisturbed in the glory of their personal accomplishments, Charlton Heston actively and eagerly continues to seek new stages and new roles. Today he is as much a prophet and an integral part of America's public conscience as he is a great actor. The voice remains strong, the vision remains clear. And the nation has been made better off because he was born among us, a relentless and gifted patriot, a one-of-a-kind American, a lesson in what it means to be a legend, and a model for living life with the courage to be free.

Wayne LaPierre
Washington, D.C.
August 2000

CHAPTER ONE

Why Freedom Takes Courage

I tremble for my country when I reflect that God is just.
— Thomas Jefferson

Do you have the courage to be free?

Most of us think of American freedom as something we're just born into. The doctor slaps our newborn bottoms and from then on, freedom is ours. It's handed to us along with our name, race, and citizenship. Like air to breathe and water to drink, this precious thing called American freedom just comes with the territory. It's a blessing all right, but once we've got it, it's a fixed possession. Freedom is our ultimate entitlement.

Courage, on the other hand, is for heroes. It seems to be the domain of soldiers in distant trenches, mothers in dangerous labor, or high school quarterbacks in overtime. We know that occasionally life may demand courage of us in those rare moments of emergency, injury or illness, like when you come upon a highway accident, or your doctor delivers a sobering diagnosis. If the rescue or recovery is courageous enough, we may be rewarded with a headline or a chest-pin or an engraved plaque.

But as a rule, Americans – especially our young – are indifferent to the principle of freedom. It's a yawner. And indifference, not cowardice, is the opposite of courage. So we don't think of courage as a personal daily regimen that's absolutely essential to the preservation of our personal freedoms.

We had better start thinking that way. Because our personal freedoms are under mortal attack in a merciless cultural war that, frankly, we are losing. Winning those freedoms back begins with you, by realizing and rekindling your individual, personal courage to be free.

That's why this is a book about war, and how to win it.

In these essays I want to reflect on the principal erosions, distortions, and perversions of American freedom that I've observed from my three-quarter-century-old vantage point. I want to reflect on ways I've tried to come to their defense. With each treatise I'll recommend a step you can take personally toward living a more courageous life in defense of freedom.

And in the end, I will ask you to make a new covenant with yourself, in the privacy of your own soul, to muster the courage – and then *model* the courage – it takes to be free.

The Nature of Cultural War

We're in sore need of soldiers to fight this war. That's why I enlisted.

My current role is that of sentinel. And for that post, I am grateful. My Creator has given me a talent to entertain you, move you, and perhaps connect you with the hearts and minds of the many great men I have played. My Creator has let me spend my life helping you feel what, perhaps, you didn't know you could feel. I hope to use that same gift here to herald the grave danger that shadows our doorsteps and threatens our Bill of Rights.

I seek to resurrect your greatness of purpose as a citizen of the greatest nation on earth, to reorient the compass of patriotism and conviction that already dwells in your heart, and to move you to action. I want to challenge you first to examine your own heart for the courage to be free, and then to do what it takes to live out that destiny. If I do my part well, the battle will be engaged by one more voice that refuses to let our most basic freedoms as a people be taken captive – *yours*.

While dedicating the memorial at Gettysburg more than a century ago, Abraham Lincoln said of America, "We are now engaged in a great Civil War, testing whether this nation, or any nation so conceived and so dedicated, can long endure." Lincoln was right back then, and if breath were to awaken his soul again, he would survey our social landscape and repeat those words today.

We are once again engaged in a great civil war. But this time it's not a war that divides us North from South, or black from white. It's a cultural war.

To lose this war is to be stripped of our most basic birthright.

To delay in engaging in this war is to diminish the pulsing life blood of freedom that caused this nation to erupt from mud, men, and malfeasance into the miracle that it is.

But let me back up a bit. How do I know this war is raging? Where did I first feel its blows?

In early 1997 I was elected as an officer of the National Rifle Association, a 3.5 million member coalition that preserves and protects the Second Amendment right to keep and bear arms. No sooner than I began my service to this organization than I became a moving target for the media, which has called me everything from "ridiculous" and "duped" to a "brain-injured, senile, crazy old man."

O.K., I admit I'm pretty old. But I sure Lord ain't senile, duped, or brain-injured.

As I've stood in the crosshairs of those who want to shoot down our Second Amendment freedoms, I have realized that I'm not the only target, and firearms are not the only issue. What is at stake is much bigger than firearms or any one man. A cultural war is raging across our land, storming our values, assaulting our freedoms, and killing our self-confidence in who we are and what we believe.

I have proven this premise in meeting after meeting across this nation. Without preface, I pause mid-speech and ask flatly, "By the way, how many of you own a gun? Can we have a show of hands?"

After an awkward moment of collective shifting in chairs and some flustered muttering and furtive glances, a few hands cautiously rise.

Then I ask, with even more command, "All right, how many of you own a *bunch* of guns?"

No additional hands go up. A few even lower their hands quietly sighing in relief.

Now, wait just a minute. I know that, statistically, at least half of my audience is composed of gun owners, and since those statistics are much higher at pro-gun gatherings, *most* of those present own at least half a dozen firearms. I must wonder – How many of those in my audience own guns but choose not to raise their hands? How many almost revealed their conviction about and exercise of a constitutional right, but then thought better of it? What would *you* have done?

If you feel even fleeting doubt, then you're a victim of the cultural war that's raging in our hearts and homes. You're already a casualty of the cultural battle being waged against traditional freedom of beliefs and ideas.

Now maybe you don't care much one way or the other about owning a gun. But I could have asked for a show of hands of Pentecostal Christians, or proud union members, or pro-lifers, or right-to-workers, or Promise Keepers, or school voucher supporters, and the result would be the same. Would you raise your hand if Dan Rather were in the back of the room with a film crew? What if the same question were asked at a PTA meeting in the gym at your child's school?

With an unrelenting barrage of criticism, Americans have been assaulted and robbed of the courage of their convictions. Our pride in who we are, and what we believe, has been ridiculed, ransacked, and plundered. And the result is a willingness to tolerate the erosion of our freedom. Any time a citizen of the United States of America, arguably the freest people on this earth, is shamed into silence because he or she embraces a view at odds with cultural elitists, that citizen has been taken "captive". His freedom has been curtailed.

Cultural war is fought without bullets, bloodshed or armored tanks, but liberty is lost just the same. If we lose this cultural war, you and your country will be less free. You and your fellow citizens will be an increasingly humbled and defeated people.

None of us really *wants* to fight this war. We didn't pick this fight. Most rank-and-file Americans I know *resent* the fact that this war has been foisted upon them. They already go to war for their families every day. They fight to hold down a job, raise responsible kids, make their payments, keep gas in the car, put food on the table and clothes on their backs, and still save a little to live their final days in dignity.

They prefer the America *they* built – the America where you could pray without feeling naive, love without being kinky, sing without profanity, be white without feeling guilty, own a gun without shame, and raise your hand to say so without apology. They long for leaders who will muster some guts, stand on principle, and lead them to victory in this cultural conflict. They are tired of being under siege for their principles and values that have been declared good, right, and just for more than two centuries.

And they are increasingly bewildered and confused when they awaken each morning to find themselves regarded as "lesser citizens" who are "out of touch." After enough breakfast-table trash TV promos enticing their kids not to miss tattooed sex slaves on the next Jerry Springer show...after enough gun-glutted movies and tawdry tabloid talk shows...after enough revisionist history books and prime-time ridicule of religion...after enough Saturday morning commercials for Johnson & Johnson's "Endangered Species" shampoo shaming kids into "saving the earth" by buying their products...after enough cultural cues both subtle and blatant, Americans begin to believe that indeed, *maybe I am out of touch!*

The message from the cultural warlords is everywhere, delivered with the arrogant swagger of absolute confidence. Summarized, it is this: Heaven help the God-fearing, law-abiding, Caucasian, middle class, Protestant (or even worse *evangelical*) Christian, the midwestern or southern (or even worse *rural*) hunter, apparently straight or admitted heterosexual gun-owning (or even worse *NRA-card-carrying*) average working stiff, or even worse still *male* working stiff, because not only do you not count, you're a downright obstacle to social progress. Your tax dollars may be just as welcome and green as you hand them over, but your voice deserves no hearing, your opinion is not enlightened, your media access is virtually nil, and frankly mister, you need to wake up, wise up, and learn a little something about your new America.

And until you do, why don't you just sit down and shut up!

Too many Americans are doing just that. That's why I'm here with a wake-up call.

A Call To Awaken Our Courage

I'm proclaiming a simple, obvious fact as forthrightly and boldly as I can, in as many arenas as I can. We are in danger of becoming numbed by the barrage of cultural messages being hurled at us by the elitists – messages that make the majority feel like they're the minority. We are in danger of being conned out of our constitutional birthright – that not all races deserve rightful pride in their heritage, and not all people are welcome in the warm embrace of freedom. We are in danger of forgetting that red, white, and blue stand for valor, purity, and vigilance.

It's time to say, "Enough!"

Are you a black Republican who speaks good English?

Are you a housewife who considers raising children an important full-time job?

Are you a soldier who shudders at the thought that a woman may someday take a bayonet in the belly and die beside you on some distant battlefield?

Are you a Christian who believes that Southern Baptist is not a synonym for redneck hillbilly?

Do you sometimes wish that homosexuals would keep their lifestyle a matter of personal conviction, not constant controversy?

Do you own a firearm and wish it were once again an honorable responsibility?

Do you realize that each one of these demands courage to be truly free?

If so, you understand the need for this book and the reason why I choose to fight for what I believe during these most meaningful years. Our nation is still a great ship. Those at her helm, however, have let her drift off course.

I hope you find strength and courage in this book that might help us set our ship of state straight again, on course, and flying the banner of personal freedom from her mast.

I hope you feel the indignant passion of Sam Adams, who wrote:

If ye love wealth greater than liberty, the tranquillity of servitude better than the animating contest for freedom, go from us in peace. We ask not your counsels or arms. Crouch down and lick the hands which feed you...and may posterity forget that ye were our countrymen.

My friend, *we shall lick no hand.*

CHAPTER TWO

My Life on the Front Lines

Courage is almost a contradiction in terms: it means
a strong desire to live taking the form of readiness to die.

— Gilbert Keith Chesterton

The U.S. Constitution was handed down to guide us by a bunch of wise, old, dead, white guys who invented our country.

Many people flinch when I make that remark in speeches. Why?

The fact is, what I say is true. The framers of the Constitution *were* white guys, old and undeniably wise, and they sure Lord invented the country. Most of those boy-soldiers who died opposing slavery at Lincoln's invitation in the 1860s were white, too. Why should I be ashamed of them?

Why is "Hispanic pride" or "black pride" a good thing, while "white pride" sounds evil, conjuring images of shaved heads or white hoods?

Why was the Million [black] Man March on Washington in 1995 celebrated as progress, while the Promise Keepers March on Washington in 1997 was greeted with suspicion and ridicule? I'll tell you why: class division.

I've stood against class division before, and I stand against it today.

How can Chuck Heston get away with saying that he's proud of those wise, old, dead, white guys who were our Founding Fathers? Because Chuck Heston was on the front lines of cultural warfare in an earlier era when class distinction was the divisive issue.

It was back in the 1960s and that time, the class division was drawn along racial lines. I was one of the first white soldiers in the civil rights movement's version of cultural warfare, long before it was fashionable in Hollywood...or anywhere else, for that matter.

My first foray on those front lines was but a skirmish; as you'll see, far larger engagements loomed ahead. I was en route to L.A. from shooting *El Cid* in Spain when my dear friend Jolly West, the youthful head of the Department of Psychiatry at the University of Oklahoma and an early advocate for civil rights, called me and asked, "How would you like to come here on your way home and raise a little hell with me?" Several Oklahoma City restaurants still refused to serve blacks and he wanted me to join a small group to picket them. I signed on.

MGM, who still had *Ben-Hur* in release, was very upset. "It's a bad idea, Chuck. You're going to alienate your audience. Keep out of it."

"For pete's sake," I said, *"Ben-Hur's* been in the theaters since 1959. Everyone's seen it at least twice. *El Cid* won't be out for another six months. You think they're going to boycott your movie because I'm picketing to let some poor black kids buy lunch in a dime store? If I generate any publicity, it will only make people want to watch the chariot race one more time!" (The picketing actually did open a few lunch counters in Oklahoma, without any violence in the process. There were an awful lot of TV crews present, I'm glad to say.)

On the Front Lines with Dr. King

The civil rights movement had loomed like a brewing thunderhead on the political horizon that year. The Kennedy Administration was walking a scrupulously cautious line on this issue at the time, perceiving it as a fight they didn't want to get mired into. I figured I'd already gotten into it, so I was glad to accept a breakfast date with Dr. King to discuss the absence of blacks in the Hollywood technical unions. I had succeeded Ronald Reagan as President of the Guild, so he thought I was the guy to see.

Many men who knew him better than I have written about Martin Luther King, Jr. I can't match their eloquence. But I can confirm what they've written. He was a special man, put on this earth, I do believe, to be a twentieth-century Moses for his people. Over coffee and toast in his hotel, I found him to be a very quiet man. Passionately quiet.

"You tell me, Mr. Heston, that there are *no* blacks on Hollywood film crews. As president of the Screen Actors Guild, what can you do about that?"

"I'm afraid not much, sir," I said. "Our Guild has always welcomed black actors, but I must tell you, the technical unions not only won't accept black members, they wouldn't accept me, or anyone who isn't the son of a member. I'm glad to speak for SAG at the inter-guild conference you've called with the studios, but I don't believe you have much of a chance with the technical unions."

I was dead wrong. At the conference that afternoon, Dr. King talked them around. They agreed to eliminate the family rule and accept black apprentices. Amazingly, they also began to take in non-family whites and women, which wasn't even on Dr. King's agenda. He was an awesomely persuasive man, even unintentionally. (Chalk it up to stunning irony that some thirty-five years later, a gifted young Hollywood film director named Spike Lee, a beneficiary of my efforts and Dr. King's persuasion, would suggest to a press corps that I should be shot in the head for my political beliefs.)

At the time I met Dr. King, he was already planning his march on Washington at the end of August, almost two months later. Although Dr. King and his main men were organizing the event, along with the NAACP and the Urban League and some other black groups, the march was open to everyone.

Some of us in the film community decided to organize a group from the arts. Our original thought was to include stage people and writers and painters as well, although I don't recall that we got many volunteers there. For that matter, we didn't get as many film people as I had hoped. I was voted honcho of our little band, probably because the SAG presidency gave me some official status (though I was careful every time I spoke publicly about civil rights to make clear that I was speaking for myself, not for the entire Guild).

I had made a bold statement to MGM to defend my modest Oklahoma City demonstration. But when I left Los Angeles for the blistering, high-profile streets of Washington, D.C. in August of 1963, this actor wondered if I might be an ex-actor when I got back.

We had a good group, though: Burt Lancaster, Jim Garner, Marlon Brando, Paul Newman, and several others. Sidney Poitier and Harry Belafonte signed on, but we had no other prominent black performers.

You can figure out for yourself who should have been there and wasn't. For that matter, I arm-wrestled more than a couple of prominent white actors and directors who opted out – some of the town's most prominent liberals, too! Well, it's been a long time now. They know who they are and I'd just as soon let it rest.

Anyway, Marlon Brando provided enough passion for us all. At our last planning session at my house, he was eloquent on the potential for confrontation. "We should chain ourselves to the Lincoln Memorial," he said. "We'll lie down in front of the White House and block Pennsylvania Avenue."

"No, we won't," I said. "We live in a country where we get to demonstrate peaceably, and that's the way we're gonna do it, or I ain't going." More important, that was the way Dr. King wanted it. And that's the way it was.

As history recorded the event, the march was an enormous success. Before it happened, however, there were faint hearts on every side. Gloomy predictions of civil disorder were common. President Kennedy had invited the leaders of the various groups involved to a reception at the White House afterwards – this was scaled down to a somewhat furtive meeting between President Kennedy and Dr. King.

Our little group arrived in Washington the night before the march for a tactical meeting. I keep saying "our little group" just to make clear how small a number we were among the throngs Dr. King drew together that day. We were twenty or thirty at most, counting some New York people who came down for the day. Per capita, of course, we had more public faces than anyone this side of Dr. King.

Our job was to get as much ink and TV time as possible. Each of the better known actors had a different media statement. I was to speak to the press as we welcomed the last of our New York bunch at Washington's National Airport (now, proudly, Ronald Reagan Washington National Airport). The organizers of the event asked me if it would be okay for James Baldwin to write my statement. He had flown over from Paris to join us and he wanted to make a contribution.

I wasn't crazy about the idea. Jimmy Baldwin was on the left fringe of the civil rights movement and I didn't know how Dr. King felt about his being there. Nevertheless, he was there. When an awful lot of good parlor liberals didn't show in case things turned nasty, Jimmy did. I decided to read whatever Jimmy wrote for me. To my surprise, the speech he wrote wasn't what *he* might have written, but instead, was very close to what I wanted to say. That's the mark of a truly great writer: I was proud to make his words my own, even as he had made my ideas the framework for his words.

For the rest of that shining time in Washington, D.C., we walked behind Dr. King and stood on the steps of the Lincoln Memorial to hear him deliver those powerful, timeless lines, "I have a dream..." We were essentially extras in the event that validated his dream, but we were there. In a long life of activism in support of good causes, I am proud of having stood in the sun behind that man on that morning.

My wife Lydia had come with me to Washington, simply to be there, though she wasn't credentialed to walk with us behind Dr. King. His personal security was paramount, of course, and the FBI had advised Lydia against joining the main body of the march. "We don't know how this will turn out," they said. "You stay in the hotel and watch it on TV." Well, that's not the line to take with my girl. She photographed the crowd from our hotel room balcony, then ran down to join the march on her own, walking alongside a wizened old black man with holes in his shoes. "I'll bet we had a better time than you big dogs up front," she said afterwards. I'll bet she did, too.

After the assassination of John Kennedy, the sky darkened. Still, there were consoling moments. I stood in the Senate Gallery as our senators debated the Civil Rights Act in 1964. Many had questions: "Are we talking about quotas here? Set-asides? Preferential treatment?"

Hubert Humphrey, God rest his soul, stood on the floor of the Senate, held the bill over his head, and swore to eat it page by page if anyone could find in it any mention of special preference. That was a shining moment in American history.

My memories of those days are as clear as I see their parallel with today. It wasn't fashionable then, but in 1963 I marched with Dr. Martin Luther King to uphold the Bill of Rights. It isn't fashionable now, but as an officer of the NRA, I'm doing the same thing. Supporting equal rights of blacks wasn't popular in 1963; supporting the right to gun ownership isn't popular now. Yet it's what I believe is right.

I believe the rights of the Constitution are for every American, not just for some.

I believe the Bill of Rights is just as applicable today as it was two hundred years ago.

I believe in equality before the law. Many of the issues spawned by the current cultural warmongers, however, do not make demands on the principle of equality before the law. They are more concerned about the currency of cultural war – money and votes – than about principle.

The courage to be free requires that we put our time and energy into what we believe. That's why I've formed Arena PAC, my own political action committee. I've chosen to remain personally involved in every way I can. Although I'm physically and financially comfortable, and have a wonderful family and grandchildren I cherish and miss deeply when I'm away from home, I've chosen the rough road of public activism – catching red-eye flights, speaking at rallies in Seattle, and eating pancakes in Bangor and chicken dinners in Des Moines. Sure, Chuck Heston could find less strenuous, more glamorous, and Lord knows more lucrative things to do with his time than stump for conservative issues and candidates out there in Anytown U.S.A. But it's a job I can do better than most, because most can't or won't.

Drawing Lines: Being Right vs. Being Popular

Being right is not the same as being popular. Sadly, our nation seems more concerned these days with popularity than with principle.

Perhaps I should have known what to expect when the earth-shoe generation skipped into the White House with a paisley carpetbag full of social experiments and revisionist history. Bill and Hillary Clinton have been the pied pipers of a cultural revolution that has absolutely nothing to do with the preservation of legal rights. Theirs has been an adolescent uprising bent on burning bridges, not building them – even though they seem especially fond of including bridge-building references in their speeches.

Our president's personal troubles are dramatic proof that cultural war is not merely a clash over the facts, or even between competing philosophies. Rather, it's a clash between the morally principled and the unprincipled.

I'm not talking about whether President Clinton did or did not commit the many foolish transgressions of which he has been accused – so many now that they rule out rational doubt by their sheer volume. I am talking about an entire administration of people who cannot comprehend moral absolutes, and a nation too often willing to accept their conclusions without questioning them. Night after night we are trapped in the silly spectacle of having our values measured by daily polls, as if the definition of the "right thing" changes like a national mood ring.

"What do you think of the president?"

"Wait – after his speech, now how do you feel?"

"Wait – after the White House spin on the issue, now how do you feel?"

"Wait – after the stock market has reacted, now how do you feel?"

"But wait – after the First Lady's interview, now how do you feel?"

Behavior is judged and rejudged based not upon what's right, but upon what seems acceptable at any given moment. The popular opinion poll is one of the favorite weapons used by cultural warriors because it's pure situational ethics couched in the false credibility of numbers.

It's a widely accepted fact that throughout his career, Bill Clinton rarely, if ever, made a decision without first consulting the polls, through which he weighed public opinion and by which he sought to keep his popularity ratings high. Sadly for all of us, this meant that even the president of the United States – and through him, much of our foreign and domestic policy – was held hostage by the talk shows, movies, and television news that formulate public opinion.

Since the media today presents an agenda rather than a simple telling of facts, the public opinion played back to pollsters is actually a predetermined outcome. Most often, this agenda and intended outcome is at odds with traditional, conservative views.

Have we really reached that point in time when our national social policy originates with Geraldo, Oprah, Ricki Lake, and Rosie O'Donnell? If so, I think it's time to pull the plug.

Henry Wadsworth Longfellow wrote about those who knew their cause was just, their values true, and their leader supremely capable:

> By the rude bridge that arched the flood,
> Their flag to April's breeze unfurled,
> Here once the embattled farmers stood,
> And fired the shot heard 'round the world.

The soldiers who fought behind George Washington in the Revolutionary War stood behind him for nine long years. Where is the leader today who proclaims what is true and what is just? From what I can tell, "true" and "just" have been traded in for "correct" and "government-approved."

In my position as president of the National Rifle Association, I have been called many names in recent years...few of them resembling anything good. Plain and simple, our Constitution guarantees law-abiding citizens the right to own a firearm. Why then, if I stand up and remind Americans of this legal right, am I assaulted by the media with such cutting derision?

The reason is simple: Today, the right for the common man to keep and bear firearms – even though that man or woman is a good-hearted, morally decent, law-abiding, and tax-paying citizen – is an increasingly "incorrect" and "unapproved" concept.

The fact that I speak out in behalf of the Second Amendment to the Constitution, the amendment that guarantees every law-abiding citizen the right to keep and bear arms, has cost me some goodwill within my Hollywood community. To have effect, blacklisting doesn't need formalized government persecution like McCarthyism; whispers at cocktail parties can be just as damning. The term "conservative" today can be just as damaging as the term "commie" was back then.

Does that make me want to sit down and keep quiet?

On the contrary.

I am a firm believer in the words of Abraham Lincoln: "With firmness in the right, as God gives us to see the right, let us finish the work we are in...and then we shall save our country."

I am going to confront the increasingly perverse version of America that is being painted by the cultural warlords of the liberal left. *I am going to do the right thing.* I am going to demand of myself and others that we marshal and brandish the courage to be free.

And that is courageous step #1: *Find ways to influence government in all of its forms.* (You'll see more about this on page 150).

CHAPTER THREE

Society Doodled on a Desktop

Every news story should, without any sacrifice of probity or responsibility, display the attributes of fiction, of drama. It should have structure and conflict, problem and denouement, rising action and falling action, a beginning, a middle, and an end. These are not only the essentials of drama; they are the essentials of narrative.

— Reuven Frank,
NBC News memorandum
quoted from Edward Jay Epstein,
News from Nowhere, 1963

"War," as Gen. William Tecumseh Sherman said, "is hell." And often at a level of horror that spins new myth in the culture of both winner and loser, and for a useful purpose.

Some soldiers bring home battlefield memories so deeply disturbing they won't talk about them. The butchery and savagery of both the victor and the vanquished, the piercing screams of the defeated, the frothy blood belching from throats of men writhing in death throes – these horrific images become hushed stories shared around the embers of campfires as petrified youth listen with riveted attention, and learn. Thus, war's awful impact can actually prevent war, at least for a generation.

Cultural warfare, while no less a transfer of power from one group to another, is for the most part seemingly painless. There are no tortured screams or bloody wounds, no limb-strewn nightmares to haunt a generation. In fact, cultural warlords seek to *keep* the battle from becoming bloody. Modern media fills the cultural airwaves with a mist of anesthesia, so that principles and values are slowly desensitized to the coming onslaught. The new culture arrives on the heels of this propaganda. It simply moves in and takes over, like slipping a fine new glove over a numbed hand. The outcome of the war is just as devastating, but without bombs bursting, twisted bodies to bury, or rubble to rebuild. A new class, a different culture, simply takes over.

Cultural war is fueled with one high-octane vapor: elitism. All societies have created layers of elitists who, by virtue of descent or skin color or religious distinction or physical prowess or code of conduct, were deemed superior to others. The preferred class is by definition hard to join. I invite you to try breaking into the caste system of India where an Untouchable has no chance of becoming a Brahmin, or try moving among social classes in Haiti or Libya or communist China.

This is precisely the bigoted system our Founding Fathers sought to overturn. In a capitalist republic, arguably the best system history has produced, anyone willing to work hard enough can join because the Bill of Rights protects everything that anyone needs to pursue happiness.

But in twenty-first century America, it works differently. Just by signing on to a point of view or certain social agenda, you become part of the preferred class. By quietly agreeing that corporate America is inherently evil, or that southern Christians are somewhat dumb and misguided, or that guns are dangerously prevalent, or that Asian lesbians (insert whatever prevailing interest group name here) have more informed views, or that any us-versus-them class concept is superior, you sign on and you're one of the elite.

That's how a bubbly but brainless twenty-five-year-old TV reporter banking on two years at a third-rate journalism school learns to cock her lovely head, cluck her tongue, look down her nose, squint in pained empathy, and parrot what's politically correct. She's set for life.

Maybe it's your favorite sitcom actor instead. In early 2000 it was revealed that the federal government used financial incentives to get the TV networks to put its "policy messages" in the scripts of popular TV shows. I'm talking about high-profile shows like *The Practice* and

ER and *The Drew Carey Show* and *Beverly Hills 90210* and *Chicago Hope*. In fact, the networks actually submitted scripts to the White House for review, who valued the messages it had approved at $22 million. In this case, the messages were drug-related. But it doesn't matter. Where is freedom of speech when TV shows can get government money for writing plotlines the government likes? What does it mean when the White House can quietly weave its agenda into the storylines of the most powerful medium in history?

By no more than agreeing that certain views are better than others, or parroting the government's script, you can gain entry into the preferred class, whose occupants hold views that are considered more valid than yours.

It's the lowest-priced initiation fee in history. But friend, you get what you pay for.

We Used to Beat Up Bullies

In many ways our nation has been vigilant in guarding against elitism, especially on the grand scale. When the time came and there was no turning back, we fought to hold these United States together and abolish the wretched specter of slavery, a social evil that besmirched the honesty of our "free and more perfect union."

At the turn of the century we embraced a flood tide of European immigrants and proved without a doubt that the torch in the hand of Lady Liberty illuminated freedom's path for those of all nationalities, races, and religions. All she asked was good citizenship and an allegiance to the Constitution in return.

Was it wise to throw open our doors to what some called the world's "chaff"? Maybe we best find the answer to that question in the fact that hard-working immigrants who crossed our threshold often rose to a stature higher than those who held the door open to them. Who better epitomizes the America our Founding Fathers dreamed of than leaders who are the descendants of immigrants only decades off the boat?

By World War I, we realized that freedom here at home was contingent upon a broader-based freedom throughout the world, and so we fought. We knew our way was better.

By World War II, we had totally outgrown our adolescence and had become the "terrible swift sword" of liberty that was needed to stop the ruthless spread of fascism advanced by the Axis powers. We had muscle to flex that would blunt aggression, and we stopped the communist march in Korea. It was a new role for a free America, an international agenda that appears inevitable when you put it all in perspective. Fortunately we were strong enough internally to thwart enslaving schemes on an international scale. We were like the quiet, strong, morally incorruptible kid on the school yard whose sudden presence sends the bullies scrambling when they're caught picking on those incapable of fighting back.

At this point in our national adolescence we weren't perfect, of course, but there was much to be proud of as we managed to define a national character during less than one hundred and fifty years of tempestuous growth. I believe in my heart that, up until the Vietnam War years, the world knew that America stood for something. And Americans knew they stood for something, too.

That "something" was clean, honest, and easy to define. We weren't reluctant heroes – we *wanted* to be heroes. In fact, we were passionate in our desire to be heroic. We were Teddy Roosevelt at the bottom of San Juan Hill, country boy marksman Audie Murphy winning medals with his bravery against the Nazis, and General MacArthur wading ashore at Corregidor. We won and were heroes because we expected to win with God on our side for a cause that was right. We were, in real life, a nation that resembled John Wayne playing his best part.

So who would have thought that at this point in our national prime of life our character would begin to crumble? In many ways we seemed oblivious to the decay that started in our national soul, like a kid chewing the candy that'll give him bad teeth.

The unraveling of America's moral fabric began with indifference, the relaxing of the eternal vigil that men like Washington, Jefferson, and Adams warned us about. It happened in the sixties, and since that time too many of us have wrung our hands and sought to spread the blame like barnyard fertilizer when in fact each of us bears a certain amount of responsibility. To quote that great American comic strip philosopher Pogo, "We have met the enemy and he is us."

As a culture, we cornered awfully hard in the sixties. We hit a hard left turn with two wheels off the ground that have never found tread again.

In many ways, the careening is still underway. It can be seen in the ongoing seduction by the entertainment and news-speak industries that continue to undermine our grasp of convention and classical knowledge. It can be heard on the campaign stump in the poll-tested orations of pandering candidates. It can be witnessed in those who espouse the mantras of the sixties even though they wear the garb of the new millennium: the Zegna suit with a pony tail.

What Happened?

What was it that happened in the sixties?

In a simple summary, the mainstream culture became fragmented into a mishmash of mini-cultures, each of which was exploited by the entertainment industry, most notably television news. (It doesn't take much imagination for me to see my journalist friends of that era and before wincing with indignation, their red editing pens moving swiftly to strike the use of "news" in conjunction with the phrase "entertainment industry." Today, however, no one thinks twice about news being *part* of the entertainment industry, forever and inextricably fused – and confused.)

The politicization of the entertainment industry, in turn, spilled over into mainstream news. News from Vietnam was orchestrated rather than reported, which put in motion a trend that has continued to this day: News people see their mission more to perpetuate an agenda than to relay fact. Ask them; they'll proudly tell you they're not just reporting change, but *leading* change.

We began to see stories pushed into our faces as a way to promote political policy. The premise was easy enough. Networks found they could capture public sentiment through a bombardment of orchestrated coverage. Then, when polls reflected the effectiveness of this blanket coverage, vote-counting political leaders started to twitch.

The news machine emerged as a public power broker, and the sad fact is that a few elite reporters managed to unravel our military effort in Vietnam. Facing declining public support at home, politicians increasingly pulled away from the tough decisions required to win that undeclared war. The man on the street saw a military effort corrupted and kids in sweaty fatigues caught in a jungle fight nobody understood, all ten thousand miles away. We became confused as a nation and almost overnight, we lost our nerve and moral compass.

It is little wonder that on the heels of the Vietnam debacle, every fringe group and radical coalition was quick to realize that a prime-time soundbite on their behalf was worth countless hours of lobbying for political power. Every little egotistical tin horn punk suddenly became a cultural dictator emerging from the closet with ambitions to make the evening news. We watched the Black Panthers, the American Indian Movement, Students for a Democratic Society, and many others of the same ilk rise to a false prominence on eighteen-inch screens in our living rooms.

By this time the poison was in the cultural wellspring. Every influential wannabe with a self-styled agenda was lining up to take a drink at the media trough. Rather than trust our instincts and rely upon the hard-won lessons of heritage and tradition, Americans became like a nest full of baby starlings swallowing the sound bites of their media mother. The star-spangled screen became our Zen master and holy land, a fermenting blend of cleverly concocted patter designed to infatuate and titillate, rather than inform. Is it any wonder then that today's young people confuse what they've seen in movies and on TV with textbook applications of history?

The blistering, mesmerizing power of the media has sullied simple truths in countless arenas in recent years: traditional male/female relationships, traditional families, immigration, foreign relations, the military, the environment, the workplace, unions, schools, educational systems and standards, traditional moral and sexual practices, hunting, fishing, and firearm ownership – you get the picture.

A powerful few, including studio bosses and network executives, have teased apart and then reassembled what were once considered commonplace values in America. They have used the tools at their disposal – the very powerful tools of radio, television, contemporary music, and movies – to sandpaper away at our heritage and put in its place a new cultural veneer of their own choosing, a shiny varnish that makes a good first impression but is only a fleck deep. They profiteered with a form of cultural escapism that, in effect, produced cultural division.

Five Reasons Some Doodles Count More than Others

It's not at all difficult for me to imagine a powerful network executive, one with a cultural agenda all his own, sitting at a big desk where he spends each early morning with a cup of coffee and pen in hand, busily doodling away on the back of a customized note pad, making little lines between circles and boxes that represent the new America that will serve his purposes – the one you are to believe in. If those executives can paint that picture vividly enough for you, with enough drama and adrenaline and lust and greed, they can hook you into watching more and more of their message. And the more of their message that you and your kids watch, the more you will come to believe in that reality.

What is this reality that the media hopes to create?

• *First, it is a one-world, global-view, quasi-socialist world.* The ideal world being portrayed is one in which the masses have merged into a broad, lower/middle class that is economically prosperous (to a specified and limited degree) and lives for the pleasure of the moment. The ideal world of the media has few authority figures apart from media superheroes, few nuclear families, and very few expressions of mainstream religion. It has few who embody Horatio Alger dreams of personal accomplishment. The masses live for the next sexual conquest, the next crime event, the next "good time," the next supernatural, abnormal, or paranormal event. I challenge you to tell the difference between sets on the vast majority of primetime sitcoms. All of America seems to live in the same apartment with only minor variances in couch pillows.

• *Second, this ideal world of the elitists is a world filled with aberrant behavior.* And by the sheer weight of its volume, that behavior becomes regarded as the norm. Talk show hosts make sure that every form of behavior and moral decay is given a full hearing – and showing – until viewers conclude that the entire world must be filled with people void of values or morals, and those with values or morals are the perceived aberration.

• *Third, people who count are too few to count.* In this ideal media-manufactured world, the really *important* people are the talk show hosts and news commentators and movie stars, with an occasional emergency-room physician, lawyer, or marine biologist given a smattering of applause. Television is considered to be the great teacher of these new cultural norms.

On Saturday mornings, children learn what is socially acceptable from cartoons that are filled with superheroes who use mind powers to subdue enemies and that portray a world largely of children ruling over adults, a fact that subliminally instills, drip by drip, Saturday by Saturday, a deeply rooted disregard for adult authority.

The values taught by television on Saturday morning are borrowed off the vegetarian platter of the New Age left: The hero despises guns in the hands of the unwashed masses, loves all animals more than his fellow man, hates meat, wants to save the rain forest, considers homosexual relationships more enlightened than heterosexual ones, and sniffs at the inherent evil of all corporate enterprise. And the bad guys? Well, they generally turn out to be not so bad after all – they seem ready and willing to be saved by a few sage words, sent off to rehab, and are soon transformed into someone you'd like to date your teenaged sister. As soon as they give up eating beef, that is.

Genuine individuality, creativity, values of individual freedom and personal responsibility, respect for authority, and legal due process are all but gone. I tell you, Patrick Henry would have sent them all packing in a heated minute.

And yet, the seduction of star power, movies, and TV is so strong that we cling to these images like a heroin addict clings to a syringe. To win the cultural war we must break the pattern, starting with the familiar "test pattern" that once began and ended our family day.

• *Fourth, in this ideal world of the elitists, what is "right" is based upon opinion, not principle or fact.* A definition of what is "right" that is rooted in opinion can fluctuate widely, of course, depending upon which audience is being polled for its opinion at any given time. It can be adjusted quickly to accommodate the audience that is contributing the greatest amount of money or votes toward the elitist camp. The political left, it seems, will let anyone in their tent if there's a donkey on the hat, a check in the mail, or some yen in the fortune cookie.

Issues related to the gay and lesbian movement provide an example of this. Many hugely talented artists and executives – dear friends of mine – are homosexuals. I do not denigrate their lifestyle, though I don't share it. As long as gay and lesbian Americans are as productive, law-abiding, and private as the rest of us, I think America owes them absolute tolerance. They share the identical set of constitutional rights as any other child born beneath these precious American skies.

Nevertheless, I find my blood pressure rising when Clinton's cultural shock troops participate in *gay*-rights fund-raisers while they indignantly boycott *gun*-rights fund-raisers. I find it the height of hypocrisy for politicians to declare that guns are morally "wrong" and then in the very next speech, claim it's morally "appropriate" to place homosexual men in tents with Boy Scouts, morally responsible to pass new laws that elevate and favor a gay lifestyle, and morally acceptable to suggest that sperm donor babies born into lesbian relationships are somehow better served and more loved than babies born to married heterosexual couples.

In fact, in Iowa, you can now get a college scholarship just for being a gay high school student. According to an Associated Press story, three scholarships a year covering tuition, fees, and books will be given to "openly gay high school students" who want to attend the University of Northern Iowa, Iowa State University or the University of Iowa. The funding comes from an openly gay Des Moines businessman and was announced by Iowa governor Tom Vilsack in early 2000. Apparently earning the scholarship is not a matter of achievement in academics or sports, but prowess at overt displays of homosexual preference – as a *teenager*, no less. The scholarships cover tuition, fees, and books at any of three Iowa universities. I have to wonder…just how do applicants compete for that scholarship?

The left has an amazing ability to declare which legal rights are "in" and which are "out," and which legal rights are currently "moral" and which are "immoral." In most cases, those rights that are "in" and "moral" are those that are backed with the most money.

Furthermore, when what is "right" is based solely on opinion, the consequences of being "wrong" can also be defined by opinion. A case in point is the issue of sexual crime. We have numerous examples in our nation's recent history of the truth that sex between consenting adults can shatter the career of the army's most senior enlisted man. A sexual infraction can wreck the life of a corporate executive. In fact, sexual gossip *alone* can forever impugn the integrity of a Supreme Court nominee. Yet with the right spin by the right people, and by taking the right polls, the top political officeholder of the nation can be declared clearly culpable but gleefully forgiven. Why? Because the polls don't support punishment. The crime is not in question; the potential value of punishment is in question.

We don't need to look far or wide to see examples of these practices at work again and again. That's how cultural war operates. It's a war of declaring opinions to be the truth. It's a way of declaring that the elite – and only the elite – dictate opinions. It's a war of intimidation, name-calling, word-parsing and situational ridicule.

• *Fifth, in the world of the elitists, everybody is assigned a moniker.* Without stereotypical classification, how are they to tell who's who? How are they to determine which classes of people and which classes of ideas are in or out?

I remember when European Jews were forced to wear labels to identify themselves as a group of people who were declared to be inferior, unwanted, ridiculed. The Nazis pinned them with yellow stars as identity badges, many all the way to the gas chambers.

What kind of "star" is being figuratively pinned on your chest today?

Which label is it that puts you on the "outside" of the elitist camp?

How are they trying to tag you?

The current battle on the Second Amendment front is all about labels and tags. Owners are being defined as "good gun" and "bad gun" owners. Armed with the overwhelming intimidation of greedy lawyers, the Clinton Administration is even defining "good" gun manufacturers versus "bad" gun manufacturers.

Of course, there are no good or bad guns or manufacturers, only good or bad people. But with phony labels like "high-capacity," "Saturday Night Special," "assault weapon," "rapid fire," "cheap import," or "non-sporting," the result of the tagging is the same. There may not be a Gestapo officer on every street corner, but the influence on our culture is just as suffocating and pervasive. Freedom, bit by precious bit, is lost.

I mention guns because gun owners, especially, have taken an uppercut to the chin. But so, too, have evangelical Christians, anti-abortionists, heterosexuals, hunters, stay-at-home mothers, rural landowners, home schoolers, and others who have sought to maintain America's heritage. If you noticed how each label conjured a stereotype in your head, then you see that the labelling campaign is quite effective, indeed.

I'm not saying that those listed above are any more "right" or "wrong" than those who hold different views, or that the list above is complete. I mention these only to stress that in an America protected by the Bill of Rights, we have a right to believe and do and be what is legal, without being subject to a collusion of cultural censorship and condemnation.

I'm saying we have a moral right to live free of labels that tag us as inferior or suspect.

We have a right to live according to the rule of law and the principles of moral decency, rather than according to a system based upon cultural doodling.

We have a right to live according to majority rule, not social engineering.

Our ancestors in this nation declared that we have room here in America for those who may seem out of step, who march to what poets call a different drum, as long as they do no harm. Including conservatives. Including gun owners. Including religious people with moral values. Including all law-abiding citizens of every color, race, and cultural persuasion.

To declare any one group in our nation to be hopelessly out of step or out of touch is to denigrate that group into a status of perpetual ridicule and bigotry. It is also to pave the way for that group to be annihilated – just ask those who were found to be out of step at Waco and Ruby Ridge. There must have been a tear in the eye of Lady Liberty when those flames soared and those bullets flew.

Breaking Free to Be Free

If our nation is going to break free of the cultural stranglehold the media and entertainment industry has imposed, we are going to have to exert enormous willpower backed up by a healthy distrust of the sugarcoated prime-time offerings intended to seduce us.

We are going to have to turn off a significant portion of the media messages we are currently ingesting without a burp, and start thinking for ourselves. And that won't be easy. The infiltration of television, radio, and newspapers into our social structure is strong. Millions of our children now regard rock music icons as prophets. Millions of adults look upon television news anchormen as saints. We've developed a dizzying crush on the entertainment business, and no one knows better than I that celebrities must weigh their words and deeds carefully. We do not always invite it, but much we do and say is digested with earnest devotion.

There are many, many good people in the media industry. There are still some tough, no-nonsense reporters and news anchors who will not tolerate meddling with the truth. Unfortunately, they're vastly eclipsed by propaganda mill puppets with little to offer other than attractive faces advancing titillating tragedy as news. Very often they are the ones used to front the agendas aimed at the sterilization of our nation and the ones used to fight our traditions, fight our heritage, and fight our cultural institutions and individual freedoms with their cynical clucking. We are going to have to ferret out the differences between media voices and choose to listen only to those who back up what they say with verifiable facts, historical precedent, and credible context. And we're going to have to engage in thoughtful debate and refuse to accept split-second "spin" on issues that are important to the preservation of our freedoms.

Faster Isn't Always Better, Just Faster

I don't apologize, but instead appreciate, that my view is the circumspect product of three-quarters of a century of observation.

I wasn't born at a particularly easy time in American history. The Great Depression was skulking just around the corner, and after that came World War II and a call to duty. Countless American lives were lost, and that war seared scars on my soul as well as on the souls of most veterans. Freedom, however, demands a premium price. We who fought knew that, and we were willing to pay to the point of putting our lives on the line. I sometimes wonder now if our nation still has the courage and conviction to fight such a war. Or would the pundits talk us out of it, and find it easier to make a deal with the devil?

I shuddered at the blinding glare over Hiroshima, yet thanked God we would not have to fly air cover for the landings on the main islands of Japan. I agonized over the unrelenting bloodshed in Korea, the first war I felt the politicians wouldn't let us win decisively.

I despaired when the Russians beat us with Sputnik, and rejoiced when Americans touched down on the moon. The twentieth century spawned more change than mankind had witnessed in all the other preceding centuries combined. More human drama was played out in the twentieth century than in the entire prior history of the world.

The rapid change in my lifetime has sometimes made me wistful for simpler days. On the other hand, it has also kept me mentally tough and on my toes. Those who slowed their pace during the twentieth century were left behind the rest. Survival was the state of grace bequeathed to those of us who chose to keep learning.

Sadly, though, the pace of modern America has left little time for contemplation or reflection. My grandfather's people plowed with mules and, as a direct result of that tedious process, the straight furrow they cut was a source of pride. Then came the tractor, and multiple furrows were possible with one pass of the field. The emphasis necessarily shifted to speed and quantity, with quality often left in the dust.

The same might be said concerning the emergence of the electronic media and its emphasis on instant news and instant cultural commentary. The old tintype press created an exercise in deliberate news gathering, balanced reporting, and precise fact checking.

It required the consumer of the finished product to read, think, and digest.

Modern journalism is vastly different. News is gathered and issued and consumed in the half hour before either reporter or listener has a chance to put the facts through a filter of meaning and values. Deliberation and balance, being second with the story but getting the facts right, are considered as old-fashioned as a mule-drawn plow in a cornfield.

There simply are no rewards given for plowing the straight furrow, for telling the whole story, for pausing for reflection that gives context, and for mustering the restraint to speak without spin.

Americans, by choice, have less and less "think" time. The result is that they either find themselves confused by the constant barrage of conflicting and "updated" information that originates from a variety of camps and undisclosed, yet touted as reliable, sources. Or they simply grow apathetic and withdraw from the process, adopting the attitudinal watchword of our day, "whatever."

To remain viable as a free, moral nation we must always seek the truth, simply because it *is* the truth. We must demand clarity, character, and honesty from those who lead us, and be willing to fight for it if fighting is what it takes. If we don't, then our rights are going to be buried under an avalanche of pandering political rhetoric and the sleazy, speakeasy slander of modern news entertainment.

In addition to valuing facts more than opinions – and demanding thoughtful debate rather than "spin" – we are going to have to refuse to abandon the look-alike, act-alike, think-alike, dress-alike, talk-alike media society. I seem to recall that as the Chairman Mao syndrome.

We are going to have to reassert our individuality, and celebrate our individuality as decent, commonsense people, and refuse to buy the media "image" and definitions of success, prosperity, morality, and freedom.

If ABC or MSNBC or Jenny Jones or *Dateline* knows best, I haven't seen it evidenced yet. The result seems to be even more gratuitous sex, seedy social commentary, and brutal violence dished up in the name of entertainment. If this is the mirror of the America they seek to sculpt, I will oppose it.

There is much you and I can do to resist being put into the mass-media-created mold.

First, refuse to run for cover when the cultural cannons roar. Remember who you are and what you believe, then raise your hand, stand up, and speak out. Don't be shamed or startled into lockstep conformity by seemingly powerful people.

Second, defeat the criminals and their apologists. Oust the biased and bigoted. Disavow the self-appointed social puppeteers whose relentless arrogance fuels this vicious war against so much that we hold so dear. Do not yield. Do not divide. Do not call truce.

Third, focus on those things you can do, rather than on those things you think you can't do or shouldn't do.

You can resist revisionism and cultural manipulation with the same passion our forefathers reserved for their resistance of the crown.

You can speak out and vote against those who seek to perpetuate with legislation the agenda created by the media.

As a free, independent, strong-willed American citizen, you can boycott the movies that undermine our cherished heritage and traditions.

You can talk to your children or grandchildren about what they listen to on their boom boxes, watch on TV, and access on the Internet. You can offer alternative viewpoints for them to ponder.

You can attend church and PTA, volunteer for scouting programs, and write letters to the editors of the papers you read.

You can support organizations like the National Rifle Association and others that support constitutional rights.

You can campaign, run for office, and vote in every election – not just every four years.

You can attend town hall and city council meetings and let your opinions be known.

I know these things are hard to do. They take time and effort and courage of conviction. But friend, it takes courage to be free. It takes energy to battle networks and studios armed with millions of dollars. It takes passion to remain free Americans united by the Bill of Rights rather than obedient lemmings divided into manageable factions.

It takes vigilance not to fall prey to a sly news-anchor eyebrow lift. It takes bravery to voice an opinion different from a blistering commentary seen and heard by millions.

You and I must fight on doggedly when and how and where we can. It is tougher, more arduous, and more lonely down here in the trenches than in some command post called a news desk. But while we are here in the trenches, let us share good company and good cheer with the spunk and spirit of our Founding Fathers.

They promised us life, liberty, and the *pursuit* of happiness. They didn't promise us happiness, remember…only the chance to chase it. And being politically correct is not the way to get there.

If our ancestors believed in political correctness, we would still be King George's boys, subjects bound to the British crown. Seek to be politically competent, yes; politically confident and politically courageous, yes; but never politically correct.

This leads to courageous step # 2: *Be willing to disobey* (discussed more on page 151).

The elitists may have society doodled on their desktops, but we-the-people still have the right to reject what they say and what they show – if we have the courage to do so. Remember: In the end, we own the pen with which they write and the paper on which they scribble.

CHAPTER FOUR

How We Lost More than the Farm

Take me home, country roads,
To the place I belong...

— "Take Me Home, Country Roads"
by John Denver, Bill Danoff & Taffy Danoff

Not long ago, I was traveling by car through America's heartland, and I discovered a place I would have sworn had disappeared, at least according to what the news media tells me.

It was an election year with lots of political races to speak at, whistle-stop style. We had started out on our journey early that day and I was ready for some mid-morning coffee and a chance to stretch my legs. An interstate highway sign held out the hope of a small community just off the four-lane turnpike. I was eager to slow down for a few minutes and fill my eyes with the sight of foot-high wheat and grazing cattle and perhaps spot a black and white heifer grazing in front of a big red barn, a tractor churning up rich loamy dirt, and maybe some fresh white sheets flapping on a clothesline.

I miss such things. These are memories from my midwestern youth and I harbor a faith that they still exist in the heartland of America. So, we turned off the well-manicured and sterile lanes of turnpike asphalt and dipped the nose of our car down into a little road without a yellow stripe but richly lined in summer green grass.

The place wasn't big by any stretch, even counting the cows. The sign said the population hovered about 3,150, but I barely saw a soul. The streets were empty. The cafe's neon sign was turned off. There wasn't a tractor in sight. The gas station with its ancient red pumps and spic-and-span restrooms seemed abandoned.

I guess I've spent too much time in a big city because my first thoughts weren't pretty. My imagination ran along the lines of a mass murder or plague. Then I remembered. It was Sunday morning!

We hooked a right turn onto a side street and there they were: long rows of pickup trucks, some rusty, some shiny new, along with station wagons, mini-vans, and Fords and Chevys galore, and one motorcycle, all lined up on the parking lot of a place of worship. Then another. And another. One brick, one whitewashed wood, one stucco and glass. Each one proudly standing underneath a cross. The town had gone to church on the Sabbath Day.

For twenty minutes we cased that town like a robber might, and I can say in all honesty that barely a soul was stirring outside of those churches. In my mind I could hear the hearty singing of hymns ricocheting off freshly painted walls, and for a moment my soul sang along. A few minutes later we headed back toward the interstate, where we found a gas station open and hot coffee brewing. I commented that the little town had sure seemed quiet that day. The attendant, an old geezer even older than I, hit me with a hard stare totally lacking in celebrity recognition and snapped back, "It's Sunday morning. What did you expect?"

I answered back, more truthfully than he will ever realize, "Nothing quite so wonderful."

I may be branded an old-fashioned square, if that's even the proper terminology these days, but I can't hide my admiration for a community that gathers around an altar on a Sunday morning. What I'd witnessed in that small midwestern hamlet was a living Norman Rockwell painting. Quaint, sure. But an American still life painted from real life. I could sense the moral fiber that bound that community together. I was only there a few minutes but I knew that a place that prayed together was also a place that played together and that honored the traditions of freedom and clung to long-standing rules of fairness, honesty, individual responsibility, and collective caregiving.

It saddens me that many of our small towns out there in the breadbasket are dying and that rural communities today may be ghost towns tomorrow. It also saddens me that such a place would seem laughable to the body-pierced hordes of young people who hang out in what now passes for my home town.

From the days of the colonial Founding Fathers – when Thomas Jefferson considered the "yeoman farmer" to be the best steward of virtue and liberty – to urban centers and suburban sprawl of today, our nation has undergone a profound transformation. We've grown from one society into two.

Let me draw the distinctions in broad strokes. On one side, we have a rural society based on farming, with a belief in independent self-determination, individual initiative, and mutual trust. On the other side stands an urban culture in which the individual is subordinate to the group, where transience and congestion alienate man from the land and from his fellow man, where upheaval and social decay give way to crime and a climate of fear, and where many are satisfied to sacrifice essential liberty for the illusion of safety.

So who started the cultural war, and why?

For the answer, meet me at the city limits. That's the symbolic battleground.

A Cultural Collision at the City Limits

As you become a more astute observer of the cultural war in which we find ourselves, you will find that the stinking root of most of the conflict grows from a vicious rift between urban and rural American values. In almost every act of cultural war, it's there somewhere: the fight between the city boys and the country boys. Look past the facts and faces of issues under debate, and you'll see one party calmly chewing on a wheat stalk while the other is flip-phoning 911.

In rural America, the clouds naturally skywrite "No Trespassing." Here prevail the tradition of taking care of one's own, a presumed independence from intrusion, a history of looking after our families, our land, and our property, and a culture where we take responsibility for these things personally.

Not so when you cross the big city limits.

In urban America a different notion thrives: almost complete dependence upon and full delegation of responsibility to others for one's safety and well-being. This is a new concept in our history, but one familiar to European serf descendants. (This mentality is one reason the recent gun confiscation in England met with such weak resistance.) City dwellers have come to see the government as the surrogate to take care of one's person and property, much the way serfs relied upon the king's armies to patrol the castle walls.

Thus our nation is increasingly at odds with itself.

Rural residents look at our cities and see uncontrolled crime and blight, and city-slickers who want to deprive them of their rights when they can't even keep the trash picked up on time.

Urban dwellers, in turn, look out at the farmland and see backwards, backwoods rustics too outdated or stupid to understand the "realities" of the modern world. And the media wielded by these urban dwellers reflects this bias – brutally.

The result is mutual distrust: two sides vying for the heart of the nation with little room for compromise anywhere near the middle.

How did this happen? And, how can we regain at least some of our lost common ground?

Whatever lifestyle differences there might have been were compounded by a divisive lava flow of economic opportunity in the nineteenth century. The Industrial Revolution was the engine driving the split. Abandoning their farms, people moved closer to the factories, which in turn built cities along the rivers of the East, the railroads of the West, and later, the modern-day airline hubs and fiber-optic backbones of the Information Age. It was a natural evolution that built the America of today. We gained a great deal. But we also lost a lot in the bargain.

We grew less independent. In time, people came to depend on the mills and their paternalistic managers; they literally began to owe their souls to the company store. As the farm gave way to the factory, citizens found themselves dependent upon others for everything from food and fuel to transportation and shelter. In time, a class hierarchy akin to medieval serfdom developed, as the Andy Carnegies of management built their own neighborhoods and schools, looking down from their mansions upon the Ed Nortons on the factory floor and across the railroad tracks.

With so many families depending on so few employers, the shutdown of a mill could mean economic collapse. So during the Depression, social programs were enacted to shield families from hardship. As good an idea as it was at the time, this safety net slowly became a hammock that ultimately supported a Great Society of social ills – from chronic unemployment to welfare dependency, drug abuse, the breakdown of the nuclear family, and entitlement as a new birthright.

As our work ethic changed, so did our relationship to the land. The "back forty" became the suburban yard and city park. The kitchen garden and family cow were replaced by the supermarket, the milkman, and the time-installment loan.

Relationships between neighbors also changed. Earlier the door was unlocked even if Dad knew where the key was, and behind it stood a shotgun – not for any burglar or midnight rapist, but as a standard implement of rural life, like a hammer, hatchet, or the Case knife in every country boy's pocket. If you needed a hand to slaughter a hog in the fall, or stand up a pole-barn in the spring, you knew you could count on your neighbors and in turn, they counted on you.

By contrast, in many of today's cities, you're lucky to learn your neighbors' names before they're transferred to another city where they'll nod to their new neighbors on the way to their passcode-validated sanctums of work and home. Along with urban transience and social decay, a distrust has developed in our cities – a distrust for the individual, and a disdain for the freedoms that criminals abuse.

I've often wondered if the "gang problem" wouldn't disappear if we had a few more barns to pitch full of hay and a few more cows that needed a 4 A.M. milking. Vandalism was almost unheard of when we all knew the faces behind the mailboxes and spoke directly to those faces at school social events. In small schools of 300 or 400 students, each child has an opportunity to participate, either in clubs or athletics. In schools of 3,000 or 4,000 students, many children become little more than numbers and are lost in the shuffling masses. Too often these children turn to trouble in a desperate, adolescent urge to be counted as a member of the human race.

Once our churches delivered groceries to families in need. Today those groceries come in a van delivered to your door by state or federal agencies. Thus, the hungry too often have no one to thank personally, the charitable too often have no one to love personally, and the children too often have no one to learn from personally. What is missing is the face-to-face caring, the strong social bonds that held us together as a people united, the sense that America is for Americans and that we are all family, bolstered by the unbreakable bonds of our similarities and strengthened by the pride we take in our differences.

The high priests of the cultural conversion promised they could provide a better life, and for higher and higher taxes, they proffered more guarantees. What they have delivered are overpriced, shoddy goods and services, and only to those who know how to work the system or those willing to totally abandon their pride. The chicken in every pot came with a much bigger price tag than the cost of the chicken and the pot combined.

The stratification of class in cities has bred crime and led to an emasculation of individual responsibility and personal initiative. Mega-metropoli create compressed, distrustful little sub-societies that are willing to sacrifice privacy and surrender individual rights so they can be collectively protected by "the system" – a complex, expensive, self-perpetuating bureaucracy with a manifesto that is generally self-defeating and pointlessly unenforceable.

The Cost of Freedom Lost

Consider the absurd extent and obscene cost of this collective helplessness.

City-dwellers seek to live in communities gated by ironworks and, if they're lucky, a little hut with a convincing guard in an ill-fitting uniform to befuddle would-be criminals. Apartment, condo, and car alarm systems chirp, scream, and wail to an indifferent populace, intended not so much to warn their owners of intruders but ostensibly to notify *someone else* to do something about it. In fact, few urban sounds provoke more indifference and annoyance than a yelping siren from a parked luxury car.

Businesses and neighborhoods hire private police forces to patrol their properties. Entire blocks of buildings are surrounded by a moat of keycards, security code pads, swipe panels, and video monitors. Metal detectors, motion sensors, and security cameras routinely greet us at doorways to places both public and private.

Urban citizens increasingly huddle behind the uncertain protection of frustrated and embittered law enforcement agencies, while criminals dart through gaping cracks left by societal and political disarray. In return for no gain in freer social intercourse or personal safety, we are barring our windows and scanning our bodies, ever elevating the suspicion with which we eye one another and, by example, we are teaching our children that to live in fear of others is normal behavior. All of this only leads to less and less personal freedom, to mutual distrust, and in turn, to the divisive effect of cultural conflict.

The result is that the uniform freedom that once blanketed us from one shining sea to the other has been shattered into shards governed by geography. Some places are, literally, more free than other places. Cross this state line or that city limit, and the quality of your freedom elevates or declines.

From opposite rims of this chasm carved by the cultural warmongers, we look at each other with accusatory misunderstanding and arrogance. The rural citizen looks at his urban brother and sees a wholesale abandonment of freedom, while the city dweller looks at his rural counterpart and sees an anachronism.

Taking Sides vs. Mending Fences

Who's right?

Who should prevail?

If the choice were mine to make, I think I'd err on the side of the rural. And that's not borne of sentimental nostalgia or lamenting loss of something that never was.

I like what I see when I look at the rural enclaves of the North, South, East, and West today. The boys and girls there are different somehow. More confident, maybe. Less afraid of the conventional aspects of life. And certainly less inclined to turn to drugs to relieve the reality that some youths misread as boredom.

Rural youth still reflect a richer time, when boys worked with their fathers and even emulated their walk and talk. Through the years, country boys seemed to grow into men eagerly and early because we gave them the opportunity to do so. They had to hunt and fish for the table, trap for hides to sell for cash, fix their own brakes and adjust their own carburetors, plow a field when Dad had calves to pull, stretch barbed wire, toss a seventy-five-pound square bale of hay on a truck with everything they had – essentially 150 pounds of sixteen-year-old bone, gut, sweat, and sinew – and learn animal husbandry by delivering a new lamb.

Their sisters grew to womanhood learning to manage, feed, and heal the household. Country girls at an early age could run things almost as well as their mothers could, and nobody considered their work a shameful task. "Housewife," "cooking," and "sewing" were noble words. Women weren't afraid to be strong in their femininity and reach out with unrestrained toughness to hold a family together, often functioning as teacher, preacher, and psychologist. Country women were nearly always considered to be a full partner – separate but equal – and they were proud of their vital role in taming the land and creating a culture of freedom and strength. They did not insist their men adopt feminine qualities, but jealously guarded those traits for themselves.

Country people carried firearms openly in their farm truck gun racks. They lived behind open windows and unlocked doors. In their communities, rape was an aberration and murder was almost nonexistent.

You may remember Truman Capote's chilling book, *In Cold Blood*, about two drifters who murdered an all-American farm family in Kansas because they had heard a rumor that money was stashed in their house. That was the crime of the decade that shocked the nation. Now such savagery is nightly headline news.

Yep, if I have to make the choice between the nightly humming of katydids in the country and the nightly humming of police and ambulance sirens in the city, I'll take the country.

I suspect our Founding Fathers would, too.

When the Founding Fathers framed the Constitution, they had their descendants of the heartland in mind. Our system of government was designed to work from the bottom up, a sort of pyramid of freedom with a broad base of power in hamlets and cities, then counties and states, with a small pinnacle of federal government way up there at the tiny sharp point.

This sensible concept has gone the way of the horse and buggy, but the trip has certainly not been worth the price of the ticket. When politicians inverted that pyramid, all the power flowed to the tip, and small towns and rural areas lost their voice, their hope, and their political muscle. Changes in tax codes made it impossible for small family farms to stay small and in the family, and the mayors of the big cities usurped the political clout once administered by men and women of the soil.

So now we have city-states where faceless throngs fight for space on freeways. We live in subdivisions where neighbors rarely speak or in apartment complexes where residents don't even bother to meet their neighbors at all. In such a culture, children can starve or be brutally abused, and crime victims can lie bleeding where they fall without anyone knowing or caring, even though hundreds of fellow citizens live only a few feet away. Compare that to an earlier America where "welfare" came in the form of neighbor helping neighbor, and where extended families included entire communities that stretched for miles.

No wonder rural Americans stare at urbanites and see the wholesale abandonment of personal freedom. And urban Americans look at their rural cousins and envision a return to the days of the Neanderthal. And right in the big fat middle of this clash of cultural beliefs is each faction's views of government, crime, and the ownership of firearms.

Gun Ownership: Symbol of the Clash

The firearm stands as a symbol dividing these two worlds, because it gives the common man or woman the most uncommon of personal freedoms.

For the urbanite, the gun is a symbol of universal menace. It's the icon chosen to display over the news anchor's shoulder on each day's TV reports of crime and murder. It's the engine of hatred and mayhem, the sign of bloodshed and fear.

For the rural resident, the gun remains an emblem of responsibility, self-sufficiency, personal independence, and the security of hearth and home.

A good many of those trucks that I described in the opening story of this chapter had guns in gun racks gleaming through their back windows. Now I don't believe those were outlaws doing penance on the Sabbath, do you? Of course not. (At this writing, presidential candidate Al Gore is proposing a ban on firearms at churches, as if worshippers were liable to fall into Satan's hands at any moment.) No, those trucks were owned by men and women who use firearms as a working tool on their farms and ranches. No doubt the gun racks also held a coil of rope and a pair of fencing pliers. I wonder if the media commentators would like to ban those tools, too.

It's through the glasses of urban-rural conflict that a teenager's birding shotgun has been transformed from a "tool" of life into, in the words of President Clinton, "a crime or an accident waiting to happen." The rugged individualism of Jefferson's self-reliant "yeoman farmer" – with shovel and gun equally slung over the shoulder in useful, law-abiding intent – has given way to an image that is far different. The urban citizen now sees the rural gun owner as a threat to public safety, an unpredictable joker in the pack, a laughable leftover of some bygone era. You see his image regularly in the movies: the imbalanced rural bumpkin with bad teeth, suppressed sexuality, a worn Bible, and a gun.

Because of gangs and firearm abuses in places like Philadelphia, Boston, and Los Angeles, we've essentially made criminals out of farm boys and girls who carry guns in the vehicles they park at school in hopes of getting in a few hours of hunting after class. Consider the image now called to mind when you hear the innocent phrase "teenager with a gun." That's the problem we face when laws flow down from the top of an all-powerful government rather than bubbling up from the strength of a million small communities.

And what about the response of city and urban citizens to laws related to freedom? Take the "right to carry" laws in some three dozen states as an example. The outraged liberal press predicted a return to some movie version of the "wild, wild west" – they vividly predicted street corner shootouts where disputes would invite armed response, and road-enraged drivers would routinely take potshots at one another. Nothing of the sort has ever materialized.

In fact, in the many states that have passed laws allowing law-abiding citizens the right to carry firearms in public, violent crime rates have declined universally and often sharply.

Of course! The beauty of concealed carry laws is that the ninety-six percent of citizens who do *not* carry firearms benefit from the four percent who *do* carry firearms, because the bad guys don't know the difference. Criminals are leery of approaching, let alone attacking, a potential victim who might be armed. That's why one of the fastest-growing groups of Americans buying handguns today is single women – many of whom have a couple of kids, an absent or dead-beat husband, a night-shift job cleaning an office building, a 3 A.M. bus to catch, and a dark walk to their homes six blocks from the bus stop. Are we surprised they would choose to carry a gun when given the legal opportunity?

Liberals and urbanites don't understand this phenomenon.

Heartland citizens understand it immediately and completely. It's called freedom, and individual responsibility is its watchword.

Small-Town Values: A Big Idea

So how might we proceed, given the fact that this urban/rural dichotomy exists?

Let me quickly assure you that I know we can't and shouldn't roll America back to the agrarian society that sustained us just a few short decades ago. It's not only unwise but probably impossible to do so. The movies that are shown, the CDs that spin, and the videos for rent in the country town are the same as those one might find in Miami, Pittsburgh, or Atlanta. Kids who hunt, fish, sew, and raise calves for the spring livestock show are also seduced by the Howard Sterns and the Dr. Dres and the bloody violence Hollywood dishes up in five-channel surround sound.

One common theme of modern media is that the trends of the East and West Coasts should be adopted by the center of the nation. It's a big lie. Let me tell you from firsthand experience that there is nothing in Hollywood or New York that is any better than the friends and neighbors and churches and schools of the place where you live. The trees on your street are just as beautiful as those that line the streets of Beverly Hills or shade Central Park. The plays at your local high school are just as important as those performed on Hollywood sound stages. (After all, as a kid I got my start in high school and community theater out in the Midwest.)

Simply because the urban world is so pervasive in its tentacles into the rural world does not mean, however, that we should abandon the values that a hard-working, freedom-loving, independent rural society came to represent. We've been pressed into cities because that is where the jobs are. A sense of community, however, does not have to die somewhere out there on the outskirts of the city.

To begin with, we must learn to abandon the idea that big government or a president or a bureaucratic clique will provide the answers to our hopes and prayers. The conservationists have a slogan, "Think Globally, Act Locally." That may be a good idea to adopt as we begin to rebuild the basic formation and foundation of how our society works. Here's what I mean:

• First of all, think of it this way: *where you are – your street, your block, your neighborhood – is the most important place in the universe.* Even large cities have neighborhood boundaries that seem to present themselves naturally, and those neighborhoods must become your priority. Make your neighborhood your nation within a nation, one of those tried-and-true building blocks that holds our democracy above defeat.

• When you have the chance, *elect congressmen and senators who reflect that place where you are.* Even more important to you and the lives of your children are city councils, chambers of commerce, boards of education, and churches. These are key organizations in binding your community together and beating the cultural generals who seek to own the heart and soul of America.

• *Be an active part of where you are.* Adopt rural neighborliness for your neighborhood. Sponsor block parties. Go to school functions. Support neighborhood children in their school activities. Help elect local representatives who will work for the streets, schools, utilities, and law enforcement in the place where you live. Write letters and make telephone calls concerning issues that affect your neighborhood. Most of all, take pride in your street, your block, your neighborhood, your township, your community, your city, your county, and your state – in that order.

When you do this, you turn things right-side-up again; the power in freedom's pyramid returns to the base where we, the people, dwell. It returns us to the way the Constitution intended for our nation to function.

"Community-thinking" and "community-acting" give an opportunity for the values of good citizenship to take root and flourish. This kind of thinking and acting takes us back to a time when crowing cocks and lowing cattle welcomed the morning. We can once again be as that traditional America was, simply by bringing those same values and beliefs to the places we call home today.

We *are* the neighborhood cop, the local priest, and the butcher down at the corner grocery. Learn to know your neighborhood clerks and shopkeepers by name. Greet them with kindness and concern for their families. Our cold, cruel big cities can become a system of warm and friendly small towns if we'll only think of them that way.

Forget the contemporary model of "big brother takes care of us" that the cultural reformers hope we'll buy. Let's get it back to "neighbor-cares-for-neighbor," no matter where your neighbor resides, and in so doing, be free again.

If you think locally, if you establish a sense of community where you live, then the law will reflect your morals and mores, rather than those of a news anchor or a Washington politician or some other self-appointed cultural savior. The elimination of elitism starts on your street and on your block, at your church, and in your school. It happens because you participate in the planning, well-being, and long-term best interests of your very own home.

If we learn to act locally, and to believe in our community and form strong social bonds there, then our churches, schools, and local government will be a reflection of who we are. And that requires courageous step #3: *Take absolute and resolute pride in your own values* (see page 152).

That, I believe, is what the Founding Fathers intended.

CHAPTER FIVE

Raging Revisionism

God cannot alter the past, but historians can.
— Samuel Butler, English novelist

Look at me.

Where else but in America could a lanky country kid named Charlton sprout in the anonymity of the Michigan north woods and forge a life that makes a difference?

My country put the gift of freedom into my hands and said, "Here, kid. Let's see what you can do with it." That's why I so deeply love this great nation and the Constitution that defines it.

Just about everything good about me – who I am and what I've done – can be traced back to some smoking muskets and a radical Declaration of Independence by ragtag rebels. Wearing threadbare coats and marching on bloody feet, they defeated the finest army assembled in that century, and they gave the world hope. Within them flowed an undercurrent of personal freedom and a relentless sense of what is right, and it flowed so irresistibly strong that they simply could not abandon it.

But today's cultural warriors are trying hard to do just that. They're revising and rewriting historic truths, and attempting to yank the Bill of Rights from our lives like a weathered handbill stuck under a windshield wiper.

They're trading tradition for whatever teases with more immediate reward. Self-gratification is displacing honor, greed is erasing good taste, and the desires of the moment are undermining basic morality. We are fast becoming a self-serving, boorish, and arrogant people quick to dismiss anything of substance that obstructs indulging our undisciplined desires.

As a tool of cultural derailment, revisionism knows no equal. The power to bewitch is there, and the incantations are not only easy to swallow, they are eagerly sought by our television-addicted society. Think on these things when you behold the power of our enemy, the seducers who would circumvent our pride and reinvent our national heritage. They, my friends, are the storm troops that lead the assault in the cultural war.

Increasingly we are becoming victims of the cultural war's Big Lie.

Victims and Variations of the Big Lie

To me, the Big Lie isn't just the parade of duplicities of the past twenty-five years, but also our country's collective acceptance and apathy toward deception in general. Without large numbers of believers, there can be no Big Lie.

The Big Lie can be as simple and profound as Bill Clinton saying he didn't when he did. The Big Lie is renewed whenever an influential person in our culture says or presents something as true which is not verifiably true.

But come on, you say. Does it really make a difference that sometimes people speak lies and believe lies and repeat lies? Sure it does!

Suppose for a minute that you have a loved one who is serving in the armed forces. What if the leader of our nation says that your son or daughter in the military must face a wartime deployment because "the cause is just"? Your willingness to send your child off to war can only be as strong as your belief that the cause truly is just. Your support for the war in which your child is involved is only as strong as your conviction that what your leader is telling you is true. This is how the secure girders that underpin our country can quickly rust and crumble from cultural dishonesty.

Revisionism surrounds us, clouding our view of the past and its hard-earned lessons. Consider the popular renewal and redefinition of relations with Viet Nam. Modern journalists have written off to fading history the horrors inflicted upon the Southeast Asian peninsula of

Cambodia, Laos and Viet Nam, where the second-largest campaign of genocide in the twentieth century took place. As we go to press, the fight over the future of a little Cuban boy named Elian Gonzalez, who washed up on the Miami shore, has revealed a chilling level of acceptance of that contentious communist island nation, an embracement unthinkable just years ago. Somehow, suddenly, "Cuba's not so bad."

Everywhere we turn we are confronted by similar incarnations of the Big Lie. And perhaps no place more insidiously so than in our schools and in the textbooks our children are reading.

I may not agree with much of what Pat Buchanan has to say these days, but one of his essays a few years ago made this point. He accurately noted that Benedict Arnold's treason at West Point has been dropped from many history texts, as has the story of Nathan Hale, the boy-patriot who spied on the British and whose only regret facing the gallows was having "but one life to give for my country." Buchanan pointed out:

> They teach that our Constitution was plagiarized from the Iroquois and that Western science was stolen from sub-Sahara Africa. The name Custer has been stricken from the battlefield where his unit fell. Demands are heard through the South that replicas of the Battle Flag of the Confederacy be removed from state flags and public buildings.

Buchanan goes on, addressing the stealthy evidence of revisionism:

> We see it in the altered calendar of holidays we are invited – nay, instructed – to celebrate. Washington's birthday disappears into Presidents Day. States like Arizona, that balk at declaring Martin Luther King's birthday a holiday, face political censure and convention boycotts. Easter is displaced by Earth Day, Christmas becomes Winter Break, [and] Christmas Day a day to reflect on the cultural imperialism and genocidal racism of the "dead white males" who raped this continent while exterminating its noblest inhabitants.

That doesn't sound like America anymore to me. Although my years are long, I wasn't there to help pen the Bill of Rights. And popular assumptions aside, the same goes for the Ten Commandments. Yet, as an American and a man who believes in God's mighty presence, I treasure both. And I lived in, fought for, and cherish an America that valued both.

Guns: The Revisionists' Favorite Target

Perhaps in no more clearly defined area has one issue been subjected to revisionism: firearms and firearm freedoms. Among the cultural revisionists and contemporary thought police, guns are the symbol of evil most often invoked against an old-fashioned, traditional, constitutional American culture. Firearms personify the struggle between traditional and New Age political reckoning, between the Constitution and contemporary revisionist theory that seeks to rewrite both history and the Bill of Rights.

I say "personify" because in this clash, inanimate guns have been assigned human attributes. Guns literally are portrayed as having the power to think ("smart" guns), to act ("assault" guns), to choose between right and wrong ("crime" guns), to move about (guns "flood" or "are awash in the streets"), to convey timely intent ("Saturday Night Special"), and even commit crime ("people are killed by guns"). Guns seem to be endowed by the media with the capability to maim and kill at random, as if no human hand ever placed a finger upon a trigger.

Guns are also portrayed as sinister devices capable of some mystifying power that can turn a good man bad. Simply touching one of these precisely machined tools of wood, plastic, and steel can supposedly bring out the beast in an otherwise kind and loving heart. Guns turn Dr. Jekyll into Mr. Hyde and choir boys into mass murderers. It's as if anyone who has the audacity to gaze upon or touch one of these treacherous and devious tools of doom should be suspect.

The fact, of course, is that a gun is a gun is a gun. The technological advances are nice for efficiency, accuracy, and durability. But they're irrelevant to the *purpose* of a firearm. That's divined only by its user. A gun fires a projectile with a charge of powder that exits the barrel and ends up as an extension of the eye of the shooter. That's all. A gun won't, can't, and will never do anything more.

The Tactics of Revisionism

The gun issue reveals several tactics of revisionism that apply to other areas of American culture as well – labelling, vilifying, and catastrophizing.

For two decades, gun owners have been so busy dodging phony salvos about "plastic guns" or "assault weapons" that we have ignored the source of these attacks – journalists who are in pursuit of a utopia in which there is no Second Amendment. All the nonsensical chatter about "cop-killer bullets" and "Saturday Night Specials" and "clip capacity" and "high power" and "rapid fire" has drowned out the critical fact that the media wants to eliminate the presumption that our Second Amendment rights are as sacred as their First Amendment right to free speech. Were it otherwise, these mythical issues would have vaporized on principle alone. Because the truth is that firearms in the hands of good people are a threat to no one except bad people.

I have talked to gun owners all across the nation and they ask the same question over and over. How, they ask, can we believe anything the anti-gun media says when they can't even get the nomenclature right? When it comes to gun issues, reporters rarely call the NRA, America's firearm authority; instead they parrot manufactured statistics and fabricated technical support from organizations that wouldn't know a semi-auto from a sharp stick. That's why the media has so little credibility on gun issues among more than seventy million gun owners, more than fifteen million hunters, and among the millions of veterans who learned the hard way which end of a gun the bullet comes out.

Firearms and firearms ownership have been subjected to massive misinformation and a dearth of objective coverage by a media that, on any other issue, would deploy investigative reporters and researchers without hesitation. They seem to possess little regard for the *facts* because they already know their *feelings*. Revisionists say what they say and facts fall where they may, which is generally a fair distance from the truth.

Take, for instance, the trumped-up myth of "Saturday Night Specials." The catchphrase has endured because it paints a memorable but fraudulent picture of crooks buying shoddy handguns to commit crimes on Saturday nights. The commonly-used curse of "cheap handguns" is another favorite from the gun-hater's lexicon that commits linguistic trickery because the phrase reduces a human being's right of self-defense to a price point. When did affordability become a crime? How does choosing a tool of less-than-the-best quality suggest criminal intent?

Freedom can't be restricted by the price point of the tools used to exercise it. Many young couples and grandmothers, for example, choose to buy a lower-priced, lower-quality hammer. It might be used to hang a picture or two, but never for serious carpentry. In fact, it may lie unused for a lifetime. The same applies to a firearm. Must lower-income Americans be excluded from gun ownership because they choose to spend $150 instead of $900 on a handgun? (Of course, the only firearm that truly deserves exclusion is one of such poor quality it doesn't fire properly or is unsafe to use. Like any other product unsuitable for its intended use, such guns, if any, should be eradicated under product liability law.)

Nonetheless, the gun-ban crowd and their media allies have spent three decades telling us that "Saturday Night Specials" are the "weapon of choice" of criminals, when in fact nobody can define what a "Saturday Night Special" is. When a ban on so-called "Saturday Night Specials" was debated in the Maryland Legislature, the toughest problem lawmakers faced was defining the gun they hoped to ban!

What it came down to was this: They eventually blacklisted the figment of some public relations firm's imagination. But the "weapon of choice of criminals" was never actually any such thing, according to the police. Crooks don't want a small, inexpensive handgun. Small, inexpensive handguns are the choice of senior citizens so they can defend themselves, of single moms and others on limited incomes, and of folks who have obtained concealed carry permits and want just such a gun for personal protection in case of an emergency.

No, according to police, criminals want the biggest, baddest, most expensive handgun they can steal or buy on the black market, which is where almost all of them get their guns anyway. Even so, a concocted story about the inherent evil of small, inexpensive handguns grew into a sinister chapter of contemporary American folklore. And such guns are now banned in Maryland – if you can figure out what they are.

Semi-Automatics, Semi-Intellects, and Right-to-Carry Revisionism

When new synthetic polymers and rugged plastics came along that were found to work well in firearm construction and be almost impervious to the elements, the anti-gunners went straight up the wall. They invented a new nonexistent bogeyman, the "plastic gun." They didn't like old guns, much less new and improved ones. Never mind that law enforcement agencies around the world were adopting the new, lighter, tougher models as quickly as they came off the assembly lines.

Suddenly the gun-banning cultural reformers had a novel tactic. They claimed that so-called "plastic guns" couldn't be detected by airport security devices and should therefore be banned. Overnight they invented "hijacking guns." But the NRA proved in scientific tests that the firearms they sought to ban had more than ample metal in them to trigger the alarms. The "plastic hijacker's gun" was another media myth.

The same guns that were almost made extinct by negative press a few years ago are today commonplace, state of the art, highly reputable, and carried by the majority of peace officers across the nation. (And to my knowledge, not once used to defy airport security.) Had they been banned, it would have been the equivalent of banning automatic transmissions in automobiles. That's how much the anti-gun crowd hates progress. They don't want any guns on hand, much less better and more efficient ones.

In America, however, we are a nation of craftsmen. We make good tools better. The old lever-action repeaters that came to symbolize the West didn't look much like the cap and ball firearms that preceded them, either. Styles change, mechanisms evolve, technology improves.

The invention of repeating firearms came about more than a century ago. Skilled craftsmen figured out a way to make a gun use its own recoil and gasses to reload itself. When the trigger was pulled, the firearm simply ejected the spent shell and slid another into the chamber to be fired. No magic and end-of-the-world distress were involved in this invention, or in the announcement of this invention at the time. It was just a simple mechanical action that saved the operator the effort of working a lever, slide, or bolt. Everybody loves convenience, right?

Today semi-automatic firearms are regularly criticized in many circles of novices exclusively because they *look* like military firearms. Indeed, some of them *do* look military, but Jeeps and dozens of other products also resemble their military counterparts. A military *appearance* may say something about a tool's quality and durability. Yet on this tide of ignorance and misinformation, many popular semi-autos have been banned based *solely on cosmetic features*, not how they function. Many others are on the current hit list, and sporting arms could follow if the latitude of the laws is expanded as the anti-gunners hope it will be.

Gun haters are still attacking semi-autos to this day, trying to sell the public the lie that semi-autos fire like fully-automatic machine guns when, in fact, they can't and don't. They're trying to sell the public on the notion that semi-autos are now the favorite gun of criminals, which is also not true, according to police data. (By the way, anti-gunners never seem to mention the fact that fully-automatic firearms, properly called machine guns, have been virtually banned since 1934 and are only strictly registered and licensed under close government scrutiny.)

Today's semi-autos are functionally *identical* to those of Teddy Roosevelt's day. But now this hundred-year-old firearm technology has been redefined by revisionists as something new and sinister. Media reporters are fed press releases that drop the "semi-" off the "semi-automatic" and infer that semi-autos operate like "rapid-fire" fully-automatic military firearms, when they do not, never have, and never could. Semi-autos fire one bullet for each trigger squeeze, just like a bolt or lever or pump action. The only difference is that the gun reloads itself. Most expert shooters can fire double-action revolvers faster than semi-autos – I have seen displays of such skill. But that's not the issue. The point is that the *facts* about guns and gun crime are routinely distorted or ignored.

That's especially true of the most fundamental but false revisionists' tenet, that outright gun bans and gun confiscation make us safer. That's why the gun haters howled as, state by state, legislatures have passed right-to-carry permit provisions for law-abiding citizens. Every time, the anti-gunners forecast all sorts of dire consequences about gunfights in the streets that recalled matinee posters of old-time western movies. Nothing of the sort ever materialized. Nothing even close.

In fact, as mentioned earlier and worthy of repeating, right-to-carry states have not only uniformly experienced a reduction in violent crime, they have enjoyed this result with almost no problems with permit holders – a handful of incidents law enforcement official reports call "statistically insignificant."

On the other hand, police officers have documented many instances in which concealed-carry firearms were used to thwart a crime in progress or an attempt on a permit holder's life. Which means countless thousands of other crimes have been averted and gone unreported, simply because *nothing bad happened.*

That's the Second Amendment in action. That's the way the right to keep and bear arms is supposed to work. And that's the way it does work, as long as you and I and generations to follow understand the truth about the Second Amendment and fight the revisionists to keep that right for the common man and woman.

Otherwise the elitist cultural revisionists will succeed with their penitential cleansing of lawful firearms from our nation. They are unwilling to do what is necessary to defeat armed crime, which is to enforce plentiful and potent existing laws. They prefer that lawful gun owners be shamed and blamed for the crimes of others and seek absolution by surrendering their guns.

That's been under way for some time in England and Australia. I have seen lines of submissive citizens, whose only alternative is imprisonment, bitterly surrendering family heirlooms – guns that won their freedom – to the sawblade and blast furnace. If this fact does not unsettle you, then you're already anesthetized. You're already a casualty of the cultural war.

Reconnecting with Your Unrevised World

How can we reconnect with the truth and get back to an America that is "unrevised"?

Let me offer three suggestions that compose an antidote for revisionism.

• *First, connect with your past.* Not just the historic past of our country's origins and its foundations of freedom, but the ancient past that echoes only in your soul. It sounds spacy, but it's important. And you don't need a time machine to connect with the beginning of time.

To connect with the past, simply walk outside on the next clear night and gaze upward at the stars. In an instant you're transported back to epochs in the universe long before eyes existed to perceive it. You're seeing the past in exquisitely perfect detail, looking at things precisely as they appeared seconds, minutes, years, and millions of lightyears ago. Follow the outline of the Big Dipper and, if you're about my age, you're looking at light that left those stars near the date of your birth. When you glance at the night sky, your view embraces a million snapshots in time at once, from moments ago to infinitely long ago.

If you stand there long enough, gazing into the infinity of space and time past, you'll no doubt come to the conclusion that few things in life matter as much as the courage to freely navigate our own course through life, and to do so with self-respect, dignity, and integrity. You'll gain some perspective on what's important in life. You'll gain some insight into *why* you need to make your life count for something, and *why* you need the courage to stand up for what is enduring and true.

• *Second, connect with your present.* One of the best ways I know to do this is to become familiar with the members of your local school board. If you have children or grandchildren in school, get to know their teachers. Read their textbooks.

You're likely to find some things in your child's textbook that make your blood run cold. You may very well discover that things you *know* to be true are represented as fiction, or maybe as "theory only," or considered unimportant, or ignored altogether. You may find huge gaps between the truth that you were taught, what life has taught you, and the opinions that are taught today.

Even if you don't have kids or grandkids in the local school system, do your homework, do your research and do it well, and then voice your opinions to your local school board. Talk to other parents and encourage them to join you at the school board meeting. Refuse to remain silent.

Any time you encounter something that you *know* has been revised so that the truthful representation of the facts is no longer in evidence, take issue with the revisionists. Write the principal, call the station, talk to the teacher, write the newspaper, ask questions, raise hell.

• *Third, connect with your future.* This is easier than it sounds. Again, you don't need a time machine. All you need to do is to stare deeply into the eyes of a child you love. If that child is over the age of seven, his or her values are already fixed. You are literally looking into the decades that lie ahead, and through that youngster, to generations yet unborn.

If you look at and listen long enough to a child you love, you'll feel a tremendous responsibility welling up within you to ensure that this child walks in freedom, not ignorance and bondage. In order for this child you love to walk in freedom, he or she must walk alongside other children who are equally informed and free, and who together, live in a society that is based upon fundamental and inalienable rights of self-determination, self-expression, and self-value.

You'll probably also feel a profoundly unsettling sense, as I do, that we are on the verge of allowing the flame of freedom's once white-hot torch to grow cold. If the precious torch that burns in you and me is extinguished by the revisionists' fog of falsehoods, and is discarded as archaic and irrelevant, it will be because we did not teach our children about the real courage it takes to nurture freedom.

These three concepts are the underpinning for courageous step #4: *Defend America as the peerless ideal – period.* (Please turn to page 153 for more about this important conviction.)

CHAPTER SIX

The Second Amendment: America's First Freedom

A well regulated militia being necessary to the security of a free state, the right of the people to keep and bear Arms, shall not be infringed.

— Amendment II
The Constitution of the United States of America

Prepare for some of my prideful heresy.

No history teacher may say so, and certainly few journalists would admit it, but the Bill of Rights are numbered one through ten almost by pure chance. The numbers do not indicate value or preeminence. The numbers do not appraise the amendments, only count them. Indeed, such hairsplitting over their order would annoy our Founders. They would admonish us that trying to analyze the ordinal value of the Ten Amendments is as absurd as trying to analyze the ordinal value of the Ten Commandments.

I propose, however, that there is a first among equals.

Consider this. Let's say you had to start a free country from scratch and could pick just one freedom from the list of ten – just *one* of the ten items in the Bill of Rights to start things off on a good footing. Which one would it be?

If the Bill of Rights lists the supreme laws for humans to live in freedom, as I claim it does, then which right among them comes first?

There's no argument. It must be the Second Amendment right to keep and bear arms.

Popular culture ignores this fact completely. Today the Second Amendment is not only *not* ranked as first in importance, many do not even regard it as the second, third, seventh, or eleventh. In fact, the right to keep and bear arms is essentially off the list, treated like America's crazy uncle in the attic, an embarrassing and regrettable reality acknowledged only with the wishful prayer that a merciful death might come soon.

I've made my life's work delivering the words of other men. So I naturally stand strong in defense of the First Amendment's guarantee of free speech. Certainly a free nation must have a free press and free speech to battle injustice, unmask corruption, and provide a voice for those desperately in need of a fair and impartial stage. But I wonder how many journalists would agree with me that the Second Amendment, the right to keep and bear arms, is not only *equally* vital, but *more* vital to protect all the other rights we employ and enjoy?

The Second Amendment is, in order of importance, the *first* amendment. The Second Amendment is America's first freedom, because it is the one right that protects all the others. Among the freedoms of speech, of the press, of religion, of assembly, of redress of grievances, it is the first among equals. The right to keep and bear arms is the one right that permits "rights" to exist at all.

It's the right that says free men and women may take up arms to defend their lives, their families, their property, and their country. In the entire Bill of Rights, only the Second Amendment right to keep and bear arms creates the absolute capacity to live without fear and, therefore, to pursue happiness.

No other people on earth can get this close: If you want to feel the warm breath of freedom upon your neck, if you want to touch the pulse of liberty that beat in our Founding Fathers, you may do so through the majesty of the Second Amendment. Because there, in that wooden stock and blued steel of a firearm, resides what gives the most common man or woman the most uncommon of freedoms. When ordinary hands are free to own this extraordinary symbol, representing the full measure of human dignity and liberty and self-determination, that is as good as it gets. Yet this precious freedom exists on a fragile piece of parchment barely a hair's breadth thick, and is manifest only when we honorably live out its words.

The Second Amendment alone is gloriously unique in the world. It's not about owning a firearm alone, but about what such ownership represents. It doesn't matter whether its purpose is to defend our shores or your front door, whether it's a rite of passage for a young man or a tool of survival for a young woman, or whether it brings meat for the table or trophies for the shelf. Without respect to age, gender, race, or class, the Second Amendment right to keep and bear arms connects us all, with all that is *right*.

This chapter, then, is an essay about guns – why we have them, why the Bill of Rights guarantees that we can have them, and why my right to own a gun is ultimately more important than the media's right to rail against it.

A Freedom as Fresh as Today's Headlines

The right to keep and bear arms is not archaic. It is not an outdated, dusty idea some old guys dreamed up in fear of redcoats, and it existed long before they found this land. It is just as essential to liberty today as it was two hundred years ago. That may be a bitter truth for some to swallow (when I spoke at the National Press Club in 1997 these words did not play well), but those who occupy the booths at the corner bar and grill intuitively understand the need for the Second Amendment – especially those who have lived through riots, anarchy, earthquakes, floods, hurricanes or other natural disasters that trigger collapse of social order.

What's worse, media efforts to undermine the Second Amendment, to deride it and degrade it, to readily accept diluting it and willingly promote redefining it, threaten not only the physical well-being of millions of Americans but also the core concept of individual liberty our Founding Fathers struggled to perfect and protect.

In fact, in a two-year study the Media Research Center found that network TV news was biased *ten to one* against firearms rights advocates. Network news has become "the communications division of the anti-gun lobby," said Brent Bozell, the center's chairman. The group analyzed 653 morning and evening news stories from 1997 to 1999 and found stories advocating gun control outnumbered those opposing it by a ratio of ten to one. That's not journalism; that's advocacy.

Let me provide a short refresher course in constitutional history.

The original amendments we call the Bill of Rights contain ten of what the Constitution's framers termed "inalienable rights." These rights were drafted in random order and were linked by their essential equality. The Bill of Rights came to us with blinders on. This document does not recognize color or class or wealth. The rights it protects are not only the rights of actors or editors or reporters, but they extend even to those we love to hate, and with good reason.

The beauty of the Constitution can be found in the way it takes human nature into consideration. We are not a perfect species capable of coexisting within a perfect society under everlasting benevolent and wise rule. Instead, we are what we are: egotistical, corruptible, vengeful, and sometimes even a bit power mad. The Bill of Rights recognizes this and builds the barricades that need to be in place to protect the individual. That's why even the most heinous of criminals has rights until he is convicted of a crime.

In a very real sense, there is no such thing as a free nation where police and other military and government agents are allowed the force of arms while individual citizens are not. According to the history books (if they haven't been tampered with) every nation in which only one segment of the population has arms becomes a big-brother-knows-best theater of the absurd that has never boded well for the peasant class, for the working class, or especially for journalists who don't toe the party line. Our media forgets this fact.

We're all familiar with the peasant revolts of centuries past, where pitchforks were pitted against powder and ball, and sticks were all that stood between a precarious existence and the swords of aristocrats' armies. Not that many years ago, we watched the Soviet Union send soldiers and police to round up the hunting rifles of workers in satellite nations that were suddenly coming apart at the seams.

Change the costumes and climate, and what happened in the Soviet Union could have been Boston on the eve of our Revolution, when red-coated British soldiers went door to door demanding firearms. We fought back, much like the working-class men and women in the Soviet satellites fought back. And in both instances, the end result was a profound change in the way people lived, believed, and behaved toward one another. Democracy arose and despotic rule declined.

Can democracy ascend without an armed citizenry? I think not. Our Constitution provides the doorway for news and commentary to pass through free and unfettered. But the doorway to freedom is framed by muskets, the same flintlocks that stood between a vision of liberty and absolute anarchy at a place called Concord Bridge.

Many think of this battle to bear arms as a modern-day struggle. In fact, the clash over the right to keep and bear arms predates the American Revolution. Did you know that the lowliest class had a right to bear arms under English common law? It's ironic that colonists here had to fight for a right that ostensibly was already theirs as subjects of the British crown. But fight they did!

The muskets of the Revolution were in the hands of farmers, not trained soldiers or police. They assembled and stood their ground as if to say, "Don't tread on me." That remains an excellent way to say how Americans feel about government today. They say, "Do the job we elected you to do. But don't you dare cross that bridge."

Firearm ownership is the oldest and most pronounced of all freedoms. Why? Because gun ownership makes us equal when divisions of power are assessed. To those who desire a cultural hierarchy with an elite in power, a gun is a threatening symbol of *equality* of power.

I Bet They Don't Teach *This* in School

I won't rehash the Revolutionary War on these pages, but I will share with you some of the thinking of our Founding Fathers as they grappled with the details of formulating the first truly free state in the history of the world.

George Mason, one of the co-authors of the Second Amendment, had this to say concerning the right of free citizens to keep and bear arms:

> I ask, sir, what is the militia? It is the whole people...To disarm the people is the best and most effectual way to enslave them...

Fiery Patrick Henry, beseeching his fellow patriots to take up arms against their British oppressors, declared:

> They tell us...that we are weak – unable to cope with so formidable an adversary. But when shall we be stronger?... Will it be when we are totally disarmed, and a British guard shall be stationed in every house?...Three million people, armed in the holy cause of liberty...are invincible by any force which our enemy can send against us.

Shortly thereafter the British denied the colonists the right to keep and bear arms. Their denial of this basic British right became the driving force behind the outbreak of armed resistance. And write about it, they did.

Thomas Jefferson wrote, "No free man shall be debarred the use of arms within his own land."

John Adams commanded, "Arms in the hands of citizens may be used at individual discretion...in private self-defense."

James Madison recognized the rarity of this American freedom, writing:

> [The Constitution preserves] the advantage of being armed which Americans possess over the people of almost every other nation... [where] the governments are afraid to trust the people with arms.

Our famous first firebrand and pamphleteer, Thomas Paine, wrote:
> ...arms discourage and keep the invader and plunderer in awe, and preserve order in the world as well as property...Horrid mischief would ensue were [the law-abiding] deprived of the use of them.

Among Thomas Jefferson's collection of quotes is this gem from European Cesare Beccaria:
> Laws that forbid the carrying of arms...disarm only those who are neither inclined nor determined to commit crimes... Such laws make things worse for the assaulted and better for the assailants; they serve rather to encourage than to prevent homicides, for an unarmed man may be attacked with greater confidence than an armed man.

For those who misunderstand our Founders' eighteenth-century use of the word "militia" in the Second Amendment, I'll let American Revolutionary leader Richard Henry Lee clarify:
> A militia, when properly formed, are in fact the people themselves...and include all men capable of bearing arms...To preserve liberty it is essential that the whole body of the people always possess arms and be taught alike...how to use them.

Finally, it can't be said any more clearly than in the words of Revolutionary icon Samuel Adams, who wrote:
> The Constitution shall never be construed to prevent the people of the United States who are peaceable citizens from keeping their own arms.

Meanwhile Benjamin Franklin articulated the dangers of complacency in his famous warning:
> Those who would give up essential Liberty to purchase a little temporary Safety, deserve neither Liberty nor Safety.

I couldn't have said it any better myself.

The Founding Fathers believed that a standing army presiding over an unarmed nation was little more than a dictatorship, and that seems to be the way it has generally worked out in every nation that has gone down that path. The armed individual was a "premise" of freedom and the antithesis of tyranny. And mind you, they never mentioned owning guns simply for sporting use. The Second Amendment was never about hunting.

Modern anti-gunners simply shrug and say, "Well, that was then, this is now."

And I'll be the first to agree with them. This is the *now* that has witnessed entire villages of unarmed native people shot down in cold blood in the former Soviet Union, and in South America, Iraq, Central America, Somalia, China, Iran, Mexico, and many more. This is the *now* that has seen unarmed innocents butchered in Libya and Uganda and other emerging African nations. Even in "civilized" Europe, we've witnessed years of unspeakable slaughter in the former Yugoslavia.

The right to keep and bear arms isn't old, it isn't new, it is simply vital. Even in our own "modern" nation, more than 2.5 million crimes are thwarted each year with a self-defense firearm! And by the way, that estimate isn't one that's been snatched out of thin air, as many of the statistics used by anti-gunners seem to be. It's the consistent result of studies conducted by criminologist Gary Kleck at Florida State University.

Think for a moment about the carnage we would have in our nation if decent citizens were denied the right to keep and bear arms. Think about 2.5 million additional murders, robberies, rapes, or assaults. The right to keep and bear arms isn't just about sport. It's still a life and death matter.

Lessons Learned, but Unreported

In his book *Guns, Crime, and Freedom*, my friend Wayne LaPierre, the CEO of the National Rifle Association, writes about the intolerable episode several years back when young armed criminals in Florida were targeting foreign tourists for assault and robbery. Several young thugs were asked why they chose tourists, often distinguished by decals on their rental cars. The terrorists' answer was clear and predictable: Florida citizens have a right to carry guns for self-protection. They knew foreigners wouldn't be armed.

Justice Department studies tell us that law-abiding citizens armed with guns are less likely to be harmed when they thwart a criminal attack than those who resist in any other way. A gun says something very serious to an armed intruder. Almost always, just the presence of a brandished firearm is enough to stop an attempted criminal attack.

Anti-gun groups are quick to say that the police provide enough protection. Yet how can you station a police officer on every doorstep of every home, at all hours of the day and night? Despite the proficiency and bravery of our nation's law enforcement officers, they are neither legally nor morally obliged to be present to protect all of us in every situation.

Police couldn't stop the riots in the wake of the Rodney King trial verdict in Los Angeles. I know. I was there.

I was at home in the Los Angeles area when those riots broke out just a few miles away. And I was armed. Like everyone within a radius of fifty miles of those riots, I was concerned when I realized that the Los Angeles Police Department could not, or would not, control the carnage and vandalism.

The fear ran so quickly and so deeply throughout the Los Angeles basin that even my liberal friends were frightened. My phone rang day and night. As TV news choppers hacked through smoke-darkened skies over L.A., I got a phone calls from firmly anti-gun friends in clear conflict.

"Umm, Chuck, you have quite a few...ah, *guns*, don't you?"

"Yes, I do."

"Shotguns and...like that?"

"Indeed."

"Could you lend me one for a day or so? I tried to buy one but they have this fifteen-day waiting period..."

"Yeah, I know; I remember you voted for that. Do you know how to use a shotgun?"

"No, I thought maybe you could teach me. This is getting a little scary."

"I noticed. It does that sometimes. I could teach you, but not in an hour. The Marines are coming up from Pendleton; that'll end it. When it does, go buy yourself a good gun and take some lessons. It doesn't get so scary then."

In the heat of the hour, California's onerous waiting period laws suddenly looked lethally absurd to law-abiding residents eager to purchase some self-protection. They didn't want to get caught "waiting" and they sure Lord didn't want to get caught "without" should the riots spread in their direction.

After the riots subsided, several of these liberal friends rushed to purchase self-defense firearms like so many sudden converts rushing the altar at a massive tent revival.

Pass It On or Give It Up

It's time our progeny learned the truth about the Second Amendment. They need to learn that firearm ownership is constitutional, not criminal.

In fact, few pursuits can teach a young person more about responsibility, safety, conservation, history, and heritage – all at once – than responsible gun ownership. But what must young Americans think when President Clinton proclaims that "a firearm in the hands of youth is a crime or an accident waiting to happen"? He is wrong, and somebody needs to stand up and say he is wrong.

It is time that the members of America's next generation learn that when they reach legal age, and if they do not break our nation's laws, they have a right to choose to own a gun. They have the right to choose a handgun, a long gun, a small gun, a large gun, a black gun, a purple gun, a pretty gun, an ugly gun – and they have the right to use that gun to lawfully defend themselves and their loved ones or to engage in any lawful purpose they desire, without apology or explanation to anyone, ever.

This does not mean I must personally and individually defend every firearm and every bullet anyone anywhere might ever dream up. I don't.

The parallels are obvious. To defend freedom of speech, I don't have to agree with every word spoken. To defend freedom of religion, I don't have to approve every prayer whispered or every doctrine followed. To defend freedom of the press, I don't have to endorse every opinion printed. And to defend the right to keep and bear arms, I don't have to approve of every gun fired. I reserve the right to have First Amendment opinions about Second Amendment instruments. There are lots of firearms out there I do not like and would never possess. But to paraphrase Voltaire, I may not like the gun you own, but I will defend to the death your right to own it.

Not long ago I received a letter from a distraught old gentlemen who lives in the Midwest. He is in his eighties now, and left his farm for only one period in his life – to serve honorably against the Germans in World War II. He wrote:

> Mr. Heston,
>
> I am worried about an old friend of mine. It is a Browning Sweet 16 shotgun. I bought it with my mustering out pay when the war ended in '45.
>
> Since that day that gun has fired thousands of rounds and brought hundreds of quail to our table. It is scratched and dented a bit, but still beautiful, and though some of the parts are worn a bit smooth, it hasn't been to the doctor nearly as much as I have.
>
> Of all my possessions that shotgun is one of the most treasured, and when I pass away I plan for my son to have it, and maybe someday his son will also hold it in his hands. There are good memories in that gun, reflections of great dogs and wonderful days afield. I hope those memories will live on in that shotgun after I'm gone.

> But now I'm worried, Mr. Heston. That Sweet 16
> is an old autoloader and I've heard talk of
> semi-auto bans. Could it be true that right here
> in America they would take this family heirloom
> away from me or my family? Have we all gone
> insane to even consider such a notion? Isn't
> this what I fought against when I went to war?

My answer wasn't much help, I'm afraid. I had to tell him the sad truth – about England, where treasured family firearms, valuable sporting arms and mementos from two wars were confiscated from private citizens and destroyed. This is going on as I write these words, just as it is going on in Australia and will soon happen in Canada and other previously proud, independent nations. It's also part of the plan for America, if the National Rifle Association and vigilant gun owners ever drop their guard.

In attacking the very amendment that defends their homes and protects their wives and children, the cultural elitists have denied those of us who defend *all* the Bill of Rights a fair hearing, much less the courtesy of an honest debate. Groups like Handgun Control, Inc., and its sister groups, people who know almost nothing about guns, provide the media's text for almost all gun-related stories in this nation. Yet if the National Rifle Association attempts to challenge their assertions, it's ignored. And if the NRA tries to purchase advertising time or space to set the record straight, all too often it's denied. How's that for First Amendment freedom?

Too many have used freedom of the press as a weapon not only to strangle the NRA's free speech, but to erode and ultimately destroy the right to keep and bear arms as well. In doing so, the press has promoted its profession to that of constitutional judge and jury, more powerful even than our Supreme Court, more prejudiced than the Inquisition's tribunals. It's a frightening misuse of constitutional privilege.

It's my great respect for the Second Amendment that led me to the NRA, or perhaps more accurately, led the NRA to me. When

NRA officials asked me to run for office, I felt duty bound. Now that I've served as NRA president, I find myself striving even harder to defend this most cherished of freedoms. I felt it was my duty to stand up for my constitutional right to keep and bear arms as a citizen of my nation. Do you have that same sense of duty?

Do you believe as I do that our Second Amendment rights are being threatened by political theatrics, piecemeal lawmaking, talk-show psychology, extremely bad taste in the entertainment industry, an ever-widening educational chasm in our schools, and a conniving and irresponsible media, all of which adds up to cultural warfare against the idea that guns ever had, or should now have, an honorable and proud place in our society? If so, I encourage your membership in the NRA.

In closing, let me share a chilling story that resonates with evidence of my commentary.

A remarkable episode took place a couple of years ago in a multi-dwelling unit of the Chicago Housing Authority. Fearing violence among drug traffickers, the Housing Authority unilaterally banned ownership of firearms by any occupant for any reason. To enforce the rule, they began to conduct unannounced, door-to-door, war-rantless searches randomly throughout the projects to find and collect guns in supposed violation of their gun ban. President Clinton, of course, endorsed the idea.

But to me, the real jaw-dropper wasn't the blatantly unconstitu-tional kick-in-the-door presumption of guilt by the law enforcement authorities. It was the fact that, when polled, the majority of the housing project occupants *agreed to permit this infringement of their rights.*

They were willing to give up their constitutional freedom from unreasonable, warrantless search and seizure, and surrender the privacy of their personal property and effects, in return for what they perceived to be Big Brother taking care of them. (See Benjamin Franklin's quote above.) They weren't casualties of the cultural war –

they were happily surrendering as POWs, kneeling before the cultural warlord's dominion.

All but one family, that is. One family had the courage to defend their freedom. The father of the family, a lawful gun owner, filed a lawsuit against the Housing Authority to stop the door-to-door searches on the grounds that even public housing occupants were protected by the Bill of Rights from gun bans and warrantless searches. It took a fight, but *they won.*

Let's strive to be such models of the courage to be free. Let's embrace courageous step #5: *Fiercely preserve all the rights outlined in the Bill of Rights* (there's more on page 155). I believe that's the only way our rights, including the first-among-equals right to keep and bear arms, can be delivered into the next century as pure and intact as they came to us at the beginning of the last century.

I believe the freedoms that provided my generation with so much opportunity must remain the birthright of each generation that carries the torch forward. Traditionally, the passing of that torch is from an elder's hand down to an eager, young one.

I gladly offer my gnarled old hand.

CHAPTER SEVEN

Dr. King Didn't Dream of Ice-T

*It is an unavoidable conclusion that gangsta rap is
negatively influencing our youth. This explains why
so many of our children are out of control and why we
have more blacks in jail than we have in college.*

— C. Delores Tucker,
chair of the National Political Congress of Black Women

1963. It was not quite the summer of love. It most certainly was
a summer of strife.

I had a compelling reason to travel to the nation's capital that
summer – the most important reason of all, in my estimation.
American citizens were gathering there to march peacefully through
Washington, D.C., to call attention to civil rights, or better stated, the
lack of civil rights. Most of the marchers were black men, women, and
children following their brilliant leader, Dr. Martin Luther King, Jr.

Oh, there were quite a few white faces –red and yellow, too –
among the thousands of freedom marchers. But for me it wasn't so
much a matter of color as it was a matter of the Bill of Rights.

Dr. King was in Washington to lead an army fighting for personal
freedom, and I wanted to be a soldier in it. I was in the prime of
health, headed for the summit of my career. But times were different
then, and Hollywood wasn't quite ready to open its doors to "the
coloreds."

Blacks weren't even welcomed as stage hands back then, and it
didn't matter much to studio executives that I thought all people,
regardless of race, color or creed, deserved a chance at life, liberty,
and the pursuit of happiness under the Constitution. As the hot tar
blistered the soles of our shoes, I couldn't help but think about

the shoeless soldiers of George Washington's army who marched through snow banks. I felt fortunate by comparison.

We marched, the world watched, and a nation listened. I recall that somewhere behind me I heard a small black boy, maybe five years old, ask his sweat-drenched mother for a drink.

A March Away from Decency

Thirty years later I would remember that child's face and the tears in his eyes and recall his innocent belief in Dr. King's dream. What a far, far cry from that day to the day I had my senses assaulted by these lyrics:

I Got My 12 Gauge Sawed Off,
I Got My Headlights Turned Off,
I'm About To Bust Some Shots Off,
I'm About To Dust Some Cops Off!

Wonderful reading, right? Just the kind of "poetry" you'd want blasting over the radio to inspire a youthful gang roaming your streets on a Saturday night?

I'm A Cop Killer,
Better You Than Me,
I Know Your Family's Grieving, Fuck 'Em!
But Tonight We Get Even, Ha Ha Ha Ha Ha!

You have just been introduced to some of the lyrics of a black man who calls himself Ice-T. An entertainer of sorts, he is a minor young Hollywood character actor, a rapper who makes money by encouraging violence, perversion, racist hatred, and bloodshed.

No. This is *not* the message that Dr. Martin Luther King, Jr., marched to promote. And no, Ice-T is not the only creator of such lyrics. I use him here only as an example of a rampant musical cancer our media doesn't even recognize as an illness.

Let me tell you how this became a personal story for me.

Ice-T is actually Tracy Marrow, an entertainer from Los Angeles via New Jersey. His medium is a raw, driving form of music known as rap. As a prominent musician I know defines it, "rap" is sung by people who can't sing, can't play an instrument, and can't write lyrics. It's vocal graffiti – just a temper tantrum with a beat.

You've probably heard rap blasting at you from boom boxes or from slowly prowling automobiles driven by young men who've adopted a tough-guy persona and play the music to match. Rap often celebrates the violence of inner-city neighborhoods, and some black performers excel at it, while greedy entertainment magnates rake in millions from the messages of hate and promiscuity it often inspires. As far as I know, the media has ducked the issue and never deployed its vast resources to study, investigate, or criticize this most virulent, violent form of music.

With the release of the rap CD *Cop Killer*, marketed in cute little body bags, Ice-T was at the height of his incendiary power, the cream of an explosive crop. His sinister albums were raunchier, dirtier, more grotesque, more gruesome, and more inflammatory than the rudest of all the rest. He quickly became the bad boy of the L.A. riots, and his recording company, owned by Time Warner, was cashing in.

I did a press conference about the CD because *Cop Killer* had outraged just about every policeman in the nation. Time Warner was stonewalling, and the media was tiptoeing around the issue because Ice-T is black. Time Warner backed down to the extent of changing the CD's name from *Cop Killer* to *Body Count*.

Ice-T's success was not generated by talent. He was more of a black, less skilled Howard Stern, turning drug- and sex- and violence-filled lyrics into the musical equivalent of raw meat. Ice-T set straight out to make a name for himself by grinding the last shreds of decency under his heel. His own songs say it best. So here, again, I bring you more "poetry" of a young black man with a self-issued license to incite, Mr. Tracy Marrow, Ice-T on stage, angry rapper with a message he wanted children to learn by heart:

Got My Brain On Hype,
Tonight'll Be Your Night,
I Got This Long Ass Knife,
And Your Neck Looks Just Right!

Many remember how an obscure record called "Louie, Louie" recorded by a group called the Kingsmen became a huge hit just because it was scrutinized until the grooves were worn flat after some imaginative teenagers thought they could discern certain four-letter words within the mumbled lyrics that might have aroused their prurient interests –if it had been for real. It wasn't.

If that was the tip of the iceberg, then Ice-T's poisonous *Body Count* was the whole North Pole. Think about what the songs on that CD advocated: the rape and sodomy of children (including the nieces of the Vice-President of the United States), the murder of police officers, the treatment of all women as "bitches" and "whores," even torturing and murdering one's mother. It might have been different if Mr. Marrow had quickly disclaimed his lyrics as a work of fiction, a flight of fantasy fueled by imagination never to be enacted, believed, or made real. To the contrary, he stood behind every word with defiant glee.

Poet Percy Shelley wrote that poets are the unacknowledged legislators of the world. I believe that. I also recognize that perhaps the biggest lie of the rap movement is that rappers are presumed to be poets who are parlaying street violence into social truth so the world can scan the soul of a lost generation through their lyrics. In fact, most rappers are just young entertainers in eager search of a greedy piece of the economic pie, twisting their own race into a gruesome antagonist in an effort to reach out and grab a lucrative slice. Most rappers can't sing. Luckily for them, their "music" doesn't require that ability. It would be redemptive if they could just write better verse. Bob Dylan can't sing either, but he can sure write.

No, Ice-T is no poet, but if ever there was an anthem that not only proclaimed that it was morally acceptable for black youth to murder, but actually incited them to do it, he wrote it.

Ah, but the critics were strangely silent while the cash registers rang away:

> *For Your Freedom, Fuck The Police,*
> *Don't Be A Pussy, Fuck The Police,*
> *Have Some Mother Fucking Courage,*
> *Fuck The Police!*
> *Sing Along, Fuck The Police*
> *What Do You Want To Be When You Grow Up?*
> *Fuck The Police!*
> *You Have A Choice, Fuck The Police!*

And if the silence wasn't enough, some myopic critics and commentators covered their cultural behinds by surrounding this surly young thug with a folk hero aura, claiming he spoke of life on the streets "as it was," rather than how it should be abolished. Some even praised gangsta rap as a contemporary art form, though what most of the young "artists" needed was a damn good spanking and a few promoters with some scruples and the courage to apply them.

I am perplexed to this day by the mysterious shroud of silence that at first insulated Ice-T from rightful outrage. How could gangsta rap evolve free of press criticism, mostly as a way for some greedy entertainers to enflame the passions of minority youth and thus, literally and figuratively, make a killing at the expense of police, frightened women, America's elderly, and many other law-abiding citizens?

The lifestyle celebrated by rap albums like *Body Count* is evidence that something's gone wrong. But I don't think white oppression is at the root of it.

What Happened? A Bad Rap

The fact is that after the doors of opportunity were swung open to minorities through the herculean efforts of Dr. King and his disciples, not all blacks chose to walk through them.

After Dr. King's death, the civil rights path seemed to split in two directions. One path was followed by those who carried the dream on to trade schools, college, and law and medical schools. The other path was one marked by crack cocaine abuse, welcome-wagon welfare programs for women willing to produce small armies of unwanted children, indifference or hostility toward job training and formal education, and an almost fanatical fascination with the alleged "get rich quick" siren songs of sports, drugs, and criminal activity. It is this second path that dead-ends in Ice-T's mean streets, mayhem, and murder.

Yes, Dr. King opened the door to the tower of potential. There was plenty of space left open for advancement. The only requirements were desire, ambition, and vision. Yet while some took this tedious upward road toward long-term opportunity, others disdained the day-in, day-out work ethic required.

I've had business people tell me, "Hey, I grew up in the sixties. My conscience is still heavy with some of the guilt they doled out at the time. If a qualified ethnic applicant would just walk through the door, I'd hire him in a minute. But hardly anyone even bothers to apply. They just don't even try."

Meanwhile, experimental concepts like racial quotas and affirmative action tried to accelerate progress through artificial means. Certainly I understand the feeling of impatience; it had been a long wait. But success was a long wait for every race, including the indentured Irish, the Italians who lived in the black hell of our coal mines so their families could find freedom in America, or the Asians who labored to build America's railroads, some of them literally working themselves to death. For that matter, it was a long wait for the first Caucasians who came to North America's shores.

No, of course it wasn't easy for blacks. Slavery remains a blight on our national conscience. Yet let's not forget the tens upon tens of thousands of white people who gave their lives so every American – black or white – could be free.

Urged on by the self-serving leaders who struggled for power in the wake of Dr. King's death, some young blacks of the sixties and seventies shouted that they wanted it all *now*, even though the youth of other races were still struggling to undertake traditional steps like education and training to achieve higher goals. With passions inflamed and no shortcuts in sight, the minority community stood by and watched while a few young rabble burned their own communities to the ground.

Very few of my generation will forget the terrible sadness we felt when fires consumed Watts, just a few miles from downtown Los Angeles, and later, other areas of the Los Angeles basin. We had marched and put our careers and perhaps even our lives at risk so young blacks could have equal opportunity. The doors were open. But some put them to the torch and nearly crushed the very spirit of Dr. King's work with looting, pillage, and even murder.

Obviously, there is no social or cultural "quick fix" to absolute economic equality. I wish simple answers existed, but real life is driven by longer rhythms. Positive cultural change is a matter of time hinged to vision and hard work. A successful style of change abides by rules, and it takes the concerted efforts of multiple generations.

Those with the Ice-T mentality don't see it that way. They want wealth, prestige, and status in a tumultuous microsecond. The doors they seek to push through with their "gangsta" mentality are framed by crime and drugs. And the "success" they seek is temporary at best, often evaporating into a sense of lost morality and despair even before it is grasped.

Those who use illegal means to achieve the success they desire fill our overcrowded prisons. The claims are made, of course, that Lady Justice is a white racist, but the facts support a different conclusion: young blacks commit a disproportionate number of violent crimes.

Now obviously one can't lay all the ills of America's sometimes deplorable race relations at the feet of an idiom called gangsta rap, nor do I single out Ice-T as the only source of lurid and lousy song lyrics. There are hundreds or thousands of others of every race who share or strive to share the mean-spirited spotlight he occupied for his fifteen minutes of fame. Yet if the laws of cause and effect still exist, then I believe it's appropriate to suspect a connection between the hopeless violence of gangsta rap and the hopelessness that drives one twelve-year-old to murder another twelve-year-old for nothing more than the sports logo on his coat or sneakers idolizing some overpaid hoopster.

I don't think it's much of a stretch to say that senseless drive-by shootings have roots in the rap anthems that rumble along some of our city streets. This music is lyrical strychnine consumed in mass quantities. "We shall overcome" has been overtaken by "I know your mama's grieving, fuck her, tonight we get even." Rap and its vision of America are at the opposite end of the spectrum of those who hope to raise honest, decent, productive citizens –and it is time we recognize that as the truth.

What We Can Do (And What I Did) About It

In the end, the cycle comes back to profit. There is big profit in gangsta trash, either on video tape or compact disks. Just on the record industry side alone, rap music and hip hop earn more than $1 billion annually, surpassing country music as the third best-selling genre in the domestic music market.

Frankly, that statistic should scare the hell out of a lot of decent people. These are "artists" who often call women "bitches" and "holes," and glorify suicide, gangbangs, copkilling and even necrophilia.

This is not to say that this musical celebration of crime, murder, rape and animal lust isn't abhorred, not only by us old white guys but by black women's groups who find the songs dangerous and repulsive beyond belief. Many of them say they've grown sick and tired of a generation of young black men who strut and swagger in the streets, yet find it difficult to stay home and show some responsibility for the children they've sired. Far too many of these young men actually exalt prison life above the workaday world of wife, job, and children.

"This music has poisoned our community," said Leroy Warren, Jr., a member of the national board of the National Association for the Advancement of Colored People (NAACP). I couldn't have said it better.

Of course the question is, can anything be done? Yes, it can – if you're willing to get involved and invest some personal courage and effort.

Because I owned a few hundred shares of Time Warner stock, I was able to appear at a Time Warner shareholders meeting that year and protest their release of Ice-T's *Body Count* album that featured songs like "Evil Dick," "KKK Bitch," "Momma's Gotta Die Tonight," and "Cop Killer."

I appeared not as an actor or a celebrity, but as a stockholder and as a private citizen totally repulsed by the idea that Time Warner would profiteer at the expense of common decency. The press – print, TV, and radio – were barred from the shareholders meeting of the largest communications conglomerate in the world. Ironic, ain't it?

When I rose and read aloud the lyrics of Ice-T's hate- and violence-filled "songs," the audience – several hundred Time Warner shareholders – sat in stunned silence. Imagine a sea of faces frozen in shock. There were hushed shudders of disgust from many, especially at the lyrics in which Ice-T and his thuggish friends fantasized about anally raping Tipper Gore's two twelve-year-old nieces. Nor did they appreciate the selection in which the "artist" suggested that children who grow angry with their mothers should consider murdering them. Many of those present were visibly and rightfully shocked.

As I left the hall, Time Warner chairman Gerald Levin was feebly defending his profit-making rapper. Fifteen or twenty media people were waiting for me outside the meeting, of course. When I read the lyrics that had disgusted the stockholders still inside, a *Los Angeles Times* reporter said, "We can't print any of this, you know."

"I know," I replied with some relish, "but Time Warner is still selling it."

Not for long, I'm proud to say.

Within weeks the *Today Show* aired videotape of an Ice-T interview during the Los Angeles riots. The rapper advocated killing police officers and said he'd personally like to blow up some police stations. Of course, that let the wind out of Levin's statement that the lyrics in *Body Count* didn't actually mean what they said.

Soon after, Time Warner announced that Ice-T was "voluntarily" removing the song "Cop Killer" from his CD. (It may have helped that all of America's professional police organizations were outraged and up in arms, too.)

Still, the rest of the songs – songs that even *Time* magazine described as "vile and irresponsible" – were still in stores to be bought by teenage kids. Unlike some people, I support the First Amendment as vigorously as I do the Second. As an advocate of the Bill of Rights, I'll fight to defend free speech. But this was more than that. This was incitement to riot. It was a vicious call to rape and murder. It was over the line, past the fringe, beyond the pale. Everything, even art and free speech, has a common sense line that one shouldn't cross. Ice-T stepped over it.

Still, the Dream Lives On

As a postscript, I'd like to add that over the months and years that followed we kept up the heat on Time Warner concerning their release of unsavory and inflammatory gangsta rap songs and lyrics. As a result today, I challenge you to find a copy of *Body Count* in any reputable record store across the nation. Time Warner ultimately fired Ice-T. It took time, but I think our combined efforts in this case did make a difference. Maybe the moral of this story is that morality still matters.

On the other hand, the cultural war rages on. When Ice-T felt the heat of audio meltdown, he quickly headed for videoland. Sad to say, the Hollywood moguls were more than happy to translate his lyrical violence onto celluloid, just to capitalize. At last check, Mr. Marrow is making B movies that revolve around lots of blood and bullets, his well-practiced persona of a dour young black hood providing a perfect fit for cheap films full of bombs, machine gun blasts, and obedient women with cavernous cleavage.

What continues to appall me is that Time Warner, a global corporation with the power to influence millions, was willing to hide behind the protection guaranteed by the First Amendment freedom of speech to shield their profits under the guise of airing a self-appointed spokesman for angry young men.

Furthermore, at the same time that Time Warner and its corporate bosses were hiding behind the First Amendment, they were among the most powerful enemies of the Second Amendment. Their *Time* magazine declared war on gun ownership and condemned guns as tools of criminal violence, while its mother company profited from youthful rants that pitted young blacks against police, sons against mothers, and men against women.

Does this make any sense? Of course not. Cultural wars never do, except to those who prevail, become the elite, and gain profit and/or power as a result. And chances are I won't get lots of movie offers from the Warner people.

But of one thing I am absolutely certain: Dr. King didn't have Ice-T's goals in mind when he said, "I have a dream." And I hope that the thirsty little five-year-old boy at the back of that 1963 Freedom March, where I put my career on the line, has grown up to be as disgusted with gangsta rap and its message of hate as I am.

My final thought here represents the power of courageous step #6: *Find the way to your loudest possible voice, and speak.* (You'll find some examples on page 156).

I believe that if Dr. King were here, and he witnessed his grandchildren listening to blacks referring to their women as "bitches" and "whores," and black entertainment sold as advocacy of killing cops;

if he saw black athletes with green hair shoving referees and black football players thrusting a bump-'n-grind in end zones; if he saw black singers grabbing their groins or black boxers biting off opponents' ears, he would ascend the steps of the Lincoln Memorial a second time, summon together the legions of today's timid black leaders and tight-lipped press members, and he would put a permanent end to it.

I'll be proud to stand alongside any black leader with the courage to take such a stand in his place.

CHAPTER EIGHT

Hollywood's Heroes: The Entertaining and Retraining of America

Hero worship is strongest where there is least regard for human freedom.

— Herbert Spencer, English philosopher

America has always had more than its share of action heroes. They were born in the dime novels of the American West, a genre that gave us two-fisted lawmen with a gun on each hip, buffalo hunters sporting heavy-barreled Sharps that could heave a bullet a mile or more, and Indian fighters that rode a hundred dusty miles to save captive maidens held in huts made of animal hide. Our original heroes were horsemen, wilderness ramblers, and westerners – tough, true blue, strict adherents to a code of moral conduct. And yes, gunmen. Very good gunmen in fact. In their make-believe world, a person survived only if he had a quick wit and a quicker draw.

After the turn of the nineteenth century, our fighting men joined the ranks of western action heroes. Books and eventually movies celebrated not only the cowboy but the citizen soldier – the Rough Riders and Yanks who rooted the Spanish and the Huns out of their trenches. On the heels of these tough hombres we were treated to the ultimate comic-book action hero of heroes, Sgt. Rock.

Then came G.I. Joe, whose red, white, and blue military ways had little in common with the new brand of action hero that has followed in his wake. Instead he (and increasingly, she) was a hardboiled, deadpanned, straight-and-narrow exponent of the law, and he carried a gun and used it both as a means of self-protection and for the betterment of mankind. Who can forget Detective Joe Friday or, later, the stubbled chin and gritted teeth of Dirty Harry challenging, "Make my day."

Still, except for the means of transportation and the cut of the suit, little really changed much from the days when the dime novelists elevated the status of frontier toughs like Wild Bill Hickok and Wyatt Earp to lawmen extraordinaire throughout the teeming cities of the East. Who was Dirty Harry other than *Gunsmoke's* Matt Dillon minus the big buckskin horse and wide-brimmed hat?

Role Models for the Noble Good

Heroes, real or imagined, are made for emulation. And emulate them we did. Kids from coast to coast played games in which they bragged, "I'm Sergeant York" or "I'm Wild Bill," then pointed a finger and shot the bad guy. Good versus bad was clearly defined, and that was the point of it all.

(Sadly, such natural boyhood behavior is now flagged as a horrifying sign of brewing violent tendencies. In April 2000, four six-year-old boys were suspended from their Sayreville, New Jersey kindergarten for pointing fingers at each other and saying the customary "bang bang, you're dead" during a playground game of pretend cops and robbers.)

As America's sense of its own character began to fray a little around the edges, our good guys shed a few skins as well. Cowboys came riding across the cinema sawdust trail a little less Tom Mix natty and a whole lot more dirty linen showing, inside and out. The good guys watched the size of their hats shrink while the amount of womanizing, drinking, brawling, and plain ol' bad behavior increased in ten-gallon increments. But, in the end, there were still good guys and bad guys, and the good guys triumphed over the dark side. When the smoke cleared from their guns, the bad guys rightfully occupied their graves in the dusty gutter.

Cops as good guys suffered the same fall from grace, and some of our badge-toting action heroes were at first glance not much elevated from the criminals they struggled to catch. Yet whether in cactus country or concrete jungle, the stage was always set for a miraculous comeback of both a moral and physical nature. Blazing away at the bad guys, our good guys experienced a sense of personal renewal that allowed them to triumph in the end. We knew our action heroes were tough enough physically to tame any back alleyway or even all of Arizona. Left hanging in uncertainty was our hero's sense of morality. But after all, action heroism in either dime novel or feature film is nothing but an old-fashioned Greek morality play in the making.

With some exceptions, this slightly soiled script still runs true to form. The heroes may seem a little scruffier and their foibles fit for an analyst's couch, but in the end, they still manage to snatch their personal failings as well as the gist of the plot from the hungry jaws of evil intent, generally doing so with some fancy gunplay, fast driving, hard fighting, and the help of a woman who now delivers more than a kiss. In many ways we are still watching Wyatt Earp in action, except that now he is better armed and probably a whole lot more real than the drugstore novelists dared to invent. We have the action hero as a human being, and that's not a bad kind of hero to have.

I've played some flesh-and-blood action parts in my time, and I have no quarrel with portraying history as it truly was when ranchers lynched and Indians scalped. Let's not forget that pirates killed and plundered on the high seas, or that cowboys murdered during the range wars. I believe my craft grew as an art form and as a mirror of society when we advanced our action heroes from Gene Autry and his pearl-handled revolvers to a much more earthy John Wayne as Rooster Cogburn in *True Grit*.

What I do ask, however, is that heroes be rooted in the *reality* of historical context. It seems we're fast approaching the day in the entertainment industry when nothing will be produced unless it has a cultural point to make. (One blatant example is the angry anti-gun cultural agenda woven into the script, props, and scenery of *Lethal*

Weapon 4, while the movie itself otherwise trades on abundant gun violence.) A fantasy that offers an escape, a reality that offers a lesson – these are being replaced by stories of changes that need to be implemented in our society. Every plot has an agenda.

Take, for instance, the practice of revising history to make it fit Hollywood's "new and improved" morality. The vastly popular *Roots*, a generations-spanning black family epic, was billed as biography when in fact it was a work of fiction. Why not call it a work of fiction? Because the story was "politically correct" and it advanced Hollywood's social agenda.

Dances with Wolves certainly corresponds with Hollywood's romantic view of Indians, even though honest history isn't nearly as sentimental or forgiving as the producers and director of this movie. Indians raped, tortured, and pillaged; whites raped, tortured, and pillaged; blacks raped, tortured, and pillaged; and all three racial groups sold their fellow man into slavery when economic opportunities presented themselves.

We are, after all, the family of man and not a rainbow coalition. As far as I'm concerned a rainbow coalition implies that we have *differences* that run deeper than skin color, that we are different shades of souls standing side by side on the spectrum. I see mankind as a family in which underneath a few millimeters of skin pigmentation, character is amazingly alike. Our hearts are all the same color and have equal capacity for good and evil. It's how we open our hearts to one another that matters, and will always matter. History should reflect an honest appraisal of events without an overlay of what we "wished" had been the context in which they took place.

By not merely dramatizing but contriving facts, movies and television present children with a cultural re-education rather than a factual education that explores the way the heart of man responds in various situations. That's wrong.

Ultimately, the point is this: How we portray ourselves and our history both in movies and on television actually *means* something.

I spoke of movies earlier as an art form, but they are much more than that. Media messages are powerful, and increasingly so. Modern children grasp far more of their heritage and culture through movies and television than from textbooks and fiction books. Just decades ago both movies and television were little more than benign entertainment vehicles; today's stars carry the cultural impact of minor deities while the screenplay and even the television sitcom shape the morals and manners of our society more than any combination of teachers, preachers, and parents did in generations past.

This underscores a new obligation among these industries to be accurate and truthful. I can stomach graphic carnage inserted simply to shock the senses more easily than I can abide those who tinker with the truth just to make a personal or political point. After all, classics like *A Tale of Two Cities* or even *The Odyssey* are rife with violence. Portrayed tastefully and truthfully, these stories continue to tell us much about our social evolution and ourselves.

Allowing the entertainment industry to have power over our lives far exceeding the scope of mere entertainment opens the door to other dangers as well. If we believe what we see on the screen in its entirety, and if we elevate the status of our actors above their ability as entertainers, we leave ourselves open to a fanciful brand of brainwashing that can quickly spill over into the everyday politics of our real world.

Can Hollywood make truly *good* movies without intentionally misrepresenting the people and places it portrays? Absolutely! I know, because I've appeared in more than one of them. Throughout most of my career I've been called upon to play roles that have been historical in nature, and my love of history has made it easy to research each part thoroughly and portray it as truthfully as possible on screen or stage.

I've always loved this aspect of my work because history is just a succession of humans proving they're only human. During my readings, it has become more and more apparent to me that, even with our sweeping technological advances, the human frailties that haunted a Julius Caesar or a Pontius Pilate or Napoleon Bonaparte or a Russian czar are, in fact, still the curse of humanity today. The drama of the human heart is still the heart of any movie or play. As a diligent researcher I resent those who seek to revise the historical context of human-heart drama to support their contemporary cultural views, whether the stories are about Italians, blacks, cowboys, Jews, Indians, or the freedoms ordained by the Bill of Rights.

The Action Hero vs. Action Sicko

What we don't need – and I must emphasize this – is for the action hero to reflect a cultural agenda. There is a line beyond which a "conflicted hero" is no hero at all, merely a pawn in a political drama, and it's that line that we have begun to cross.

Let me explain.

The detective who is frayed, bumbling, prone to eat, drink, smoke, or womanize too much or surrender to dark moods due to stress can be, with good writing and acting, a flawed character that harkens back to the best of Shakespeare. This character can be a hero if and when, through the progression of the plot, he or she flips the switch from moral and physical ineptitude to a new-found strength that triumphs over the dark forces at work both inside and outside his being. In these "heroes," we find a sequence of inner transition, of moral and spiritual growth.

But now, Hollywood and television sometimes seem intent on presenting what I call an anti-hero. We find the main character in our morality plays to be totally devoid of any personal strength or conviction. What we're offered are psychotic alcoholics or drug abusers who seethe with an inner anger that fuels their careers but erupts into destructive violence. They destroy their own lives bit by bit, they wreck relationships and families, and ultimately, they sell out the moral passion that once lay at the core of the "self."

In essence, we're left with an action hero as an aberration of society, little more than human debris. There are few redeeming qualities, no transitional catharsis, and minimal effort at rehabilitation and some form of ultimate victory. Instead, our "hero" either sinks deeper into his or her personal trash heap or calls it a draw with the villain (since right and wrong are situational) to either avoid judgmentalism or offer a sequel. This script has become more prevalent in recent years, and it leaves us little reason to wonder why young people find themselves confused as to how to handle situations in which good must confront evil.

What does Hollywood offer us in the place of the traditional action hero? Well, you might turn to the Saturday morning cartoons some time to get a small yet blatantly in-your-face taste of the substitute: special effects and gratuitous mechanical violence without clear heroes. You'll find repeated and bombastic ninja-art and vaporizing special effects that are not at all rooted in personal heroism, but rather, are techniques or means of furthering a very specific social agenda.

Sex and Violence Do Beget Sex and Violence

As of last year, on average, one act of *serious* brutality was found for every *four minutes* of entertainment. That's the bottom-line bad news from the Center for Media and Public Affairs, a nonpartisan research group, whose exhaustive study reviewed television and movies combined.

Today's action movies glory in violence, and to some degree that's what action heroism is all about. Violence is not pretty, and people who die violently shed lots of blood. In *Gunsmoke* that's all you saw, the gun smoke. Today with advanced technology there's little left to imagination. Human flesh reacts gruesomely to the impact of a nine millimeter bullet. Ask any soldier or police officer who's been there. Or if you saw the 1999 release *Three Kings*, you don't have to ask.

Let's stop kidding ourselves, however, about the effects of violence on the screen. For too long the so-called "media experts" have been trying to convince us that violence on TV and in movies is unrelated to crime statistics. They've been wrong and while we've intuitively known it as a nation of viewers, the statistics now confirm the bloody reality.

Today's average preschooler watches more than twenty-seven hours of television per week, and all this at an age when he is unable to distinguish fantasy from reality. This is important, because by age sixteen this same child will have witnessed 200,000 acts of violence on television, including at least 40,000 murders.

In light of this, epidemiologist Dr. Brandon Centerwall of the University of Washington looked at various communities in the U.S. and abroad, and analyzed murder rates before and after the introduction of television. In the communities he studied, Centerwall found murder rates doubled, as if by clockwork, ten to fifteen years after the introduction of TV. Explaining that delay, Centerwall wrote, "If TV exerts its behavior-modifying effects primarily on children, the initial 'TV generation' would have had to age ten to fifteen years before they would have been old enough to affect the homicide rate."

Centerwall's conclusions are even more chilling. Calling exposure to TV "a risk factor for violence," the epidemiologist determined that it had a clear, cause-and-effect relationship with "approximately half" of all murders and "a major proportion" of rapes, assaults and violence in the U.S. Researchers point out that if exposure to television violence causes only eight percent of our population to become more aggressive, the national homicide rate could double as a result.

Music videos, shock TV, "reality" shows, both network and cable movies, and even violent news and cartoons are at fault. From 1993 to 1996, while the U.S. homicide rate dropped by twenty percent, USA Today reported that coverage of murders on network evening news programs rose an average of 721 percent. In a single day, picked at random by a survey group, 1,846 acts of violence were shown on television programming. Cartoons alone portrayed 471 violent scenes in this single day. In all of the programming as a whole, some 362 scenes involved the violent misuse of a firearm.

Research data from the American Psychological Association, the Centers for Disease Control, the National Institute of Mental Health, the Surgeon General's Report, and the U.S. Attorney General's Task Force on Family Violence, among many others, all showed that watching TV violence during childhood is directly related to aggressive, violent, and criminal behavior later in life.

Let's consider sex. The Parents Television Council in April 2000 reported that while levels of television violence have remained steady over the past ten years, overall sexual content has tripled and references to homosexuality have increased dramatically. The study, "What A Difference A Decade Makes," revealed that references to genitalia on network TV rose sevenfold in that time and that "bitch," rarely used in 1989, was commonplace in 1999. There were also huge jumps in references to oral sex, pornography, masturbation, and kinky sex.

As for violence and sex in the entertainment industry, first of all we have to acknowledge that for years much of the violence has been embarrassingly gratuitous. It's time we call upon the Hollywood and television network creative cartel to come out of the closet and admit that they've used needless violence to appeal to the worst in human nature and profit as a result. It's time to force them into admitting that violence in movies and on television *does* have a direct bearing on the violent crime, both adult and juvenile, that has haunted America during the past twenty years.

Certainly the entertainment industry would rather blame the carnage that has resulted in our society on firearms rather than upon their own distasteful fare. Yet a measured form of tacit admission came as of this writing, when 197 creative programming artists joined to form the Committee to End Violence, promising to cut down on the "gratuitous, excessive, and unpunished violence" that we and our children watch every day. I hope this is a sign that the scapegoat era is about over, and that Hollywood and the networks will take a long overdue look in the mirror.

Hollywood's Duplicity about Guns

When it comes to guns, I see no greater example of hypocrisy than what I see on screen and behind the cameras in the television and movie industry.

Our entertainment culture entertains young boys with relentless volleys of gun violence. At the same time, studio heads and network executives preach against gun ownership and are aghast when organizations like the National Rifle Association suggest that young people appease their natural curiosity about firearms by handling and shooting guns in a safe, supervised environment. If we glorify guns in our art yet condemn them in real life, we're creating a dichotomy in the minds of impressionable, curious youth.

It seems to me we're in something of an intellectual quandary. From the president on down we like to rent a video tape and cheer on our action hero as he sometimes singlehandedly (with a gun in that hand, of course) manages to subdue the world's worst terrorists. But then the following morning comes and we find our neighbors staring at us in disgust as we take our son and a couple of guns to the trap or shooting range.

On screen, law-abiding gun owners are grouped together with the worst sort of lawbreakers, even though the two groups are lightyears apart in action and intent in the real world.

The news media delights over a juicy double homicide to boost ratings, especially if they and their news cameras get there first. Hollywood's belly feeds on gun profits while Hollywood's mouth defiles gun rights. Just ask yourself: When was the last time *you* saw an action movie that didn't feature multiple scenes of bullet-ridden hailstorms of firearm violence?

As a result of all these mixed messages, kids find themselves confused. Their entertainment action heroes use guns to defeat and destroy the bad guys, and thus guns should be good, right? Yet if the child expresses a desire to hold a gun or shoot a gun or someday own a gun to hunt, target shoot, or maybe even stop a real-life criminal from committing a crime, he is told guns are bad. A firearm then becomes a sort of psychological contraband. When firearms are celebrated and condemned simultaneously, kids find themselves in a cultural and moral Catch 22. Is it any wonder that kids are intrigued to seek out guns for themselves, to experiment with them in secret, and then show them to their friends?

A fascination with firearms is not only rational, but international in scope. Every culture on this planet has armed itself at one time or another, and young men have looked upon the ownership of tools ranging from a rifle to a spear to a bow and arrows as a rite of passage into manhood and the adult world. That age-old image of a boy's pointed finger and the vocalized "Bang!" that accompanies it echoes from African savannas and Japanese gardens as much as from the suburban lawns of Atlanta.

A young person's fascination with weapons is going to persist and grow as long as responsible adults and action heroes keep and use firearms in fiction or fact – even though vast merchandise chains might ban toy guns. These giant retailers may tell the hand-wringing women's groups that they'll reduce toy gun inventories, and the toy-makers themselves may strive to make the toy guns look more like candy dispensers, but the demand doesn't ebb even when the supply won't rise to meet it. Kids see guns and are captivated by them. It's a romance as old as humanity itself, and the schizoid head-in-the-sand approach many have taken to defuse kids' interests isn't working and never will.

Why is there such a cultural stigma about youngsters learning the truth about guns? Kids once learned about guns as a matter of course, long before gunplay dominated family entertainment media. Today, even teaching the history of guns in America is socially forbidden while firearms themselves are shamefully hidden from view. Should we even have to consider, then, why children regard firearms as an object of wonder?

It is even more perplexing that, with proper firearm safety training denied to children in our schools and in a growing number of youth organizations, kids in fact have to turn to movies and television for invariably wrong information about a subject to which they conspicuously give their undivided attention. There is cultural pressure to keep youth and guns galaxies apart. So instead of learning firearm responsibility and safety from an early age from educated and law-abiding adults, the child turns to the latest bullet-butchered thriller where he sees the worst possible display of erroneous firearm use and abuse. That makes no sense.

Worst of all, illusions become their own reality. Not only children but many adults seem to draw absurd notions about guns from watching too many Hollywood thrillers. (Trust me on this one – Hollywooders will always excuse themselves from any gun bans they help pass.) Check the latest techno-savagery crime flick and you'll see bad guys with every sort of fully-automatic military firearm spraying bullets like water from seemingly endless capacity clips. Ain't no such thing.

Yet in real life, FBI crime statistics tell us that semi-automatic military-looking firearms are involved in less than one-tenth of one percent of all criminal assaults. Bans on contemporary "assault weapons" (just military-looking semi-autos with less power than most hunting rifles) have materialized not from real-life situations, but from what our society has come to *believe* to be the truth based upon movies and television programs. Film directors love technical one-upmanship, and cinematic displays of firepower range from the ridiculous to the bizarre. You'd think that television commentators and newspaper reporters would consider the source and seek the technical truth before they call for limitations, restrictions, and even outright bans. But they don't, and there's little reason to believe they will.

Young Americans love to cheer for their action heroes. Nine times out of ten those heroes settle their differences with a firearm. Isn't it time we realized the impact this has on young minds?

Isn't it time we gave our kids the proper technical and psychological tools to piece together the often contradictory messages they receive about guns?

I believe it's time our kids were taught the technical truth about guns, about the Constitution's rights to keep and bear arms, about firearm history, and about gun responsibility and safety. The place to start is in our schools, where firearms can be demystified for young people – instead of having their first experience with a gun come at some late night party or during a heated emotional confrontation they cannot control.

Hollywood, Hypocrisy, and How It Came to Be

Many of my brethren are fair game for commentary here – both the hypocrisy I see among some of my fellow actors, and the hypocrisy I see in the way they're often treated by their adoring fans.

Swashbuckling heroes who kill dozens of enemies per movie – and who are praised by their fans for their daring feats with massive firepower – are personally censured in real life if they appear at a pro-gun event. Actors have been urged to boycott some of my pro-Second Amendment gatherings, even though these same actors portray gun-toting tough cops, private detectives, and armed space commandos on screen. It's a strange double standard, to be sure, but today's cultural war is conducted with few commonsense rules.

I know one of the world's most famous directors who owns numerous guns and who loves to shoot, but only in private. He'd take too much heat if he appeared at a public range.

I have spent most of my adult life living and working in the biggest and most influential of these entertainment wonderlands. Hollywood, USA, may be the one address that just about everyone in the world recognizes. Hollywood is a city larger than life, the place where legends become movies and movies become legendary. And the people who make the movies? Well, many become larger than life, household names, box office magnets, and in the most common of words, "stars."

Star power is an interesting phenomenon. Stardom certainly doesn't make one God, but it can make one believe that he is somewhat godlike, imbued with the power to move, to persuade, and inevitably to bring about cultural change.

Star power is a power of tremendous magnitude. It's little wonder that Hollywood is so heavily courted by aspiring politicians from both sides of the fence, but especially the left, the direction the Hollywood fence increasingly slants these days.

It wasn't always so. Back when, actors like Clark Gable, Gary Cooper, and Jimmy Stewart were politically conservative, and a liberal like Humphrey Bogart was the exception, not the norm. The work of actors like John Wayne was steeped in the old-fashioned brand of American conservatism. But as the cultural war took its toll over the years, things changed.

Today, it doesn't take two hands to tally the number of Hollywood luminaries willing to reveal their presence in the conservative corner. The most famous, of course, was Ronald Reagan, a visionary who channeled his acting success into a role as a conservative spokesman, then governor of California, then one of the most popular presidents and most potent political craftsmen in world history. It's a revealing miscarriage that so few in our Hollywood community today acknowledge that it was one of their own who was responsible for ending the Cold War. Without Reagan's leadership the Soviet threat might still be real, and nuclear winter rather than global warming would be the catastrophe lifted up as the specter to haunt our children's future.

Will Reagan ever receive the honor overdue him from the community that helped launch his career and where he toiled faithfully for so many years? I doubt that it will happen in my lifetime. Today's Hollywood is decidedly a wide swing to the other side of any spectrum that Ronald Reagan espoused, and were his story told today, it would either be couched in cynicism or rife with revisionist history. In all fairness to my friend Ron, I hope they'll wait and get it right.

Like Ronald Reagan, I was a Democrat early in my acting career. That was during the Kennedy years, at a time when the Democratic Party was playing the lead in working for equal rights for all Americans, and not just some Americans. A Kennedy Democrat then would be considered a conservative Republican now. Over the years I watched with dismay as my party drifted farther and farther away from constitutional principles and began arms trading in a cultural war.

It was during this time that the media and entertainment industry realized it had tremendous power to sway opinion and even revise history to make it agree with its political agenda. Once again I found myself on the outside: first as a civil rights Democrat, then as a conservative Republican, as the Democratic Party boarded a runaway train down a liberal track.

My views have cost me a certain amount of goodwill within the industry. But my midwestern values make it difficult for me to sacrifice my integrity for the few shekels such sacrifice might earn.

As actors, Ronald Reagan and I have learned from a lifetime of experience to be thick-skinned about how we are received and reviewed personally. When I chose to become a spokesman for the National Rifle Association, I was immediately branded a "muddle-minded old man" and worse by those among the media and entertainment industry who do not believe that the Bill of Rights guarantees the right to keep and bear arms. While I'm not thrilled by their badmouthing, I refuse to compromise my personal convictions to pay homage to a cultural agenda that defies the very rights on which our nation is built.

You don't see many Hollywood luminaries writing books or speaking out for conservative causes these days. The reason is *not* because there aren't any conservative Hollywood luminaries. It's because they find it very hard to take the heat. They hardly dare speak out for fear of ABC or CBS or NBC or CNN or worst of all, the IRS. The rising, young, conservative filmmakers in Hollywood are understandably careful about what they say, and to whom. Their livelihood may be at stake. I have often said there are more conservatives than homosexuals in Hollywood's closets.

That's a damn shame. Those who back this cultural war have set the price extremely high for standing up for what you believe. Speaking with the courage of your conviction can be very costly, not only in terms of dollars and cents but in terms of friendships, working relationships, and reputation. Not paying the price of principle, however, is to sacrifice your integrity and ultimately, to lose your freedom.

Why Hollywood Liberals Act Like, Well, Liberals

The history of the acting profession may explain some of the paranoia and insecurity that seems rampant today in a community that often seems contradictory. Actors have been a minority group from the beginning, dating back to when they were fighting off the castle dogs of Athens for the last shreds of gristle on discarded bones. Even during the last century, some of the world's most famous hotels have barred entry to those of my chosen profession, solely because actors were thought to be of inferior social and moral caste.

One of my favorite stories is about Jimmy Stewart, who was checking into the noted Ritz Hotel in Madrid. The personnel recognized him as an actor, of course, yet did not know that Stewart was also a general in the Air Force Reserve, and was then on active duty in Spain.

As Stewart set down his luggage the manager said, "Oh, forgive me, Señor Stewart, I am overwhelmed with distress to tell you that we do not accept members of your profession in our hotel."

Stewart drawled back, "'Zat so? Well, for the next four weeks I'm Brigadier General James Stewart, United States Air Force." With that he picked up his key and went up to his room.

In the early days of my career I played summer stock in towns where actors were asked not to mingle with the respectable members of the community. It was something I grew accustomed to, yet was never comfortable with. So maybe it's natural that most members of the acting community tend to feel a sort of kinship with the world's estranged people, and less comfortable with the self-sustaining heritage and traditions of conservatism. It has only been recently, as part of this evolving cultural war, that this alignment with the "downtrodden" has been used as a weapon to divert traditional American beliefs and reinvent history to make it agree with revisionist theories regarding race and class.

Of course that does not explain why, back in the 1960s when I marched for equal rights with Dr. Martin Luther King, Jr., I was shunned in Hollywood for what was considered "inappropriate" activities at the time. Possibly it was because I did not seek, nor receive, the permission and blessings of my peers. Actors are a close-knit and often judgmental tribe, probably owing to the harassment and lack of respect they themselves have suffered through the ages.

During World War II the Hollywood community turned out in force to help the war effort, with stars appearing in promotional films and selling war bonds, and studios aiding in whatever way possible to unite the American public behind our fighting men overseas. Many had admirable combat records.

Then years slipped by and something changed. By the Vietnam era, Hollywood seemed bent on undermining our military efforts abroad, and today you won't find a single feature film on the video shelves that celebrates Reagan's victory in the Cold War, or the fall of the Berlin Wall, or the way that a Republican Congress devoted dollars and sense to increased military technology – the technology that brought us victory in Desert Storm in a matter of days and brought our fighting men and women home with minimal casualties.

The entertainment industry would rather put a spin on these accomplishments, and sadly, it's a spin that demeans and belittles the vitality of what these events truly mean to the American people. We won our freedom for the second time when we emerged out of the shadow of nuclear destruction by the Soviet Union. We kept the world's free markets from collapsing when we defended Kuwait against invasion by Iraq and preserved an unrestricted flow of petroleum out of the Middle East. Someday the truth will have its day, and our citizens will see more clearly the magnitude of these historic achievements.

Hollywood rallied within itself during the McCarthy hearings on un-American activities in the 1950s, but since then, most actors have remained a bit distant and aloof from the mainstream. Part of it is the nature of the business, since actors are trained to "play" other people. Playing oneself requires an entirely different regimen of hard work, and many actors shy away from personal appearances and taking personal stands because who they *really* are may be in conflict with the successful characters they have played.

In a nutshell, we actors are much desired socially, but oftentimes only as entertainers and not as equals. Only in recent times have we learned to be powerful spokespersons on social issues, and thus, to earn our way into a society that in many sectors has shunned us for centuries.

I personally was not impressive at public speaking early in my career. Public speaking is very different from acting. Still, I felt it was necessary to work hard and learn to do what most actors consider an unbearable chore. I wanted to have a voice, even if it was only a voice in an interview. Most actors never face the public "as themselves" unless it's to receive an award, stand behind a lectern for a second or so, and say "thank you" while they hold their prize in the air.

With all of this background in mind, you would think that the entertainment community would be rock-solid conservative in its approach to preserving something as precious as the Bill of Rights. Instead, the tendency is toward a sort of convoluted socialism, one with a distinct hierarchy, a promiscuous social allegiance that dashes from one cause to another, and a community that often fails to practice what it preaches.

Where Do We Go from Here?

Though I possess no crystal ball, I've lived long enough and seen enough trends within the business to safely predict that the power and scope of the entertainment industry will only multiply in the years ahead. Our reactions to it comprise courageous step #7, *Embrace change*, on page 158.

The emphasis will continue to be on theatrical reinventions of the American way of life, so that it will correspond to the cultural patterns that are most predictable and profitable to Hollywood and mainstream media. Control is, after all, the heart and soul of any cultural war – control of votes, ratings, purse strings, pocketbooks, policies, lifestyles, and most of all, children's attitudes. Those who seek control want to manipulate *how* you think so that your resulting lifestyle will profit them and not their competitor. Those who seek control want you to think in such a way that you will buy their products, tune in to their stations, watch their movies, read their magazines and newspapers, support their causes, and spend your money in a way that *reinforces* your newly adopted beliefs, and causes you to buy still more products.

What I believe our response should be at this point is to repeatedly expose the hypocrisy between what Hollywood says on screen and what Hollywood power brokers and stars then say on the public dais.

We also need to demand that a degree of morality be brought back into the industry. Whatever sense of moral values that may once have guided the media has been lost in today's onslaught of nonstop insipid commentary and tiresome displays of aberrant behavior.

As a nation, we need to learn to hold the entertainment industry in healthy distrust. We need to recognize the profiteering agenda at work: the fragmentation of our society and the creation of more and more labeled factions, cults, and cliques that can be marketed to, each with products that often exclude or ridicule the others.

Above all, we need to trust what we know to be true, not what we see portrayed as truth on the silver screen.

We must keep fighting the revisionists and reformers as they seek to cloud selected issues, recast certain characters, and alter various historical facts. It's only right that we battle for a free and honest voice in the midst of all this media programmed confusion and chaos. Liberty deserves no less than that.

If individualism, morality, tradition, heritage, and advocacy for constitutional rights are old-fashioned, then I don't mind being old-fashioned. I don't mind being culturally out of step, if that's what it takes to be free.

CHAPTER NINE

Hunting: A Tradition in the Crosshairs

*To combat hunting in your area, post 'No Hunting' signs on
your land, join or form a local anti-hunting organization, protest
organized hunts, play loud radios, and spread deer repellent or
human hair (from barber shops) near hunting areas.*
— from a fact sheet published by
PETA (People for the Ethical Treatment of Animals)

What the animal rights terrorists dare not mention in their training
manuals are their more offensive methods of attack, such as tossing
human feces around, planting tire-impaling spikes into the soil of back
roads, feeding poisoned meatballs to hunting dogs (resulting in their
death), and screaming saliva-slinging epithets in the faces of hunters.

Such radical assault upon lawful hunters is resulting in not only
the loss of a sport or pastime, it is a blatant assault against the legal
rights of law-abiding citizens. It is yet another tragic casualty of the
cultural warfare being conducted by the ignorant urban radical
against the rural traditionalist. It's an irreversible trend, troubling
and regrettable.

Hunting, like no other hobby or passion, provides an open-air
classroom for teaching an entire curriculum of important lessons to
young people: conservation, compassion, wildlife studies, life cycles,
vegetation, weather and seasons, safety and planning responsibility,
orienteering, survival preparedness, and communication. Of equal
importance, hunting provides a forum for camaraderie between
members of different generations. The impending loss of this heritage
is a national tragedy.

Hunting in wilderness areas is uniquely American. In England,
wild game belongs to the Crown. In America, it belongs to all of us.

Yet more and more I see a modern America where parents don't believe they have the right to take their kids shooting or hunting. Some are afraid of the social consequences if they do so. An increasing number of parents are concluding that it is easier to bow before the politically correct pressure to disavow anything that has to do with guns and hunting, than to teach their children the vital lessons *learned best* through firearm education and hunting.

But I'm a predator just as you are, no more or less than a hawk on the wing or a weasel squeezing into a tight underground refuge to accomplish the permanent taming of the shrew. We are predators by nature, and no apologies should be made or required. The urge to hunt is a primal biological urge, just as the desire to procreate or to test another boy's strength in a childhood tussle.

Hunting is also ritual. It's almost impossible, for even the most accomplished wordsmith or thespian, to describe the essence of hunting to a non-hunter.

But I will try.

Reflections on the Instinct and Ethics of Tradition

To this day I remember the first quail I shot with my little 20-gauge shotgun on my very first trip afield with grown men. The bird fell clean from a single shot and the dog went to retrieve it. Dutifully the little retriever brought the bird to heel and placed it in my hand. There was just a tiny fleck of dark red blood on the cock's black and white striped head.

Then suddenly the quail shuddered, the wings fluttered weakly, then it was still. At that moment I realized it had died in my hand. Heart pounding, face flushed with excitement, I was also suddenly overwhelmed with sadness at the bird's death.

These are difficult sentiments to balance, even though their coexistence is entirely natural in the outdoors. Even so, as long as we share this planet with other creatures and as long as we take from the earth for our sustenance, balance them we must. I have never outgrown those opposite yet united emotions – the adrenaline surge that precedes and follows the hit, and the sweet sorrow at recognizing that a living creature has died. Nor have I ever outgrown a love for pan-fried quail smothered in brown gravy. It's especially good after a hard day in the field and a good shot at a fast bird bursting out of cover.

The joy of hunting may be beyond the realm of explaining. It is something that is best experienced. And experience it I have, most of my life.

When I was a boy growing up in Michigan's wild north woods, autumn was a time of exhilarating unrest. Geese migrated overhead, announcing their passage through the pale blue skies with their strange angst of untamed, migratory music. Those of us bound to the earth below watched them wistfully and wished that we, too, could take wing and see the smoldering crimson blaze of maple leaves from their lofty vantage point.

Our dogs, content to sleep under the porch through the summer months or to tag along lazily as we fished during the long daylight hours of July, sensed that something changed with the first frost. It was as if they picked up on the increasing enthusiasm in the men who gathered around the steps of the local country store to tell tales of bucks and venison.

Of course, there were always young boys squeezed into the tight huddle of adult conversation, squirming our way into the inner circle as best we could. The dogs barked and wagged their tails as each story grew longer, more elaborate, and most likely, less true than the one before it. But that was part of the autumn ritual. A good story-teller knew how to embellish without defrocking the dignity of his words. There is, you know, a big difference between a lie and a properly exaggerated hunting or fishing story. Some may find it hard to distinguish – unless you've stood near steps like those, smelled the tobacco smoke, strained to pull each word into your heart over the snarl of sporadic dogfights in the background, and listened while men breathed life into events long past.

The talk was always of dogs, guns, knives, deer on the run, game on the wing, warm clothes, cold winds, and sheer survival. And the talk formed a bond that linked us together, generation to generation. It's a tradition I know my son will pass along to my grandson. America will be less of a nation, I believe, should we ever let these rites of passage fade away. Those days for me were a form of magic.

As we boys walked home from school we often wished aloud that this might be the year when a father, or an uncle, grandfather, or older brother would casually say, "Think you're ready to go out to camp with us this season?"

The invitation was part of an initiation. The rite of passage included greasing our leather boots, oiling the guns, and an afternoon sighting in. It was all so exciting that it seemed to each of us youngsters that we might fairly well explode from the images that raced like hounds through our heads. It was a sobering experience as well.

Winter meant snow, lots of it, and strong winds that swept straight down out of the heart of the frozen north, raw and savage and with a searing bite. You remember those winds with both respect and just a little bit of fear if you've ever spent much time outdoors in the north country.

I think of those seasons still when the calendar says the landscape should be white and the blizzards should be howling. They were wonderful days spent rambling in a faint, gray, frozen light, days when wood smoke curled from stovepipe chimneys and heavy leather boots, soaked through with snow, sizzled next to the cast iron stove where they sat drying.

Winter in the woods was a strict teacher. Nature is a harsh taskmaster in the frigid north, and mistakes in judgment can be deadly. As a boy, I listened attentively as men talked of their outdoor experiences and adventures. The passing of nature's wisdom from one generation to another was not all that different in my Anglo-Saxon "tribe" than it has been for American Indians in generations before mine. Elders have always gathered their sons, nephews, and grandsons around crackling campfires to pass on the secrets of survival and successful conquest of the wild.

There were rules that governed every hunt, and if you broke them, you carried the stigma for the rest of your life. Bad tidings as well as good made up the stories the older men told. They could be cruel and unforgiving in their evaluation of a poacher, or game hog, or someone reckless with a firearm. Woe be unto the man or boy who left the field without tracking and retrieving wounded game. They were shamed by both elders and peers, sometimes even shunned.

I learned to hunt from my elders in traditions that were unspoken and unwritten, but exact nonetheless. My teachers were often grizzled locals with stubble on their chins, patches on their clothes, and dogs that seemed forever to be scratching. They were country men who talked rough and lived even rougher. Still, they knew the rules and they made sure we obeyed them.

Some of these men, God rest their souls, would be puzzled today if they could see the emerging culture that condemns everything they held dear and that often held their families together. To them, guns were tools, and any man worth his salt used his tools wisely and correctly.

We boys listened closely, because the telling of the tales was an integral part of the learning process. Little or no allowance was made for the errors of youthful exuberance. We didn't need a government agent to police our hunts. The graybeards among us could do it with no more than a piercing flash out of the corner of their age-glazed eyes.

I *practiced* hunting in the most wonderful way possible – through time spent "a roaming" the woods near our home, just a boy, his dog, cathedral-tall trees, and solitude. I would rise at daylight, dress and pull on my boots, lift my .22 rifle off the rack, stuff something in my pocket to munch on, and then whistle up the pup and watch him go directly from a deep sleep into a quivering dynamo eager for adventure.

When my thoughts wander back to those moments in my life that approached perfection, many are of those woods. I recall days spent tramping through deep snow drifts in February, my breath rising like a plume of smoke amidst the stark evergreens. I recall bright crimson stains on a windswept drift that signaled the point where a rabbit had been stopped in its tracks, soon to become the main ingredient of a stew stirred on a wood stove. I recall placing my well-oiled little .22 back on the gun rack as darkness fell, and my dog, sated by table scraps, surrendering to his moaning wolf dreams and running in place where he slept in a corner out of the cold. By that time my own dreams were drifting away with the bear and the moose and the caribou and the wondrous heroes who might chase them, all part of the vast universe that I read about.

Those north woods were my childhood wilderness, even though much of the timber had long since been harvested and the landscape was thick with brush, brambles, berries, and second growth. It was irresistibly beckoning country for a boy who knew that a rabbit in the pot was welcome fare for his family.

Like many rural Michigan families we did without and yet had plenty. Mostly what I had as a youth was space – space to roam, space to hunt, space to shoot, space to absorb a way of life that stretched far back beyond the arrival of Columbus. I hunted rabbits and made each bullet count. I learned wingshooting as I crashed through those rugged thickets, practicing my lead on upland birds that fell to a 20-gauge that was actually far too long for my adolescent arms, although I didn't know it at the time.

Still to this day I am proud of the fact that I remain a decent wingshot, although hunters' etiquette compels me to remain humble. My schedule and hip surgery don't permit much hunting these days. But I still love wingshooting and I bust a few clay birds whenever I can. As for hunting, it's enough to know that should the opportunity arise, I would have more than a fair chance of adding game to the bag. My family and I would eat. And that instinctive sense of self-destiny and self-reliance, more than anything else, is still at the core of why I hunt, and I suspect it lies at the core of the reason most hunters hunt.

Certainly there were days when it seemed the rabbits ran faster than a speeding bullet and the birds seemed to slip through a mysterious hole in my shot pattern. All of us who hunt have had those days when the hand, eye, and the hunted never seemed to align themselves successfully. We will continue to have such days, as well we should. The joy of just being outdoors is as much a part of hunting as the joy of bringing home some game.

There were deer in those Michigan woods and we hunted them as much for meat as for sport at a time when money was scarce and beef was scarcer. As I look back, it seems remarkable that so many of our neighbors kept such strict allegiance to game laws. It would have been easy to poach, but these were proud men and they took their deer on the license. We were also a community, and as in any community, there were families that were sometimes down on their luck. Those people did not go hungry. What was hunted from the land was shared.

I am saddened when these memories and rituals of hunting are slandered. I am angered when I hear of attempts to outlaw hunting through radical legislation. I am disheartened when I see the continuing exodus from rural grassroots that signals a loss of many things I hold to be precious beyond measure.

But I take courage when I hear that they still close the schools in some parts of the South when deer season arrives so the youngsters can spend this particularly cherished time out in the woods among friends and family. Hunting connects generations to values deeply embedded in family, place, space, legend, and the keeping of timeless human rituals.

I find it ironic that as a nation we raise millions of dollars to protect hunters of the rain forest in South America, but at the same time spawn anti-hunting groups to lobby and protest against organizations such as the Boy Scouts of America and the NRA, which teach young people the most basic hunting and wildlife conservation ethics here in the United States.

It was in the woods of Michigan where I learned that boys are more than blank hard drives ready for programming by MTV and video games. They are men in the making. And as far as I am concerned, hunting is one of the most beneficial means of helping a boy make a transition to responsible manhood.

The Courage to Say Teenager and Gun in the Same Sentence

Look into the eyes of any teen, male or female, as they hold a firearm for the first time. There is wonder and magic in their face, not evil.

The attraction of guns and shooting is strong in the young. In my estimation it's as strong as ever, although increasingly misunderstood and maligned. What appears to be less strong is a determination to provide our youth with the space, freedom, and instruction it takes to correctly absorb and apply our special heritage of firearms and hunting. We're a nation of city dwellers now, so timing and planning related to hunting are of even greater importance. Even so, parents need to be encouraged that any time spent outdoors with their youngsters is time well spent. It's an investment that pays dividends for a lifetime.

It's imperative we teach our youth the right ways to hunt and the right ways to handle a gun. Toward that end, there are no finer hunter safety and gun safety courses than those of the National Rifle Association. Our first formal hunter safety course took shape in New York state in 1949. Since then, that basic program has been adopted in all fifty states and across Canada.

Does it work? Ask the National Safety Council. According to their statistics, hunting now involves fewer injuries than playing basketball, tennis, or even ping-pong!

More than 600,000 new hunters complete hunter safety courses every year, and for more than a decade, the NRA's Youth Hunter Education Challenge (YHEC) program has offered "graduate studies" for them with some of the most advanced hunter skills and safety training available. With exercises designed to simulate situations hunters encounter in the field, YHEC helps young hunters develop the knowledge and decision-making skills they need for a lifetime of safe and memorable hunting. Programs are in place in more than thirty states now, plus Canada and Mexico.

The NRA also has an affiliated organization, the NRA Special Contribution Fund, which owns and operates the Whittington Center in the northeast corner of New Mexico, the largest non-governmental shooting facility in the world. There you'll find young men and women from across America gathering to strike out across tens of thousands of high, dry, and rugged rimrock acres, fight through clinging juniper, pinion, and cactus, hike around rattlesnakes, and climb the jagged mesas in an attempt to learn what Anasazi youth learned before them thousands of years ago.

Upon completion of Whittington Center courses, these young hunters will know tracking, how to read vegetation and game signs, how to stalk, gauge wind, judge animal movements, conserve water, and how to camp, cook, and hike through rugged country in pursuit of wild quarry that have lured hunters there since the Ice Age.

The NRA also serves as a central networking clearinghouse to link charitable hunters with meat processors, food banks, and government agencies who participate in "Hunters for the Hungry," an effort to provide high-protein, low-fat game for the needy. We're now working with thirty-six state agencies to raise money through grants and donations for their programs, since many states find they have more venison available than funding to see it processed, packed, and distributed.

The NRA's political victories on behalf of hunters are too numerous to recount fully. The NRA has fought to keep federal lands open, defeat anti-hunting referendums on state ballots, protect hunters from the outrageous and dangerous activities of animal-rights protest groups, and establish a positive working relationship between sportsmen's groups and government regulatory bodies.

In my own way, and through the NRA, I hope I'm helping to keep the important tradition of hunting alive.

A Final Word to Anti-Hunters

For those who cannot connect with the joys that hunting brings to the breast, I hope to find common ground of appreciation, at least, for its many blessings for wildlife. Some strongly believe that we, as the thinking, spiritual animal, should be content to remain stewards only, rather than harvesters, of wildlife. That is wistful idealism with no firm basis in science or even common sense.

Talk these days seems cheap when it's aimed against hunting. It's best we remember, for example, that the dollars that saved the whooping crane can be traced back to men who killed deer. It's time more people understood the relationship between those who hunt and the wildlife they enjoy. It's time to open up lines of communication between those who hunt and those who condemn the sport as cruel and unusual. The fact is, starvation or a slow death from parasites is not a pretty sight. That could be the fate of many of our large-game species should their numbers be left unchecked.

Biologists estimate there are now more white-tailed deer on the North American continent than on the day the Pilgrims first arrived at Plymouth Rock. At the beginning of the twentieth century, these animals were all but extinct in many parts of their former range. In less than one hundred years, however, this outstanding game animal has come back from the brink of extinction to become abundant, and even a pest in many parts of the eastern United States. This is true of many game species.

What happened?

By the middle of the nineteenth century, noted naturalists and adventurers were lamenting the indiscriminate slaughter of America's wildlife resources for hungry markets along the eastern seaboard. Late in the century the slaughter had reached a crisis, and outdoorsmen and politicians such as Theodore "Teddy" Roosevelt pledged to turn the tide. As president, he established a series of wildlife refuges across the continent to protect birds and non-game animals, as well as huntable species. He also established the first national forests, was a strict enforcer of game laws and bag limits, and was the engineer of a conservative heritage of wildlife conserva-tion – a heritage such modern notables as Presidents Richard Nixon and George Bush not only endorsed but further developed.

The emergence of scientific wildlife management can be attrib-uted to hunters, especially Yale forester Aldo Leopold, who early in the century began to catalog relationships between native plants, animals, and the land. The result was the science we now call ecology. Leopold believed it would take the establishment of a "land ethic" to save dwindling wildlife species and their natural habitats, and he preached the sermon of conservation even as he worked to set aside wilderness hunting areas in the Southwest.

Today, we depend upon scientific management to balance wildlife populations and dwindling land resources. We depend upon the hunter to pick up the tab for these management costs. Taxes on sporting arms and ammunition pay for wildlife restoration efforts, wild lands acquisition, refuges, game wardens, research, and endan-gered species monitoring. You name it and the hunter pays for it, and pays willingly.

In 1937, American hunters imposed a federal excise tax on themselves specifically to pay for wildlife conservation efforts. These Pittman-Robertson (P-R) funds, as they're called, are collected through an eleven percent tax on firearms, ammunition, and hunting-related equipment and supplies. Each year, hunters and shooters kick in more than $190 million to this fund – money that improves habitats, builds ranges, pays game wardens, teaches young hunters gun safety, and more.

Add to that the more than half a billion dollars each year that Americans spend on hunting licenses, permits and stamps, and the bottom line is that hunters are underwriting wildlife conservation in this nation to the tune of nearly two million dollars *every day*.

What do we get for this money? Pittman-Robertson funds alone have allowed states to buy more than four million acres for habitat and hunting. In many cases this money accounts for three-quarters of a state's conservation budget.

Thanks in large part to the projects these funds have made possible, we have forty-five times as many turkeys, nineteen times as many elk, thirty times as many bison, and thirty-six times as many whitetail deer as in 1907.

And it's not only game species that benefit. Bald eagle nesting pairs have risen from four hundred to more than 4,500 in the lower forty-eight states, plus 40,000 individual eagles in Alaska. Trumpeter swans have come back from a low of seventy-three birds to more than 16,000. It's a good deal, especially when you consider we achieved all that with what amounts to about three days' worth of interest on the national debt.

Hunters also help fuel our general economy. Add up what they spend on travel, lodging, equipment, supplies, and so forth, and you'll find the average hunter contributes $1,500 to the general economy each year, for a total of about $14 billion each year.

In Texas, big game hunting contributes almost one *billion* dollars a year to the state's economy. In the state where I grew up, Michigan, deer hunting brings in enough money to fund more than 10,000 well-paying jobs.

Hunters are often anglers, who make major contributions, too. Following the lead set by hunters with Pittman-Robertson, fishermen set up the Dingell-Johnson Sport Fish Restoration Act and Wallop-

Breaux Act, which established federal excise taxes on boats, motors, fishing tackle, equipment, and supplies. Since 1951, Dingell-Johnson has generated nearly $3.6 billion for fisheries and related projects.

In 1996 (these numbers are compiled only every five years), anglers bought 26 million fishing licenses, tags, permits, and stamps for $579 million, which provided dependable annual funding for programs that established and restored fisheries all across the nation. If you want to understand the benefits of this money to sport fishing, just ask a Chesapeake rockfish angler, a shad angler on the Delaware or Potomac, or a bass enthusiast on reservoirs nationwide. Also take a look at the Great Lakes towns that have been brought back from near collapse by tourists and fishermen seeking out the sport made possible by the rejuvenated salmon fisheries there.

Even though these moneys come from hunters and anglers, they benefit game and non-game species, and citizens in general whether they hunt or fish or not. Hikers, campers, bird watchers, boaters, "camera hunters," and just about everyone who enjoys the outdoors all share in the bounty that hunters and anglers make possible.

I'm proud that our National Rifle Association provides substantial support for many of these efforts. Our Environment, Conservation, and Hunter Outreach (ECHO), for example, works with state and local agencies and organizations on wildlife conservation projects every year.

No other nation in the world can boast of the accomplishments we've achieved here with our wildlife management and wild-lands conservation efforts. All these programs came about at a great cost. Yet general tax revenues were not tapped because hunters, men and women with firearms, were willing to pay extra through their taxes and license fees to finance the vision of Roosevelt and Leopold and other conservation greats.

When a handful of shrill people today dispute the role the hunter has played in conserving America's wildlife resources, let's have the courage to speak the truth. More importantly, let's employ courageous step #8: *Find myriad avenues to pass on your convictions* (see page 158). Few have been as willing to reach into their pockets and put their money where there mouth is on matters of conservation as hunters and fishermen.

For them and for me, hunting remains the natural thing to do in a natural world. I believe this natural world is still yours and mine. Let's do what we must do to protect it, and to protect the way we harvest its game species.

CHAPTER TEN

A Colorblind Nation...
Unless You're White

Prejudice, which sees what it pleases, cannot see what is plain.
— Aubrey Thomas de Vere, Irish author

As often as possible when I speak publicly about our history, and as I opened Chapter 2 of this book, I refer to America's Founding Fathers as a "bunch of wise, old, dead white guys."

I do it for a reason.

Generally, several members of the audience cringe when I make this statement. Others look at their shoes or alternatively fix their gaze on me to avoid eye contact with those around them. Why these reactions?

What I say is true. Our Founders' skin color may not be a relevant point, but it is an indisputable fact. There wasn't a black, Hispanic, Indian, or Asian among the lot of them, and that's a part of our heritage the revisionists will find themselves challenged to rewrite.

Still, it is part of the unspoken code of cultural warfare that "white makes blight." Ask any third grader who is to blame for black slavery or Indian displacement or for that matter, global warming.

Of course, no race is free of historical judgment or fault. That is not my claim. My claim is this: Far too many children are being brainwashed into believing that white people are the root of all evil in our society. It's truthful, not racist, to observe that white people were the founders of the freest nation on the planet. It was indeed a bunch of wise, old, dead white guys who brought us to this dance: one nation, indivisible, with liberty and justice for all.

Why does stating this historical fact upset so many sensitivities? How did being white fall into such disrepute? Because guilt-driven class division is one of the basic tactics of the elitists who wage cultural war.

Being White Isn't a Black and White Issue

The original colonies were settled by white people – mostly English, French, Dutch, German, and Swedish in origin. Certainly when they arrived here some other immigrants met their boats. These people we came to call Indians, although they bore no relation to the people of India at all. These "Indians" were, in fact, the descendants of roaming hunters from the steppes of Asia and Siberia, cousins to the Tartars and Mongols, who had somehow worked their way across the Bering Strait to America at an undetermined time, as the Vikings did across the North Atlantic.

America was, and indeed has remained, a melting pot. Later in our history, Chinese and Pacific Rim natives would immigrate here to labor up and down the West Coast, while Irish and Italian and other European immigrants would sail to this nation to do the same along the eastern seaboard. Migrants came up from Mexico – the descendants of Aztec, Mayan, and Yaqui tribes mingled with Spanish blood – and would push north to claim land inhabited by the Pueblo peoples, descendants of Asian immigrants in centuries past.

For all of history, slavery was a booming global business. Black people from Africa would arrive on our shores by ship after being captured and enslaved by other African blacks, who sold them to slave traders in Africa, who sold them to southern plantation owners, who themselves were likely to be the descendants of immigrants who fled to America to escape the enslaving traditions of monarchical rule.

And so the pot was stirred, and so the human soup thickened, and so we grew into a nation that, by all that is sensible and sacred, should have been by the very nature of its origin, growing more and more colorblind. Unfortunately, that has not been the case.

It seemed we were on the verge of it in the sixties when Dr. Martin Luther King began to break down the remaining vestiges of racial barriers in the South. For a brief and shining moment, it seemed the dream of life, liberty, and the pursuit of happiness would finally apply to *all* Americans, not to any one segment, and certainly not to Anglos only, men only, the wealthy only, or those with blue eyes and freckled noses only. For a few years at least, the dream of our Founding Fathers was almost within our grasp. Then in the seventies something strange happened, and a wedge began to appear.

In the divide-and-conquer process, only one group has been left wondering where it fits into the newly subdivided America. And that group, my friends, is the *majority* – the white, middle-class, hard-working, law-abiding, churchgoing, education-pursuing, yawn-inspiring, gun-owning mainstream. Average America found itself somewhat like vanilla ice cream in the same store with fifty-seven exotic flavors – overlooked, unexceptional, and well, a bit too plain vanilla.

If you were average, middle class, and Caucasian – which remains the profile of the majority of people who work, achieve, persevere, and endure in this nation – you were considered too common for the avant garde media and contemporary political schemers to pursue.

The result has been a form of reverse discrimination that is not only an issue for courtroom decisions, but a pervasive attitude in certain sectors of our nation. Repeatedly in recent years the average white man has been the object of ridicule, a social obstructionist and considered suspect, while other races are exalted.

For example, the September 1997 cover of *Time* magazine pictured several white men seated in a stadium, their arms raised in prayer, with the headline, "Promise Keepers, men who assert their manhood, rally in Washington. Are they to be cheered – or feared?" Compare that to the gushing, fawning coverage of Louis Farrakhan's Million [black] Man March on Washington.

Time magazine praised black women gathered in Philadelphia for singing the Black National Anthem. Imagine if anyone proposed to sing a *White* National Anthem; they'd be regarded as a dangerous supremacist and probably placed under armed FBI surveillance.

Nobody wants a nation embroiled in the controversy that continues to plague the former Yugoslavia. Ethnic clashes there have demolished a proud civilization and demoralized a once-proud people. Do you remember the Winter Olympic Games of Sarajevo? Can you recall the beauty of the countryside, the health and radiance of the local citizenry, and the magnificence of the city's art and historic buildings? Most of that is gone now, destroyed in a heartbeat of history because of racial, religious, and ethnic division and hatred.

Will we awaken before we experience the same consequences of cultural division?

Class Division vs. Class Tolerance

Stage one in cultural war "division" requires the introduction of dissension and hate between classes or racial groups. The "mask" may include terms such as affirmative action, retroactive retribution, ethnic purity, and other terms designed to make the people in one or both classes feel good. At the core, however, is a desire to drive a stake into the heart of real brotherhood and create dissension, distrust, and a disruption of the status quo. Class division of this type is the antithesis of the liberties proclaimed by our Constitution and Bill of Rights.

America's Founding Fathers invented democracy from the bottom up. It was the only way that class distinction and discrimination could be eliminated and the term "liberty and justice for all" could be elevated to its rightful stature. Today, our freedom is protected both by our courts and by the checks and balances imposed upon various branches of government. It is also held above harm by the heritage and traditions of men and women who have had their taste of freedom and found it worthy of any sacrifice. We threw the concept of a ruling class overboard a long time ago, along with a couple of dozen bales of British tea.

Now, however, class warfare is back among us. It has reared its ugly head again. This time those who are advocating a privileged class are those in high political power and those who control the media and entertainment industry. They, in turn, have enlisted the support of those in higher academia and high society.

Members of this gang of cultural terrorists are of their own choosing, and the rules they have made are of their own imagination. It's a safe bet that you and I and millions of ordinary, everyday working stiffs won't be on the list of these elites.

Newer forms of class division may not be immediately recognizable because they are largely faceless and invisible. One emerging and frighteningly powerful example being practiced by business people – who may call themselves conservatives – excludes common citizens from participating in Initial Public Offerings. The dirty little secret is that dot-com millionaires are being made every day, from IPOs and other transactions in a stock market where only giant institutions and insiders get to play.

Class distinction is not a new concept. Any gathering of animals, including man, produces a hierarchy. Class distinction within a species, most biologists would assert, has been a factor in the betterment of breeds through the centuries. Class distinction in the human species, however, is another matter when it comes to government. Class distinction may allow a society to function more efficiently, but most definitely not more freely.

No, elitism is not new in history.

Neither are its "divide-and-conquer" tactics.

Divide, Conquer, Then Pour an Iced Mocha

The principle of divide and conquer dates back at least to the Trojan War and very likely before that time. The principle operates like this: Divide a people, and then rule each of the ragged remnants of the fragmented society.

Ask the Romans if powerful nations have ever fallen as a result of cultural division. There are ruins around the world that were once the smug centers of small-minded, arrogant elitism. Could it be possible that rather than evaporate in the flash of a split atom, as so many feared for so many decades, we may instead succumb to a divided culture?

Politicians naturally gravitate to this policy of divide and conquer because the more factions that can be defined, the greater the suspicion that can be raised to pit one group against the next. Those suspicions in turn spawn targeted promises made to each group. The net result is more votes.

The media has used the same tactic. The more factions that can be defined, the more advertisers and program creators can generate specific programming, increase the market share and the cost of commercials. The net result is more money. Divide-and-conquer tactics have been used to sell everything from shoes to cigarettes to movie tickets to CDs.

This same divide-and-conquer mentality has been used by gun abolitionists. During Reconstruction following the Civil War, many southern states sought to limit ownership of firearms by newly freed blacks. Early in the twentieth century, when Irish and Italian immigrants were considered second-class citizens, political power-brokers in large eastern cities sought to keep firearms out of their "inferior" hands.

An elite class engaged in divide-and-conquer tactics is *precisely* the state that our Founding Fathers were determined to sidestep. In a capitalist republic, arguably the best economic system history has produced, anyone willing to work hard enough can join a higher socioeconomic stratum. All who keep the law in our system of government are afforded an equal opportunity to the courts and the legislative process. All have equal opportunity to prove themselves worthy of prestige, privilege, and status.

The Bill of Rights protects everything anyone needs to *pursue* happiness.

In twenty-first century America, however, just by signing on to a point of view or specific social agenda, a person can become part of the preferred class. In other words, by no more than posturing and parroting the party line, a person gains otherwise effortless admittance to the "us" and rejects the "them."

As I pointed out in Chapter 3, the entrance fee to the elite class is at an historical all-time low, requiring only that a person agree to the general tenets, for example, that white males are disposable, corporate America is inherently evil, southern Christians are somewhat dumb and misguided, guns are dangerously prevalent, and lesbian Islamic rainforest biologists (or name any other interest group you like) have more worthwhile views than other people. By no more than learning the language of political correctness, taught by modern media, you're more enlightened.

What are the benefits offered to those who buy into the class-distinction agenda?

In today's world, those who gain entrance into the preferred class are rewarded with almost unlimited access to the mass media, as long as they print in big lines or speak in loud voices against those people they hold to be inferior and whose beliefs they hold to be wrong. The mighty pen becomes the mighty sword for ensuring that the cultural battle rages on.

Since the sixties our courts have bombarded us with rulings willing to seek parity in America by promoting factionalism among race and class. Rather than elevate the time-honored traditions of individualism that a free society recognizes, our counselors on high have shown themselves determined to mete out welfare sustenance rather than encourage – or better yet, demand – the personal achievement that can only come through hard work and self enterprise. The *pursuit*, as our Founding Fathers so aptly put it.

I can clearly remember the first time I saw those massive highrise buildings built by our tax dollars in the great city of Chicago, buildings constructed to house a new subculture that the government had decided to micromanage. The "projects" were an invitation to failure, and fail we did when we began subdividing American citizens and pinning labels on them. The results were disastrous.

I find it deplorable that we have insulated and isolated minority Americans from the ebb and flow of mainstream society and called it "civil rights" and "social welfare." Socialism masquerading as civil rights has done little over the last thirty years except to disassociate and alienate one essential segment of our population.

The factors that eventually bring people together are often those that are measured on economic scales. Those made comfortable in a welfare system are those who eventually "die" emotionally and psychologically in that same system. A "father knows best" government mentality of providing all needs for all people has robbed an entire group of people of education, social skills, and simple good citizenship.

The cost has been high. Literally billions of dollars in tax money has been used to widen the gap of race and economic strata in America, rather than suture the wounds. Welfare programs have served primarily to *keep too many* people dependent upon government rather than to *free* people by giving them skills and an impetus to work and achieve something on their own.

We should all be skeptical about politicians who sermonize about "creating jobs." The real goal should be to "create employers." Had government stepped aside to let a freer market provide better jobs and steady economic growth for all our citizens, racial and poverty issues would be much closer to resolution.

Dr. King opened the door to equality. The do-gooders who followed flaunted welfare as a shortcut to a better life. In fact, it was just slavery in another form, a modern incarnation of dependency on someone other than yourself.

Welfare thus turned out to be a crime cloaked in guilt. Its mindless, mechanized redistribution of wealth gave and gave and gave, while welfare recipients used and too many abused. The welfare culture forgot about one very important word that helps steer the ship of a free society: pride. Pride in ownership, pride in achievement, pride in accomplishment – such pride is directly related to freedom.

At a civic club speech I gave, a businessman told me, "I hired a young Hispanic woman as a secretary because the employment agency gave her a high rating. Race wasn't an issue. Then, after she typed some dictation, I noticed she wasn't much of a speller. I politely asked her to spend some time working on it. She was furious. She flew into a rage and accused me of being prejudiced against Hispanics. Then she quit and filed a grievance against me. The truth is, had a white secretary performed so poorly, I'd have fired her."

For me, the most enduring and saddening ethnic challenge is why black households are more likely than white households to be headed by a woman without a husband, father, or partner living there. As of 1999, the situation had improved little; while married couples headed 47 percent of the country's 8.4 million black households, about 45 percent were led by women without partners present. Of all white households, only 13 percent are headed by women alone.

This situation may have old roots. Rather than instill pride that motivates hard work and creative initiative, the welfare advocates of the sixties and seventies built housing projects and funded endless states of unemployment. This fostered a cesspool of inhuman violence, broken families, drug addiction, and child abuse. The housing projects became a nightmare of blood, broken glass, screams in the night, wide-eyed children huddled in fear, and souls virtually stripped away from children at birth. This was the lifestyle gangsta rap often reflects while complaining, "The white man did this to us." But at its heart, the collective contempt is not really so much against the white man or any color of man, but against their own failure to realize their greatness.

What a Riot Revealed

In an earlier chapter I mentioned the fear that swept through the Los Angeles basin after the Rodney King trial verdict. It was a frightful time, owing to old ethnic and racial hatreds fanned to a full flame by media and special interests sensing that new jockeying for power might arise from the ashes of this agony, bloodshed, and destruction.

The phenomenon of thousands of people literally burning themselves out of house and home in a fit of rage is a deplorable spectacle and intolerable response to a court verdict. It is even more deplorable when you consider that in the months that followed the destruction, this criminal element actually demanded that our government rebuild, with tax dollars from law-abiding citizens, all that they had destroyed in their fury. The tax base dutifully coughed up the funds.

The riots in the wake of the Rodney King verdict will long be remembered as a social outrage. However, few are likely to remember that much of the explosive hatred, originally aimed at white cops and the white community, was quickly widened to target the Korean business community that had moved into an economically deprived area. Through hard work and determination, the Koreans had built thriving businesses, just as the Constitution had promised they had the right to do.

During the riots, many threatened Korean storekeepers posted giant signs in their windows that read, "YOU LOOT, WE SHOOT." The looters left those stores alone. My guess is those signs had as much influence stopping the burning, vandalizing, looting, murdering mob as the L.A. police.

It appeared that when blacks felt an injustice had been done to them in the court system, they vented their hatred and anger not at the courts, and not even at whites, but rather, at the Koreans. Somehow these dissidents, wetnursed on a lifelong welfare system, felt that they had been shortchanged their piece of someone else's pie. They internalized their perceived injustice of the court as a perceived injustice of the economy, right in their own back yard, though they had full constitutional rights to pursue businesses of their own had they been willing to do so.

The doors that Dr. King opened on one side of the cultural spectrum seemed to result in doors that the black community slammed shut on moral issues. One of the sad legacies of the welfare state is that mature morality recedes and childish entitlement flourishes. Jealousy, rage, vandalism, and looting are never a means to resolve grievances, I don't care what color you are or how rightful your grievances.

A Bright Present, A Brighter Future

To place racial dissension in America in perspective, remember that the Constitution guarantees the right to *pursue* happiness. It doesn't *guarantee* happiness. We are all given equal opportunity to the chase, but the catch remains a matter of personal initiative and determination. The widespread success of those who *have* chosen this route is grossly underreported.

Author and management consultant Peter Drucker, writing in *Atlantic Monthly*, has said that no group in world history has ever made so much economic progress so fast as American blacks have since World War II to the present day. Three-fifths of African-Americans have risen into middle-class incomes, whereas before World War II, the figure was one-twentieth.

While nobody would call America a totally colorblind workplace yet, you rarely hear the progress reports. John Leo cited America's "addiction to bad news" regarding race relations in *U.S. News & World Report* and countered:

> The black dropout rate from high school has come way down and is now 5 percent, vs. 4 percent for whites. There are almost seven times as many black college students today – 1,410,000 – as there were in 1960. Among college-educated, full-time workers, 28 percent of blacks have executive, administrative or managerial jobs, vs. 30 percent for non-Hispanic whites – a dramatic improvement. Doors are opening every day.

What's more, Leo continued:

Hispanic immigrants are succeeding, assimilating and inter-marrying with native stock at about the same rates as the white ethnic immigrants of a century ago. The wages of second-generation Mexican-Americans are nearly identical to those of similarly educated non-Hispanic whites – quite an accomplishment. My own Irish and Italian immigrant ancestors took much longer to reach parity, under far better economic conditions. But don't breathe a word of this. It's good news.

No one I know objects to any qualified, talented person of any color or persuasion earning their way into any production. But directives from "diversity coalitions" strike me as something less than colorblind.

For example, as I write, all four major broadcast networks have bent to pressure from the NAACP and committed to a more ethni-cally diverse fall television season. The NAACP had threatened lawsuits if more minorities weren't included in programming. "These agreements will bring real, meaningful change," said Kweisi Mfume, president of the National Association for the Advancement of Colored People.

Two questions occur to me. First, how will the relative ethnicity of make-believe TV shows constitute "real, meaningful change"? And second, I wonder how the NAACP would react if those same forced ethnic quota characters on TV referred to themselves as "colored people," reflecting their benefactors' namesake? By the way, Mfume also said his next focus is similar pressure on the motion pic-ture industry.

As it stands, the twenty-first century promises to become one of our most ethnically-challenged centuries yet. Census data in 1999 predicted that America's populace will become even more diverse in this century; the black population will rise to 59.2 million in 2050 – which represents a seventy percent increase.

That's why I'm alarmed that too many leaders perpetuate racial and cultural divisions that divide black and white, black and yellow, red and white, red and black and yellow, Arab and Jew, black and Jew, Christian and Jew, urban and rural, men and women, young and old, liberal and conservative, gay and straight, religious and agnostic, Mexican and American. There's plenty of venom to go around, to be sure, yet too little regard for the all-embracing arms of the Statue of Liberty and her promise that the Constitution and the Bill of Rights extend to all citizens and never just to the factional flavor of the day.

It may take sacrifice, which is the point of courageous step #9, *Accept that sacrifice is just part of the deal,* on page 159.

But I look forward to the day when we dismiss the factions created by greedy advertisers and power-hungry politicians. I look forward to the day when every child born into this nation is not subjected to infinite forms of class division, but is instead judged by how he or she deploys his or her God-given potential, and not by ethnic history or the color of skin – including those who are born white.

I believe that our many heritages are to be welcomed and celebrated, both in their uniqueness and their juxtaposition. Like exciting cuisines and art found where two cultures meet, our diverse peoples should be complementary catalysts for greatness. In America's contrasts we have always found vitality. There is energy in our diversity, and we should extract it.

I look forward to the day when we all find strength, not strife, in our differences. And I'm going to do all I can to hasten that day.

CHAPTER ELEVEN

A Tent Revival for Tolerance

Give me that old time religion, give me that old time religion,
Give me that old time religion, it's good enough for me.
— Traditional gospel song

The same Bill of Rights that protects our right to keep and bear arms guarantees each American citizen a right to worship as he or she pleases. Freedom of religion is as deeply ingrained in our Constitution as any of the other personal liberties framed by our Founders. In fact, it was a desire to escape religious intolerance in the old countries that was a principal factor in pilgrims of a number of faiths coming to our shores in the seventeenth and eighteenth centuries.

Therefore, the Founding Fathers were adamant when it came to guaranteeing freedom of religion. Faith, and the free expression thereof, was vitally important to free men and women of that era. They had endured spiritual suffocation from governments with a prescribed national church and religion. They burned with eagerness to express their connection to God in a manner of their own choice, and they saw this not only as a privilege for the devout, but as a right that was divine.

In the United States of America we have no state church. It is this way by constitutional design.

Our Constitution declares that we have a right to worship as we choose, or not at all. While this has been interpreted to mean a separation of church and state, I believe it also means that the government can neither establish a state religion nor discriminate against, seek to abolish, or destroy any religion that certain members of the government, press, or media determine to be "unfashionable" or "outside the accepted social order."

Sadly, were the Founding Fathers suddenly to step forward onto the stage of contemporary events, they might feel that modern government, in concert with the cultural reformers with whom our government seems to ally itself, has been overwhelmed by spiritual indifference and even a certain cynicism toward expressions of faith.

Does Faith Have a Prayer?

As it stands today, what I refer to as the "designer religions" remain very much in vogue. But woe be unto you should you feel the urge to take up serpents as a religious rite, as some of our brethren in the rural South still choose to do. Oddly, it is somehow not as culturally sacrosanct as the equally sacred practices of consuming peyote cactus to induce visions, or even the Hopi Snake Dance, celebrated rites known to Native Americans. But more about that later.

Even though practices such as snake handling as an expression of faith may revolt some, this practice is just as spiritual in the eyes of its practitioners as a prayer offered in a synagogue or church is to others. And therefore, constitutionally speaking, it's a protected practice.

As the self-styled executors of change in America, cultural reformers often deride fundamentalist and evangelical religions, and especially those that remain popular in rural areas. They infer upon them a lesser level of intellect, a surly affinity for firearms, a general ethnic intolerance, and a brimming dose of paranoia. Certain religious expressions have, pardon the pun, come under the same "cultural gun" as the right to keep and bear arms. Both are out of fashion among a faction who view themselves as enlightened.

The cultural conquerors, sadly, are not content merely to privately scorn the religious practices they disdain. Rather, with holier-than-thou self-righteousness, they publicly ridicule and stereotype styles of faith that vary from those they favor. They are no less religious tyrants than the royalty who forced the monarchy's religion on English commoners and motivated shiploads of devout men and women to set sail for Plymouth Rock.

Several decades ago, the cultural elitists declared that God was dead in America. Many remember the infamous *Time* magazine cover that declared His demise. Since then God has recovered, rebounded, and proved His resilience. Despite a cultural spin that sought to reduce religion to backwoods superstition, the majority of people in America still find solace in religious traditions.

In order to *practice* their religion freely, however, many Americans are being forced to wade through a thick muck of egotistical and elitist posturing that I doubt the Almighty is proud to witness.

Those of the Jewish faith seem perpetually caught in the political crossfire of issues in Israel and feel the need to explain and re-explain their various positions on matters that have nothing to do with the expression of their faith in America.

Christians wrongly feel a need to tiptoe cautiously around Jews and to continue to apologize for past sins against them, even though the vast majority of those Christians and their ancestors had absolutely nothing to do with the Crusades, the Inquisition, or the Holocaust.

Catholics at times feel under intense pressure to modify their traditions to conform to cultural norms.

And Christian evangelical fundamentalists and those who speak in tongues and sing songs to the backbeat of tambourines and guitars under brush arbors struggle just to stay out of the limelight of prime-time criticism.

And all of that's just the tip of the prayer cloth. Such prejudice in the name of God is both terribly sad and an affront to the Constitution that defines religious freedom under the broadest of revival tents. Our Bill of Rights does not forbid religious intolerance solely in the name of Baptists, Jews, Catholics, or Pentecostals. The Bill of Rights, as I and the best of America's constitutional scholars read it, embraces religious opportunity for shakers and glossolalians as well as believers who receive communion at gothic-cathedral altars, as well as Quakers who quiver under the Spirit, as well as those who carry Torah scrolls high on their shoulders, as well as Hispanics who bear the lash of the Penitentes. Religious freedom in America is not reserved territory for Episcopalians, Methodists, Presbyterians, or Lutherans. Religious tolerance here must also embrace religious practices which some – perhaps even the majority – find bizarre and perhaps even offensive.

The Bizarre and the Blessed

A fairly recent high court decision finally came down on the side of "favor" for the use of peyote cactus sacraments by the Native American Church. For many years members of this church were harassed by law enforcement officials because peyote buds, used in Indian rites to induce religious ecstasy, were also classified as a dangerous narcotic on the street, where its possession was declared unlawful. As a result, the Native American Church was driven underground and its rites were considered illegal until the courts decreed that peyote could be obtained and possessed by tribes as long as it was used solely as part of religious observances.

Even with the court's decision, however, we were left with the enigma of a narcotic that leads a strange sort of double life as a potion for religious sacrament and an illegal street drug. Compounding the enigma are all sorts of obvious yet sticky questions. Is peyote legal only for those of Native American ancestry, or only those who can prove membership in the Native American Church? Could an American Indian who happens to be a Methodist be arrested for possession of peyote? What about a white man who attends services in this predominately American Indian religious group – should he be allowed to participate in their sacrament?

A smart lawyer or good constitutional scholar could sort all this out for us, but my main point in raising the issues here is this: Our courts have bent over backwards to observe what the Founding Fathers felt strongly about and what the Constitution decrees. Our right to worship as we choose, even if it flies in the face of stereotypical religious aberration, must not be abridged. Citizens of the United States of America are free to immerse themselves in the rituals of their own faith, as long as the rights of others are not degraded.

Cultural reformers find this a cocklebur to swallow, and for the most part, they continue to overlook the legal and obvious, and continue their relentless attacks of caricature and innuendo against certain religious practices that they regard as backward.

The Christian Caricature

Who among us hasn't seen fundamentalist, evangelical, and charismatic religious practices ridiculed in made-for-TV movies or television sitcoms? Rarely will you find, on any given Sunday morning, a worship service of one of the more conservative denominations given equal time on network broadcasting. These denominations and the parachurch organizations that grew up around them were forced years ago into buying their own air time, and later, into establishing their own networks, in order to give their message a public platform.

This certainly wasn't the result of a lack of popularity of these religions. Fundamentalist faiths are immensely popular in the small towns and villages of rural America, and they are also popular in certain urban enclaves of more conservative states. In fact, if popularity were the basis on which Sunday morning programming was based, networks would be standing in line to air these programs. No, forcing these religious groups to purchase time and networks of their own has been the result of cultural warfare. These religions were simply deemed "out of social fashion" by the elite.

Fashionable or not, rural religions have numbers and a voice. They have spawned an entire media industry of their own – cable outlet networks, independent publishing, bulletins, newspapers, booklets, bookstore chains, and direct mail appeals. Millions of fundamentalist Christians who can't find someone who looks like them or sounds like them on major television network programming or in the *New*

York Times are flourishing quite nicely, thank you, without the mainstream press or media moguls.

What many Americans do not realize is that when they read the list of "top 10" books, fiction or nonfiction, or the "top 10" television programs, they are *not* reading a list that includes any books or programs produced by those who publish or broadcast outside the venues controlled by the cultural elitists.

Hundreds of thousands of copies of books are sold or distributed by authors and publishers in the non-mainstream outlets by evangelical and charismatic groups – in numbers that would automatically secure "best selling" status on any New York list – yet these titles are totally ignored when it comes time for awards, best-seller status, or critiques.

In the same way, non-network religious, evangelical, and charismatic television programs draw millions of regular viewers, yet these numbers are never counted or even recognized by any mainstream, market-share analysts.

Once again, it's useful to draw an analogy to legal ownership of firearms by law-abiding American citizens. Cultural elitists tend to view the "religious right" as a rural phenomenon that should be shoveled aside like so much barnyard manure. They stereotype those who participate in "old-time religion" in many of the same ways they stereotype gun owners – ignorant, hay-chewing, inferior human beings. They make old-time religion practitioners the brunt of "intelligent comedy" in the same way gun owners become the punchline for redneck jokes.

Left without a forum to appeal their case to the majority they themselves represent, old-time religion practitioners have resorted to their own means and venues for communication among themselves. So too, gun owners. Gun owners and advocates of the Second Amendment must purchase advertising when and where they can, and create media vehicles with money from their own pockets to get their word out, not only to the public at large, but to the majority of the public they represent.

Agnostics and atheists with a New Age theory to promote are often given major coverage in today's media. Theirs is the religion that rules the big screen. And their messages regarding abortion, homosexuality, euthanasia, and censorship are the messages aired freely and widely without question. Those who might advocate the existence of God, the importance of morality, the heritage of religious values, right to life, heterosexuality, anti-pornography and anti-euthanasia legislation, or censorship of vile and repugnant displays in public galleries are stifled – not merely stifled, but choked into silence. Their messages are dismissed out of hand as unenlightened, extremist, and reactionary. In order for their opinions to be heard, they must *buy* outlets for their message anywhere they can.

Conversely, anti-gun forces get a free ride on network broadcasts and the pages of the world's most powerful presses, while law-abiding, constitutionally protected gun owners must search diligently to find an outlet that will even accept their paid advertising.

In the rural South, West, and Midwest, of course, fundamentalist churchgoers and gun owners are often one and the same. These people are equally protective of their right to worship as they choose and their right to own a gun. I know from traveling across America and talking to these people face-to-face that they resent the ongoing efforts of the cultural elitists to sweep their fundamentalist heritage and their constitutional privilege under the cultural rug.

Firearms, Faith, and Freedom

It should not go without notice that those who occupied Ruby Ridge and Waco's Mount Carmel were identified principally as cultural fringe separatists who – you guessed it – owned guns. Both groups literally "holed up" to protect themselves from armed federal agents who were ostensibly there to arrest them on gun charges, but who also were suspicious of the practices that were going on behind their closed doors. The outcome was a slaughter of both the family at Ruby Ridge and the sect at Waco in police-state-style blitzkriegs that resulted in the death of innocent children.

Even the battering ram assault upon that Miami household to seize Cuban refugee Elian Gonzalez involved excessive force. Who can forget the photographic image of a SWAT-uniformed federal agent training an MP5 machine gun on a terrified boy in a closet – all because they had heard "there might be guns in that house."

Who gave our federal government even the *notion* that it had a right to assault a religious sect with military-style firepower? It certainly wasn't the Constitution of the United States, which guarantees *every* citizen the free expression of religion and the right to bear arms.

It was a sad day when our nation's federally owned tanks rolled against a religious compound occupied by American citizens, and those accidental but lethal flames leaped skyward, straight from a hell of our own political making. It was a sad day when federal sharp-shooters were called out to take on a family, one or two of whose members may have been technically on the outside of some gun laws, but who were not dangerous or criminal by any account from those who knew them. It's not illegal to be eccentric, odd, strange, fanatic, separatist, zealous, or reclusive.

Who among us can fail to see the obvious solution to both of these situations – a quiet "walking away" and "waiting out" that would eventually have resulted in the questioning of one or two individuals on very specific charges? Who gave the federal government even the vaguest idea that it had a right to approach either of these groups with big-gun, big-media-attention, big-government fury?

These government reactions were just as condemnable as the mob violence and looting in the aftermath of the murder of Dr. Martin Luther King, Jr., or the Rodney King verdict. Rather than restoring law and order, the incidents at Waco and Ruby Ridge only unleashed massive discontent and suspicion for the federal government, and an increased desire on the part of both fundamentalist religious practitioners and gun owners to seek greater privacy and refuge.

The obvious ties in these two related incidents – fundamentalist beliefs and firearms use – have never been closely explored by the mainstream press. Nevertheless, those ties are there. And while the government would deny vigorously that it was engaged in religious persecution, it most certainly must admit that it allowed a detonator of suspicion and fear to be ignited that blew the cap off federal rage. Was that suspicion and fear of an illegal gun or two, or was it a fear of what these people *stood for*, including what they stood for in the arena of their beliefs and faith?

The Constitution is very clear on the point of religious freedom. If we expect to heal some of the deep wounds in our nation, we are going to have to adopt a new level of tolerance. Not the tolerance that the cultural elitists advocate for agnosticism, atheism, social aberrations, and their "cause of the week," but tolerance for the majority of Americans who are people of faith, morality, and religious practice.

Let us adopt courageous step #10: *Commit to the daily process of private prayer* (see page 161). Won't somebody say Amen?

CHAPTER TWELVE

Ten Covenants of Courage

One man with courage makes a majority.
— Andrew Jackson

In this collection of essays, I admit I've been critical of societal bullies, posturing elitists, cultural warlords, and other self-appointed engineers who would remodel the Bill of Rights. They should rightfully be "outted" and revealed for the damage they're doing.

But I hope you've noted my admonition that the final solution isn't to accuse and condemn them, hoping they'll become converts while we commiserate and lament for a better world. That's a futile waste, since we have an infinitely more powerful weapon at our disposal.

No, the path to victory in cultural war, as it is in most matters of personal conviction, is to live by example – and live *loud*.

All true teaching, like parenting, is best conveyed not by talking it up, but by living it out. Conversion starts with the person you face in the mirror in the morning and the family with whom you share your breakfast table. Your doctrine gains disciples not by the life you describe, but by the life you lead.

With each essay of observations, I concluded by offering a specific principle or action plan that could lead us a step closer to salvation of freedom – a way to live courageously. All of these taken together comprise the Ten Covenants of Courage that, if made manifest and alive by millions of us, I believe can indeed salvage our precious freedoms. (No, I did not arrive at "ten" because of the ten amendments contained in the Bill of Rights, or the biblical Ten Commandments with which I'm widely associated. Indeed, one could count ten *thousand* covenants or more. I just stopped at ten because it felt right, and that's how many fingers I see tapping on my keyboard.)

Tragically, you'll notice that the religion of political correctness preached by the media and the government rebukes or derides most of them.

How to Have the Courage to Be Free

1. Find ways to influence government in all of its forms.

Vote. How basic, but oh, how many don't exercise their ballot-box rights. Election after election in our nation is decided by a *minority*, not the majority, of the population. Take time to study the issues at stake and the candidates who are running. Not just in national elections, but in all elections – city elections, school board elections, school bond issue votes, and county and state elections.

The exercise of representative rule isn't limited to the public arena. The democratic process holds sway in corporations, clubs, and churches in America. Literally hundreds of decisions that may affect you are put to a vote each month.

Do you know what decisions are being made by the leaders of the corporations in which you have purchased stock? Are you an active, *voting* shareholder (see my relevant story on page 87)? Do you know what decisions are being made by your union leaders, or by the leaders of various groups to which you belong – such as your neighborhood or community organization, the local PTA, or your church? Do you attend meetings, inform yourself of issues, and voice your opinion through the power of your vote?

Voting is only the beginning, of course. There are other vital ways of influencing the process at all levels and in all sectors. Your contributions to various groups bear weight. Your voice at meetings and your attendance at certain functions, even "silent" attendance, is noted. Your running for an office is a means of increasing your voice, even if you don't win. And for those who do win, the holding of an office – no matter what the organization or hue of the political spectrum – becomes a powerful forum for making decisions and voicing opinions that build up and bolster our heritage of freedom.

I've never met a patriot who was too busy to vote, too busy to speak up in a crowd, or too busy to support those who are on the front lines of the cultural war. As H. L. Mencken has said, "In war, the heroes always outnumber the soldiers ten to one." Your role may not be as a front-line soldier. It may be a supporting role as a contributor, voting member, or silent "presence." You are a hero nonetheless.

2. Be willing to disobey.

Be willing to say "no" through your acts when powerful people expect submission. Be willing to disobey.

Peaceably, yes. Respectfully, of course. Nonviolently, absolutely. But disobedient nonetheless. I learned the awesome power of disobedience from Dr. King, who learned it from Gandhi and Thoreau and Jesus, and every other great person who led those in the right against those with the might.

Disobedience is in our DNA. We feel innate kinship with that disobedient spirit that tossed tea into Boston Harbor, that sent Thoreau to jail, that spurred Rosa Parks' refusal to sit in the back of the bus, that protested a war in Viet Nam. In that same spirit, you must be willing to disavow cultural correctness with personal and collective disobedience of rogue authority, social directives, and onerous law that weaken personal freedom.

There are marches worth joining. There are times when standing up or raising a hand is important. There are placards worth carrying. There are places worth walking into. There are situations worth walking away *from*, refusing participation.

Certainly with nonviolent disobedience you accept risk and perhaps incur some loss. You must be willing to be humiliated, to endure the modern-day equivalent of the police dogs at Montgomery and the water cannons at Selma. You must be willing to experience discomfort.

I'm not complaining, but my own decades of social activism have taken their toll on me. I have consistently disobeyed using language approved for public consumption. When I told an audience recently that white pride is just as valid as black pride or red pride or anyone else's pride, I was called a racist. When I drew an analogy in a speech between the singling out of innocent Jews in World War II days to the singling out of innocent gun owners today, I was called an anti-Semite. When I once challenged an audience to oppose the cultural assaults of those who are trying to redefine our nation, I was compared to Timothy McVeigh!

How might you disobey today? Here are some examples, reflecting current headlines. When you read that a mugger is suing his elderly victim for defending herself, call your friends and collectively jam the switchboard of the district attorney's office.

If your favorite university is pressured to lower its standards to the point that eighty percent of the students graduate with honors, choke the halls of the board of regents annual meeting.

When an eight-year-old boy pecks a girl's cheek on the playground and gets hauled into court for sexual harassment, march on that school with pickets and block its doorway.

When someone you elected is seduced by political power and betrays you, petition them, oust them, banish them.

When a magazine or network or corporation takes a stance against the values or faith that you not only hold dear but which form the very fabric of your soul, boycott their product, or refuse to watch or participate in their endeavor.

It's time we practice the power of disobedience. And I think Dr. King would agree.

3. Take absolute and resolute pride in your own values.

If you believe in your values, say so. You can't reconcile pride in your values with keeping quiet about them. If you are ashamed, you will not speak out.

Let me explain myself with an attempt to reconnect you with what pure freedom feels like.

As a boy roaming the woods of northern Michigan, I imagined I was a thousand different heroes. I was free to dream about all I might become. Maybe you remember that feeling of real freedom, when you were a kid. That was in a time before time, before clocks and mortgages, before taxes and laws and government. Before life and its liars built fences around your dreams, when possibility was limitless and freedom flowed through you like fresh air.

The dawn of day needed no alarm clock. Each new day exploded with possibility. Every tree dared a climb, every hill challenged a look over it. Every car or plane or train was a ticket to adventure. Every bicycle could fly, every pet could talk, good guys won the day, and a new occupation was possible every hour. You were told that in America anyone can be president, and you considered that a serious career option – before romping off into the next what-if and by day's end, fighting sleep for fear you'd miss something.

That's the very essence of freedom – the sheer exhilaration of exploring one's potential and possibilities defined by one's values in life. It's an intoxicating natural high.

It was in these moments of unbridled gallop that your sense of freedom intersected with your set of values, and your life gained the guideposts that would define its geography forever. Your values did not materialize from trivial etiquette primers, but from a deeply-rooted sense of self cultivated by unbounded freedom.

Be proud of that product. Wear it on your chest. And in time, pass it on.

4. Defend America as the peerless ideal – period.

First, commit yourself to clearly understanding the American model, its origins, its history, its Constitution, its standards of freedom. Then, *defend it as the unrivaled, incomparable master achievement of political man in the entire history of the world.* Rather than consider lowering ourselves to the admission price of the "world club," let's help the world elevate its standards and aspire to our model of freedom.

Remember that George Washington and his raggedy rebels in arms defeated the finest army on earth; then the Founding Fathers created the first – and to this day most successful – democracy since the Roman Republic.

Remember that you live in the nation that defeated Communism, defended Europe against the heels of Hitler and Stalin, and rebuilt country upon country after helping win their wars against tyranny. You live in the one nation that still defends democracy around the world. You live in the one nation where you can freely express yourself, freely defend yourself, freely gather together to worship, and freely face others in debate, discuss, or otherwise voice your opinions.

I hear about the "ugly American" with all of his flaws of arrogance, presumption, and pride. What I don't hear much about, and should, is how many tens of millions of people long to come to this nation and would quickly board any means of transportation possible and give any amount of wealth in their possession to reach our shores, even to the point of boarding leaky dinghies, crossing barbed-wire barriers in the freezing dark of night, wallowing in the seasick squalor of cargo holds, and enduring days in stifling overheated vans. We're the only ones with the statue emblazoned with "Give me your tired, your poor..."

And let's forget this "experiment in freedom" stuff. Measured against a Chinese dynasty or Roman civilization, America's little experiment in freedom – only 225 years old – may be an eye blink. But I propose that by every historical standard, this "little experiment" has already stood the test of time. History is the story of change, and our world has changed more in the past two centuries than in all the time before it.

Where history used to be measured by ages – the Iron or Bronze or Dark Ages – or by empires or dynasties like Elizabethan or Chin, today we define time with the breakneck speed of *generations*: the Depression generation, the Baby Boomers, the Generation Xers, and now the Tweeners. We're down to history so swift it's defined by decades: the Twenty-somethings. We in America have compressed into two tiny centuries the perils of an eternity of challenge and change. Yet we have prevailed.

I declare that America is no longer an experiment. It's an accomplishment. It's the best system in the world, and we're not giving it up for anyone's one-worldism.

5. Fiercely preserve all the rights outlined in the Bill of Rights.

You can't cherry pick the Bill of Rights. You can't say I believe this part, but not that part. You can't claim that freedom of the press belongs to Time Warner but not NRA, or that free speech belongs to CBS but not John Rocker, or that gun ownership belongs to body-guarded celebrities but not defenseless commoners. The same rights protect us all, despite our diverse beliefs. That's why the rights of *all* must be protected.

That is, all but the insanities of political correctness gone berserk. In his book, *The End of Sanity*, Martin Gross writes that:

> ...blatantly irrational behavior is rapidly being established as the norm in almost every area of human endeavor. There seem to be new customs, new rules, new anti-intellectual theories regularly foisted on us from every direction. Underneath, the nation is roiling. Americans know something without a name is undermining the nation, turning the mind mushy when it comes to separating truth from falsehood and right from wrong. And they don't like it.

Let me repeat a handful of incidents he mentions, which the Bill of Rights does *not* embrace, that might elicit a smirk but represent the seriousness of our predicament.

• At Antioch College in Ohio, young men seeking intimacy with a coed must get verbal permission at each step of the process from kissing to petting to final copulation...all clearly spelled out in a printed college directive.

- At William and Mary, a group of students tried to change the name of the school team, "The Tribe," because they thought it might insult local Indians. They quickly learned that authentic Virginia chiefs actually liked the name. So did alumni who had been "Tribe" fans for decades. (Just for the record, I happen to be a blood-initiated brother of the Miniconjou Sioux.)
- In San Francisco, city fathers passed an ordinance protecting the rights of transvestites to cross-dress on the job, and for transsexuals to have separate toilet facilities while undergoing sex change surgery.
- In New York City, children who don't speak a word of Spanish have been placed in bilingual classes to learn their three R's in Spanish solely because their last names *sound* Hispanic.
- At the University of Pennsylvania, in a state where thousands died at Gettysburg opposing slavery, the president of the university officially set up a *segregated* dormitory space for black students.

Not too long ago, the head of a Washington, D.C., Office of Public Advocate, David Howard, used the word "niggardly" while talking to colleagues about budgetary matters, and within days, he was forced to publicly apologize and resign. Of course, niggardly means scanty or stingy and has no racial overtones. But since when do we demand an apology from a public official solely because a word he used might "sound like" a racial slur?

Since when are we so overly sensitive to such words that they take on such great importance and meaning, when the real issues of importance are dismissed with the wave of a hand – issues such as the right of a person to own a firearm, the right of a people to demand law-abiding behavior of their leaders, and the right of a people to demand that government abide by what the framers of the Constitution stated so clearly. In other words, *all* of the Bill of Rights.

6. Find the way to your loudest possible voice, and speak.

Society and modern technology offer a surprising array of communications channels available to you. Some can thunder while others just whisper. Find your most compelling way to speak your values, then make them resonate. Express yourself despite the culture of self-censored silence and negative thought that permeates many churches and schools.

You may not be a thespian or a political speaker. But that doesn't mean you don't have a stage on which to play out your most important role as a patriot.

Your stage might be standing up in a school cafeteria to voice your opinions at a PTA meeting. It might be moving to the microphone that's open to public expression at a school board meeting or a city council meeting.

Your stage may be the letters-to-the-editor forum in your local newspaper, a personal web page on the Internet, a news group, or multi-user mail service.

Your stage may be set in a union hall, a church hall, or a town hall. Or in a corporate boardroom, a chamber-of-commerce planning session, or a meeting of corporate shareholders.

Your stage may be the lectern of a Kiwanis, Rotary, Lions, Shriners, or other community-service club or organization. It may be in the form of a "program" to deliver to a book club, garden club, missionary-support club, or church group.

Your stage may actually *be* a stage. If by chance you happen to work in the media industry or marketing or the press, take another look at the opportunity that has been given to you. Are you just "playing a part" that has been scripted for you by someone above you, or are you truly voicing what you *believe?* You have a tremendous opportunity for influence on the side of freedom, heritage, and time-honored values. Take advantage of it.

And always, your stage is the family dinner table, the car in which you drive your children to and from their many activities, and the beach or nature trail along which you walk with your children for times of reflection about what is truly important in life. Rehearse your lines if you must. I do. Know what you believe and why.

Don't be discouraged if you receive no applause. Remember that those who voice politically approved views display no bravery. It takes no courage to parrot back the culturally correct drivel of the day.

It *does* take courage to stand up and say "no" to those who seek to exert power and control in unlawful or immoral ways, to value others and to allow them the full expression of their constitutional rights, and to build lasting and meaningful bridges among groups of people. It takes courage to march on the side of what is right, and to walk out onto any platform that offers you the opportunity to say so.

7. *Embrace change.*

This mandate may seem at odds with themes of preserving our heritage, but it's not. If you've been blessed with four or five decades of life, you know we have no choice but to embrace change. The only individuals who successfully oppose all change are residents of the cemetery.

Change is often scary, often unfair, but usually necessary. Change alone is not evil; it's nature's way. Society is always modernizing itself, even if it seems to step back twice to make one step forward.

It is important that we do not confuse superficial diversions (trendy music and art, for example) or cosmetic novelties (hemlines and hairstyles come to mind) with what doesn't change: our values. To elevate transient fads to the status of genuine societal change misdirects energy and confuses people.

My purpose with this covenant is to remind you that it takes courage to understand, interpret, accept, and gracefully integrate change. And that genuine values always survive change.

8. *Find myriad avenues to pass on your convictions.*

There's no way for your values to outlive you if you don't.

Your number-one audience is always going to be the children or grandchildren who watch your life, listen to your words, and follow in your footsteps. Make sure they follow those footsteps to the voting booths, to the town meeting, to the church pew, and to the display of their work at their school's open house.

Teach your children that every person born beneath American skies has rights nobody can take away, rights that were theirs from the beginning. That fact alone makes them utterly special among all peoples of the earth.

Each of us has a birth certificate, but it didn't give us life. It just puts on paper what we already know: We are alive. In the same way, the Bill of Rights doesn't give us rights. It just puts on paper what we already know: We are free to speak and write and think and work and worship as we choose.

If you consider yourself to be a freedom-loving patriot, you must not shirk your duty to teach America's young people about the Bill of Rights. You must teach them to revere it, embrace it, and defend it. And then in their turn, to bequeath it to others.

You must be a *teacher* to the children you know and love, regardless of what your occupation may be. That includes children everywhere in your sphere of influence. Model for them that you are willing to do the right thing, not just once, but all the time. Model for them how to tolerate others who express differing views and beliefs.

There's no more effective way to instill in children the message of the Golden Rule than to embody it yourself – to do unto others just as you would have them do to you – *where children can observe it.*

9. Accept that sacrifice is just part of the deal.

Life in America simply has a higher price of admission – because the whole production is better from beginning to end. We sacrifice more and get more in return. There's no place in the vanguard of freedom for wimps, whiners, and self-absorbed bluebloods.

Since our nation's founding, free people in America understood they'd have to pay a premium for a freer life. I believe they instinctively accepted more pain, clashes of opinion, personal sacrifice, harsher inconvenience, more distant wars, the proud duty of voting, and political activism, just for starters.

Think back for a moment to the people whose sacrifices instilled in you the flame of freedom. Think about the constellation of selfless people who orbited around you, pulling here and pushing there, shaping your beliefs and molding your character until you became who you are today. Do you remember their sacrifice?

Parents who didn't just talk about values but *lived out* those values.

The gym coach whose knotted rope taught you to pull your own weight.

The scoutmaster who surely had a job and family to tend to, but always made time for you.

The clergyman whose moral compass was always there to guide your way.

The grocery store owner who took time to play along with Mom in a scolding that ended your candy pilfering days forever.

The principal whose handmade paddle was somehow comforting because it meant punishment was certain – but so was forgiveness.

The disabled veteran down the street whose silence after the war taught you unspoken truths about war.

The underpaid teacher who stood up for the weak and stared down the bully.

The neighborhood cop who didn't just know the law, but also knew exactly what you were thinking.

The older stranger you watched at the football game who, during the national anthem, unknowingly guided you by his example to place your hand over your own heart.

And that woman next to him, her eyes fixed on the flag, who taught you that patriotism isn't just for guys.

All those people sacrificed, knowingly or not, as threads in the tapestry of your life that taught you right and wrong, faith and freedom. You, too, have been and always will be called upon by freedom's flame to sacrifice, so its flame may light the American way.

10. Commit to the daily process of private prayer.
Because nobody can lie to God.

Dear reader, these are, in my view, the Ten Covenants of Courage we're all obligated to honor to sustain America's freedom. These are the ten commitments you must personally make in your heart, covenants between you and whomever you consider your Maker to be.

And then you must walk the walk, not just talk the talk.

But take heart – for your courage is contagious. And with each step along the way you will, by your example alone, confound adversaries, make converts, inspire believers, and cast countless seeds for unborn future followers who will someday cultivate their own courage to be free.

An Appendix of Selected Speeches

I'm thankful for the many invitations I accept each year to speak at gatherings of every stripe and regret the many more I can't fulfill. Public speaking is not something most actors seek or even enjoy, especially if your political soapbox isn't the most popular brand of the day.

But I cherish the opportunity, perhaps the duty, to speak my mind. And however frank my words, my audiences are universally gracious and tolerant – as Americans functioning under the First Amendment ought to be. For that, I am grateful, too.

As I wrote this book, I drew upon many ideas I've offered audiences over recent years. Not all of my opinions always passed such a tough field test, of course, but they were no less heartfelt. As I peruse these various addresses, I can see my political and social thought being reviewed and refined through the lens of fresh news events, but always with the fundamental theme in focus: That personal courage, mustered with each sunrise and practiced with conviction, is the true fuel of freedom.

So I offer a selection of those speeches here. Thanks for listening.

Charlton Heston
Hollywood, California
August 2000

REMARKS BEFORE THE 125TH ANNUAL MEETING OF MEMBERS OF THE NATIONAL RIFLE ASSOCIATION

March 30, 1996 Dallas, TX

I REMEMBER MY SON, WHEN HE WAS FIVE, EXPLAINING TO HIS KINDERGARTEN CLASS WHAT HIS FATHER DID FOR A LIVING. "MY DADDY," HE SAID, "PRETENDS TO BE PEOPLE."

THERE HAVE BEEN QUITE A FEW OF THEM. PROPHETS FROM THE OLD AND NEW TESTAMENTS, A COUPLE OF CHRISTIAN SAINTS, GENERALS OF VARIOUS NATIONALITIES AND DIFFERENT CENTURIES, SEVERAL KINGS, THREE AMERICAN PRESIDENTS, A FRENCH CARDINAL AND TWO GENIUSES, INCLUDING MICHELANGELO. IF YOU WANT THE CEILING REPAINTED I'LL DO MY BEST. I DON'T MEAN TO BOAST... PLEASE UNDERSTAND. IT'S JUST THAT THERE ALWAYS SEEM TO BE A LOT OF DIFFERENT FELLOWS UP HERE, AND I'M NOT SURE WHICH ONE OF THEM GETS TO TALK.

ONE OF THE MOST REMARKABLE MEN, ONE OF THE THREE PRESIDENTS, WAS THOMAS JEFFERSON, WHO IS GENERALLY RECOGNIZED AS THE ONLY GENIUS TO EVER OCCUPY THE WHITE HOUSE. WHEN JOHN KENNEDY WAS ENTERTAINING SEVERAL DOZEN NOBEL LAUREATES IN THE EAST ROOM, HE SAID TO THEM, "I'M SURE THERE'S NEVER BEEN SUCH A CONCENTRATION OF BRAINPOWER ASSEMBLED IN THIS ROOM SINCE TOM JEFFERSON ATE HERE ALONE."

ONE OF HIS BIOGRAPHERS SUMMED UP JEFFERSON'S CAPACITIES MORE SUCCINCTLY: "HE COULD BREAK A HORSE," HE SAID, "AND DANCE A MINUET AND TIE AN ARTERY. HE ALSO WROTE THE DECLARATION OF INDEPENDENCE." BY ANY MEASURE, THOMAS JEFFERSON WAS A GREAT MAN.

SO LET US CONSIDER GREAT MEN. I KNOW THERE ARE GREAT WOMEN, TOO, BUT I DON'T GET TO PLAY THEM.

GREAT MEN WOULD BE SUSPECT TODAY, PERHAPS BECAUSE WE DON'T HAPPEN TO HAVE MANY OF THEM AROUND. WE HAVE GOOD MEN... GIFTED MEN...GOD KNOWS WE HAVE PLENTY OF FAMOUS MEN...BUT THAT'S NOT THE SAME THING. ANYONE CAN BE FAMOUS, AND THE FAMOUS ARE LIKE ANYONE.

BUT VERY FEW CAN BE GREAT, AND THE GREAT ARE LIKE NO ONE ELSE. MEN LIKE THOMAS JEFFERSON AND ANDREW JACKSON, THOMAS MORE AND CARDINAL RICHELIEU, MARC ANTONY AND MICHELANGELO, MOSES AND JOHN THE BAPTIST.

OF ALL THE GREAT MEN I'VE HAD THE GOOD FORTUNE TO PLAY, THE MOST TOWERING, BOTH IN THE RECORD OF HIS LIFE AND HIS IMPACT ON HUMAN HISTORY, WAS MOSES. LAWGIVER TO THE JEWS, WARRIOR PROPHET OF ISLAM TO THE MOSLEMS, FIRST AMONG THE PROPHETS TO CHRISTIANS. THAT'S HOW FAR THE SHADOW OF THE MAN, MOSES, REACHES. BUT HE WAS A MAN, REMEMBER. NONE OF THE THREE RELIGIONS THAT REVERE HIM CALL HIM DIVINE. HE WAS A MAN, AND FLAWED, LIKE ALL OF US.

BUT MOSES STOOD FOR FREEDOM. FOR MORE THAN TWENTY-FIVE CENTURIES, HE HAS INSPIRED THOSE WHO SEARCH FOR LIBERTY.

IT'S NO COINCIDENCE THAT THE FIRST TIDE OF OUR PROTESTANT FOREFATHERS IN AMERICA BORE THE NAMES FROM THE EXODUS: MOSES AND AARON, ABRAHAM, JOSHUA AND ISAAC. GENERATIONS OF BLACK AMERICAN MEN BORE THOSE NAMES HERE, TOO, FIRST SEARCHING FOR FREEDOM, THEN CELEBRATING IT.

THE WORDS MOSES SPOKE AS HE WATCHED HIS PEOPLE CROSS OVER JORDAN, FREE AT LAST, ARE CUT IN THE RIM OF OUR LIBERTY BELL: "PROCLAIM LIBERTY THROUGHOUT ALL THE LAND UNTO ALL THE INHABITANTS THEREOF."

THE INSTINCT FOR FREEDOM...IT SEEMS TO BE PART OF THE HUMAN CONDITION, DOESN'T IT? ...LIKE BREATHING, FREEDOM IS INSTINCTIVE.

SO AS I PONDERED OUR 125TH BIRTHDAY VISIT TONIGHT IT STRUCK ME: IF MY CREATOR ENDOWED ME WITH THE TALENT TO ENTERTAIN YOU, THE GIFT TO CONNECT YOU WITH THE HEARTS AND MINDS OF THESE GREAT MEN...IF MY CREATOR HAS LET ME SPEND MY LIFE HELPING YOU FEEL WHAT YOU DIDN'T KNOW YOU COULD FEEL...THEN I CHOOSE TO USE THAT SAME GIFT NOW, TO RECONNECT YOU WITH A GREATNESS OF PURPOSE THAT ALREADY RESIDES IN YOU.

YOU SEE, I BELIEVE THAT IN THIS AGE OF MEDIA STIMULATION, YOU'VE BECOME NUMB TO THE MAJESTY THAT SURROUNDS YOU. YOU HAVE FORGOTTEN THAT THE RED, WHITE AND BLUE STAND FOR YOUR VALOR, PURITY AND VIGILANCE. YOU HAVE BEEN HIJACKED AND JADED, CONNED RIGHT OUT OF YOUR OWN BIRTHRIGHT. YOU NO

LONGER TRUST THE PULSING STUFF INSIDE YOU THAT MADE THIS COUNTRY ERUPT FROM MUD INTO THE MIRACLE THAT IT IS.

WELL, IT IS STILL THERE. "THOSE WHO CANNOT REMEMBER THE PAST," SAID SANTAYANA, "ARE CONDEMNED TO REPEAT IT." I AGREE. STRONGLY. I'M CONVINCED HISTORY IS NOT ONLY THE MOST IMPORTANT SUBJECT, IT IS THE ONLY SUBJECT. AND YOUR HISTORY IS A WINNER.

I KNOW, I KNOW. MEASURED AGAINST A CHINESE DYNASTY OR ROMAN CIVILIZATION, AMERICA'S "LITTLE EXPERIMENT" IN FREEDOM – TWO HUNDRED YEARS – IS BUT AN EYE BLINK. BUT I PROPOSE THAT BY EVERY HISTORICAL STANDARD, THIS "LITTLE EXPERIMENT" HAS ALREADY STOOD THE TEST OF TIME. HISTORY IS THE STORY OF CHANGE. AND OUR WORLD HAS CHANGED MORE IN THE PAST TWO CENTURIES THAN IN ALL THE TIME BEFORE IT.

WHERE HISTORY USED TO BE MEASURED BY AGES – THE IRON OR BRONZE OR DARK AGES...OR BY EMPIRES OR DYNASTIES – ELIZABETHAN OR CHIN...TODAY WE DEFINE TIME WITH THE BREAK-NECK SPEED OF GENERATIONS: THE DEPRESSION GENERATION, THE BABY BOOMERS, THE GENERATION XERS, AND NOW THE TWEENERS. WE'RE DOWN TO HISTORY SO SWIFT IT'S DEFINED BY DECADES: THE TWENTY-SOMETHINGS. WE IN AMERICA HAVE COMPRESSED INTO TWO TINY CENTURIES THE PERILS OF AN ETERNITY OF CHALLENGE AND CHANGE. YET WE HAVE PREVAILED.

I PROPOSE THAT AMERICA IS NO LONGER AN EXPERIMENT. IT IS AN ACCOMPLISHMENT. FREEDOM WORKS. YOU INHERITED IT. AND YOU DARE NOT NEGLECT IT. BUT BEQUEATH IT.

THAT MEANS YOU MUST FIND IT AND FEEL IT AND CHERISH IT AGAIN, RECONNECT WITH ITS ESSENCE. HAVE YOU FORGOTTEN HOW?

IF YOU WANT TO RECONNECT WITH AN ANCESTOR, YOU TOUCH HIS TINTYPE PHOTO, OR SMELL THE BRITTLE PAGE OF HER DIARY, OR IF YOU'RE LUCKY, YOU FEEL THEIR PRESENCE IN A FAMILY TRADITION. YOUR HAND CAN TOUCH THE WELLSPRING OF YOUR FAITH, TRACING THE SAME SURFACE AS THE PROPHETS ON THE WAILING WALL IN JERUSALEM OR THE TABERNACLE IN SALT LAKE CITY.

IF YOU YEARN FOR THE CAMARADERIE OF YOUR SCOTTISH FORE-FATHERS, IMMERSE YOURSELF IN THE LONGING LYRIC OF AULD LANG

SYNE. PUT A NAUTILUS TO YOUR EAR, AND YOU CAN CONTEMPLATE THE SAME OCEAN ROAR THAT SOCRATES CONTEMPLATED.

CHILDREN RECONNECT WITH LOST FATHERS PROBING NAMES ETCHED IN THE VIET NAM MEMORIAL. YOU CAN BE DWARFED BY THE SAME GLORY AS WERE WORSHIPPING PEASANTS...BY BEHOLDING THE VERY SAME CATHEDRAL OF NOTRE DAME. MUSLIMS RECONNECT EACH MORNING, HEARING THE SAME HORN THAT CALLED MUHAMMAD TO PRAYER. HINDUS RECONNECT AS THEY BATHE IN THE SACRED WATER OF THE GANGES.

YOU CAN TASTE A COLONIAL BREAKFAST IN THE SPRING SAP SYRUP OF NEW ENGLAND. YOU CAN FALL IN AWE OF THE SAME ANCIENT BEAUTY AND SYMMETRY AND LONGEVITY WHERE THE PYRAMIDS RISE FROM THE FLAT PLAINS OF EGYPT. OR YOU CAN SENSE THE REPUGNANT EVIL BLACKNESS THAT WAS ADOLPH HITLER IN THE GAS CHAMBERS OF AUSCHWITZ AND TREBLINKA.

YOU CAN FEEL YOUR HEART QUICKEN, AS DID YOUR ANCESTORS, STANDING AT GETTYSBURG, WHERE BROTHER BUTCHERED BROTHER OVER WHETHER YOU SHOULD BE AN AMERICAN, OR A SOMETHING ELSE.

AND IF YOU WANT TO FEEL THE WARM BREATH OF FREEDOM UPON YOUR NECK...IF YOU WANT TO TOUCH THE PULSE OF LIBERTY THAT BEAT IN OUR FOUNDING FATHERS, YOU MAY DO SO THROUGH THE MAJESTY OF THE SECOND AMENDMENT. BECAUSE THERE, IN THAT WOODEN STOCK AND BLUED STEEL, LIES WHAT GIVES THE MOST COMMON OF COMMON MEN THE MOST UNCOMMON OF FREEDOMS. WHEN ORDINARY HANDS ARE FREE TO OWN THIS EXTRAORDINARY SYMBOL, REPRESENTING THE FULL MEASURE OF HUMAN DIGNITY AND LIBERTY, THAT IS AS GOOD AS IT GETS.

IT DOESN'T MATTER WHETHER ITS PURPOSE IS TO DEFEND OUR SHORES OR YOUR FRONT DOOR...WHETHER IT IS A RITE OF PASSAGE FOR A YOUNG MAN OR A TOOL OF SURVIVAL FOR A YOUNG WOMAN...WHETHER IT BRINGS MEAT FOR THE TABLE OR TROPHIES FOR THE SHELF...WITHOUT RESPECT TO AGE, OR GENDER, OR RACE, OR CLASS, THE SECOND AMENDMENT RIGHT TO KEEP AND BEAR ARMS CONNECTS US ALL – WITH ALL THAT IS RIGHT.

THAT IS THE NRA'S CONTRIBUTION TO AMERICAN FREEDOM. WITHOUT THE NRA THIS WOULD BE A DIFFERENT USA. WITHOUT

THE NRA, AMERICAN FREEDOM WOULD BE MORE LIKE CANADIAN FREEDOM, OR ARGENTINE FREEDOM, OR AUSTRALIAN FREEDOM.

BUT IT'S PURE, BECAUSE NRA HAS STAYED TRUE TO ITS MISSION. FOR 125 YEARS, YOU HAVE AVOIDED THE TRENDY AND TRANSIENT. YOU HAVE NOT BEEN WARPED BY GENERATIONAL INFLUENCES OR THE CONVENIENCE OF POLITICS. YOU DIDN'T SURRENDER YOUR PRINCIPLES OR ABANDON YOUR CHAMPIONS.

AND NO AMOUNT OF OPPRESSION, NO FBI, NO IRS, NO BIG GOVERNMENT, NO SOCIAL ENGINEERS, NO MATTER WHAT AND NO MATTER WHO, THEY CANNOT CLEAVE THE GENES WE SHARE WITH OUR FOUNDING FATHERS.

REMEMBER, THEY GUARANTEED US LIFE, LIBERTY, AND THE PURSUIT OF HAPPINESS. THEY DIDN'T PROMISE US HAPPINESS, ONLY THE CHANCE TO CHASE IT. AND BY THE WAY, BEING POLITICALLY CORRECT IS NOT THE WAY TO GET THERE. IF AMERICANS BELIEVED IN POLITICAL CORRECTNESS, WE'D STILL BE KING GEORGE'S BOYS – SUBJECTS ENSLAVED TO THE BRITISH CROWN.

PLEASE, PLEASE LET OUR CHILDREN BE POLITICALLY COMPETENT...LET THEM BE POLITICALLY CONFIDENT...POLITICALLY COURAGEOUS...BUT NEVER INSIST THEY BE POLITICALLY CORRECT.

AND TO THOSE WHO SAY THE SECOND AMENDMENT DOESN'T MEAN WHAT WE SAY IT MEANS: LET'S SETTLE IT. THE PURPOSE OF THE BILL OF RIGHTS WAS TO PROTECT PEOPLE FROM THE STATE. OUR FOUNDERS REFUSED TO RATIFY A CONSTITUTION THAT DIDN'T PROTECT INDIVIDUAL LIBERTIES. MAYBE THEY'RE JUST A BUNCH OF WISE, OLD, DEAD, WHITE GUYS, BUT THEY MEANT WHAT THEY SAID. THE SECOND AMENDMENT ISN'T ABOUT THE NATIONAL GUARD OR THE POLICE OR ANY OTHER GOVERNMENT ENTITY. IT IS ABOUT LAW-ABIDING, PRIVATE U.S. CITIZENS, PERIOD.

YOU ARE OF THAT SAME BLOODLINE. YOU ARE SONS AND DAUGHTERS OF THE BOSTON TEA-SPILLERS. WHAT YOU'RE FEELING IS THE PURE PEDIGREE OF FREEDOM...A LINEAGE OF LIBERTY...CONCEIVED IN THE MAGNA CARTA, PROCLAIMED IN THE DECLARATION OF INDEPENDENCE AND GUARANTEED BY THE U.S. CONSTITUTION. OF COURSE IT IS YOUR INSTINCT, AND I SAY THEREFORE IT IS YOUR DUTY, TO TAKE BACK THIS COUNTRY, REPOSSESS THIS GOVERNMENT, AND RESTORE AMERICA'S FUNDAMENTAL UNIT OF GREATNESS: INDIVIDUAL RESPONSIBILITY.

AND YOU DON'T NEED ANYBODY'S PERMISSION OR SO-CALLED EMPOWERMENT. THE MINUTEMEN OF THE AMERICAN REVOLUTION WERE NOT THE BEST TRAINED, OR BEST EQUIPPED, OR BEST FINANCED ARMY AROUND. THEY WERE A COMMON-MAN BAND OF FARMERS AND LABORERS WHO WERE NOT EVEN ESPECIALLY HANDY WITH A MUSKET. BUT THEIR REAL ARSENAL BEAT IN THEIR CHESTS. THEY WERE EXPLODING WITH MOTIVATION, BECAUSE THEIR FAMILIES AND FARMS AND CHURCHES WERE ON THE LINE.

IT IS NO DIFFERENT FOR YOU HERE. YOUR FAMILIES AND THEIR FUTURES ARE ON THE LINE, AND IT IS YOUR TURN TO MUSTER. OR SOON YOUR COUNTRY WILL FEEL FOREIGN TO YOU, AND YOUR POSTERITY WILL INHERIT A PERVERSE VERSION OF WHAT AMERICA WAS MEANT TO BE.

HOW CAN WE RECONNECT WITH WHAT AMERICA WAS MEANT TO BE?

OVER THE YEARS I PUT TOGETHER A CLIP FILE NOTING WHAT EXTRAORDINARY AMERICANS HAVE SAID ABOUT AMERICA THE PAST TWO CENTURIES. ONE DAY I SPREAD OUT SOME OF THESE FILE CARDS AND, IN MINUTES, FITTED THEM TOGETHER INTO A SINGLE PARAGRAPH WITH AN EASE THAT STUNNED ME. THESE WORDS FROM DIFFERENT MEN, FROM DIFFERENT BACKGROUNDS, FROM DIFFERENT CENTURIES, FROM DIFFERENT GENERATIONS, THEY SEEMED TO SPEAK TO US WITH THE SAME VOICE FROM ACROSS THE AGES...THESE WORDS OF MARTIN LUTHER KING, JR., F. SCOTT FITZGERALD, TOM PAINE, SAMUEL ELIOT MORISON, WILLIAM FAULKNER AND ABRAHAM LINCOLN:

"I HAVE A DREAM. I REFUSE TO ACCEPT THE END OF MAN. I BELIEVE HE WILL ENDURE. HE WILL PREVAIL. MAN IS IMMORTAL, NOT BECAUSE, ALONE AMONG GOD'S CREATURES, HE HAS A VOICE, BUT BECAUSE HE HAS A SOUL...A SPIRIT CAPABLE OF COMPASSION...AND SACRIFICE...AND ENDURANCE. "ABOUT AMERICA, AND AMERICANS, THIS IS PARTICULARLY TRUE. IT IS A FABULOUS COUNTRY, THE ONLY FABULOUS COUNTRY...WHERE MIRACLES NOT ONLY HAPPEN, THEY HAPPEN ALL THE TIME.

"AS A NATION WE HAVE, PERHAPS UNIQUELY, A SPECIAL WILLINGNESS OF THE HEART...A BLITHE FEARLESSNESS...A SIMPLE YEARNING FOR RIGHTEOUSNESS AND JUSTICE THAT IGNITED IN OUR REVOLUTION A FLAME OF FREEDOM THAT CANNOT BE STAMPED OUT. THAT IS THE LIVING, FRUITFUL SPIRIT OF THIS COUNTRY.

"THESE ARE THE TIMES THAT TRY MEN'S SOULS. THE SUNSHINE PATRIOT AND SUMMER SOLDIER WILL IN THIS CRISIS SHRINK FROM SERVICE. BUT HE THAT STANDS AND SERVES HIS COUNTRY NOW WILL EARN THE THANKS OF MAN AND WOMAN.

"WE MUST BIND UP THE NATION'S WOUNDS. WITH FIRMNESS IN THE RIGHT AS GOD GIVES US TO SEE RIGHT, LET US FINISH THE WORK WE ARE IN."

I BELIEVE THAT SAYS IT ALL. THANKS. IT'S BEEN A PLEASURE.

REMARKS BEFORE THE CONSERVATIVE POLITICAL ACTION CONFERENCE

January 25, 1997 Washington, D.C.

"Be Yourselves, O Americans"

THIS YEAR, AMERICA WILL CHOOSE BETWEEN THE QUICK AND THE DEAD. BETWEEN AN AMERICA THAT CAN LIVE AGAIN...OR MORE OF THE LETHAL LIBERALISM THAT IS KILLING IT.

THIS IS A PIVOTAL MOMENT BECAUSE EITHER WE ARE AMERICANS, OR WE ARE SOMETHING ELSE. EITHER WE KNOW WHO WE ARE AND WHAT WE STAND FOR, OR WE SURRENDER TO SITUATIONAL EVERYTHING, WHERE THERE IS NO ABSOLUTE TRUTH, NO UNRELENTING CONVIC- TION, NO UNSHAKABLE POLICY.

THIS IS A DEFINITIVE MOMENT FOR AMERICA'S IDENTITY. VERY MUCH LIKE A MOMENT IN THIS NATION'S FIRST STUMBLING MONTHS OF FREEDOM FROM BRITAIN.

IT WAS A SCALDING AUGUST DAY IN PHILADELPHIA IN 1776, BARELY ONE MONTH AFTER THEY HAD SIGNED THE DECLARATION OF INDEPENDENCE. OUR FOREFATHERS FOUND THEMSELVES FEELING MUCH AS YOU DO TODAY. ENERGIZED...EXHILARATED...RESOLUTE...

A LITTLE SURPRISED...AND YET DEEPLY HUMBLED BY THE VAST RAW MATERIAL OF DEMOCRACY, THE INFINITY OF POSSIBILITY THAT LAY BEFORE THEM. THEY HAD FINALLY CLAIMED WHAT WAS RIGHTFULLY THEIRS: A FREE PEOPLE, SOVEREIGN RULE, A FERTILE SOIL, A POWERFUL ARMY, A CONSTITUTION. YET AS THE WORLD WATCHED, IN THEIR HEARTS, I THINK SOME WONDERED IF THEY WOULD FALTER.

BUT THEN SAMUEL ADAMS TOOK THE FLOOR AND ANY DOUBT VANISHED, AS HE COMMANDED THEM TO BE GUARDIANS OF THEIR OWN LIBERTY AND AUTHORS OF THEIR OWN DESTINY, WITH WORDS THAT THUNDERED IN THEIR EARS AS THEY SHOULD IN YOURS TODAY: "BE YOURSELVES, O AMERICANS!"

YOU ARE OF THAT SAME BLOODLINE. OF COURSE IT IS YOUR INSTINCT, AND I SAY THEREFORE IT IS YOUR DUTY, TO "BE YOUR-SELVES, O AMERICANS!" TO TAKE BACK THIS CITY, REPOSSESS THIS GOVERNMENT AND RESTORE AMERICA'S MOLECULAR UNIT OF GREATNESS: INDIVIDUAL RESPONSIBILITY.

WHAT BEACON LEADS US THERE? I HAVE REACHED THAT MILESTONE IN LIFE WHEN, LIKE MOST GRANDFATHERS, I ASSESS ANY MATTER OF REAL IMPORTANCE IN GLARING RELIEF AGAINST THE SHINING FACE OF MY GRANDSON. HIS NAME IS JACK. WHAT COURSE MIGHT WE TAKE, THAT WILL BE BEST FOR JACK?

WELL, WHAT WILL BE BEST FOR JACK...IS TO MAKE IT POSSIBLE FOR JACK TO BE HIMSELF.

TO GIVE JACK THE FREEDOM TO FIND GUIDANCE WITHIN HIMSELF – NOT IMPOSED BY SOME DISTANT, FEDERAL DECISION-MAKING FORCE IN HIS LIFE. TO GIVE JACK AN AMERICA IN WHICH HE SEEKS SOLUTIONS IN HIS LIFE THAT ARE FIRST INDIVIDUAL...THEN FAMILIAL...THEN COMMUNAL...THEN LOCAL...AND FINALLY, REGION-AL...AND AT A VERY DISTANT LAST...FEDERAL.

YOUR FAMILIES AND THEIR FUTURES ARE ON THE LINE, AND IT IS YOUR TURN TO MUSTER. OR VERY SOON YOUR COUNTRY WILL FEEL FOR-EIGN TO YOU, AND YOUR POSTERITY WILL INHERIT A POISONED AND PERVERSE VERSION OF AN AMERICA THAT COULD HAVE BEEN.

BEFORE YOU THINK I'M LOST IN SOME SENTIMENTAL, NOSTALGIC NEVER-WAS NEVER-LAND, LISTEN TO THIS. I RECALL HEARING ABOUT HOW RESEARCHERS GATHERED TOGETHER A COLLECTION OF INNER-CITY GANG MEMBERS AND GHETTO KIDS. THEY SHOWED THEM

'50S-VINTAGE MOVIES, NEWS CLIPPINGS, '50S-ERA MEMORABILIA, TV SHOWS LIKE BEAVER AND LUCY AND FATHER KNOWS BEST...PORTRAYING TRADITIONAL FAMILY UNITS, COPS WHO'RE ON YOUR SIDE, CLERGY WHO AREN'T KOOKY, SAFE SCHOOLS, CERTAIN PUNISHMENT, MANAGEABLE CONFLICT.

WHAT HAPPENED? THE RESEARCHERS HYPOTHESIZED THAT THIS CROWD OF CYNICAL, MTV-BRED MALCONTENTS WOULD GREET OZZIE AND HARRIET WITH DERISIVE LAUGHTER AND CATCALLS. BUT INSTEAD, THEY WATCHED IN LONGING SILENCE, WITH EACH PASSING MINUTE YEARNING TO LIVE WITHIN WHAT THEY SAW, INTUITIVELY UNDERSTANDING THE VALUES OF A LIFE THEY'D NEVER LED. THE PARTICIPANTS LATER REPORTED THEY WISHED THEY COULD GO TO THAT FARAWAY PLACE. THAT PLACE WHERE A TEENAGER'S TOUGHEST CHOICE WAS WHICH COLOR WOULD LOOK BEST AT THE PROM, NOT WHICH COLOR WOULD GET YOU KILLED ON THE STREET.

AMERICA YEARNS TO BE TRUE TO ITSELF AGAIN, TO RETURN TO THAT WARM FIRESIDE OF COMMON SENSE AND COMMON VALUES. REMEMBER HOW WE ONCE FELT ABOUT OUR SAFETY, OUR SCHOOLS, OUR POLICE, OUR EMPLOYERS, OUR MEDIA, OUR PARENTS, OUR NEIGHBORS? REMEMBER WHEN WE TRUSTED THE FEDERAL GOVERNMENT TO DO THE RIGHT THING? TODAY ONLY ONE IN FOUR OF US DOES.

AMERICANS WANT LESS GOVERNMENT, A BALANCED BUDGET, MORE INDIVIDUAL RESPONSIBILITY, LESS TAXES. AMERICANS WANT TO REWARD INDUSTRY, NOT IDLENESS. AMERICANS WANT TO BE AMERICAN AGAIN.

AMERICANS CLEARLY WANT THE FUTURE WE OFFER.

BECAUSE WE ARE RIGHT, AND WE'VE BEEN RIGHT ALL ALONG. THE PROOF OF THIS IS THAT THE ARTFUL DODGER, BILL CLINTON, HAS STOLEN OUR SCRIPT.

IN FACT, WE'RE SO RIGHT THAT CLINTON IS FINALLY SAYING IN 1996 WHAT WE WERE SAYING BEFORE THE ELECTIONS IN 1994. FOR THAT MATTER, CLINTON IS SAYING WHAT SOME OF US WERE SAYING IN 1964!

LAST MONTH, WHEN BILL CLINTON ADDRESSED BOTH HOUSES OF CONGRESS IN HIS STATE OF THE USURPATION ADDRESS, HE MOUNTED CLASS WARFARE BY DEMONIZING YOU, THE VERY PEOPLE WHO PROPOSE WHAT POLL AFTER POLL SHOWS AMERICA WANTS.

AND NOW THE DEMOCRATIC NATIONAL LEADERSHIP IS SLINGING GREASEPAINT LIKE A BACKSTAGE FAST-CHANGE ARTIST, TRYING TO CARICATURE CONSERVATIVES AS COLD-HEARTED, CRUEL VILLAINS. THEY WANT TO COPY YOUR CONTENT, BUT CONDEMN YOUR INTENT. THEY WANT TO CO-OPT YOUR SUBSTANCE, BUT VILIFY YOUR STYLE.

I DON'T THINK YOU WILL LET IT WORK. FIRST, BECAUSE THEIR BRAND OF CRADLE-TO-GRAVE SOCIALISM IS ON THE RETREAT EVERYWHERE IN THE WORLD EXCEPT HERE. AND SECONDLY, BECAUSE THEIRS IS NOT THE AMERICA YOU OR I OR MOST AMERICANS WANT.

IN OUR AMERICA, YOU KNEW YOUR OWN NEIGHBORS, YOU PAID YOUR OWN DEBTS, AND YOU CARED FOR YOUR OWN POOR. BUT IN THEIR AMERICA TODAY, DO PEOPLE IDENTIFY MORE WITH THE INHAB-ITANTS OF THE HOUSE NEXT DOOR OR THE INHABITANTS OF THE WHITE HOUSE?

DO PEOPLE FEEL MORE OBLIGATION TO A PERSONAL IOU, OR TO THE FACELESS IRS?

DO THE POOR FEEL KINDNESS WHEN YOU REACH INTO YOUR WALLET, OR DO THEY FEEL ENTITLEMENT WHEN CLINTON REACHES INTO YOUR WALLET?

SINCE HE HAS APPROPRIATED YOUR IDEAS, MR. CLINTON CAN ONLY MALIGN YOUR CHARACTER AS RUTHLESS AND HEARTLESS, WHILE HE CONTRASTS HIMSELF AS THE COMPASSIONATE I-KNOW-YOUR-PAIN HANDWRINGER FROM CENTRAL CASTING. WELL, ANY KID'LL TELL YOU, IF YOU CONSUME ENOUGH SUGARCOATING, YOU WILL GET NAUSEATED.

MR. CLINTON, WHAT IS SO COMPASSIONATE ABOUT YOKING OUR KIDS WITH BREATHTAKING DEBT? WHERE IS THE CHARITY IN BANK-RUPTING MEDICARE? WHERE IS THE KINDNESS IN RAIDING SOCIAL SECURITY? SPENDING AMERICA OUT OF GREATNESS IS A FAVOR TO NO ONE.

BILL CLINTON REMINDS ME OF THE WELFARE FATHER, OR DEADBEAT DAD, WHO ONLY SHOWS UP TO BASK IN A FLASH OF GLORY. HE'S NEVER THERE TO DO THE REAL WORK, TO CHANGE THE DIAPERS, TO TUCK YOU IN, TO TOSS THE BALL, TO TEACH DISCIPLINE, TO INSTILL VALUES.

NO, HE ARRIVES JUST IN TIME FOR DESSERT WITH PRESENTS AND SMILES, TO BOUNCE YOU ON HIS KNEE, MAKE YOU FEEL GOOD, AND

DISAPPEAR AGAIN. THIS GIMME-A-FIX ADDICTION HAS DISMANTLED THE COMMUNITY THAT ONCE GAVE US A SENSE OF PLACE AND PURPOSE, A SENSE OF WHO WE ARE AND WHAT WE CAN ASPIRE TO BE.

WELL IT'S TIME TO "BE YOURSELVES, O AMERICANS." YOUR ANCESTORS KNEW EXACTLY WHAT SAM ADAMS MEANT. AND WITHOUT A WORD OF FURTHER HISTORICAL EXPLANATION, SO DO YOU.

YOU KNOW WHAT TO DO. THE SOLUTION STARTS, NOT WITH CHANGING THIS COUNTRY, OR THIS CONGRESS, OR EVEN THIS CONFERENCE. BUT WITH REGAINING RENEWED CONFIDENCE IN YOUR OWN CONVICTION.

YOU NEED ONLY HEAR YOUR HEART, TRUST YOUR HERITAGE, AND ABIDE ITS MESSAGE.

YOU NEED ONLY BE YOURSELVES, O AMERICANS, WITH COURAGE AND WITHOUT APOLOGY.

WE CAN BE TOUGH BUT FAIR.

WE CAN CUT TAXES BUT STILL CARE FOR OUR OWN.

WE CAN BE TRUE TO OUR FOUNDING FATHERS WITHOUT HARMING THEIR POSTERITY.

WE CAN RECLAIM SELF-RESPECT, WITHOUT TAKING IT AWAY FROM ANYONE ELSE.

WE CAN DEFEAT BILL CLINTON AND EVERYTHING HE REALLY STANDS FOR.

LET'S NOT WASTE ANOTHER FORTY YEARS AND FIVE TRILLION DOLLARS.

WE ARE IN THE ARENA, AND WE ARE IN THE RIGHT.

FOR MY JACK, AND FOR YOURS, HAVE THE COURAGE NOW TO "BE YOURSELVES, O AMERICANS."

THANK YOU.

REMARKS BEFORE THE NATIONAL PRESS CLUB

September 1, 1997 Washington, D.C

"The Second Amendment: America's First Freedom"

TODAY I WANT TO TALK TO YOU ABOUT GUNS: WHY WE HAVE THEM, WHY THE BILL OF RIGHTS GUARANTEES THAT WE CAN HAVE THEM, AND WHY MY RIGHT TO HAVE A GUN IS MORE IMPORTANT THAN YOUR RIGHT TO RAIL AGAINST IT IN PRINT.

I BELIEVE THERE COMES A TIME IN EVERY GOOD JOURNALIST'S LIFE WHEN HE OR SHE NEEDS TO KNOW WHY THE SECOND AMENDMENT, THE RIGHT TO KEEP AND BEAR ARMS, MUST BE CONSIDERED MORE ESSENTIAL THAN RIGHTS THAT GUARANTEE FREEDOM OF THE PRESS AND OF SPEECH.

THIS MAY BE A BITTER PILL TO SWALLOW, BUT THE RIGHT TO KEEP AND BEAR ARMS IS NOT ARCHAIC. IT IS NOT AN OUTDATED, DUSTY IDEA SOME OLD, DEAD, WHITE GUYS DREAMED UP IN FEAR OF RED-COATS. NO, IT IS JUST AS ESSENTIAL TO LIBERTY TODAY AS IT WAS IN 1776. THESE WORDS MAY NOT PLAY WELL AT THE PRESS CLUB, BUT IT'S STILL THE GOSPEL DOWN AT THE CORNER BAR AND GRILL.

AND EVEN MORE IMPORTANTLY, YOUR EFFORTS TO UNDERMINE THE SECOND AMENDMENT, TO DERIDE IT AND DEGRADE IT, TO READILY ACCEPT DILUTING IT AND WILLINGLY PROMOTE REDEFINING IT, THREATEN NOT ONLY THE PHYSICAL WELL-BEING OF MILLIONS OF AMERICANS BUT ALSO THE CORE CONCEPTS OF INDIVIDUAL LIBERTY OUR FOUNDING FATHERS STRUGGLED TO PERFECT AND PROTECT.

SO NOW YOU KNOW: I BELIEVE STRONGLY IN THE RIGHT OF EVERY LAW-ABIDING CITIZEN TO KEEP AND BEAR ARMS, FOR WHAT I THINK ARE VERY CLEAR AND GOOD REASONS.

LET'S BEGIN WITH A SHORT REFRESHER COURSE IN CONSTITUTIONAL HISTORY. THE ORIGINAL AMENDMENTS WE REFER TO AS THE BILL OF RIGHTS CONTAIN TEN OF WHAT THE CONSTITUTIONAL FRAMERS TERMED UNALIENABLE RIGHTS. THESE RIGHTS ARE RANKED IN RAN-DOM ORDER AND ARE LINKED BY THEIR ESSENTIAL EQUALITY. THE

BILL OF RIGHTS CAME TO US WITH BLINDERS ON. IT DOESN'T RECOGNIZE COLOR, OR CLASS, OR WEALTH. THE RIGHTS IT PROTECTS ARE NOT JUST THE RIGHTS OF ACTORS, OR EDITORS, OR REPORTERS, BUT EXTEND EVEN TO THOSE WE LOVE TO HATE, AND WITH GOOD REASON.

THAT'S WHY THE MOST HEINOUS OF CRIMINALS HAVE RIGHTS UNTIL THEY ARE CONVICTED OF A CRIME. THE BEAUTY OF THE CONSTITUTION CAN BE FOUND IN THE WAY IT TAKES HUMAN NATURE INTO CONSIDERATION. WE ARE NOT A PERFECT SPECIES CAPABLE OF COEXISTING WITHIN A PERFECT SOCIETY UNDER EVERLASTING BENEVOLENT AND WISE RULE. INSTEAD WE ARE WHAT WE ARE. EGOTISTICAL, CORRUPTIBLE, VENGEFUL, SOMETIMES EVEN A BIT POWER MAD. THE BILL OF RIGHTS RECOGNIZES THIS AND BUILDS THE BARRICADES THAT NEED TO BE IN PLACE TO PROTECT THE INDIVIDUAL.

YOU, OF COURSE, REMAIN ZEALOUS IN YOUR BELIEF THAT A FREE NATION MUST HAVE A FREE PRESS AND FREE SPEECH TO BATTLE INJUSTICE, UNMASK CORRUPTION AND PROVIDE A VOICE FOR THOSE DESPERATELY IN NEED OF A FAIR AND IMPARTIAL STAGE.

AND I AGREE WHOLEHEARTEDLY THAT A FREE PRESS IS VITAL TO A FREE SOCIETY. BUT I WONDER: HOW MANY OF YOU WILL AGREE WITH ME THAT THE SECOND AMENDMENT, THE RIGHT TO KEEP AND BEAR ARMS, IS NOT JUST EQUALLY VITAL, BUT THE MOST VITAL AND DESPERATELY NEEDED TO PROTECT ALL THE OTHER RIGHTS WE EMPLOY AND ENJOY?

I WOULD SAY THAT THE SECOND AMENDMENT IS, IN ORDER OF IMPORTANCE, THE FIRST AMENDMENT. I BELIEVE THE SECOND AMENDMENT IS AMERICA'S FIRST FREEDOM, THE ONE RIGHT THAT PROTECTS ALL THE OTHERS. AMONG FREEDOM OF SPEECH, OF THE PRESS, OF RELIGION, OF ASSEMBLY, OF REDRESS OF GRIEVANCES, IT IS THE FIRST AMONG EQUALS. THE RIGHT TO KEEP AND BEAR ARMS IS THE ONE RIGHT THAT ALLOWS "RIGHTS" TO EXIST AT ALL. IT IS THE RIGHT THAT SAYS FREE MEN AND WOMEN MAY TAKE UP ARMS TO DEFEND THEIR LIVES, THEIR FAMILIES, THEIR PROPERTY. IN OTHER WORDS, ONLY THE RIGHT TO KEEP AND BEAR ARMS CREATES THE ABSOLUTE CAPACITY TO LIVE WITHOUT FEAR.

IN A VERY REAL SENSE, THERE IS NO SUCH THING AS A FREE NATION WHERE POLICE, MILITARY AND GOVERNMENT AGENTS ARE ALLOWED THE FORCE OF ARMS AND INDIVIDUAL CITIZENS ARE NOT. THAT'S A "BIG BROTHER KNOWS BEST" THEATER OF THE ABSURD THAT HAS

NEVER BODED WELL FOR THE PEASANT CLASS, THE WORKING CLASS OR EVEN FOR REPORTERS, ACCORDING TO THE HISTORY BOOKS.

WE'RE ALL FAMILIAR WITH THE PEASANT REVOLTS OF CENTURIES PAST, WHERE PITCHFORKS WERE PITTED AGAINST POWDER AND BALL, AND STICKS WERE ALL THAT STOOD BETWEEN A PRECARIOUS EXISTENCE AND THE SWORDS OF ARISTOCRATS' ARMIES.

AND JUST RECENTLY WE WATCHED THE FORMER SOVIET UNION SEND SOLDIERS AND POLICE TO ROUND UP THE HUNTING RIFLES OF WORKERS IN SATELLITE NATIONS THAT WERE SUDDENLY COMING APART AT THE SEAMS.

CHANGE THE COSTUMES AND CLIMATE AND IT COULD HAVE BEEN BOSTON ON THE EVE OF OUR REVOLUTION, WHEN RED-COATED BRITISH SOLDIERS WENT DOOR TO DOOR DEMANDING FIREARMS. WE FOUGHT BACK, MUCH LIKE THE WORKING CLASS MEN AND WOMEN IN THE SOVIET SATELLITES FOUGHT BACK. AND IN BOTH INSTANCES THE END RESULT HAS BEEN A PROFOUND CHANGE IN THE WAY PEOPLE AROUND THE WORLD LIVE, AND BELIEVE, AND BEHAVE TOWARD ONE ANOTHER.

COULD IT HAVE HAPPENED WITHOUT AN ARMED CITIZENRY? I THINK NOT. OUR CONSTITUTION PROVIDES THE DOORWAY FOR YOUR NEWS AND COMMENTARY TO PASS THROUGH FREE AND UNFETTERED. BUT THAT DOORWAY TO FREEDOM IS FRAMED BY MUSKETS THAT STOOD BETWEEN A VISION OF LIBERTY AND ABSOLUTE ANARCHY AT A PLACE CALLED CONCORD BRIDGE.

THOSE MUSKETS WERE IN HANDS OF FARMERS, NOT TRAINED SOLDIERS OR POLICE. THEY ASSEMBLED AND STOOD THEIR GROUND AS IF TO SAY, "DON'T TREAD ON ME." THAT REMAINS AN EXCELLENT MOTTO FOR THE WAY MOST AMERICANS FEEL ABOUT GOVERNMENT TODAY: THEY SAY DO THE JOB WE ELECTED YOU TO DO, BUT DON'T YOU DARE CROSS THAT BRIDGE.

UNFORTUNATELY, THE MEDIA CROSSED THE BRIDGE WHEN YOU LAUNCHED YOUR CRUSADE TO UNDERMINE THE RIGHT TO KEEP AND BEAR ARMS. I DOUBT THAT VERY MANY OF YOU WOULD PREFER A ROLLED-UP NEWSPAPER AS A WEAPON TO THWART THE CRIMINAL ADVANCES OF AN INTRUDER. YET IN ESSENCE THAT IS WHAT YOU HAVE ASKED OUR LOVED ONES TO DO, THROUGH AN ILL-CONTRIVED AND TOTALLY NAIVE CAMPAIGN AGAINST THE SECOND AMENDMENT.

YOU SHOULD KNOW THAT A FEW MORE AMERICANS MIGHT HAVE SWALLOWED YOUR STORY IF YOU HAD ONLY TAKEN THE TIME TO GET A FEW FACTS RIGHT. IN THE PAST FEW YEARS I HAVE TALKED TO GUN OWNERS ALL ACROSS THE COUNTRY, AND THE MAJORITY MENTION THE SAME THING OVER AND OVER AGAIN.

HOW, THEY SAY, CAN WE BELIEVE ANYTHING THE ANTI-GUN MEDIA SAYS WHEN THEY CAN'T EVEN GET THE NOMENCLATURE RIGHT? FOR TOO LONG YOU HAVE DEPENDED UPON MANUFACTURED STATISTICS AND FABRICATED TECHNICAL SUPPORT FROM ORGANIZATIONS THAT WOULDN'T KNOW A SEMI-AUTO FROM A SHARP STICK. AND IT SHOWS. YOU FALL FOR IT EVERY TIME.

THAT'S WHY YOU HAVE VERY LITTLE CREDIBILITY AMONG MORE THAN 70-MILLION GUN OWNERS, MORE THAN 20-MILLION HUNTERS, AND AMONG THE MILLIONS OF VETERANS WHO LEARNED THE HARD WAY WHICH END THE BULLET COMES OUT. AND WHILE YOU ATTACKED THE AMENDMENT THAT DEFENDS YOUR HOMES AND PROTECTS YOUR WIVES AND CHILDREN, YOU DENIED THOSE OF US WHO DEFEND ALL THE BILL OF RIGHTS A FAIR HEARING...OR EVEN THE COURTESY OF AN HONEST DEBATE.

GROUPS LIKE HANDGUN CONTROL INCORPORATED PROVIDE THE TEXT FOR A MAJORITY OF GUN ISSUE-RELATED STORIES IN THIS COUNTRY. YET IF THE NRA ATTEMPTS TO CHALLENGE YOUR ASSERTIONS, WE ARE IGNORED. AND IF WE TRY TO PURCHASE ADVERTISING TIME OR SPACE TO ANSWER YOUR CHARGES, MORE OFTEN THAN NOT WE ARE DENIED. HOW'S THAT FOR FIRST AMENDMENT FREEDOM?

CLEARLY THEN, TOO MANY HAVE USED FREEDOM OF THE PRESS AS A WEAPON NOT ONLY TO STRANGLE OUR FREE SPEECH, BUT TO ERODE AND ULTIMATELY DESTROY THE RIGHT TO KEEP AND BEAR ARMS AS WELL. IN DOING SO YOU PROMOTED YOUR PROFESSION TO THAT OF CONSTITUTIONAL JUDGE AND JURY, MORE POWERFUL EVEN THAN OUR SUPREME COURT, MORE PREJUDICED THAN THE INQUISITION'S TRIBUNALS. IT IS A FRIGHTENING MISUSE OF CONSTITUTIONAL PRIVILEGE, AND I PRAY THAT YOU WILL COME TO YOUR SENSES AND SEE THAT THESE ABUSES ARE CURBED.

AS A VETERAN OF WORLD WAR II, AS A FREEDOM MARCHER WHO STOOD WITH DR. MARTIN LUTHER KING LONG BEFORE IT WAS FASHIONABLE, AND AS A GRANDFATHER WHO WANTS THE COMING CENTURY TO BE FREE AND FULL OF PROMISE FOR MY GRANDCHILDREN,

I AM TROUBLED BY THE EROSION OF OUR BILL OF RIGHTS.

I BELIEVE THAT ALL OUR RIGHTS, INCLUDING THE RIGHT TO KEEP AND BEAR ARMS, MUST BE DELIVERED INTO THE 21ST CENTURY AS PURE AND MEANINGFUL AS THEY CAME TO US AT THE BEGINNING OF THIS CENTURY.

AND I BELIEVE THE FREEDOMS THAT PROVIDED MY GENERATION WITH SO MUCH OPPORTUNITY MUST REMAIN THE BIRTHRIGHT OF EACH GENERATION THAT CARRIES THE TORCH FORWARD. TRADITIONALLY THE PASSING OF THAT TORCH IS FROM A GNARLED, OLD HAND DOWN TO AN EAGER, YOUNG ONE. SO NOW, AT 72, I OFFER MY GNARLED, OLD HAND.

I HAVE ACCEPTED A CALL FROM THE NATIONAL RIFLE ASSOCIATION OF AMERICA TO HELP PROTECT THE SECOND AMENDMENT, BECAUSE AS A FIRM BELIEVER IN THE CONSTITUTION OF THESE UNITED STATES, I FEEL IT IS MY DUTY TO DO SO. I BELIEVE THE RIGHT TO KEEP AND BEAR ARMS IS THREATENED BY POLITICAL THEATRICS, PIECEMEAL LAW-MAKING, TALK SHOW PSYCHOLOGY, EXTREME BAD TASTE IN THE ENTERTAINMENT INDUSTRY, AN EVER-WIDENING EDUCATIONAL CHASM IN OUR SCHOOLS AND A CONNIVING AND IRRESPONSIBLE MEDIA, THAT ALL ADD UP TO CULTURAL WARFARE AGAINST THE IDEA THAT GUNS EVER HAD, OR SHOULD NOW HAVE, AN HONORABLE AND PROUD PLACE IN OUR SOCIETY.

NO ONE IS TELLING THE TRUTH ABOUT THE SECOND AMENDMENT EXCEPT THE NATIONAL RIFLE ASSOCIATION – AND YOU'VE MADE IT HARD TO BE HEARD. SO I WILL DO WHAT I CAN TO HELP GET THE MESSAGE OUT. IT WILL BE A TALL ORDER, YET I THINK THERE ARE SEVERAL MILLION OF US OUT THERE WHO REMAIN EQUAL TO THE TASK.

MY VISION FOR THIS ORGANIZATION AND THE CONSTITUTIONAL RIGHT IT PROTECTS CAN BE SUMMARIZED IN THREE SIMPLE PARTS. FIRST OF ALL, IN THE THREE YEARS THAT REMAIN BEFORE WE ENTER THE NEXT CENTURY, I WILL EXPECT TO SEE A PRO-SECOND AMENDMENT PRESIDENT IN THE WHITE HOUSE.

SECONDLY, I EXPECT TO BUILD AN NRA WITH THE POLITICAL MUSCLE AND CLOUT TO KEEP A PRO-SECOND AMENDMENT CONGRESS IN PLACE. TO ACHIEVE THIS WE WILL INCREASE OUR MEMBERSHIP AND ACCUMULATE A WAR CHEST THAT WILL BE THE ENVY OF DEMOCRATS, REPUBLICANS, THE CHRISTIAN COALITION, THE SIERRA CLUB,

ANY AND ALL. WE ARE GOING TO WORK HARD DURING THE NEXT THREE YEARS.

THIRD, IS A PROMISE TO THE NEXT GENERATION OF FREE AMERICANS. I HOPE TO HELP RAISE A HUNDRED MILLION DOLLARS FOR NRA PROGRAMS AND EDUCATION BEFORE THE YEAR 2000. AT LEAST HALF OF THAT SUM WILL GO TEACH OUR KIDS ABOUT THE SECOND AMENDMENT, AND WHAT THE RIGHT TO KEEP AND BEAR ARMS REALLY MEANS TO THEIR CULTURE AND COUNTRY.

IT IS TIME THEY LEARNED THAT FIREARM OWNERSHIP IS CONSTITUTIONAL, NOT CRIMINAL. IN FACT, FEW PURSUITS CAN TEACH A YOUNG PERSON MORE ABOUT RESPONSIBILITY, SAFETY, CONSERVATION, THEIR HISTORY AND THEIR HERITAGE, ALL AT ONCE. YET WHAT MUST YOUNG AMERICANS THINK WHEN THEIR PRESIDENT PROCLAIMS THAT "A FIREARM IN THE HANDS OF YOUTH IS A CRIME OR AN ACCIDENT WAITING TO HAPPEN"? HE IS WRONG.

IT IS TIME THEY FOUND OUT THAT THE POLITICALLY CORRECT DOCTRINE OF TODAY HAS MISLED THEM, AND THAT WHEN THEY REACH LEGAL AGE, AND IF THEY DO NOT BREAK OUR LAWS, THEY HAVE A RIGHT TO CHOOSE TO OWN A GUN – A HANDGUN, A LONG GUN, A SMALL GUN, A LARGE GUN, A BLACK GUN, A PURPLE GUN, A PRETTY GUN, AN UGLY GUN – AND TO USE THAT GUN TO DEFEND THEMSELVES AND THEIR LOVED ONES OR TO ENGAGE IN ANY LAWFUL PURPOSE THEY DESIRE WITHOUT APOLOGY OR EXPLANATION TO ANYONE, EVER.

THIS IS THE MOST BASIC FREEDOM AND WITHOUT A DOUBT THE FIRST FREEDOM – THE FREEDOM THAT FOUGHT FOR AND WON ALL THE REST. IF YOU SAY IT IS OUTDATED, THEN YOU HAVEN'T READ YOUR OWN HEADLINES. IF YOU SAY GUNS CREATE CARNAGE, I WOULD ANSWER THAT YOU KNOW BETTER. DECLINING MORALS, DISINTEGRATING FAMILIES, VACILLATING POLITICAL LEADERSHIP, AN ERODING CRIMINAL JUSTICE SYSTEM AND SOCIAL MORES THAT CONVENIENTLY KICK CHARACTER OUT THE BACK DOOR WITH THE DOG ARE MORE TO BLAME – CERTAINLY MORE THAN ANY LEGALLY OWNED FIREARM.

WE HAVE RAISED A GENERATION OF YOUNG PEOPLE WHO THINK THAT THE BILL OF RIGHTS COMES WITH THEIR CABLE TV. GIVE THEM THE CHANCE TO CHANNEL SURF AND THEY'LL REMAIN OBLIVIOUS TO HISTORY AND HERITAGE, AND TO TRADITIONS THAT TRULY MATTER.

AND YES, OBLIVIOUS ALSO TO THEIR VERY OWN INDIVIDUAL RIGHTS. FREEDOM WON'T SURVIVE LONG IN SUCH A WASTELAND OF AN ENVIRONMENT. NOT EVEN TO THE END OF THIS CENTURY, MUCH LESS INTO THE NEXT.

SO I BELIEVE IT IS TIME TO ACT. I BELIEVE THE HOUR IS AT HAND TO RESCUE THE SECOND AMENDMENT FROM AN OPPORTUNISTIC PRESIDENT, AND FROM A PRESS THAT APPARENTLY CAN'T COMPREHEND THAT ATTACKS ON THE SECOND AMENDMENT SET THE STAGE FOR ASSAULTS ON THE FIRST.

I WANT TO SAVE THE SECOND AMENDMENT FROM ALL THESE NITPICKING LITTLE WARS OF ATTRITION – FIGHTS OVER ALLEGED SATURDAY NIGHT SPECIALS, PLASTIC GUNS, COP-KILLER BULLETS AND SO MANY OTHER MADE-FOR-PRIME-TIME NON-ISSUES INVENTED BY SOME PRESS AGENT OVER AT HANDGUN CONTROL HEADQUARTERS THAT YOU GUYS BUY TIME AND AGAIN.

AND I WANT OUR YOUNG PEOPLE TO KNOW THE REAL STORY ABOUT THE SECOND AMENDMENT AND WHY IT IS CURRENTLY FASHIONABLE TO SUPPRESS IT. I SIMPLY WILL NOT STAND BY AND WATCH A RIGHT GUARANTEED BY THE CONSTITUTION OF THE UNITED STATES COME UNDER ATTACK FROM THOSE WHO EITHER CAN'T UNDERSTAND IT, DON'T LIKE THE SOUND OF IT OR FIND THEMSELVES TOO PHILOSOPHICALLY SQUEAMISH TO SEE WHY IT REMAINS THE FIRST AMONG EQUALS: THE RIGHT WE TURN TO WHEN OTHERS COME UNDER FIRE.

A FEW YEARS AGO, WHEN LOS ANGELES WAS GRIPPED BY RIOTS, SOME OF MY MORE LIBERAL FRIENDS – THOSE WHO HAD ARGUED MOST PASSIONATELY AGAINST THE RIGHT TO KEEP AND BEAR ARMS – SUDDENLY HAD THE TELEPHONE RINGING OFF THE WALL.

"CHUCK," THEY SAID, WITH MORE THAN A LITTLE ANXIETY IN THEIR VOICES. "DO YOU KNOW WHERE WE CAN GET A GUN... IN A HURRY?"

"NO, NOT WITH CALIFORNIA'S WAITING PERIOD IN PLACE," I REPLIED.

AND THEN THE LONG NAUSEATED PAUSE. THEY NO LONGER WANTED THE POPULARITY OF POLITICS. THEY WANTED PROTECTION. BECAUSE SUDDENLY THEY WERE AFRAID. I FELT AFRAID, TOO – FOR THEM, AND FOR WHAT THEY'D WROUGHT.

FEAR CAN DO THAT TO CERTAIN CAUSES. WHAT SOUNDS SO GOOD OVER COCKTAILS CAN SEEM PRETTY EMPTY WHEN THE STREETS ARE TEEMING WITH HATE.

OUR FOUNDERS REMEMBERED THAT. YOU HAVE FORGOTTEN IT. THERE CAN BE NO FREE SPEECH OR FREEDOM OF THE PRESS WITHOUT ARMED CITIZENS TO FIGHT FOR IT. IF YOU DON'T BELIEVE ME, JUST TURN ON THE NEWS TONIGHT: CIVILIZATION'S VENEER REMAINS TOO THIN. THANK YOU.

REMARKS BEFORE THE CONSERVATIVE POLITICAL ACTION CONFERENCE

January 27, 1998 Alexandria, VA

"Armed with Pride"

THANK YOU FOR THAT VERY KIND INTRODUCTION. SOME DAY I'LL ARRIVE AT ONE OF THESE EVENTS IN A CHARIOT JUST TO LIVE UP TO YOUR EXPECTATIONS. BUT ONLY IF SOME OF YOU GUYS WILL VOLUNTEER TO CLEAN UP AFTER THE HORSES. AFTER ALL, YOU'VE BEEN CLEANING UP AFTER THE DEMOCRATS FOR A LONG TIME.

DEDICATING THE MEMORIAL AT GETTYSBURG MORE THAN A CENTURY AGO, ABRAHAM LINCOLN SAID OF AMERICA, "WE ARE NOW ENGAGED IN A GREAT CIVIL WAR, TESTING WHETHER THIS NATION...OR ANY NATION SO CONCEIVED...AND SO DEDICATED...CAN LONG ENDURE." LINCOLN WAS RIGHT. FRIENDS, LET ME TELL YOU: YOU ARE ENGAGED AGAIN IN A GREAT CIVIL WAR...A CULTURAL WAR THAT'S ABOUT TO HIJACK YOU RIGHT OUT OF YOUR OWN BIRTHRIGHT. AND I FEAR THAT YOU NO LONGER TRUST THE PULSING LIFE BLOOD INSIDE YOU THAT MADE THIS COUNTRY RISE FROM MUD AND VALOR INTO THE MIRACLE THAT IT STILL IS.

LET ME BACK UP. ABOUT A YEAR AGO I BECAME A VICE PRESIDENT OF THE NATIONAL RIFLE ASSOCIATION, WHICH DEFINES AND PROTECTS THE RIGHT TO KEEP AND BEAR ARMS. I RAN FOR OFFICE, I WAS ELECT-

ED, AND NOW I SERVE...I SERVE AS A MOVING TARGET FOR THE MEDIA WHO'VE CALLED ME EVERYTHING FROM "RIDICULOUS" AND "DUPED" TO A " BRAIN-INJURED, SENILE, CRAZY, OLD MAN." I KNOW...I'M PRETTY OLD...BUT I SURE, LORD, AIN'T SENILE.

AS I HAVE STOOD IN THE CROSSHAIRS OF THOSE WHO WANT TO SHOOT DOWN OUR SECOND AMENDMENT FREEDOMS, I HAVE REALIZED THAT FIREARMS ARE NOT THE ONLY ISSUE...I AM NOT THE ONLY TARGET. IT'S MUCH, MUCH BIGGER THAN THAT.

I'VE COME TO REALIZE THAT A CULTURAL WAR IS INDEED RAGING ACROSS OUR LAND...STORMING OUR VALUES, ASSAULTING OUR FREEDOMS, KILLING OUR SELF-CONFIDENCE IN WHO WE ARE AND WHAT WE BELIEVE.

HOW MANY OF YOU HERE OWN A GUN?

HOW MANY OWN A BUNCH OF GUNS?

THANK YOU. I WONDER – HOW MANY OF YOU OWN GUNS BUT CHOSE NOT TO RAISE YOUR HAND? HOW MANY ALMOST REVEALED YOUR CONVICTION ABOUT A CONSTITUTIONAL RIGHT, BUT THEN THOUGHT BETTER OF IT?

THEN YOU ARE A VICTIM OF THE CULTURAL WAR. YOU'RE A CASUALTY OF THE CULTURAL BATTLE BEING WAGED AGAINST TRADITIONAL AMERICAN FREEDOM OF BELIEFS AND IDEAS.

NOW MAYBE YOU DON'T CARE MUCH ONE WAY OR THE OTHER ABOUT OWNING A GUN. BUT I COULD'VE ASKED FOR A SHOW OF HANDS OF PENTECOSTAL CHRISTIANS OR PRO-LIFERS OR RIGHT-TO-WORKERS OR PROMISE KEEPERS OR SCHOOL VOUCHER-ERS, AND THE RESULT WOULD BE THE SAME. WOULD YOU RAISE YOUR HAND IF DAN RATHER WERE IN THE BACK OF THE ROOM WITH A FILM CREW? WHAT IF THE SAME QUESTION WERE ASKED IN THE GYM AT YOUR KIDS' PTA MEETING?

YOU HAVE BEEN ASSAULTED...AND ROBBED OF THE COURAGE OF YOUR CONVICTIONS. YOUR PRIDE IN WHO YOU ARE, AND WHAT YOU BELIEVE, HAS BEEN RIDICULED, RANSACKED AND PLUNDERED. IT MAY BE A WAR WITHOUT BULLET OR BLOODSHED, BUT THERE IS JUST AS MUCH LIBERTY LOST: YOU AND YOUR COUNTRY ARE LESS FREE.

AND YOU'RE NOT INCONSEQUENTIAL PEOPLE! YOU IN THIS ROOM, WHOM MANY WOULD SAY ARE AMONG THE POWERFUL PEOPLE ON

EARTH, YOU ARE SHAMED INTO SILENCE! SO WHAT OTHER BELIEF IN YOUR HEART WILL YOU DISAVOW WITH YOUR HAND?

I REMEMBER WHEN EUROPEAN JEWS FEARED TO ADMIT THEIR FAITH. THE NAZIS FORCED THEM TO WEAR YELLOW STARS AS IDENTITY BADGES. IT WORKED. SO – WHAT COLOR "STAR" WILL THEY PIN ON GUN OWNERS' CHESTS? HOW WILL THE SELF-STYLED ELITE TAG US? THERE MAY NOT BE A GESTAPO OFFICER ON EVERY STREET CORNER, BUT THE INFLUENCE ON OUR CULTURE IS JUST AS PERVASIVE.

NOW, I'M NOT REALLY HERE TO TALK ABOUT THE SECOND AMENDMENT OR THE NRA, BUT THE GUN ISSUE CLEARLY BRINGS INTO FOCUS THE WARFARE THAT'S GOING ON. RANK-AND-FILE AMERICANS WAKE UP EVERY MORNING INCREASINGLY BEWILDERED AND CONFUSED AT WHY THEIR VIEWS MAKE THEM LESSER CITIZENS. AFTER ENOUGH BREAKFAST-TABLE TV PROMOS HYPING TATTOOED SEX SLAVES ON THE NEXT RICKI LAKE SHOW, ENOUGH GUN-GLUTTED MOVIES AND TABLOID TALK SHOWS, ENOUGH REVISIONIST HISTORY BOOKS AND PRIME-TIME RIDICULE OF RELIGION, ENOUGH OF THE TV NEWS ANCHOR WHO COCKS HER HEAD, CLUCKS HER TONGUE AND SIGHS ABOUT GUNS CAUSING CRIME, AND FINALLY THE MESSAGE BEGINS TO GET THROUGH: HEAVEN HELP THE GOD-FEARING, LAW-ABIDING, CAUCASIAN, MIDDLE CLASS, PROTESTANT, OR EVEN WORSE, EVANGELICAL CHRISTIAN, MIDWEST OR SOUTHERN, OR EVEN WORSE, RURAL, APPARENTLY STRAIGHT, OR EVEN WORSE, ADMITTED HETERO-SEXUAL, GUN-OWNING, OR EVEN WORSE, NRA-CARD-CARRYING, AVERAGE WORKING STIFF, OR EVEN, WORST OF ALL, A MALE WORKING STIFF, BECAUSE THEN, NOT ONLY DON'T YOU COUNT, YOU'RE A DOWNRIGHT OBSTACLE TO SOCIAL PROGRESS, PAL. YOUR TAX DOL-LARS MAY BE JUST AS GREEN AS YOU HAND THEM OVER, BUT YOUR VOICE BETTER BE QUIET, YOUR OPINION IS LESS ENLIGHTENED, YOUR MEDIA ACCESS SILENCED, AND FRANKLY MISTER, YOU NEED TO WAKE UP, WISE UP AND LEARN A LITTLE SOMETHING ABOUT YOUR NEW AMERICA...AND MEANTIME, WHY DON'T YOU JUST SIT DOWN AND SHUT UP!

THAT'S WHY YOU DIDN'T RAISE YOUR HAND. THAT'S HOW CULTURAL WAR WORKS. AND WE ARE LOSING.

THIS IS WHY I'VE FORMED ARENA PAC, MY OWN POLITICAL ACTION COMMITTEE...AND THAT'S WHY, THOUGH I'M PHYSICALLY AND FINANCIALLY COMFORTABLE, AND HAVE A WONDERFUL FAMILY

AND GRANDCHILDREN I CHERISH AND MISS DEEPLY WHEN I'M GONE, I GO ON THE ROAD – CATCHING REDEYE FLIGHTS, SPEAKING AT RALLIES IN SEATTLE AND EATING PANCAKES IN PEORIA AND EATING RUBBER CHICKEN IN DES MOINES. YES, INDEED…CHUCK HESTON CAN FIND LESS STRENUOUS AND MORE GLAMOROUS THINGS TO DO WITH HIS TIME THAN STUMP FOR CONSERVATIVE CANDIDATES OUT THERE IN ANYTOWN U.S.A., BUT IT'S A JOB I CAN DO BETTER THAN MOST, BECAUSE MOST CAN'T.

YOU DON'T SEE MANY OTHER HOLLYWOOD LUMINARIES SPEAKING OUT FOR CONSERVATIVE CAUSES, DO YOU? IT'S NOT BECAUSE THERE AREN'T ANY. IT'S BECAUSE THEY CAN'T TAKE THE HEAT. THEY DARE NOT SPEAK UP FOR FEAR OF ABC OR CBS OR CNN OR WORST OF ALL, THE IRS.

CULTURAL WAR SAPS THE STRENGTH OF OUR COUNTRY BECAUSE THE PERSONAL PRICE IS SIMPLY TOO HIGH TO STAND UP FOR WHAT YOU BELIEVE IN. TODAY, SPEAKING WITH THE COURAGE OF YOUR CONVIC-TION CAN BE SO COSTLY, THE PRICE OF PRINCIPLE SO GREAT, THAT LEGISLATORS WON'T LEAD…SO CITIZENS CAN'T FOLLOW, AND SO THERE IS NO ARMY TO FIGHT BACK. THAT'S CULTURAL WARFARE.

FOR INSTANCE: IT'S PLAIN THAT OUR CONSTITUTION GUARANTEES LAW-ABIDING CITIZENS THE RIGHT TO OWN A FIREARM. BUT IF I STAND UP AND SAY SO, WHY DOES THE MEDIA ASSAULT ME WITH SUCH SLASHING DERISION?

BECAUSE BILL CLINTON'S CULTURAL WARRIORS WANT A PENITENTIAL CLEANSING OF ALL FIREARMS. MILLIONS OF LAWFUL GUN OWNERS MUST FEEL GUILTY FOR THE CRIMES OF OTHERS AND SEEK ABSOLU-TION BY SURRENDERING THEIR GUNS. THAT'S WHAT'S LITERALLY UNDERWAY RIGHT NOW, IN ENGLAND AND AUSTRALIA. LINES OF SUBMISSIVE CITIZENS, THREATENED WITH IMPRISONMENT, ARE BITTERLY SURRENDERING FAMILY HEIRLOOMS, GUNS THAT WON THEIR FREEDOM, TO THE BLAST FURNACE. IF THAT FACT DOES NOT UNSET-TLE YOU, THEN YOU ARE ALREADY ANESTHETIZED, YOU ARE A READY VICTIM OF THE CULTURAL WAR.

SO HOW DO WE GET OUT OF THIS MESS? MOSES LED HIS PEOPLE THROUGH THE WILDERNESS, BUT HE NEVER MADE IT TO THE PROMISED LAND – NOT EVEN WHEN I PLAYED HIM. BUT HE DID DO HIS JOB – HE POINTED HIS PEOPLE IN THE RIGHT DIRECTION.

UNLIKE THE TEN COMMANDMENTS, THE BILL OF RIGHTS WASN'T CUT INTO STONE TABLETS. BUT THE TEXT SURELY HAS THAT SAME RIGHTEOUS FEEL TO IT. IT'S AS IF YOU CAN SENSE THE UNSEEN HAND OF THE ALMIGHTY GOD GUIDING THE SWEEP OF A GOOSE QUILL PEN, WHILE SOME REBELLIOUS OLD WHITE GUYS SWEATED OUT THE BIRTH OF A NATION. JEFFERSON, ADAMS, PAINE – THEY POINTED THE WAY, AND WE MADE IT TO THIS PROMISED LAND – THE ONE OUR IMMIGRANT ANCESTORS DREAMED OF...THE LAND ABE LINCOLN CALLED, "MAN'S LAST, BEST HOPE ON EARTH."

LOOK AT ME. WHERE ELSE BUT IN AMERICA COULD A SKINNY COUNTRY KID NAMED CHARLTON WORK HIS WAY OUT OF THE MICHIGAN NORTH WOODS AND FIND A LIFE THAT MAKES A DIFFERENCE? MY COUNTRY PUT THE GIFT OF FREEDOM IN MY HANDS AND SAID, "HERE! MAKE SOMETHING OF IT." THAT'S WHY I SO DEEPLY LOVE THIS GREAT NATION, AND THE CONSTITUTION THAT DEFINES IT.

JUST ABOUT EVERYTHING GOOD ABOUT ME...WHO I AM AND WHAT I'VE DONE, CAN BE TRACED BACK TO SOME SMOKING MUSKETS AND A RADICAL DECLARATION OF INDEPENDENCE BY THOSE RAGTAG REBELS. WEARING THREADBARE COATS AND MARCHING ON BLEEDING FEET, THEY DEFEATED THE FINEST ARMY ASSEMBLED IN THAT CENTURY, AND THEY GAVE THE WORLD HOPE. WITHIN THEM FLOWED AN UNDERTOW OF PERSONAL FREEDOM, A RELENTLESS SENSE OF WHAT IS RIGHT, SO IRRESISTIBLY STRONG THAT THEY SIMPLY COULD NOT ABANDON IT.

BUT TODAY'S CULTURAL WARRIORS ARE TRYING. THEY'RE REVISING AND REWRITING THESE TRUTHS, YANKING THE BILL OF RIGHTS FROM OUR LIVES LIKE A WEATHERED HANDBILL STUCK UNDER YOUR WINDSHIELD WIPER. THEY'RE TRADING TRADITIONS THAT ARE RIGHT FOR TRENDS THAT TEASE US WITH MORE IMMEDIATE REWARD. SELF-GRATIFICATION HAS DISPLACED HONOR, GREED HAS ERASED GOOD TASTE, THE DESIRES OF THE MOMENT HAVE UNDERMINED BASIC MORALITY. WE ARE FAST BECOMING A SELF-SERVING, BOORISH AND ARROGANT PEOPLE GIVEN TO CULTURAL BINGES, QUICK TO DISMISS ANYTHING OF SUBSTANCE THAT STANDS IN THE WAY OF OUR UNDISCIPLINED DESIRES.

THAT'S THE CULTURALLY BEREFT AMERICA WE SEE AND HEAR IN OUR MOVIES, TELEVISION, POPULAR MUSIC, EVEN THE PRIME-TIME NEWS HOUR.

I SHOULD HAVE KNOWN WHAT TO EXPECT WHEN THE EARTH SHOE GENERATION SKIPPED INTO THE WHITE HOUSE WITH A PAISLEY SUITCASE FULL OF SOCIAL EXPERIMENTS AND REVISIONIST HISTORY. BILL AND HILLARY ARE THE PRODUCT OF A CULTURAL REVOLUTION THAT HAD ABSOLUTELY NOTHING WHATSOEVER TO DO WITH THE POWER OF FLOWERS. IT WAS AN ADOLESCENT UPRISING BENT ON BURNING BRIDGES, NOT BUILDING THEM.

OUR PRESIDENT'S RECENT TROUBLES ARE DRAMATIC PROOF THAT CULTURAL WAR IS NOT A CLASH OVER THE FACTS, OR EVEN BETWEEN PHILOSOPHIES. IT'S A CLASH BETWEEN THE PRINCIPLED AND THE UNPRINCIPLED.

I AM NOT TALKING ABOUT WHETHER HE "DID IT" OR "DIDN'T DO IT." I AM TALKING ABOUT PEOPLE WHO CANNOT COMPREHEND MORAL ABSOLUTES, AND A COUNTRY THAT SEEMS TO ABIDE IT. HERE WE ARE, TWO NIGHTS AFTER THE STATE OF THE UNION ADDRESS, TRAPPED IN THE SILLY SPECTACLE OF HAVING OUR VALUES MEASURED HOURLY BY THE POLLS, AS IF THE DEFINITION OF THE "RIGHT THING" CHANGED LIKE A NATIONAL MOOD RING.

"WHAT DO YOU THINK OF THE PRESIDENT? WELL, WAIT – AFTER HIS SPEECH, NOW HOW DO YOU FEEL? OH, WAIT, AFTER THE WHITE HOUSE SPIN, HOW DO YOU FEEL? BUT WAIT, AFTER THE FIRST LADY'S INTERVIEW, NOW HOW DO YOU FEEL?"

BEHAVIOR IS JUDGED AND REJUDGED BASED NOT UPON WHAT'S RIGHT, BUT UPON WHAT FEELS RIGHT, AND TO WHOM, AT THE MOMENT.

THIS IS HOW CULTURAL WARRIORS USE SEXUAL CRIME TO DESTROY THEIR ENEMIES. SEX BETWEEN CONSENTING ADULTS SHATTERS THE CAREER OF A SENIOR ENLISTED MAN…A SEXUAL INFRACTION WRECKS THE LIFE OF A CORPORATE EXECUTIVE…AND SEXUAL GOSSIP IMPUGNS THE INTEGRITY OF A SUPREME COURT NOMINEE. YET WITH THE RIGHT SPIN BY THE RIGHT DOCTOR, OTHERS ARE GLEEFULLY FORGIVEN.

SOMEWHERE IN THIS RANCID MESS WE FIGHT TO FIND PRINCIPLE OUR CHILDREN CAN UNDERSTAND.

BUT AMERICANS SHOULD NOT HAVE TO GO TO WAR EVERY MORNING FOR THEIR VALUES. THEY ALREADY GO TO WAR FOR THEIR FAMILIES. THEY FIGHT TO HOLD DOWN A JOB, RAISE RESPONSIBLE KIDS, MAKE THEIR PAYMENTS, KEEP GAS IN THE CAR, PUT FOOD ON

THE TABLE AND CLOTHES ON THEIR BACKS, AND STILL SAVE A LITTLE TO LIVE THEIR FINAL DAYS IN DIGNITY.

THEY PREFER THE AMERICA THEY BUILT – WHERE YOU COULD PRAY WITHOUT FEELING NAIVE, LOVE WITHOUT BEING KINKY, SING WITHOUT PROFANITY, BE WHITE WITHOUT FEELING GUILTY, OWN A GUN WITHOUT SHAME, AND RAISE YOUR HAND WITHOUT APOLOGY. THEY ARE THE MASSES WHO FIND THEMSELVES UNDER SIEGE AND LONG FOR YOU TO GET SOME GUTS, STAND ON PRINCIPLE AND LEAD THEM TO VICTORY IN THIS CULTURAL WAR. THEY ARE SICK AND TIRED OF NATIONAL SOCIAL POLICY THAT ORIGINATES ON OPRAH, AND THEY'RE READY FOR YOU TO PULL THE PLUG.

NOW IF THIS ALL SOUNDS A LITTLE MOSAIC, MY PUNCH LINE IS AS ELEMENTARY AS THE GOLDEN RULE: THERE IS ONLY ONE WAY TO WIN A CULTURAL WAR: DO THE RIGHT THING.

TRIUMPH BELONGS TO THOSE WHO ARM THEMSELVES WITH PRIDE IN WHO THEY ARE AND WHAT THEY BELIEVE, AND...THEN DO THE RIGHT THING. NOT THE MOST EXPEDIENT THING, NOT WHAT'LL SELL, NOT THE POLITICALLY CORRECT THING, BUT THE RIGHT THING.

AND YOU KNOW WHAT? EVERYBODY ALREADY KNOWS WHAT THAT IS. YOU, AND I, WE KNOW THE RIGHT THING. PRESIDENT CLINTON, MADONNA, LOUIS FARRAKHAN, EVEN MARILYN MANSON, WE ALL KNOW. IT'S EASY. YOU SAY WAIT A MINUTE, YOU TAKE A LONG LOOK IN THE MIRROR, THEN INTO THE EYES OF YOUR KIDS, OR GRANDKIDS, AND YOU'LL KNOW WHAT'S RIGHT.

I PROMISED TO TRY TO RECONNECT YOU WITH THAT SENSE OF PURPOSE, THAT COMPASS FOR WHAT'S RIGHT, THAT ALREADY LIVES IN YOU. TO UNLEASH ITS POWER, YOU NEED ONLY UNBRIDLE YOUR PRIDE AND REARM YOURSELF WITH THE RAW COURAGE OF YOUR CONVICTIONS.

OUR ANCESTORS WERE ARMED WITH PRIDE, AND BEQUEATHED IT TO US – I CAN PROVE IT. IF YOU WANT TO FEEL THE WARM BREATH OF FREEDOM UPON YOUR NECK...IF YOU WANT TO TOUCH THE PROUD PULSE OF LIBERTY THAT BEAT IN OUR FOUNDING FATHERS IN ITS PUREST FORM, YOU CAN DO SO THROUGH THE MAJESTY OF THE SECOND AMENDMENT RIGHT TO KEEP AND BEAR ARMS.

BECAUSE THERE, IN THAT WOODEN STOCK AND BLUED STEEL, IS WHAT GIVES THE MOST COMMON OF COMMON MEN THE MOST

UNCOMMON OF FREEDOMS. WHEN ORDINARY HANDS ARE FREE TO OWN THIS EXTRAORDINARY, SYMBOLIC TOOL STANDING FOR THE FULL MEASURE OF HUMAN DIGNITY AND LIBERTY, THAT IS AS GOOD AS IT GETS.

IT DOESN'T MATTER WHETHER ITS PURPOSE IS TO DEFEND OUR SHORES OR YOUR FRONT DOOR...WHETHER THE GUN IS A RITE OF PASSAGE FOR A YOUNG MAN OR A TOOL OF SURVIVAL FOR A YOUNG WOMAN...WHETHER IT BRINGS MEAT FOR THE TABLE OR TROPHIES FOR THE SHELF...WITHOUT RESPECT TO AGE, OR GENDER, OR RACE, OR CLASS, THE SECOND AMENDMENT RIGHT TO KEEP AND BEAR ARMS CONNECTS US ALL – WITH ALL THAT IS RIGHT.

AND NO AMOUNT OF OPPRESSION, NO FBI, NO IRS, NO BIG GOVERN-MENT, NO SOCIAL ENGINEERS, NO MATTER WHAT AND NO MATTER WHO, THEY CANNOT CLEAVE THE GENES WE SHARE WITH OUR FOUNDING FATHERS.

REMEMBER: THEY PROMISED US LIFE, LIBERTY, AND THE PURSUIT OF HAPPINESS. THEY DIDN'T PROMISE US HAPPINESS, ONLY THE CHANCE TO CHASE IT. AND BEING POLITICALLY CORRECT IS NOT THE WAY TO GET THERE. IF AMERICANS BELIEVED IN POLITICAL CORRECTNESS, WE'D STILL BE KING GEORGE'S BOYS – SUBJECTS ENSLAVED TO THE BRITISH CROWN. PLEASE...SEEK TO BE POLITICALLY COMPETENT, YES...POLITICALLY CONFIDENT AND POLITICALLY COURAGEOUS, YES...BUT NEVER POLITICALLY CORRECT.

DON'T RUN FOR COVER WHEN THE CULTURAL CANNONS ROAR. REMEMBER WHO YOU ARE AND WHAT YOU BELIEVE, AND THEN RAISE YOUR HAND, STAND UP, AND SPEAK OUT. DON'T BE SHAMED OR STAR-TLED INTO LOCKSTEP CONFORMITY BY SEEMINGLY POWERFUL PEOPLE.

DEFEAT THE CRIMINALS AND THEIR APOLOGISTS...OUST THE BIASED AND BIGOTED...ENDURE THE UNDISCIPLINED AND UNPRINCIPLED. BUT DISAVOW THE SELF-APPOINTED SOCIAL PUPPETEERS WHOSE RELENTLESS ARROGANCE FUELS THIS VICIOUS WAR AGAINST SO MUCH WE HOLD SO DEAR. DO NOT YIELD, DO NOT DIVIDE, DO NOT CALL TRUCE. IT IS YOUR DUTY TO MUSTER WITH PRIDE AND WIN THIS CULTURAL WAR.

AS LEADERS YOU MUST DO WHAT ABRAHAM LINCOLN WOULD DO, CONFRONTED WITH A PERVERSE VERSION OF WHAT AMERICA WAS MEANT TO BE: DO THE RIGHT THING. AS MR. LINCOLN SAID, "WITH

FIRMNESS IN THE RIGHT, AS GOD GIVES US TO SEE RIGHT, LET US FINISH THE WORK WE ARE IN...AND THEN WE SHALL SAVE OUR COUNTRY."

I BELIEVE THAT SAYS IT ALL. THANKS. IT'S BEEN A PLEASURE.

☆ ☆ ☆

REMARKS BEFORE THE 127TH ANNUAL MEETING OF THE MEMBERS OF THE NATIONAL RIFLE ASSOCIATION

May 22, 1998 Philadelphia, PA

THIS IS WHERE IT ALL STARTED, ISN'T IT? RIGHT HERE IN PHILADELPHIA.

TWO AND A QUARTER CENTURIES AGO, A BUNCH OF AMAZING GUYS TRAVELED HERE. THEY HAD FREEDOM'S BUSINESS TO TEND TO. BRAVE, WISE, GALLANT MEN. THEY KNEW THEIR SIGNATURES ON THAT DECLARATION OF INDEPENDENCE TOLD EVERYBODY THAT THEY WERE WILLING TO DIE FOR IT.

BY DARING TO PUT ON PARCHMENT WHAT OUR FOUNDING FATHERS FELT DEEP IN THEIR HEARTS, THE LONG-SILENT SOUL OF LIBERTY ROSE UP FROM A COMMONER'S DREAM TO BECOME EVERY MAN'S BIRTHRIGHT. THAT IS, AS LONG AS PATRIOTS LIKE YOU KINDLE ITS FLAME.

FREEDOM HAS ONLY ONE ENEMY IT CANNOT DEFEAT, AND THAT IS NEGLIGENCE. SO YOUR PRESENCE HERE NOW TODAY IS AN ACT OF REVERENCE. OF ALL MAN'S WORKS BENEATH THE HEAVENS, NONE SHINES BRIGHTER THAN OUR CONSTITUTION. I THINK JEFFERSON AND PAINE, ADAMS, MADISON, MASON, FRANKLIN, I THINK THEY'RE LOOKING DOWN RIGHT NOW AT US. I THINK THEY UNDERSTAND WHAT WE'RE TRYING TO DO, WHAT WE STRIVE TO DO.

I CAME HERE TO HELP MAKE THEM PROUD OF US. WHY HAVE YOU COME HERE?

HAVE YOU COME HERE TO CELEBRATE OUR FREEDOM, OR TO DIVIDE THIS MEMBERSHIP?

HAVE YOU COME HERE TO SHOW THE WORLD OUR UNITY, OR TO SPLINTER IT?

BECAUSE BEFORE WE GO ANY FURTHER, I WANT TO KNOW WHO'S WITH ME…AND WHO'S AGIN' ME.

BEFORE I TAKE ONE MORE STEP ON THIS MARCH INTO THE NEXT CENTURY THOUGH, I REALLY NEED TO KNOW.

SO I WANT THOSE WHO STAND WITH ME – PLEASE, RIGHT NOW, RISE FROM YOUR CHAIRS, TAKE TO YOUR FEET AND SHOW ME, SHOW THE WORLD – STAND WITH ME.

GOOD. I THANK YOU. WELL, LET ME TELL YOU WHY I CAME HERE.

FIRST, I HAVE COME HERE TO HEAL. WE DO NOT HAVE TO AGREE WITH EACH OTHER ON EVERY POINT OF EVERY ISSUE EVERY DAY; THE SECOND AMENDMENT HAS ROOM FOR THE FIRST AMENDMENT. BUT AFTER YOU'VE HAD YOUR FREE SPEECH, YOUR SAY, AND THE VOTES ARE COUNTED AND THE DIE IS CAST, GET TOGETHER OR GET OUT OF THE WAY!

NEXT, I HAVE COME HERE TO TAKE BACK WHAT'S OURS. TOO MANY GUN OWNERS THINK WE'VE WANDERED INTO SOME FRINGE OF AMERICAN LIFE AND LEFT THEM BEHIND. I CAN TELL YOU WHY THEY THINK THAT: YEAR AFTER YEAR OF LIE AFTER LIE BY THE PRESS AND THE POLITICIANS WHO ARE HOOK-LINE-AND-SINKER STUPID ABOUT LOCK-STOCK-AND-BARREL FREEDOM!

I PROMISE YOU WE WILL WIN BACK OUR RIGHTFUL PLACE IN THE MAINSTREAM OF AMERICAN POLITICAL DEBATE.

"MAINSTREAM" DOESN'T MEAN GIVING UP ANYTHING. IT MEANS GETTING BACK EVERYTHING. EVERYTHING SHOOTING USED TO BE – A WHOLESOME SPORT AND AN AMERICAN TRADITION, PROUDLY PRACTICED IN CLUBS AND CAMPUSES AND COUNTRYSIDES, A RITE OF PASSAGE TREATED WITH REVERENCE AND RESPECT. THE MAINSTREAM IS WHERE OUR NRA SHOULD BE, SPEAKING WITH ONE, PROUD, PRUDENT VOICE. AND BELIEVE ME, YOUR VOICE RUMBLES LIKE THUNDER.

I HAVE COME HERE STANDING IN THE SHADOWS OF THE FOUNDING FATHERS TO ELECT PRO-GUN CANDIDATES.

No more leaders who toy with the truth and get away with anything, including our gun rights.

If I am not being clear, let me spell it out: Mr. Clinton, sir, America didn't trust you with our healthcare system, America didn't trust you with gays in the military, America doesn't trust you with our 21-year-old daughters, and we sure Lord don't trust you with our guns!

I have come here to educate America's children and their parents. To those who do not know us, we must reach out with open arms, not clinched fists. Never again will you think twice before saying you're an NRA member, or think twice about putting that NRA decal on your car. I can even see, believe me, a day when, for heaven's sake, some Hollywood luminary besides me finds the courage to admit they own and enjoy guns! There are more of them than you think.

And finally, I have come here because I am proud. I believe the Second Amendment is America's first freedom. Among the entire of that magnificent Bill of Rights, it is the first among equals.

It is the one freedom that makes all freedoms defensible, possible, the one right that protects all the others. I am proud of our guns, proud of how we use them, and proud of what they stand for.

No organization in the history of the world has done more to preserve personal freedom, to ensure personal security, to fight violent crime, or taught more kids and adults about firearm safety, than your National Rifle Association.

I came here today because, like you and those great men that travelled here two and a quarter centuries ago, because of them, we have freedom's business to tend to.

Thank you.

ORAL STATEMENT OF CHARLTON HESTON, PRESIDENT NATIONAL RIFLE ASSOCIATION OF AMERICA

Hearings on the Second Amendment
Subcommittee on the Constitution
Committee on the Judiciary; United States Senate

September 23, 1998 Washington, D.C.

The Right of the People to Keep and Bear Arms

THANK YOU, CHAIRMAN ASHCROFT, AND HONORABLE MEMBERS OF THE SUBCOMMITTEE. I APPEAR HERE TODAY AS PRESIDENT OF THE NATIONAL RIFLE ASSOCIATION OF AMERICA. PRESENT WITH ME ARE WAYNE LAPIERRE, NRA EXECUTIVE VICE PRESIDENT, AND STEPHEN HALBROOK, MY COUNSEL.

I'D LIKE TO BRIEFLY TOUCH ON SOME HIGH POINTS THAT ARE FULLY FOOTNOTED IN MY WRITTEN TESTIMONY.

THE BILL OF RIGHTS WAS INTENDED NOT JUST AS A RULE BOOK FOR GOVERNMENT, BUT ALSO AS AN EASY-TO-UNDERSTAND GUIDE FOR ORDINARY CITIZENS. I ASSURE YOU THAT THE NEARLY THREE MILLION MEMBERS OF THE NRA, TOGETHER WITH MILLIONS OF OTHER LAW-ABIDING GUN OWNERS, KNOW EXACTLY WHAT THE SECOND AMENDMENT MEANS WHEN IT SAYS THAT "THE RIGHT OF THE PEOPLE TO KEEP AND BEAR ARMS, SHALL NOT BE INFRINGED." BUT LET'S TALK ABOUT IT ANYWAY.

LET'S BEGIN WITH PERHAPS THE KEY TERM IN THE SECOND AMENDMENT: "THE PEOPLE." IT'S A TERM THAT IS SPRINKLED THROUGHOUT SEVERAL OF THE AMENDMENTS AND CONSISTENTLY MEANS THE INDIVIDUALS WHO COMPOSE OUR SOCIETY.

IN A 1990 DECISION BY CHIEF JUSTICE WILLIAM REHNQUIST, THE U.S. SUPREME COURT TELLS US THAT "'THE PEOPLE' SEEMS TO HAVE BEEN A TERM OF ART EMPLOYED IN SELECT PARTS OF THE CONSTITUTION" AND THAT USAGE OF THIS TERM "SUGGESTS THAT 'THE PEOPLE' REFERS TO A CLASS OF PERSONS WHO ARE PART OF A NATIONAL COMMUNITY..."

YET A CERTAIN FICTION WAS INVENTED IN THE TWENTIETH CENTURY PROCLAIMING THAT "THE PEOPLE" IN THE SECOND AMENDMENT REALLY MEANS "THE STATES" OR THE NATIONAL GUARD. THIS FICTION WOULD ASSUME THAT THE FRAMERS OF THE CONSTITUTION AND BILL OF RIGHTS WERE POOR DRAFTSMEN, PLAYING FAST AND LOOSE WITH THE LANGUAGE OF OUR CHARTER OF GOVERNMENT. CERTAINLY THEY WERE NOT.

CLEARLY THE FRAMERS KNEW HOW TO SAY "THE STATES" WHEN THEY MEANT THE STATES, AND THEY CONSISTENTLY DESCRIBED THE STATES AS HAVING "POWERS," WHILE ONLY THE CITIZENS HAD "RIGHTS." IT GOES WITHOUT SAYING THAT THE NATIONAL GUARD DID NOT EXIST WHEN THE SECOND AMENDMENT WAS RATIFIED. IN ANY EVENT, THE RIGHT PROTECTED, THE RIGHT TO KEEP AND BEAR ARMS, PLAINLY RESTS IN THE HANDS OF "THE PEOPLE."

FOR FURTHER VERIFICATION LET US TURN TO THE WORDS OF JAMES MADISON, WHO SAID THAT ANY ATTEMPT AT TYRANNY WOULD BE COUNTERED BY "HALF A MILLION CITIZENS WITH ARMS IN THEIR HANDS," REFERRING TO "THE ADVANTAGE OF BEING ARMED, WHICH THE AMERICANS POSSESS OVER THE PEOPLE OF ALMOST EVERY OTHER NATION."

AT THE SAME TIME SAMUEL ADAMS, THE GREAT REVOLUTIONARY PATRIOT, PROPOSED A BILL OF RIGHTS DECLARING "THAT THE SAID CONSTITUTION BE NEVER CONSTRUED TO AUTHORIZE CONGRESS TO INFRINGE THE JUST LIBERTY OF THE PRESS, OR THE RIGHTS OF CONSCIENCE; OR TO PREVENT THE PEOPLE OF THE UNITED STATES, WHO ARE PEACEABLE CITIZENS, FROM KEEPING THEIR OWN ARMS..." IN THE SAME VEIN ANTI-FEDERALIST LEADER RICHARD HENRY LEE WROTE THAT "TO PRESERVE LIBERTY, IT IS ESSENTIAL THAT THE WHOLE BODY OF THE PEOPLE ALWAYS POSSESS ARMS, AND BE TAUGHT ALIKE, ESPECIALLY WHEN YOUNG, HOW TO USE THEM..."

ST. GEORGE TUCKER, THE FIRST MAJOR COMMENTATOR ON THE BILL OF RIGHTS, SUGGESTED THAT, "THE RIGHT OF SELF-DEFENSE IS THE FIRST LAW OF NATURE...WHEREVER...THE RIGHT OF THE PEOPLE TO KEEP AND BEAR ARMS IS, UNDER ANY COLOR OR PRETEXT WHATSOEVER, PROHIBITED, LIBERTY, IF NOT ALREADY ANNIHILATED, IS ON THE BRINK OF DESTRUCTION."

AND THAT RIGHT OF THE PEOPLE EXTENDS TO ALL. AT THE CONCLUSION OF THE CIVIL WAR IT WAS OUR GOAL TO ERADICATE ALL

INCIDENTS OF SLAVERY. YET THE SOUTHERN STATES ENACTED "BLACK CODES," WHICH EMBODIED THE OLD SLAVE LAWS, INCLUDING BANS ON GUN OWNERSHIP BY BLACK PEOPLE. TO PROTECT THE RIGHTS OF FREED SLAVES FROM SUCH LAWS, IN 1866 CONGRESS PROPOSED THE ADOPTION OF THE FOURTEENTH AMENDMENT, WHICH PROTECTS CITIZENS' RIGHTS FROM STATE VIOLATION.

SENATOR JACOB HOWARD, WHEN HE INTRODUCED THE AMENDMENT, EXPLAINED THAT THE PURPOSE WAS TO PROTECT "PERSONAL RIGHTS" SUCH AS "THE RIGHT TO KEEP AND BEAR ARMS" FROM STATE INFRINGEMENT. THE SAME CONGRESS PASSED THE CIVIL RIGHTS ACT AND ALSO THE FREEDMEN'S BUREAU ACT, WHICH PROTECTED THE "FULL AND EQUAL BENEFIT OF ALL LAWS AND PROCEEDINGS CONCERNING PERSONAL LIBERTY, PERSONAL SECURITY, AND...ESTATE, REAL AND PERSONAL, INCLUDING THE CONSTITUTIONAL RIGHT TO BEAR ARMS."

MORE THAN ONCE THIS BODY HAS AFFIRMED THE SANCTITY OF THE SECOND AMENDMENT. JUST OVER A DECADE AGO, CONGRESS PASSED THE FIREARMS OWNERS PROTECTION ACT OF 1986, ACKNOWLEDGING THAT THE GOVERNMENT HAD EXCEEDED ITS AUTHORITY AND PASSED CERTAIN LAWS VIOLATING THE BILL OF RIGHTS.

AND JUST LAST YEAR THE SUPREME COURT HELD THAT THE BRADY ACT, WHICH COMMANDED LOCAL LAW ENFORCEMENT OFFICERS TO CONDUCT BACKGROUND CHECKS ON HANDGUN PURCHASERS, VIOLATED STATE POWERS UNDER THE TENTH AMENDMENT. IN HIS CONCURRING OPINION, JUSTICE CLARENCE THOMAS NOTED THAT – LIKE THE FIRST AMENDMENT – "THE SECOND AMENDMENT SIMILARLY APPEARS TO CONTAIN AN EXPRESS LIMITATION ON THE GOVERNMENT'S AUTHORITY."

THE NATIONAL RIFLE ASSOCIATION OF AMERICA REMAINS DEDICATED TO THE PRESERVATION OF OUR CONSTITUTION AND BILL OF RIGHTS, AND WE AGREE THAT THE RIGHT TO KEEP AND BEAR ARMS IS INDEED "THE PALLADIUM" OF THE LIBERTIES OF OUR REPUBLIC. THE SUPPORTING EVIDENCE – HISTORICAL, SOCIETAL AND JUDICIAL – IS OVERWHELMING. AS WE ENTER THE 21ST CENTURY, LET US PRAY THAT OUR DESCENDANTS WILL ENJOY THE BLESSINGS OF CONSTITUTIONAL LIBERTY THAT OUR FOUNDING FATHERS SO WISELY BESTOWED OVER TWO CENTURIES AGO.

THANK YOU.

Remarks before the Christian Coalition

September 19, 1998 Washington, D.C.

"With Firmness in the Right"

Usually at the beginning of a speech I part some waters for dramatic effect. But I hear that even if you part the waters for Dr. [Pat] Robertson, he rises to the occasion and walks across the top. But as an actor, I can't let myself be upstaged like that. Next time I'll arrive in a chariot just to live up to your expectations. But only if a few of you guys will volunteer to clean up after the horses. After all, you've been cleaning up after the liberals for a long time.

And no, I will not make a parable of our president's story tonight, because I'm sure some day there will be a film about Mr. Clinton's life. I just hope I'm old enough to be admitted to the theater.

Tonight, Shakespeare's words from *Richard II* come to mind:
O' that I were as great/As in my grief,
Or lesser than my name,
Or that I could forget what I have been,
Or not remember what I must be now.

Before I go any farther, I'd like to say how good it is to see a fellow Reaganite, Don Hodel, at the helm of this historic movement. Don, your old boss and my old friend may not be with us tonight, but Ronald Reagan's spirit fills this room, or for that matter, any room where decent people gather in the name of God and country.

I remember my son, when he was five, explaining to his kindergarten class what his father did for a living. "My daddy," he said, "pretends to be people."

There have been quite a few of them. Prophets from the Old and New Testaments, a couple of Christian saints, generals of various nationalities and different centuries, several kings, three American presidents, a French cardinal and

TWO GENIUSES, INCLUDING MICHELANGELO. IF YOU WANT THE CEILING REPAINTED I'LL DO MY BEST. I DON'T MEAN TO BOAST...PLEASE UNDERSTAND. IT'S JUST THAT THERE ALWAYS SEEMS TO BE A LOT OF DIFFERENT FELLOWS UP HERE, AND I'M NOT SURE WHICH ONE OF THEM GETS TO TALK.

BUT IF I COULD BREATHE LIFE INTO ANY ONE OF THESE GREAT MEN TONIGHT, I THINK THEY WOULD AGREE THAT THE COALITION'S WORK IS VITAL. THEY WOULD ADVISE YOU TO CARRY ON, TO KEEP THE FAITH, TO STAY THE COURSE...ON THE ROAD TO VICTORY.

THEY'D AGREE IT WAS A CRITICAL MOMENT IN OUR HISTORY WHEN DR. ROBERTSON STEPPED FORWARD TEN YEARS AGO. I'LL TELL YOU WHY: HE SET THE BAR HIGH.

PAT ROBERTSON'S BID FOR THE PRESIDENCY FORCED AN APATHETIC CITIZENRY TO FOCUS ON THIS NATION'S MORAL DECLINE. THE CHRISTIAN COALITION ROSE FROM THE GRASSROOTS TO ASSERT THE TRUTH THAT WE MUST BE, FIRST, A MORAL PEOPLE. A NATION UNDER GOD...IF YOU SO CHOOSE, OF COURSE – AND THE MAJORITY OF US DO SO CHOOSE.

AT THAT MOMENT HE PUT IN PLACE A ROCK-SOLID STANDARD BY WHICH TODAY'S EVENTS ARE MEASURED. DECENT PEOPLE EVERYWHERE ARE GRATEFUL THAT STANDARD IS STILL HELD HIGH BY THE CHRISTIAN COALITION. PAT, ALONG WITH MILLIONS OF YOUR FOLLOWERS, I APPLAUD YOU. YOU CHRISTIAN SOLDIERS HAVE SHOWN US THAT MORALITY AND POLITICS AND EVERYDAY LIFE ARE ALL INTERTWINED, LIKE FINE EMBROIDERY.

BUT AS WE APPROACH THE NEXT MILLENNIUM, OURS REMAINS A NATION OF GREAT PARADOX. ECONOMICALLY WE REVEL IN THE FAT OF THE LAND. YET SPIRITUALLY, WE HUNGER.

LOOK AROUND AND YOU'LL SEE A NATION GLUTTED BY ITS OWN TOO MUCH, YET STRUGGLING TO RESET ITS MORAL COMPASS, WHERE LEADERSHIP IS DEFINED BY OPINION POLLS, SPIN DOCTORING, LIES AND A MAD SCRAMBLE OF DECEPTION.

OUR PRESIDENT'S RECENT TROUBLES ARE DRAMATIC PROOF THAT CULTURAL WAR IS NOT A CLASH OVER THE FACTS, OR EVEN BETWEEN PHILOSOPHIES. IT'S A CLASH BETWEEN THE PRINCIPLED, AND THE UNPRINCIPLED.

I AM NOT TALKING ABOUT HIS BEHAVIOR. I AM TALKING ABOUT REACTION TO IT. I AM TALKING ABOUT PEOPLE WHO CANNOT COMPREHEND MORAL ABSOLUTES, AND A COUNTRY THAT SEEMS TO ABIDE IT. WE ARE TRAPPED IN THE SILLY SPECTACLE OF HAVING OUR VALUES MEASURED HOURLY BY THE POLLS, AS IF THE DEFINITION OF THE "RIGHT THING" CHANGED LIKE A NATIONAL MOOD RING.

"WHAT DO YOU THINK OF THE PRESIDENT? WELL, WAIT – AFTER HIS MEA CULPA, NOW HOW DO YOU FEEL? OH…NO…WAIT…AFTER THE WHITE HOUSE SPIN, HOW DO YOU FEEL? BUT WAIT, AFTER THE FIRST LADY'S INTERVIEW, NOW HOW DO YOU FEEL?"

BEHAVIOR IS JUDGED BASED NOT UPON WHAT'S RIGHT, BUT UPON WHAT SEEMS RIGHT, AND TO WHOM, AT WHAT MOMENT.

BUT WHAT'S TRULY RIGHT IS NOT SITUATIONAL. IT IS CONSTANT.

WE'VE LET THE CULTURAL REFORMERS GET THEIR HANDS ON THE WHEEL, AND NOW THEY'RE DRIVING US STRAIGHT INTO MORAL BANKRUPTCY. AND THE LEGACY OF SUCH CONVOLUTED THINKING? AMERICA IS RED WITH THE BLOOD OF IT.

LIKE SEX EDUCATION IN SCHOOLS WHERE PRAYER IS BANNED. IT SEEMS WE'RE SAYING, "WE CAN TELL YOU HOW-TO, BUT WE CAN'T TELL YOU WHY-NOT."

SO WE'VE GOT CHILDREN BEARING CHILDREN. CHILDREN KILLING CHILDREN. EVERYONE KILLING UNBORN CHILDREN. WE'RE UP TO OUR ELBOWS IN THIS BRIGHT BLOODY STAIN OF CULTURAL WARFARE. NO WONDER MAINSTREAM AMERICANS WAKE UP EVERY MORNING INCREASINGLY BEWILDERED AND CONFUSED AT WHY THEIR TRADITIONAL VIEWS MAKE THEM LESSER CITIZENS.

AFTER ENOUGH BREAKFAST-TABLE TV PROMOS HYPING TATTOOED SEX SLAVES ON THE NEXT *JERRY SPRINGER*…ENOUGH BULLET-RIDDLED MOVIES AND TEEN-MOM TALK SHOWS…ENOUGH REVISIONIST HISTORY BOOKS AND PRIME-TIME RIDICULE OF GODLINESS…ENOUGH OF THE TV NEWS ANCHOR WHO COCKS HER HEAD AND CLUCKS HER TONGUE ABOUT RIGHT-WING RELIGION, FINALLY THE MESSAGE BEGINS TO GET THROUGH:

HEAVEN HELP THE GOD-FEARING, LAW-ABIDING, CAUCASIAN, MIDDLE-CLASS, PROTESTANT, OR EVEN WORSE, EVANGELICAL CHRISTIAN… MIDWEST OR SOUTHERN, OR EVEN WORSE, RURAL…APPARENTLY STRAIGHT, OR EVEN WORSE, ADMITTED HETEROSEXUAL…GUN-OWN-

ING, OR EVEN WORSE, NRA-CARD-CARRYING...AVERAGE WORKING STIFF, OR WORST OF ALL, MALE WORKING STIFF...BECAUSE NOT ONLY DON'T YOU COUNT, YOU'RE A DOWNRIGHT OBSTACLE TO SOCIAL PROGRESS. AND FRANKLY MISTER, YOU NEED TO WAKE UP, WISE UP AND LEARN A LITTLE SOMETHING ABOUT YOUR NEW AMERICA. AND MEANTIME, WHY DON'T YOU JUST SIT DOWN AND SHUT UP!

THAT'S WHY I'VE FORMED ARENA PAC, MY OWN POLITICAL ACTION COMMITTEE. THAT'S WHY THE SABRES ARE RATTLING IN AMERICA'S MILD-MANNERED LIVING ROOMS. AMERICANS ARE READY TO FIGHT FOR THE TRUE BOOTY OF CULTURAL WAR: THEIR VALUES. AND THEY WANT THEM BACK.

THEY WANT THE AMERICA THEY BUILT WHERE YOU COULD PRAY WITHOUT FEELING NAIVE, LOVE WITHOUT BEING KINKY, SING WITHOUT PROFANITY, BE WHITE WITHOUT FEELING GUILTY, OWN A GUN WITHOUT STIGMA, SHOUT AMEN WITHOUT APOLOGY, AND PROSPER WITHOUT BEING BLAMED.

THEY'RE GRATEFUL FOR THE EVANGELICAL NETWORKS, THE CHRISTIAN CHANNELS SPRINKLED ON CABLE OUTLETS, THE NON-MAINSTREAM PRESSES THAT HAVE PROLIFERATED, THE BULLETINS, NEWSPAPERS, BOOKLETS AND BOOKSTORES THAT APPEAL TO MILLIONS OF CHRISTIANS WHO CAN'T FIND SOMEONE WHO LOOKS LIKE OR SOUNDS LIKE THEMSELVES ON A MAJOR TELEVISION NETWORK OR IN THE *NEW YORK TIMES*.

THIS IS POSSIBLE BECAUSE, THANK GOD, OUR CONSTITUTION DEFINES RELIGIOUS FREEDOM UNDER THE BROADEST OF REVIVAL TENTS.

OUR BILL OF RIGHTS DOES NOT FORBID RELIGIOUS INTOLERANCE SOLELY IN THE NAME OF BAPTISTS, OR JEWS, OR CATHOLICS OR PENTECOSTALS. THE BILL OF RIGHTS EMBRACES RELIGIOUS OPPORTUNITY FOR PEOPLE WHO SPEAK IN TONGUES AND MOUNTAINEERS WHO TAKE UP SNAKES, FOR THE NATION OF ISLAM, AS WELL AS BELIEVERS WHO RECEIVE COMMUNION, WHO SEEK GUIDANCE FROM A RABBI, QUAKERS AND SHAKERS WHO QUIVER UNDER THE SPIRIT, OR HISPANICS WHO BEAR THE LASH OF THE PENITENTES, FOR THAT MATTER.

RELIGIOUS FREEDOM IN AMERICA IS NOT JUST RESERVED FOR METHODISTS OR PRESBYTERIANS OR LUTHERANS. RELIGIOUS TOLERANCE HERE MUST ALSO EMBRACE FAITHS WHICH SOME – MAYBE EVEN MOST – FIND BIZARRE OR EVEN OFFENSIVE.

IT'S SIMILAR TO FIREARM FREEDOM. NOT LONG AGO I WAS ELECTED PRESIDENT OF THE NATIONAL RIFLE ASSOCIATION. MOST PEOPLE SEEMED TO THINK I WAS A PRETTY NICE GUY UP UNTIL THEN. BUT NOW THE ATTACKS ARE BLISTERING, BECAUSE WE FIGHT FOR A FUNDAMEN-TAL FREEDOM.

THAT'S THE WAY IT IS IN A CULTURAL WAR, BECAUSE IF YOU WANT TO BRING DOWN A MIGHTY CHURCH, YOU START BY CRACKING ITS FOUNDATION. YOU FIRST ATTACK THE MOST BASIC BELIEFS.

LIKE THE MILLIONS OF GUN OWNERS IN THE NRA, YOU HAVE TAKEN THE ONLY RECOURSE LEFT OPEN TO YOU. YOU HAVE ORGANIZED TO FIGHT FOR WHAT YOU KNOW IS RIGHT. AND YOU ARE WINNING.

A COUPLE OF DECADES AGO THE CULTURAL WARRIORS DECLARED THAT GOD WAS DEAD IN AMERICA. MANY REMEMBER THE INFAMOUS TIME MAGAZINE COVER THAT DECLARED HIS DEMISE. I AM PLEASED TO REPORT THAT SINCE THEN, GOD HAS RECOVERED, REBOUNDED AND PROVED HIS RESILIENCE! HIS PRESENCE SURROUNDS US EVERY DAY, IF WE ONLY LOOK FOR IT. AND IN THE PAST FEW WEEKS WE HAVE WATCHED A STORY UNFOLD ABOUT A MAN NAMED MARK MCGWIRE THAT HOLDS A PARABLE FOR US ALL.

HE'S NOT LIKE MOST SPORTS HEROES. HE DOES NOT YELL AT REFER-EES, STRIKE OPPONENTS, SPIKE THE BALL, DYE HIS HAIR GREEN, HAWK SNEAKERS, BITE EARS OR PIERCE HIS NOSE.

HIS AUTOGRAPH IS NOT FOR SALE. IT IS FREE. HE GIVES AWAY ONE MILLION DOLLARS A YEAR TO ABUSED KIDS.

HE SETS RECORDS THAT MAY NEVER BE MATCHED. AND WHEN ASKED HOW HE DOES IT, HE GIVES ALL THE CREDIT TO "THE BIG MAN UPSTAIRS."

BUT MORE IMPORTANT THAN THE BEHAVIOR HE DISPLAYS IS THE BEHAVIOR HE INSPIRES.

WHEN HE SMACKED IT WITH HIS MIGHTY BAT, AND IT SAILED OUT OF THE FIELD AND INTO THE HANDS OF A FAN, A NINE-DOLLAR BALL TURNED INTO A MILLION-DOLLAR BILL. A SOUVENIR SO VALUABLE THE IRS STOOD READY TO TAX IT. BUT TIME AFTER TIME, HOME RUN AFTER HOME RUN, THE FANS GAVE THEM BACK. WITHOUT EXCEPTION, THOSE PRICELESS HOME RUN TREASURES WERE RETURNED – TO TAKE THEIR PLACE IN HISTORY IN COOPERSTOWN.

IN HIS MANNER, YOU CAN SEE THE PRESENCE OF HIS MASTER: HE IS MEEK. HE SEEMS TO PERFORM MIRACLES. HE TRIES TO HEAL. HE PERPLEXES THE MONEY CHANGERS. AND HE INSPIRES ALL WHO FOLLOW HIM. IN ANOTHER ERA, THIS KIND OF CONDUCT MIGHT DESCRIBE JUST ANOTHER GOOD GUY. AGAINST TODAY'S BACKDROP, HE SEEMS LIKE A MIRACLE.

THE LESSON HERE IS BASIC: GOODNESS IS CONTAGIOUS. MORAL LEADERSHIP ELEVATES AND INSPIRES US ALL. WE GROW IN MORAL MEASURE WHEN OUR HEROES MAKE ROOM FOR US. WE BECOME AS BIG AS OUR LEADERS LEAD US TO BE. IF THEY EXPECT LESS OF THEMSELVES, SO DO WE. BUT THE HIGHER THEIR CONDUCT, THE HIGHER OUR CHARACTER NATURALLY RISES TO THE OCCASION.

ON A NATIONAL SCALE, THIS IS THE LEGACY OF YOUR WORK. KEEP IT UP. RAISE THE BAR BY SHOWING WHO YOU ARE. LIFT THE STANDARD AS YOU LIVE YOUR OWN LIFE. ELEVATE BY EXAMPLE EVERYONE AROUND YOU. AS YOU WALK DOWN THAT ROAD TO VICTORY, CHOOSE NOT TO FOLLOW, BUT TO LEAD THE WAY.

AS MR. LINCOLN SAID, "WITH FIRMNESS IN THE RIGHT, AS GOD GIVES US TO SEE RIGHT, LET US FINISH THE WORK WE ARE IN...AND THEN WE SHALL SAVE OUR COUNTRY."

THANK YOU.

REMARKS BEFORE THE REPUBLICAN GOVERNOR'S ASSOCIATION IN INTRODUCTION OF DAVID SCHILLER

November 1998 New Orleans, LA

PROMISES. PROMISES ARE THE CURRENCY OF YOUR PUBLIC SERVICE. YOU ARE HERE BECAUSE YOU HAVE MADE YOUR PERSONAL CURRENCY VALUABLE. YOU ARE HERE BECAUSE YOUR PROMISE TO THE PEOPLE, YOUR WORD, MEANS SOMETHING.

THINK HOW MANY PROGRAMS AND POLICIES HAVE PROMISED TO MAKE LIFE SAFER. THINK HOW MANY TIMES YOU'VE BEEN LOBBIED WITH THE PROMISE THAT THIS LAW OR THAT REFORM WOULD MAKE SOMEONE, SOMEWHERE, SOMEHOW, SAFER. IN FACT, THINK HOW MUCH POLICY BECOMES LAW ON THE SINGULAR PROMISE THAT "IF IT SAVES JUST ONE LIFE…" – EVEN IF IT NEVER DOES.

SUCH HOLLOW PROMISES HOLD SPECIAL AGONY FOR VICTIMS OF GUN CRIME. THEY KNOW THE CRUEL FOLLY OF THE WAITING PERIODS AND GUN BANS AND LICENSING, AND ONE-GUN-A-MONTH, AND MANY MORE PROMISES THAT HAVE YET TO PRODUCE A REDUCTION IN CRIME RATES ANYWHERE. OF COURSE THESE FAILURES DO NOT STOP THE PROMISERS FROM CONTINUING TO PROMISE. BUT THEY DO STOP THE VICTIMS FROM CONTINUING TO LIVE.

THE MOST RECENT EXAMPLE CAME TWO WEEKS AGO IN NEW ORLEANS. MAYOR MARC MORIAL'S NEW PROMISE IS TO MAKE NEW ORLEANS "THE SAFEST BIG CITY IN AMERICA" BY FILING A LAW-SUIT AGAINST GUN MAKERS. HE IS QUITE PROUD OF HIS PLAN, AND BOASTS THAT IT'S THE FIRST LAWSUIT EVER FILED AGAINST THE FIREARMS INDUSTRY BY GOVERNMENT. IN FACT, HE HOPES YOU WILL FOLLOW SUIT.

BUT LET US REMEMBER THE WORDS OF ABRAHAM LINCOLN, WHO WROTE, "WE MUST NOT PROMISE WHAT WE OUGHT NOT, LEST WE BE CALLED ON TO PERFORM WHAT WE CANNOT."

MAYOR MORIAL WILL BE CALLED UPON, BUT HE CANNOT PERFORM WHAT HE HAS PROMISED. HE KNOWS, AND YOU KNOW, AND THE PEO-PLE CERTAINLY KNOW, THAT YOU CANNOT LOOK THEM IN THE EYE AND SAY, "MY LAWYERS AND THEIR BRIEFCASES FULL OF LAWSUITS AGAINST HONEST GUNSMITHS ARE GOING TO MAKE YOU SAFE."

I MIGHT ADD THAT THE ARMED CRIMINALS OF NEW ORLEANS KNOW IT, TOO. AND THEY'RE PRETTY HAPPY ABOUT IT. BUT TODAY, YOU HAVE A CHANCE TO MAKE A PROMISE YOU CAN KEEP THAT WILL SAVE LIVES. NO HOPE-SO'S AND MAYBES, NO PASS-IT-NOW AND APOLOGIZE LATER, NO BRADY BILL SMOKE AND MIRRORS.

IMAGINE PROMISING THAT YOU CAN ACTUALLY MAKE YOUR CON-STITUENTS SAFER, AND THEN DOING SO. IMAGINE THE HEROISM OF SAYING, "MY FRIENDS, A NUMBER OF US WERE GOING TO DIE AT THE HANDS OF ARMED CRIMINALS NEXT YEAR. BUT I CAN NOW PROMISE YOU THAT ALMOST ALL OF US, INSTEAD, WILL LIVE."

AND IMAGINE...THE PLEASURE OF INVITING YOUR CONSTITUENTS TO JOIN YOU IN SCARING ARMED CRIMINALS TO DEATH. THE PROMISE IS CALLED PROJECT EXILE. THE PLACE THAT KEEPS ITS PROMISE IS RICHMOND, VIRGINIA. AND THE MAN WHO CONCEIVED AND ENGINEERED IT IS HERE TO TELL YOU ABOUT IT – A PROMISE I HOPE YOU WILL MAKE, AND KEEP.

LADIES AND GENTLEMEN, PLEASE WELCOME SENIOR LITIGATION COUNSEL IN THE U.S ATTORNEY'S OFFICE FOR THE EASTERN DISTRICT OF VIRGINIA, MR. DAVID SCHILLER.

REMARKS BEFORE THE INLAND PRESS ASSOCIATION

January 1999 Scottsdale, AZ

"The Pretending Press"

LIKE ALL ACTORS I LOVE THAT EXPLOSION OF APPLAUSE WHEN I'VE TRULY STIRRED AN AUDIENCE. BUT TONIGHT I KNOW I MAY NOT GET IT. THAT'S OKAY...TONIGHT I WANT TO STIR YOUR MINDS INSTEAD.

I THINK OF MYSELF AS AN HONEST MAN. I THINK YOU'RE HONEST PEOPLE, TOO. YOU PRESIDE OVER AN HONORABLE PROFESSION.

BUT WHEN I UNDERTAKE THE WORK I LOVE, I AM BY DEFINITION SOMETHING LESS THAN HONEST. WHEN I ACT, I PRETEND. I'M NOT REALLY DISHONEST...JUST PARTICIPATING IN A MUTUALLY CONSENTING DECEPTION. IT'S AN UNDERSTOOD COVENANT WITH MY AUDIENCE. I AGREE TO DECEIVE THEM...TEMPORARILY...AND THEY AGREE TO BELIEVE ME...TEMPORARILY. WHEN IT WORKS, IT CAN BE AWESOME. AUDIENCES LAUGH, CRY, THINK. FOR JUST A WHILE, THEY BELIEVE.

TONIGHT I SUBMIT THAT YOU ARE A LOT LIKE ME. YOU TOO ARE ACTORS, PRETENDING. I SAY THIS BECAUSE OF THE REMARKABLE SAMENESS OF YOUR SCRIPT ON NATIONAL NEWS STORIES. EVERY DAY,

COAST TO COAST, FROM PAPER TO PAPER, NEWSPAPERS READ IN SURPRISING SYNC. PUT DOWN ONE PAPER AND PICK UP ANOTHER, AND YOU THINK "OH, YES, THIS IS WHERE I CAME IN." THE STAGING IS THE SAME, THE ACTION IS BLOCKED, AND THE PLOTS UNFOLD SO AUDIENCES EVERYWHERE CAN PLAY ALONG.

I SUBMIT THAT YOUR PROFESSION, LIKE MINE, IS PRETENDING. YOU MANIPULATE YOUR AUDIENCE WITH THE EXPERIENCE THEY SEEK AND AN OUTCOME YOU CAN PREDICT. IN THAT SENSE, I'VE WORKED WITH PEOPLE LIKE YOU ALL OF MY LIFE.

DON'T GET ME WRONG – I'M NOT BLAMING YOU. PERFORMERS MUST BE SENSITIVE TO THEIR AUDIENCES TO GAIN THEIR APPROVAL AND TO PAY THE BILLS. I SEE THE TOPICS ON YOUR AGENDA REFLECT THIS. "HOW TO OVERCOME NEWS DEPARTMENT RESISTANCE TO MARKETING CHANGE"..."HOW TO LINK MARKET RESEARCH TO NEWS DEPARTMENT CHANGES." THE PRESSURE TO PRETEND, AND PRETEND WELL, IS INTENSE.

BUT AS THE TWENTIETH CENTURY CLOSES, WE MUST ASSESS THE DAMAGE OF DISHONESTY TO THE FIRST AMENDMENT FREEDOM OF SPEECH AND PRESS ...BECAUSE THEY ALONE LEAD US TO TRUTH AND THUS TO FREEDOM.

IF, FIFTY YEARS AGO, YOU SET OUT TO DESTROY FREE SPEECH, YOU'D INVENT TELEVISION AND THE INTERNET...TO INDOCTRINATE A DROWSY AND CYNICAL SOCIETY INTO THAT DUMBED-DOWN CULT CALLED "COULDN'T-CARE-LESS" WHOSE MANTRA IS "WHATEVER."

WE'RE ALMOST THERE. POLITICAL CORRECTNESS TELLS US WHAT TO THINK, SO THE POLLS TELL THE PRESS WHAT TO SAY IN ORDER TO REFLECT WHAT WE THINK, SO WE'LL FEEL NORMAL WHEN WE'RE WATCHING TV BECAUSE WE BELIEVE WHAT WE'RE BEING TOLD BECAUSE IT'S WHAT WE ASKED THEM TO TELL US. THIS IS CLINTON'S LEGACY TO AMERICAN CULTURE. LEADERSHIP BY LOOKING IN MIRRORS. POLL-PLUG-'N-PLAY PRETENDING. CLOSED-CIRCUIT CONFIRMATION OF SELF-AFFIRMING, SELF-GRATIFYING, SELF-DELUSION. AND AN AUDIENCE THAT PLAYS ALONG.

THIS MAKES YOUR DUTY FAR MORE DIFFICULT, BUT INFINITELY MORE IMPORTANT. WHEN THERE IS SO LITTLE RESPECT FOR THE WRITTEN WORD, AND SO MUCH AVERSION TO FREE THOUGHT, CAUSES CANNOT BE CHAMPIONED, AND TRUTH CANNOT BE REVERED. AS MORE

AMERICANS REJECT DEPTH TO GULP DOWN FAST-FOOD JOURNALISM, DRIVE-THRU THOUGHT PASSES ITSELF OFF AS A SELF-GOVERNING DEMOCRACY. BUT IT'S NOT. IT'S BANKRUPT BRAIN FODDER THAT'S ALL ABOUT TASTE, NOT HEALTH. IT OFFERS STIMULATION, NOT NUTRITION. AND I FEAR YOU'RE GOING ALONG WITH THE CROWD, CONVERTING EVENTS INTO BITE-SIZE BITS, MORE FACTOID AND LESS FACT. YOU'RE ACTING THE PART, JUST LIKE ME IN MACBETH...PRETENDING.

DECEPTION, LYING, DISHONESTY AND CHEATING ARE NOW EPIDEMIC IN AMERICA. WHETHER IT'S A 9TH-GRADE GEOGRAPHY TEST OR A DRIVER'S EXAM OR SATs, JOB TESTS, HONORS CLASSES AT HARVARD, TERM PAPERS OR RECRUITMENT EXAMS – OR BEFORE A GRAND JURY – CHEATING IS RAMPANT. THREE OUT OF FOUR COLLEGE STUDENTS NOW ADMIT TO CHEATING ON TESTS. WHY ISN'T THIS A BIG STORY? DOESN'T ANYONE HERE THINK IT'S NEWS THAT DECEPTION – THE ASSASSIN OF TRUTH – IS NOW AMERICA'S GREAT EXPECTATION?

NBC HAS BEEN PRETENDING. AS YOU KNOW THEY SAT ON A TAPED INTERVIEW WITH A WOMAN WHO ALLEGES THEN-ARKANSAS-ATTOR-NEY-GENERAL BILL CLINTON BRUTALLY RAPED HER IN 1978. HER STORY WAS THOROUGHLY CORROBORATED. IT BROKE IN THE WALL STREET JOURNAL LAST WEEK, SORT OF. BUT NBC SAT ON IT UNTIL LAST WEDNESDAY NIGHT, WHEN IT WAS A HANDY, 20-MINUTE DIVERSION IN ITS RATINGS FIGHT AGAINST THE GRAMMIES.

IMAGINE – IF NBC HAD A CREDIBLE WOMAN ON TAPE ALLEGING THAT THEN-ATTORNEY-GENERAL GEORGE BUSH, JR. HAD BITTEN HER LIPS AND TORN HER PANTIES DURING A SEXUAL ASSAULT IN 1978 – OR ANY YEAR – YOU'D LEAVE THIS BANQUET NOW TO FILE THAT STORY. AND TOMORROW MORNING'S FRONT PAGES WOULD IGNITE LIKE GUNPOWDER. BUT YOU PRETEND NOT TO NOTICE, AND THE AUDI-ENCE...PLAYS ALONG.

NONE OF YOU PRETENDED NOT TO NOTICE IN 1987 WHEN RONALD REAGAN SOLD ARMS TO FREEDOM FIGHTERS. EVERY PAPER COVERED THE IRAN-CONTRA SCANDAL DAILY FOR WEEKS. BUT A WEAPONS TECHNOLOGY TRANSFER TO THE RED CHINESE BY THIS PRESIDENT IS VIRTUALLY IGNORED. WE'RE TALKING ABOUT MISSILE WEAPONS TECHNOLOGY THAT GIVES THE RED CHINESE POTENTIAL FOR MAKING GLOBAL WAR, THAT DWARFS THE SMALL ARMS OF IRAN-CONTRA. BUT YOU PRETEND NOT TO NOTICE, AND THE AUDIENCE PLAYS ALONG.

BEFORE YOU CALL ME PARTISAN...IT'S NOT THAT THE DEMOCRATS GET A FREE RIDE WHILE THE REPUBLICANS DON'T. IT'S THAT THE RED CHINESE GET A FREE RIDE WHILE OUR ALLIES DON'T. IMAGINE IF WEAPONS TECHNOLOGY WAS SOLD BY OUR PRESIDENT TO THE GERMANS OR THE JAPANESE. THERE'D BE A FLOOD OF STORIES ABOUT HOLOCAUST REPARATIONS AND UNCHECKED IMPERIALISM. BUT WHEN IT COMES TO THE RED CHINESE, THE PRESS PRETENDS, AND THE AUDIENCE PLAYS ALONG.

I DON'T CARE WHAT YOU THINK ABOUT GUNS. BUT YOU HARDLY MISS A CHANCE TO REPORT CRIMINAL GUN VIOLENCE AS EVIDENCE OF NEED FOR GUN CONTROL. THAT'S DISHONEST ENOUGH. BUT WHEN LAWFULLY ARMED CITIZENS DEFEND THEMSELVES OR THWART CRIME A MILLION TIMES A YEAR...SILENCE. WHEN MILLIONS OF CONCEALED-CARRY LICENSE-HOLDERS COMMIT NOT A SINGLE CRIME BUT, BY THEIR PRESENCE, PREVENT COUNTLESS CRIMES...SILENCE. YOU PRE-TEND THERE ARE NO POSITIVE SOCIAL BENEFITS OF FIREARM OWNERSHIP, AND YOUR AUDIENCE PLAYS ALONG.

YOUR ANTI-GUN ENTHUSIASM IS RELISHING THE NEW INDUSTRY LITIGATION. WITH THINLY VEILED JUBILATION, THE PRESS REPORTS THAT GROWING RANKS OF BIG-CITY MAYORS ARE FILING LAWSUITS AGAINST FIREARM MANUFACTURERS. THEY WANT TO MAKE A LEGITI-MATE INDUSTRY PAY FOR THE ACTS OF CRIMINALS THEIR OWN GOVERNMENTS HAVE FAILED TO CONTROL.

SHIFTING BLAME FROM TWO-BIT CRIMINALS TO LAWFUL MANUFAC-TURERS IS ABSURD ON ITS FACE. BUT THERE IS ALMOST NO DEPLOYMENT OF INVESTIGATIVE REPORTING TO PURSUE THIS STORY TO ITS INEVITABLE GOAL – DESTRUCTION OF THE SECOND AMENDMENT. THE ABSENCE OF CRITICAL ANALYSIS EVEN LEADS YOUR AUDIENCE TO THE CONCLUSION THAT IT'S A GOOD IDEA.

BUT IF A FIREARM COMPANY IN CONNECTICUT IS FINANCIALLY RESPONSIBLE FOR THE CRIMES OF AN ARMED EX-CON IN NEW ORLEANS, WHAT'S NEXT? WHAT ABOUT A LEGITIMATE PHARMACEU-TICAL PRODUCT WRONGLY USED TO COMMIT DATE RAPE? WHAT ABOUT A HIGH-POWER MUSCLE CAR WRONGLY USED IN A BANK ROB-BERY GETAWAY? WHAT ABOUT YOUR NEWSPAPER'S COVERAGE OF A VISITING DIPLOMAT'S ITINERARY WRONGFULLY USED BY A SNIPER TO ASSASSINATE HIM?

IF YOU FOLLOW THE LOGIC OF THIS MIASMA OF MISPLACED RESPON-
SIBILITY, AS YOU SHOULD, ANY INDUSTRY COULD BE LITIGATED TO ITS
KNEES. AND IF GUN MAKERS ARE FORCED OUT OF BUSINESS, THERE IS
NO SECOND AMENDMENT FREEDOM. NOW THAT'S A STORY. YET
YOU PRETEND IT'S NOT THERE, AND THE AUDIENCE PLAYS ALONG.

WHETHER IT'S PANDEMIC CHEATING OR ALLEGED RAPE OR WEAPONS
TECHNOLOGY TRANSFER OR LITIGATION AGAINST THE BILL OF RIGHTS,
IT SEEMS THESE STORIES AREN'T NEWS BY YOUR STANDARDS. INSTEAD
IT SEEMS THERE'S A COORDINATED EFFORT TO IGNORE THEM.

I KNOW...YOU'RE THINKING, "HEY, PAL, WE REPORTED THAT IN OUR
PAPER." BUT I DON'T MEAN AN OCCASIONAL MENTION. I MEAN THAT
STEADY DRUMBEAT OF CRITICAL DAILY COVERAGE THAT SETS THE
AGENDA OF NATIONAL DISCOURSE FOR ALL OTHER MEDIA...I MEAN
TAKING YOUR LEADING ROLE TO ALERT THE COMMON CONSCIOUS-
NESS ABOUT UNCOMMON THREATS. AND AS LONG AS YOU PRETEND,
AS LONG AS YOU ABIDE THE DISHONESTY, YOU ARE, BY YOUR GRAND-
FATHER'S STANDARDS, COWARDS.

IF YOU SAY IT PAYS THE BILLS, I SAY IT BUYS DISASTER. BECAUSE SUR-
VIVAL BY DISHONESTY IS LIFE NOT WORTH LIVING. IT'S A HOLLOW
AND COUNTERFEIT EXISTENCE. ASK BILL CLINTON. IT'S THE DRY
RESIDUE OF SPIN SLUNG ONTO THE WALLS – ALL TALK, ALL COIFFED
HAIR, ALL SALESMANSHIP, ALL MARKETING, ALL SIZZLE AND NO STEAK.

THE CONSEQUENCE OF ALL THIS DISHONESTY IS THAT WE LOSE OUR
WATCHDOG...A FREE AND CONCERNED PRESS...WHICH MEANS WE
LOSE PERSONAL FREEDOMS. PRETENDING HAS A PRICE MEASURED IN
SAGGING SCHOLASTIC SCORES, HOMOGENIZED THINKING, SUFFOCAT-
ING POLITICAL CORRECTNESS, REPRESSED IDEAS, SIMMERING ANGER,
INCREASED DIVORCE RATES, MORE RELIANCE ON GOVERNMENT,
MORE REGULATION, EXPLODING LITIGATION, THE WILLINGNESS TO
VOLUNTARILY SURRENDER PRIVACY IN RETURN FOR GOVERNMENT
SECURITY...ALL BECAUSE THE PRESS IS NO LONGER WARNING US
ABOUT WHAT THAT SUBMISSION REALLY MEANS. AND AN AUDIENCE
THAT PLAYS ALONG CANNOT MUSTER THAT ETERNAL VIGILANCE
WHICH IS THE PRICE OF FREEDOM.

I BELIEVE THIS DISHONESTY HAS BECOME SO ROUTINELY EXPECTED OF
THE PRESS THAT THE DAILY DISTRIBUTION OF REAL INFORMATION –
THE NEWS – IS NO LONGER HAPPENING.

FOR EXAMPLE, I AM WEARY OF THE NON-STORY THAT HILLARY CLINTON DOES NOT LIVE IN NEW YORK AND HAS NOT PROCLAIMED THAT SHE HAS NOT ANNOUNCED THAT SHE IS NOT YET A SENATE CANDIDATE. IT'S NOT NEWS, IT'S NOT CERTAIN, IT'S NOT POSSIBLE FOR 18 MONTHS, IT'S NOT RELEVANT, IT'S NOT EVEN VERY INTERESTING. BUT IT GETS LOTS OF FAVORABLE PRESS...THEY'RE ALREADY RUNNING HILLARY-VERSUS-RUDY POLLS. MEANWHILE, ELIZABETH DOLE'S SPECULATION ABOUT RUNNING FOR PRESIDENT – A FAR MORE NEWSWORTHY PROSPECT – GETS A FRACTION OF THE SPACE HILLARY GETS...AND THE BAND PLAYS ON.

SO WHAT DO I WANT?

I'M ASKING YOU TO LEAVE THE ACTING TO GUYS LIKE ME. THAT'S WHAT I DO, AND IT TAKES ONE TO KNOW ONE. LEAVE THE HACKNEYED SCRIPTS AND CONTRIVED STAGING TO THE THESPIANS.

ABANDON THE PRETENDING, DECEPTION AND PLAY-ALONG-TO-GET-ALONG DISHONESTY. DO THE JOB YOU'RE SUPPOSED TO DO.

DO THE JOB YOU TELL EACH OTHER AND THE PUBLIC YOU DO. YOUR DUTY IS TO DEBUNK DISHONESTY, NOT PERPETUATE IT.

DON'T REPORT THE IRRELEVANT AS RELEVANT, DON'T SERVE UP MANUFACTURED THOUGHT AS NEWS.

AND PLEASE, DON'T GIVE SPIN ANY MORE TURNS.

YOU WILL INCREASE YOUR CIRCULATION AND REVITALIZE YOUR INDUSTRY – AND PRESERVE OUR PRECIOUS LIBERTIES – BY DRIVING OUT THE ACTORS AND SCREENWRITERS WHO POSE IN YOUR NEWSROOMS AS JOURNALISTS. UNTIL YOU DO, YOU'RE CO-CONSPIRATORS, JUST BIT PLAYERS IN PREDICTABLE DAILY DRAMAS WITH OUTCOMES THAT HAVE IMMENSE CONSEQUENCES FOR PERSONAL FREEDOMS IN OUR COUNTRY.

THAT DENOUEMENT IS THE PRECISE OPPOSITE OF WHAT THE FOUNDING FATHERS INTENDED WHEN THEY PENNED THE AMENDMENT WHICH CREATES YOU, PROTECTS YOU, AND GIVES YOU GUARDIANSHIP OF THE NOBLE AND PEERLESS WEAPON WHICH DEFENDS OUR REPUBLIC: THE TRUTH.

PLEASE...DO NOT PRETEND THERE IS ANYTHING LESS.

THANK YOU.

REMARKS BEFORE THE CONSERVATIVE
POLITICAL ACTION CONFERENCE

January 1999 Washington, D.C.

"Conservative Challenge for a New Millennium"

1998 WAS A GREAT YEAR FOR ME. I DID THREE FILMS AND HAD DUAL HIP SURGERIES. BUT THAT WAS NOTHING. I SURVIVED *TIME* MAGAZINE AND *60 MINUTES*, IN THAT ORDER.

THANK YOU FOR YOUR THIRD KIND INVITATION TO SPEAK HERE. AS YOU KNOW, I'VE CHOSEN THIS PULPIT IN THE PAST TO OFFER YOU MY MOST HEARTFELT BELIEFS. TODAY IS NO EXCEPTION, SO HANG ON TO YOUR POLITICALLY CORRECT HATS. LET ME APPRISE YOU OF THE STATE OF FREE SPEECH FOR CHUCK HESTON SINCE WE TALKED LAST YEAR.

I'VE WORKED WITH BRILLIANTLY TALENTED HOMOSEXUALS ALL MY LIFE. BUT WHEN I TOLD YOU THAT GAY RIGHTS SHOULD EXTEND NO FURTHER THAN YOUR RIGHTS OR MINE, I WAS CALLED A HOMOPHOBE.

I FOUGHT IN WORLD WAR II. BUT WHEN I DREW AN ANALOGY BETWEEN SINGLING OUT INNOCENT JEWS AND SINGLING OUT INNOCENT GUN OWNERS, I WAS CALLED AN ANTI-SEMITE.

I WAS A CIVIL RIGHTS ACTIVIST LONG BEFORE IT WAS FASHIONABLE. BUT WHEN I TOLD YOU WHITE PRIDE IS JUST AS VALID AS BLACK PRIDE OR RED PRIDE OR ANYONE ELSE'S PRIDE, THEY CALLED ME WAS A RACIST.

EVERYONE KNOWS I WOULD NEVER RAISE A CLOSED HAND AGAINST MY GOVERNMENT. BUT WHEN I ASKED YOU TO STAND AND OPPOSE CULTURAL PERSECUTION, I WAS COMPARED TO TIMOTHY MCVEIGH.

AND PERHAPS MOST BRAZEN OF ALL, I BECAME PRESIDENT OF AN ORGANIZATION SO PRESUMPTUOUS IT SEEKS TO PRESERVE THE SECOND AMENDMENT TO THE U.S. CONSTITUTION – THE NATIONAL RIFLE ASSOCIATION!

FROM MIKE WALLACE TO COLLEAGUES TO FRIENDS AND FAMILY, THEY ESSENTIALLY SAID, "CHUCK, HOW DARE YOU SPEAK YOUR MIND. YOU ARE USING LANGUAGE NOT AUTHORIZED FOR PUBLIC

CONSUMPTION!" MANY WANT TO MUZZLE ME AND REIN ME BACK INTO LINE. IN FACT, I CAN SENSE MY AGENT AND MY PUBLICIST BRACING THEMSELVES NOW.

SO TELL ME – HERE AMONG FRIENDS, MAY I SPEAK MY MIND?

WHAT DOES THIS CENSURE OF FREE SPEECH MEAN? IT MEANS THAT TELLING US WHAT TO THINK HAS EVOLVED INTO TELLING US WHAT TO SAY, SO TELLING US WHAT TO DO CAN'T BE FAR BEHIND.

IT MEANS THAT THE WAR FOR OUR NATION'S CULTURE IS NOT JUST THEORY ON PAPER, BUT RAGING IN THE LAND. THIS CULTURAL WAR HAS ESCALATED INTO A WHITE-HOT CONFLAGRATION OF OPPOSING IDEAS, A COLLISION BETWEEN THE PRINCIPLED AND THE UNPRINCIPLED, IN A FEROCIOUS FINAL CLASH FOR OUR NATION'S SOUL.

IF YOU DOUBT THAT, NOTE THAT AMERICA HAS HAPPILY DRAFTED PORN POTENTATE LARRY FLYNT TO DRAW OUR NATION'S MORAL BATTLE LINES. YOU KNOW WE ARE AT WAR!

SO HOW DO THE GOOD GUYS WIN? HOW CAN WHAT'S RIGHT TRIUMPH? HOW DOES ANY MOVEMENT PREVAIL AGAINST A BIGGER, MORE POWERFUL ARMY?

THE ANSWER'S BEEN HERE ALL ALONG.

I LEARNED IT IN THIS CITY, 35 YEARS AGO, ON THE STEPS OF THE LINCOLN MEMORIAL, STANDING WITH DR. MARTIN LUTHER KING AND TWO HUNDRED THOUSAND PEOPLE.

WE SIMPLY...DISOBEY. PEACEABLY, YES. RESPECTFULLY, OF COURSE. NONVIOLENTLY, ABSOLUTELY.

BUT WHEN TOLD HOW TO THINK OR WHAT TO SAY OR HOW TO BEHAVE, WE DON'T. WE DISOBEY. WE DISOBEY SOCIAL PROTOCOL AND WRONGFUL LAW IMPOSED TO STIFLE AND STIGMATIZE AND SUFFOCATE PERSONAL FREEDOM. SINGLY AND COLLECTIVELY, WE DISOBEY.

I LEARNED THE AWESOME POWER OF DISOBEDIENCE FROM DR. KING...WHO LEARNED IT FROM GANDHI, AND THOREAU, AND JESUS, AND EVERY OTHER GREAT MAN WHO LED THOSE WITH THE RIGHT AGAINST THOSE WITH THE MIGHT. DISOBEDIENCE PROVES THOSE WITH LITTLE MORE THAN RIGHT ON THEIR SIDE CAN PREVAIL IN THE END, IF AT FIRST THEY DISOBEY.

DISOBEDIENCE IS IN OUR DNA. WE FEEL INNATE KINSHIP WITH THAT DISOBEDIENT SPIRIT THAT TOSSED TEA INTO BOSTON HARBOR, THE DISOBEDIENT SPIRIT THAT SENT THOREAU TO JAIL, THE DISOBE-DIENT SPIRIT THAT REFUSED TO SIT IN THE BACK OF THE BUS, THE DISOBEDIENT SPIRIT THAT PROTESTED A WRONGFULLY-WAGED WAR IN VIET NAM.

DISOBEDIENCE IS INSTINCTIVE. IN CALIFORNIA RIGHT NOW, TENS OF THOUSANDS OF HONEST GUN OWNERS ARE QUIETLY REFUSING TO REGISTER THEIR GUNS BECAUSE THE LAW IS A DIRECT AFFRONT TO INDIVIDUAL, CONSTITUTIONAL FREEDOMS.

LET ME BE CLEAR: NEITHER I NOR THE NRA ADVOCATES BREAKING ANY LAW. BUT WHEN A LAW IS UNJUST, EACH OF US HAS THE INDI-VIDUAL RIGHT TO MAKE A DECISION WHETHER OR NOT TO OBEY IT.

DISOBEDIENCE SAVES LIVES. IN RICHMOND, VIRGINIA, A HANDFUL OF FEDERAL PROSECUTORS DISOBEYED THEIR BOSSES IN WASHINGTON AND DEPLOYED A PROJECT THAT CUT GUN MURDERS BY 65% IN ONE YEAR. HOW DID THEY DISOBEY? THEY ACTUALLY ENFORCED FEDERAL LAW. EVERY FELON CAUGHT CARRYING A GUN IN RICHMOND GETS FIVE YEARS IN FEDERAL PRISON. NO DEALS, NO DISCUSSION. IT'S CALLED PROJECT EXILE, IT CUTS CRIME, IT SAVES LIVES, AND IT IS NOW A NATIONAL PET PROJECT OF MY NRA. WATCH FOR AN ANNOUNCEMENT MONDAY THAT'LL SURPRISE YOU, AND SCARE THE PANTS OFF GUN CRIMINALS.

YES – I AM ASKING YOU TO WIN THIS CULTURAL WAR WITH MASSIVE DISOBEDIENCE OF ROGUE AUTHORITY, SOCIAL DIRECTIVES AND ONER-OUS LAW THAT WEAKENS THE SECURITY OF OUR PERSONAL FREEDOMS.

BUT LET ME WARN YOU. IT HURTS.

DISOBEDIENCE DEMANDS YOU HAVE THE COURAGE TO PUT YOURSELF AT RISK. DR. KING STOOD ON LOTS OF BALCONIES. YOU MUST BE WILLING TO BE HUMILIATED...TO ENDURE THE MODERN-DAY EQUIV-ALENT OF THE POLICE DOGS AT MONTGOMERY AND THE WATER CANNONS AT SELMA.

YOU MUST BE WILLING TO EXPERIENCE DISCOMFORT. I'M NOT COM-PLAINING, BUT MY OWN DECADES OF SOCIAL ACTIVISM HAVE TAKEN THEIR TOLL ON ME. LET ME TELL YOU A STORY.

A FEW YEARS BACK I HEARD ABOUT A RAPPER NAMED ICE-T WHOSE *COP KILLER* CD WAS ABOUT MURDERING POLICE OFFICERS. IT WAS BEING MARKETED BY NO OTHER THAN TIME WARNER, THE BIGGEST ENTERTAINMENT CONGLOMERATE IN THE WORLD.

POLICE ACROSS THE COUNTRY WERE OUTRAGED. RIGHTFULLY SO. BUT TIME WARNER WAS STONEWALLING BECAUSE IT WAS A CASH COW HIT CD FOR THEM, AND THE MEDIA WERE TIPTOEING AROUND IT BECAUSE THE RAPPER WAS BLACK.

ABOUT THEN I HEARD TIME WARNER HAD A STOCKHOLDERS' MEETING SCHEDULED IN BEVERLY HILLS. I OWNED A COUPLE OF HUNDRED SHARES AT THE TIME, SO I DECIDED TO ATTEND.

WHAT HAPPENED NEXT WAS AGAINST THE ADVICE OF MY FAMILY AND COLLEAGUES, AND TO THE INTENSE DISMAY OF MY FRIENDS WITHIN THE TIME WARNER ORGANIZATION. I ASKED FOR THE FLOOR. TO A HUSHED ROOM OF A THOUSAND AVERAGE AMERICAN STOCKHOLDERS, I SIMPLY READ THE FULL LYRICS OF *COP KILLER* – EVERY VICIOUS, VULGAR, DIRTY WORD THEY WERE SELLING.

"I GOT MY 12 GAUGE SAWED OFF
I GOT MY HEADLIGHTS TURNED OFF
I'M ABOUT TO BUST SOME SHOTS OFF
I'M ABOUT TO DUST SOME COPS OFF..."

THE ROOM WAS DEATH-STILL, A SEA OF SHOCKED, FROZEN, BLANCHED FACES. THE TIME WARNER EXECUTIVES SQUIRMED IN THEIR CHAIRS AND STARED AT THEIR SHOES. THEY HATED ME FOR THAT.

THEN I DELIVERED ANOTHER VOLLEY OF SICK LYRIC BRIMMING WITH RACIST FILTH, WHERE ICE-T FANTASIZES ABOUT SODOMIZING TWO 12-YEAR OLD NIECES OF AL AND TIPPER GORE.

"SHE PUSHED HER BUTT AGAINST MY..."

WELL, I WON'T DO TO YOU HERE WHAT I DID TO THEM THERE. LET'S JUST SAY I LEFT THE ROOM IN AN ECHOING SILENCE.

TWO MONTHS LATER, TIME WARNER TERMINATED ICE-T'S CONTRACT. I KNOW I'LL NEVER BE OFFERED ANOTHER FILM BY WARNER OR GET A GOOD REVIEW FROM *TIME* MAGAZINE. BUT TAKING THE RISK TO STAND UP AND DRAW A LINE ALLOWED THE RIGHTING OF A DEADLY WRONG.

DISOBEDIENCE MEANS YOU MUST BE WILLING TO ACT, INSTEAD OF TALK.

WHEN A MUGGER SUES HIS ELDERLY VICTIM FOR DEFENDING HER-SELF...JAM THE SWITCHBOARD OF THE DISTRICT ATTORNEY'S OFFICE.

WHEN YOUR DAUGHTER'S COLLEGE IS PRESSURED TO LOWER STAN-DARDS UNTIL 80% OF THE STUDENTS GRADUATE WITH HONORS... CHOKE THE HALLS OF THE BOARD OF REGENTS.

WHEN AN EIGHT-YEAR-OLD BOY PECKS A GIRL'S CHEEK ON THE PLAYGROUND AND GETS HAULED INTO COURT FOR SEXUAL HARASS-MENT...MARCH ON THE SCHOOL AND BLOCK ITS DOORWAYS.

WHEN A LAW FIRM JOINS IN THE GREEDY LITIGATION TO PUT GUN MAKERS OUT OF BUSINESS...BAR THEM AND THEIR CLIENTS FROM YOUR BUSINESS RELATIONSHIPS.

WHEN THE GUY OR GAL YOU ELECTED GETS SEDUCED BY POLIT-ICAL POWER AND BETRAYS YOU...PETITION THEM, OUST THEM, BANISH THEM.

WHEN *TIME* MAGAZINE PORTRAYS MILLENNIUM NUTS AS DERANGED, CRAZY CHRISTIANS HOLDING UP A CROSS AS IT DID LAST WEEK... BOYCOTT THEIR MAGAZINE AND THE PRODUCTS IT ADVERTISES.

WE HAVE THE NUMBERS. WE JUST NEED TO UNITE, AND THEN DISOBEY... BOYCOTT...MARCH...EMBARGO...SPEAK UP...SHOUT DOWN...DEFY... INTERRUPT...OVERWHELM...RAISE HELL UNTIL HEAVEN HEARS US!

I REALIZE NOT ALL OF YOU CAN PUT YOURSELVES AT SUCH RISK TODAY. BUT I PREDICT THAT AS THIS CREEPING CULTURAL CANCER SLOWLY INGESTS THE VITAL ORGANS OF A FREE AMERICA, MORE WILL COME FORWARD. AS THE CULTURE CRUMBLES IN THE HANDS OF THE DUBIOUS AND DUPLICITOUS, MORE AND MORE MOTHERS AND FATHERS AND SHOPKEEPERS AND ACTORS AND PATRIOTS WILL MARCH INTO THE STREETS AND SAY, "NO – I WILL DISOBEY."

LET'S FOLLOW IN THE HALLOWED FOOTSTEPS OF THE GREAT DISOBE-DIENCE MOVEMENTS THAT FOUNDED RELIGIONS, DEFINED COUNTRIES, AND DEFEATED TYRANTS.

IT WORKED 35 YEARS AGO. IT CAN WORK AGAIN. IF DR. KING WERE SITTING NEXT TO YOU, I THINK HE WOULD AGREE IT IS TIME WE SAY, WE SHALL OVERCOME.

THANK YOU.

REMARKS BEFORE THE
HARVARD LAW SCHOOL FORUM

February 16, 1999 Cambridge, MA

"The Cultural War"

I REMEMBER MY SON WHEN HE WAS FIVE, EXPLAINING TO HIS KINDER-GARTEN CLASS WHAT HIS FATHER DID FOR A LIVING. "MY DADDY," HE SAID, "PRETENDS TO BE PEOPLE."

THERE HAVE BEEN QUITE A FEW OF THEM. PROPHETS FROM THE OLD AND NEW TESTAMENTS, A COUPLE OF CHRISTIAN SAINTS, GENERALS OF VARIOUS NATIONALITIES AND DIFFERENT CENTURIES, SEVERAL KINGS, THREE AMERICAN PRESIDENTS, A FRENCH CARDINAL AND TWO GENIUSES, INCLUDING MICHELANGELO. IF YOU WANT THE CEIL-ING REPAINTED I'LL DO MY BEST. THERE ALWAYS SEEM TO BE A LOT OF DIFFERENT FELLOWS UP HERE. I'M NEVER SURE WHICH ONE OF THEM GETS TO TALK. RIGHT NOW, I GUESS I'M THE GUY.

AS I PONDERED OUR VISIT TONIGHT IT STRUCK ME: IF MY CREATOR GAVE ME THE GIFT TO CONNECT YOU WITH THE HEARTS AND MINDS OF THOSE GREAT MEN, THEN I WANT TO USE THAT SAME GIFT NOW TO RECONNECT YOU WITH YOUR OWN SENSE OF LIBERTY...YOUR OWN FREEDOM OF THOUGHT...YOUR OWN COMPASS FOR WHAT IS RIGHT.

DEDICATING THE MEMORIAL AT GETTYSBURG, ABRAHAM LINCOLN SAID OF AMERICA, "WE ARE NOW ENGAGED IN A GREAT CIVIL WAR, TESTING WHETHER THIS NATION OR ANY NATION SO CONCEIVED AND SO DEDICATED CAN LONG ENDURE."

THOSE WORDS ARE TRUE AGAIN. I BELIEVE THAT WE ARE AGAIN ENGAGED IN A GREAT CIVIL WAR, A CULTURAL WAR THAT'S ABOUT TO HIJACK YOUR BIRTHRIGHT TO THINK AND SAY WHAT RESIDES IN YOUR HEART. I FEAR YOU NO LONGER TRUST THE PULSING LIFEBLOOD OF LIBERTY INSIDE YOU...THE STUFF THAT MADE THIS COUNTRY RISE FROM WILDERNESS INTO THE MIRACLE THAT IT IS.

LET ME BACK UP. ABOUT A YEAR AGO I BECAME PRESIDENT OF THE NATIONAL RIFLE ASSOCIATION, WHICH PROTECTS THE RIGHT TO KEEP AND BEAR ARMS. I RAN FOR OFFICE, I WAS ELECTED, AND NOW

I SERVE...I SERVE AS A MOVING TARGET FOR THE MEDIA WHO'VE CALLED ME EVERYTHING FROM "RIDICULOUS" AND "DUPED" TO A "BRAIN-INJURED, SENILE, CRAZY OLD MAN." I KNOW...I'M PRETTY OLD...BUT I SURE, LORD, AIN'T SENILE.

AS I HAVE STOOD IN THE CROSSHAIRS OF THOSE WHO TARGET SECOND AMENDMENT FREEDOMS, I'VE REALIZED THAT FIREARMS ARE NOT THE ONLY ISSUE. NO, IT'S MUCH, MUCH BIGGER THAN THAT. I'VE COME TO UNDERSTAND THAT A CULTURAL WAR IS RAGING ACROSS OUR LAND, IN WHICH, WITH ORWELLIAN FERVOR, CERTAIN ACCEPTABLE THOUGHTS AND SPEECH ARE MANDATED.

FOR EXAMPLE, I MARCHED FOR CIVIL RIGHTS WITH DR. KING IN 1963 – LONG BEFORE HOLLYWOOD FOUND IT FASHIONABLE. BUT WHEN I TOLD AN AUDIENCE LAST YEAR THAT WHITE PRIDE IS JUST AS VALID AS BLACK PRIDE OR RED PRIDE OR ANYONE ELSE'S PRIDE, THEY CALLED ME A RACIST.

I'VE WORKED WITH BRILLIANTLY TALENTED HOMOSEXUALS ALL MY LIFE. BUT WHEN I TOLD AN AUDIENCE THAT GAY RIGHTS SHOULD EXTEND NO FURTHER THAN YOUR RIGHTS OR MY RIGHTS, I WAS CALLED A HOMOPHOBE.

I SERVED IN WORLD WAR II AGAINST THE AXIS POWERS. BUT DURING A SPEECH, WHEN I DREW AN ANALOGY BETWEEN SINGLING OUT INNOCENT JEWS AND SINGLING OUT INNOCENT GUN OWNERS, I WAS CALLED AN ANTI-SEMITE.

EVERYONE I KNOW KNOWS I WOULD NEVER RAISE A CLOSED FIST AGAINST MY COUNTRY. BUT WHEN I ASKED AN AUDIENCE TO OPPOSE THIS CULTURAL PERSECUTION, I WAS COMPARED TO TIMOTHY MCVEIGH.

FROM *TIME* MAGAZINE TO FRIENDS AND COLLEAGUES, THEY'RE ESSENTIALLY SAYING, "CHUCK, HOW DARE YOU SPEAK YOUR MIND. YOU ARE USING LANGUAGE NOT AUTHORIZED FOR PUBLIC CONSUMPTION!"

BUT I AM NOT AFRAID. IF AMERICANS BELIEVED IN POLITICAL CORRECTNESS, WE'D STILL BE KING GEORGE'S BOYS – SUBJECTS BOUND TO THE BRITISH CROWN.

IN HIS BOOK, *THE END OF SANITY*, MARTIN GROSS WRITES THAT "BLATANTLY IRRATIONAL BEHAVIOR IS RAPIDLY BEING ESTABLISHED AS THE NORM IN ALMOST EVERY AREA OF HUMAN ENDEAVOR. THERE SEEM TO

BE NEW CUSTOMS, NEW RULES, NEW ANTI-INTELLECTUAL THEORIES REGULARLY FOISTED ON US FROM EVERY DIRECTION. UNDERNEATH, THE NATION IS ROILING. AMERICANS KNOW SOMETHING WITHOUT A NAME IS UNDERMINING THE NATION, TURNING THE MIND MUSHY WHEN IT COMES TO SEPARATING TRUTH FROM FALSEHOOD AND RIGHT FROM WRONG. AND THEY DON'T LIKE IT."

LET ME READ A FEW EXAMPLES.

AT ANTIOCH COLLEGE IN OHIO, YOUNG MEN SEEKING INTIMACY WITH A COED MUST GET VERBAL PERMISSION AT EACH STEP OF THE PROCESS FROM KISSING TO PETTING TO FINALLY COPULATION...ALL CLEARLY SPELLED OUT IN A PRINTED COLLEGE DIRECTIVE.

IN NEW JERSEY, DESPITE THE DEATH OF SEVERAL PATIENTS NATIONWIDE WHO HAD BEEN INFECTED BY DENTISTS WHO HAD CONCEALED THEIR AIDS – THE STATE COMMISSIONER ANNOUNCED THAT HEALTH PROVIDERS WHO ARE HIV-POSITIVE NEED NOT – NEED NOT – TELL THEIR PATIENTS THAT THEY ARE INFECTED.

AT WILLIAM AND MARY, STUDENTS TRIED TO CHANGE THE NAME OF THE SCHOOL TEAM "THE TRIBE" BECAUSE IT WAS SUPPOSEDLY INSULTING TO LOCAL INDIANS, ONLY TO LEARN THAT AUTHENTIC VIRGINIA CHIEFS TRULY LIKE THE NAME.

IN SAN FRANCISCO, CITY FATHERS PASSED AN ORDINANCE PROTECTING THE RIGHTS OF TRANSVESTITES TO CROSS-DRESS ON THE JOB, AND FOR TRANSSEXUALS TO HAVE SEPARATE TOILET FACILITIES WHILE UNDERGOING SEX CHANGE SURGERY.

IN NEW YORK CITY, KIDS WHO DON'T SPEAK A WORD OF SPANISH HAVE BEEN PLACED IN BILINGUAL CLASSES TO LEARN THEIR THREE R'S IN SPANISH SOLELY BECAUSE THEIR LAST NAMES SOUND HISPANIC.

AT THE UNIVERSITY OF PENNSYLVANIA, IN A STATE WHERE THOUSANDS DIED AT GETTYSBURG OPPOSING SLAVERY, THE PRESIDENT OF THAT COLLEGE OFFICIALLY SET UP SEGREGATED DORMITORY SPACE FOR BLACK STUDENTS.

YEAH, I KNOW...THAT'S OUT OF BOUNDS NOW. DR. KING SAID "NEGROES." JIMMY BALDWIN AND MOST OF US ON THE MARCH SAID "BLACK." BUT IT'S A NO-NO NOW. FOR ME, HYPHENATED IDENTITIES ARE AWKWARD...PARTICULARLY "NATIVE AMERICAN." I'M A NATIVE AMERICAN, FOR GOD'S SAKE. I ALSO HAPPEN TO BE A BLOOD-

INITIATED BROTHER OF THE MINICONJOU SIOUX. ON MY WIFE'S SIDE, MY GRANDSON IS A THIRTEENTH GENERATION NATIVE AMERICAN... WITH A CAPITAL LETTER ON "AMERICAN."

FINALLY, JUST LAST MONTH...DAVID HOWARD, HEAD OF THE WASHINGTON, D.C. OFFICE OF PUBLIC ADVOCATE, USED THE WORD "NIGGARDLY" WHILE TALKING TO COLLEAGUES ABOUT BUDGETARY MATTERS. OF COURSE, "NIGGARDLY" MEANS STINGY OR SCANTY. BUT WITHIN DAYS HOWARD WAS FORCED TO PUBLICLY APOLOGIZE AND RESIGN.

AS COLUMNIST TONY SNOW WROTE: "DAVID HOWARD GOT FIRED BECAUSE SOME PEOPLE IN PUBLIC EMPLOY WERE MORONS WHO (A) DIDN'T KNOW THE MEANING OF "NIGGARDLY," (B) DIDN'T KNOW HOW TO USE A DICTIONARY TO DISCOVER THE MEANING, AND (C) ACTUALLY DEMANDED THAT HE APOLOGIZE FOR THEIR IGNORANCE."

WHAT DOES ALL OF THIS MEAN? IT MEANS THAT TELLING US WHAT TO THINK HAS EVOLVED INTO TELLING US WHAT TO SAY, SO TELLING US WHAT TO DO CAN'T BE FAR BEHIND.

BEFORE YOU CLAIM TO BE A CHAMPION OF FREE THOUGHT, TELL ME: WHY DID POLITICAL CORRECTNESS ORIGINATE ON AMERICA'S CAMPUSES? AND WHY DO YOU CONTINUE TO TOLERATE IT? WHY DO YOU, WHO'RE SUPPOSED TO DEBATE IDEAS, SURRENDER TO THEIR SUPPRESSION?

LET'S BE HONEST. WHO HERE THINKS YOUR PROFESSORS CAN SAY WHAT THEY REALLY BELIEVE? IT SCARES ME TO DEATH, AND SHOULD SCARE YOU TOO, THAT THE SUPERSTITION OF POLITICAL CORRECT-NESS RULES THE HALLS OF REASON.

YOU ARE THE BEST AND THE BRIGHTEST. YOU, HERE IN THE FERTILE CRADLE OF AMERICAN ACADEMIA, HERE IN THE CASTLE OF LEARNING ON THE CHARLES RIVER, YOU ARE THE CREAM. BUT I SUBMIT THAT YOU, AND YOUR COUNTERPARTS ACROSS THE LAND, ARE THE MOST SOCIALLY CONFORMED AND POLITICALLY SILENCED GENERATION SINCE CONCORD BRIDGE. AND AS LONG AS YOU VALIDATE THAT...AND ABIDE IT...YOU ARE – BY YOUR GRANDFATHERS' STANDARDS – COWARDS.

HERE'S ANOTHER EXAMPLE. RIGHT NOW AT MORE THAN ONE MAJOR UNIVERSITY, SECOND AMENDMENT SCHOLARS AND RESEARCHERS ARE BEING TOLD TO SHUT UP ABOUT THEIR FINDINGS OR THEY'LL LOSE THEIR JOBS. WHY? BECAUSE THEIR RESEARCH FINDINGS WOULD UNDER-

MINE BIG-CITY MAYOR'S PENDING LAWSUITS THAT SEEK TO EXTORT HUNDREDS OF MILLIONS OF DOLLARS FROM FIREARM MANUFACTURERS.

I DON'T CARE WHAT YOU THINK ABOUT GUNS. BUT IF YOU ARE NOT SHOCKED AT THAT, I AM SHOCKED AT YOU. WHO WILL GUARD THE RAW MATERIAL OF UNFETTERED IDEAS, IF NOT YOU? WHO WILL DEFEND THE CORE VALUE OF ACADEMIA, IF YOU SUPPOSED SOLDIERS OF FREE THOUGHT AND EXPRESSION LAY DOWN YOUR ARMS AND PLEAD, "DON'T SHOOT ME."

IF YOU TALK ABOUT RACE, IT DOES NOT MAKE YOU A RACIST. IF YOU SEE DISTINCTIONS BETWEEN THE GENDERS, IT DOES NOT MAKE YOU A SEXIST. IF YOU THINK CRITICALLY ABOUT A DENOMINATION, IT DOES NOT MAKE YOU ANTI-RELIGION. IF YOU ACCEPT BUT DON'T CELEBRATE HOMOSEXUALITY, IT DOES NOT MAKE YOU A HOMOPHOBE.

DON'T LET AMERICA'S UNIVERSITIES CONTINUE TO SERVE AS INCUBATORS FOR THIS RAMPANT EPIDEMIC OF NEW MCCARTHYISM.

BUT WHAT CAN YOU DO? HOW CAN ANYONE PREVAIL AGAINST SUCH PERVASIVE SOCIAL SUBJUGATION?

THE ANSWER'S BEEN HERE ALL ALONG. I LEARNED IT 36 YEARS AGO, ON THE STEPS OF THE LINCOLN MEMORIAL IN WASHINGTON, D.C., STANDING WITH DR. MARTIN LUTHER KING AND TWO HUNDRED THOUSAND PEOPLE.

YOU SIMPLY...DISOBEY. PEACEABLY, YES. RESPECTFULLY, OF COURSE. NONVIOLENTLY, ABSOLUTELY.

BUT WHEN TOLD HOW TO THINK OR WHAT TO SAY OR HOW TO BEHAVE, WE DON'T. WE DISOBEY SOCIAL PROTOCOL THAT STIFLES AND STIGMATIZES PERSONAL FREEDOM.

I LEARNED THE AWESOME POWER OF DISOBEDIENCE FROM DR. KING... WHO LEARNED IT FROM GANDHI, AND THOREAU, AND JESUS, AND EVERY OTHER GREAT MAN WHO LED THOSE IN THE RIGHT AGAINST THOSE WITH THE MIGHT.

DISOBEDIENCE IS IN OUR DNA. WE FEEL INNATE KINSHIP WITH THAT DISOBEDIENT SPIRIT THAT TOSSED TEA INTO BOSTON HARBOR, THAT SENT THOREAU TO JAIL, THAT REFUSED TO SIT IN THE BACK OF THE BUS, THAT PROTESTED A WAR IN VIET NAM.

IN THAT SAME SPIRIT, I AM ASKING YOU TO DISAVOW CULTURAL CORRECTNESS WITH MASSIVE DISOBEDIENCE OF ROGUE AUTHORITY,

SOCIAL DIRECTIVES AND ONEROUS LAW THAT WEAKEN PERSONAL FREEDOM.

BUT BE CAREFUL...IT HURTS. DISOBEDIENCE DEMANDS THAT YOU PUT YOURSELF AT RISK. DR. KING STOOD ON LOTS OF BALCONIES.

YOU MUST BE WILLING TO BE HUMILIATED...TO ENDURE THE MODERN-DAY EQUIVALENT OF THE POLICE DOGS AT MONTGOMERY AND THE WATER CANNONS AT SELMA. YOU MUST BE WILLING TO EXPERIENCE DISCOMFORT. I'M NOT COMPLAINING, BUT MY OWN DECADES OF SOCIAL ACTIVISM HAVE TAKEN THEIR TOLL ON ME. LET ME TELL YOU A STORY.

A FEW YEARS BACK I HEARD ABOUT A RAPPER NAMED ICE-T WHO WAS SELLING A CD CALLED *COP KILLER* CELEBRATING AMBUSHING AND MURDERING POLICE OFFICERS. IT WAS BEING MARKETED BY NONE OTHER THAN TIME WARNER, THE BIGGEST ENTERTAINMENT CONGLOMERATE IN THE WORLD.

POLICE ACROSS THE COUNTRY WERE OUTRAGED. RIGHTFULLY SO – AT LEAST ONE HAD BEEN MURDERED. BUT TIME WARNER WAS STONEWALLING BECAUSE THE CD WAS A CASH COW FOR THEM, AND THE MEDIA WERE TIPTOEING AROUND IT BECAUSE THE RAPPER WAS BLACK.

I HEARD TIME WARNER HAD A STOCKHOLDERS MEETING SCHEDULED IN BEVERLY HILLS. I OWNED SOME SHARES AT THE TIME, SO I DECIDED TO ATTEND.

WHAT I DID THERE WAS AGAINST THE ADVICE OF MY FAMILY AND COLLEAGUES. I ASKED FOR THE FLOOR. TO A HUSHED ROOM OF A THOUSAND AVERAGE AMERICAN STOCKHOLDERS, I SIMPLY READ THE FULL LYRICS OF *COP KILLER* – EVERY VICIOUS, VULGAR, INSTRUCTIONAL WORD.

"I GOT MY 12 GAUGE SAWED OFF
I GOT MY HEADLIGHTS TURNED OFF
I'M ABOUT TO BUST SOME SHOTS OFF
I'M ABOUT TO DUST SOME COPS OFF..."

IT GOT WORSE, A LOT WORSE. I WON'T READ THE REST OF IT TO YOU. BUT TRUST ME, THE ROOM WAS A SEA OF SHOCKED, FROZEN, BLANCHED FACES. THE TIME WARNER EXECUTIVES SQUIRMED IN THEIR CHAIRS AND STARED AT THEIR SHOES. THEY HATED ME FOR THAT.

THEN I DELIVERED ANOTHER VOLLEY OF SICK LYRIC BRIMMING WITH RACIST FILTH, WHERE ICE-T FANTASIZES ABOUT SODOMIZING TWO 12-YEAR OLD NIECES OF AL AND TIPPER GORE.

"SHE PUSHED HER BUTT AGAINST MY..."

WELL, I WON'T DO TO YOU HERE WHAT I DID TO THEM. LET'S JUST SAY I LEFT THE ROOM IN ECHOING SILENCE. WHEN I READ THE LYRICS TO THE WAITING PRESS CORPS, ONE OF THEM SAID, "WE CAN'T PRINT THAT." "I KNOW," I REPLIED, "BUT TIME WARNER'S SELLING IT."

TWO MONTHS LATER, TIME WARNER TERMINATED ICE-T'S CONTRACT. I'LL NEVER BE OFFERED ANOTHER FILM BY WARNER, OR GET A GOOD REVIEW FROM TIME MAGAZINE. BUT DISOBEDIENCE MEANS YOU MUST BE WILLING TO ACT, NOT JUST TALK.

WHEN A MUGGER SUES HIS ELDERLY VICTIM FOR DEFENDING HERSELF...JAM THE SWITCHBOARD OF THE DISTRICT ATTORNEY'S OFFICE.

WHEN YOUR UNIVERSITY IS PRESSURED TO LOWER STANDARDS UNTIL 80% OF THE STUDENTS GRADUATE WITH HONORS...CHOKE THE HALLS OF THE BOARD OF REGENTS.

WHEN AN EIGHT-YEAR-OLD BOY PECKS A GIRL'S CHEEK ON THE PLAYGROUND AND GETS HAULED INTO COURT FOR SEXUAL HARASSMENT...MARCH ON THAT SCHOOL AND BLOCK ITS DOORWAYS.

WHEN SOMEONE YOU ELECTED IS SEDUCED BY POLITICAL POWER AND BETRAYS YOU...PETITION THEM, OUST THEM, BANISH THEM.

WHEN TIME MAGAZINE'S COVER PORTRAYS MILLENNIUM NUTS AS DERANGED, CRAZY CHRISTIANS HOLDING A CROSS AS IT DID LAST MONTH...BOYCOTT THEIR MAGAZINE AND THE PRODUCTS IT ADVERTISES.

SO THAT THIS NATION MAY LONG ENDURE, I URGE YOU TO FOLLOW IN THE HALLOWED FOOTSTEPS OF THE GREAT DISOBEDIENCES OF HISTORY THAT FREED EXILES, FOUNDED RELIGIONS, DEFEATED TYRANTS, AND YES, IN THE HANDS OF AN AROUSED RABBLE IN ARMS AND A FEW GREAT MEN, BY GOD'S GRACE, BUILT THIS COUNTRY.

IF DR. KING WERE HERE, I THINK HE WOULD AGREE.

THANK YOU.

REMARKS BEFORE THE YALE POLITICAL UNION

April 16, 1999 New Haven, Connecticut

"Truth and Consequences"

I AM PLEASED TO BE AMONG POLITICAL THINKERS, AND I HOPE, POLITICAL ACTIVISTS.

MY LIFE HAS ALWAYS BEEN A LIFE OF ACTIVISM. I MARCHED WITH MARTIN LUTHER KING IN 1963, LONG BEFORE HOLLYWOOD FOUND IT FASHIONABLE. SUPPORTING CIVIL RIGHTS THEN WAS JUST AS POPULAR AS SUPPORTING GUN RIGHTS IS NOW. YUP, I'M CURRENTLY THE PRESIDENT OF THE NATIONAL RIFLE ASSOCIATION. CLEARLY, MY VIEWS ARE NOT BOUND BY POLITICAL CORRECTNESS. THE THOUGHT POLICE DO NOT FRIGHTEN ME. I HOPE I FRIGHTEN THEM.

SINCE YOUR POLITICAL UNION DEBATES FOLLOW TRADITIONAL STRUCTURE, MY RESOLUTION WOULD GO SOMETHING LIKE THIS: BE IT RESOLVED THAT SOCIETAL DISHONESTY CAN KILL YOU. THAT IS TO SAY, A WORLD WITHOUT CONSEQUENCES IS A WORLD WITHOUT TRUTH, AND THAT YOU CAN DIE FROM THAT LIE.

I BELIEVE THAT IN YOUR HEART YOU ALREADY KNOW SOMETHING IS PROFOUNDLY WRONG. WHEN BARTENDERS ARE RESPONSIBLE FOR DRUNK DRIVERS' ACTS, AND GUNMAKERS ARE RESPONSIBLE FOR CRIMINALS' ACTS, AND NOBODY IS RESPONSIBLE FOR O. J. SIMPSON'S ACTS, SOMETHING IS WRONG.

AS STUDENTS, YOU SHOULD SEARCH FOR TRUTH. YOUR BRAIN EVOLVED TO DEMAND REALITY. IT CAN BEST PROCESS INFORMATION AGAINST AN UNCHANGING BACKDROP OF CERTAINTY.

BUT THAT'S HARD TO FIND. YOUR WORLD IS ALL SPIN. ACTIONS ARE FURTHER AND FURTHER REMOVED FROM CONSEQUENCES. CAUSE AND EFFECT ARE, AT BEST, THEORETICAL. EQUAL AND OPPOSITE REACTIONS ARE NO LONGER PC.

THE DOW TOPS TEN THOUSAND, BUT OUR LIVES ARE NOT ENRICHED. WE ENJOY UNPRECEDENTED AFFLUENCE, BUT OUR SOULS ARE IMPOVERISHED. OUR LUNGS INHALE THE RARIFIED AIR OF PROSPERITY, BUT OUR HEARTS WANT FOR NOURISHMENT. YOU LACK THAT INVISIBLE

ANCHOR THAT TETHERED YOUR GRANDPARENTS TO REALITY – YOU KNOW WHAT I'M TALKING ABOUT.

OUR NATION'S ABUNDANCE IS LIKE A NARCOTIC THAT MASKS OUR MALADY – WE FEEL TOO GOOD TO ACKNOWLEDGE THAT WE'RE SICK. WE'RE LIKE THE COCAINE-SNORTING ROCK STAR, WHO DARES NOT LOOK IN THE MIRROR – THE GHOULISH REFLECTION WOULD RUIN THE BUZZ.

IN HIS BOOK *THE END OF SANITY*, MARTIN GROSS SAYS, "BLATANTLY IRRATIONAL BEHAVIOR IS RAPIDLY BEING ESTABLISHED AS THE NORM IN ALMOST EVERY AREA OF HUMAN ENDEAVOR. THERE SEEM TO BE NEW CUSTOMS, NEW RULES, NEW ANTI-INTELLECTUAL THEORIES REGULARLY FOISTED ON US FROM EVERY DIRECTION. UNDERNEATH, THE NATION IS ROILING. AMERICANS KNOW SOMETHING WITHOUT A NAME IS UNDERMINING THE NATION, TURNING THE MIND MUSHY WHEN IT COMES TO SEPARATING TRUTH FROM FALSEHOOD AND RIGHT FROM WRONG. AND THEY DON'T LIKE IT."

LET ME GIVE YOU TWO GOOD EXAMPLES: THIS ADMINISTRATION'S APPROACH TO CRIME AND TO WAR. OUR GOVERNMENT'S DUPLICITY PROVES MY POINT.

IF YOU DROVE INTO RICHMOND, VIRGINIA TODAY, YOU'D BE GREETED BY BILLBOARDS WITH GIANT WORDS THAT SAY, "AN ILLEGAL GUN GETS YOU FIVE YEARS IN FEDERAL PRISON." THESE WARN ALL FELONS THAT PROJECT EXILE IS IN EFFECT. PROJECT EXILE SIMPLY ENFORCES EXISTING FEDERAL LAW. PROJECT EXILE MEANS EVERY CONVICTED FELON CAUGHT WITH A GUN, NO MATTER WHAT HE'S DOING, WILL GO TO PRISON FOR FIVE YEARS. NO PAROLE, NO EARLY RELEASES, NO DISCUSSION, PERIOD.

MY, MY – INCARCERATING ARMED FELONS. WHAT A NOVEL IDEA. IT WORKS, LIKE NO OTHER ANTI-CRIME POLICY EVER PROPOSED. PROJECT EXILE, IN ITS FIRST YEAR IN RICHMOND, CUT GUN HOMICIDES BY 62%. AND AS YOU'D EXPECT, RELATED GUN CRIMES LIKE ROBBERY, RAPE AND ASSAULT ALSO PLUMMETED. THAT MEANS HUNDREDS OF PEOPLE IN RICHMOND TODAY ARE ALIVE AND INTACT WHO, WITHOUT PROJECT EXILE, WOULD BE DEAD OR BLEEDING.

FOR YEARS THE NRA HAS DEMANDED THAT PROJECT EXILE BE DEPLOYED NATIONWIDE. MAKES SENSE, HUH? THE LAWS ARE ALREADY ON THE BOOKS. JUST ENFORCE THEM.

BUT BILL CLINTON WON'T DO IT. WHEN HE SAYS HE'S SERIOUS ABOUT FIGHTING CRIME, CONSIDER THAT AS A MATTER OF POLICY – AS A MATTER OF POLICY – THE CLINTON ADMINISTRATION IS NOT PROSECUTING VIOLATIONS OF FEDERAL GUN LAW. IN FACT, THEY REVERSED THE BUSH ADMINISTRATION'S POLICY OF PROSECUTING FELONS WITH GUNS. INSTEAD, WITH PLEA BARGAINS, A WINK AND A NOD, THEY'VE BEEN LETTING ARMED FELONS OFF THE HOOK. FROM 1992 TO 1998, PROSECUTIONS HAVE BEEN CUT ALMOST IN HALF. SO WHILE PROJECT EXILE WAS SAVING LIVES IN RICHMOND, FEDERAL PROSECUTION FOR GUN LAW VIOLATIONS EVERYWHERE ELSE DROPPED BY 43%.

SUCH FRAUD COULD NOT HAPPEN WITHOUT THE NEWS MEDIA'S ALLIANCE IN THE DISHONESTY; IT GOES UTTERLY UNREPORTED. HERE ARE MORE EXAMPLES.

EVERYONE REMEMBERS THE PRESS'S PODIUM-POUNDING FOR CLINTON'S CRIME BILL AND ITS "URGENTLY NEEDED" JUVENILE GUN TRANSFER PROVISIONS. IT BECAME LAW. BUT NOBODY IS REPORTING THAT, OUT OF THOUSANDS OF CERTAIN OFFENDERS, HIS JUSTICE DEPARTMENT BOTHERED TO PROSECUTE ONLY FIVE PEOPLE IN 1997 AND SIX IN 1998.

EVERYONE REMEMBERS ALL THE PRESS SUPPORT FOR HIS "DESPERATELY NEEDED" SEMI-AUTO GUN BAN THAT OUTLAWED GUNS BASED SOLELY ON THEIR APPEARANCE. BUT NOBODY IS REPORTING THAT, OUT OF THOUSANDS OF CERTAIN OFFENDERS, THE CLINTON ADMINISTRATION PROSECUTED FOUR PEOPLE IN 1997 AND FOUR IN 1998.

EVERYONE REMEMBERS THAT MEDIA LOVE-CHILD, THE BRADY BILL. MR. CLINTON REPEATEDLY CLAIMS THAT A QUARTER MILLION HAND-GUNS HAVE BEEN PREVENTED FROM FALLING INTO THE HANDS OF CONVICTED FELONS. BUT NOBODY IS REPORTING WHAT MATTERS TO YOU: HOW MANY OF THOSE QUARTER MILLION PEOPLE WERE CONVICTED AND TAKEN OFF YOUR STREETS FOR THE FEDERAL CRIME OF BEING A FELON TRYING TO BUY A GUN? TRY NINE!

IT'S SURREAL. MR. CLINTON STANDS IN THE ROSE GARDEN WITH HIS TEN PROP COPS, LIP-BITING IN PAINED SUPPORT OF SOME NEW LAW. THE PRESS DOES ITS BEST TO GET IT PASSED. IT BECOMES LAW. THEN EVERYBODY FORGETS ABOUT IT. AND AMERICANS BUY IT OVER AND OVER AND OVER AGAIN.

MAYBE YOU THINK A POLITICIAN'S LIES CAN'T HURT YOU. BUT LET ME TELL YOU, ARMED FELONS CAN.

PASSING LAWS IS WHAT KEEPS POLITICIANS' CAREERS ALIVE. ENFORCING LAWS IS WHAT KEEPS YOU ALIVE. BUT NOBODY'S GETTING ARRESTED, NOBODY'S GOING TO JAIL, IT'S ALL A GIANT SCAM. IT'S NOT REAL LIFE. IT'S A BIG LIE, PACKAGED BY AN ALLIANCE BETWEEN THIS ADMINISTRATION AND A MEDIA THAT SYSTEMATICALLY PROPAGATES ITS DOCTRINE. FORGIVE MY SEVERITY, BUT THAT'S PRECISELY THE DEFINITION OF THE SOVIET PROPAGANDA MACHINE OF THE '50S AND '60S.

WHILE THIS ADMINISTRATION WEAVES REALITY SPUN FROM EMPTY AIR AND HEAVY BREATHING, THE NRA IS HELPING FUND PROJECT EXILE TO KEEP IT ALIVE. I SUBMIT TO YOU THAT THE CONSEQUENCE OF WHAT WE'RE DOING SAVES PEOPLE...AND THE CONSEQUENCE OF WHAT THEY'RE DOING KILLS PEOPLE.

IT'S A CERTAIN CONSEQUENCE THAT IF YOU CHOOSE NOT TO PROSECUTE CRIMINALS, PEOPLE WILL DIE. IT IS ALSO A CERTAIN CONSEQUENCE THAT IF YOU CHOOSE TO GO TO WAR, PEOPLE WILL DIE.

CONSIDER KOSOVO. THOUGH UNDECLARED, THE WAR IS REAL. WHAT IS UNREAL IS BILL CLINTON'S GRASP OF ITS CONSEQUENCES... AND PERHAPS YOURS.

FROM THE OUTSET IT APPEARS NOBODY ANTICIPATED THAT FIRST HUMAN CONSEQUENCE OF WAR CALLED REFUGEES, THAT FIRST STREAM OF TRAGEDY THAT SPILLS FROM ARMED CONFLICT. IT SEEMS OUR LEADERSHIP IS SURPRISED AND UNPREPARED, CAUGHT SHORT ON TENTS, FOOD, CLOTHES AND MEDICINE FOR TENS AND TENS AND TENS AND TENS OF THOUSANDS OF REFUGEES.

NOW, I AM NOT ONE OF THOSE CONSERVATIVES WHO REFLEXIVELY OPPOSES EVERYTHING BILL CLINTON DOES WITH KNEE-JERK UNIFOR-MITY. WHETHER OR NOT WE SHOULD HAVE GONE IS IRRELEVANT. THAT DEBATE IS OVER. SO LET'S DISCUSS WHAT REALITY DEMANDS OF US NOW. THE ONLY GOOD WAR IS A FAST AND DECISIVE WAR, WITH OVERWHELMING MILITARY MIGHT THAT RESULTS IN QUICK VICTORY.

BUT THAT CHANCE IS LOST. INSTEAD WE'RE DOLING OUT CRUISE MISSILES LIKE POPSICLES IN A POPULARITY-POLL-GUIDED WAR, CON-DUCTED BY A MAN WHO DID NOT DISPLAY THE WILL TO FIGHT AS A

YOUNGER MAN, WHOM I DOUBT WOULD GO FIGHT NOW, AND WHO WOULD NOT OFFER HIS OWN LOVED ONES TO MARCH ON KOSOVO.

WARFARE EXPERTS GRASP THE TRUTH THAT MR. CLINTON DOESN'T: NOW WE'RE IN IT, WE MUST WIN IT. THAT MEANS THAT GROUND TROOPS – DADDIES, NEIGHBORS, CLASSMATES, UNCLES, HUSBANDS, AND GOOD FRIENDS – ARE GOING TO DIE. ARE YOU WILLING TO SEND YOURS?

MORE IMPORTANTLY, ARE YOU WILLING TO TAKE A ROUND IN THE GUT? I MEAN YOU HERE TONIGHT. YOU, AND YOU, AND YOU. YOU'RE THE FLESH THAT FILLS UNIFORMS. YOU MAY SAY THAT'S MELODRAMA; BUT THIS ACTOR FILLED A UNIFORM FOR TWO YEARS IN WORLD WAR II.

YOU THERE, LISTENING POLITELY WHILE YOU PLAN YOUR NEXT DATE AND FIRST MILLION, ARE YOU WILLING TO PUT THAT ALL ASIDE – JUST AS THOUSANDS OF GOOD MEN DID ALMOST 60 YEARS AGO – AND GO FIGHT? OR ARE YOU THINKING, AS I SUSPECT, THAT IT'S SOME LESSER PERSON'S JOB? OR THAT, NESTLED SAFELY IN OUR DISTANCE AND ABUNDANCE, WE CAN JUST WIGGLE JOYSTICKS ON REMOTE CONTROL MISSILES AND WIN THIS GAMEBOY WAR?

IF YOU BELIEVE THAT, YOU HAVE LOTS OF EQUALLY NAIVE COMPANY. A CNN/GALLUP POLL THREE DAYS AGO REPORTED THAT TWO OUT OF THREE AMERICANS THINK WE HAVE A MORAL OBLIGATION TO FIGHT MILOSEVIC. BUT AN EQUAL NUMBER, TWO OUT OF THREE, WERE UNWILLING TO AGREE THAT CASUALTIES ARE AN ACCEPTABLE CONSEQUENCE. SO WE'RE ALL FOR MORAL OBLIGATION, ALRIGHT...AS LONG AS THERE IS NO PAIN, NO PRICE, NO CONSEQUENCE.

NO, THE TRUTH IS, LIFE HAS CONSEQUENCES AND MUST BE LIVED IN THAT REALITY, NOT AS IT IS PRETENDED TO BE LIVED BY PEOPLE WHO AREN'T HONEST. WE HAVE AN ARROGANT ADMINISTRATION AND CONSPIRING MEDIA WHO ARE GETTING US INTO EVENTS THAT HAVE GENUINE CONSEQUENCES.

BUT THEN, THIS PRESIDENT HAS LONG SEEN HIMSELF AS FREE OF CONSEQUENCES.

THERE IS SOMETHING WRONG WITH A GOVERNMENT THAT PURPOSELY, AS A MATTER OF POLICY, IGNORES THE CONSEQUENCES OF LETTING ARMED FELONS GO FREE, OR OF GOING TO WAR.

TO ME, THAT DISAPPOINTMENT IS THE GRAND TRAGEDY OF THE BABY BOOMERS. FOR ALL THE DREAMS WE HAD FOR THE GENERATION THAT NOW RUNS THIS COUNTRY – MY GENERATION'S CHILDREN AND YOUR GENERATION'S PARENTS – FOR ALL THE BABY BOOMERS' ACHIEVEMENTS IN COMMUNICATIONS AND SPACE AND MEDICINE, IT IS ALL FOR NAUGHT IF YOU INHERIT AND PERPETUATE SOCIETAL DISHONESTY.

SO WHAT CAN YOU DO?

I LEARNED THE ANSWER 36 YEARS AGO ON THE STEPS OF THE LINCOLN MEMORIAL IN WASHINGTON, D.C., STANDING WITH DR. MARTIN LUTHER KING AND TWO HUNDRED THOUSAND PEOPLE. YOU SIMPLY REFUSE TO GO ALONG. YOU DISOBEY. PEACEABLY, YES. RESPECTFULLY, OF COURSE. NON-VIOLENTLY, ABSOLUTELY. BUT WHEN YOU'RE ASKED TO LIVE THEIR LIES, YOU PRACTICE CIVIL DEFIANCE. YOU REFUSE TO GO ALONG WITH THE SPIN AND FACADE AND VACANT LANGUAGE OF DISHONEST PEOPLE.

I LEARNED THE AWESOME POWER OF DISOBEDIENCE FROM DR. KING...WHO LEARNED IT FROM GANDHI, AND THOREAU, AND JESUS, AND EVERY OTHER GREAT MAN WHO REFUSED TO GO ALONG. RACIAL DISCRIMINATION WAS ILLEGAL, BUT VIOLATION HAD NO CONSEQUENCES. SEGREGATION WAS ILLEGAL, BUT PROSECUTION OF OFFENDERS WAS NOT A POLICY. SO DR. KING TAUGHT US TO DEFY SOCIETAL DISHONESTY WITH ACTION – AND CHANGED OUR COUNTRY.

DISOBEDIENCE IS IN OUR DNA. WE FEEL INNATE KINSHIP WITH THAT DEFIANT SPIRIT THAT TOSSED TEA INTO BOSTON HARBOR, SENT THOREAU TO JAIL, REFUSED TO SIT IN THE BACK OF THE BUS, AND PROTESTED A DISHONESTLY-FOUGHT WAR IN VIET NAM.

OUR UNIQUELY AMERICAN GENES NATURALLY DEFY POLITICAL POSTURING. FOR EXAMPLE: WHO'S CONDUCTING THE GREATEST INTELLECTUAL REBELLION IN HISTORY RIGHT NOW? IT'S NOT THE LIKES OF THE NEW YORK TIMES OR WASHINGTON POST OR OTHER TRADITIONALLY CRUSADING JOURNALS OF AMERICAN OPINION. NO, IT'S THE INTERNET, BUILT BY AND FOR THE MINDS OF YOUNG PEOPLE LIKE YOU, PEOPLE YEARNING FOR TRUTH.

IN THAT SAME SPIRIT, I'M ASKING YOU TO DISAVOW CULTURAL DISHONESTY WITH MASSIVE CIVIL DEFIANCE AGAINST A GOVERNMENT SPOILED BY PROSPERITY...AGAINST WISHFUL THINKING MASQUERADING AS LEADERSHIP...AND AGAINST NEWS MEDIA WHO PERPETUATE

THE UNTRUTH THAT ACTION CAN OCCUR WITHOUT CONSEQUENCE.

I ASK YOU, IN LINCOLN'S WORDS, "SO THAT THIS NATION MAY LONG ENDURE," PLEASE...DO WHAT YOU MUST TO REVEAL, AND THEN REVERE, TRUTH...EXPECT AND ACCEPT THE CONSEQUENCES OF YOUR ACTIONS AND THOSE OF YOUR NATION...AND EVERY DAY, TEST WHAT YOU SEE WITH WHAT YOU KNOW IS RIGHT.

AND WHEN IT'S DISHONEST, DEFY IT. FOLLOW IN THE HALLOWED FOOTSTEPS OF THE GREAT DISOBEDIENCE MOVEMENTS OF HISTORY THAT FREED EXILES, FOUNDED RELIGIONS, DEFEATED TYRANTS, AND IN THE HANDS OF AN AROUSED RABBLE IN ARMS AND A FEW GREAT MEN, BY GOD'S GRACE, BUILT THIS COUNTRY.

IF DR. KING WERE HERE, I THINK HE'D AGREE.

THANK YOU.

REMARKS BEFORE THE 128TH ANNUAL MEETING OF THE MEMBERS OF THE NATIONAL RIFLE ASSOCIATION

May 1, 1999 Denver Colorado

(Note: Just days before the National Rifle Association was to begin its 1999 annual meetings and exhibits in Denver, Colorado, the tragic events of Columbine High School in Littleton – a few miles away from the meeting site – horrified a stunned nation. Despite very public political pressure to cancel the NRA meetings, which its bylaws require, we convened a short business meeting under these most difficult and sensitive circumstances. As it turned out, we had a packed house of several thousand proud members who'd endured intimidating media and angry protestors to attend their association's gathering.)

OPENING REMARKS

GOOD MORNING.

I WANT TO WELCOME YOU TO THIS ABBREVIATED ANNUAL GATHERING OF THE NATIONAL RIFLE ASSOCIATION. THANK YOU FOR COMING AND THANK YOU FOR SUPPORTING YOUR ORGANIZATION.

I ALSO WANT TO APPLAUD YOUR COURAGE IN COMING HERE TODAY. OF COURSE, YOU HAVE A RIGHT TO BE HERE.

AS YOU KNOW, WE'VE CANCELED THE FESTIVITIES AND FELLOWSHIP WE NORMALLY ENJOY AT OUR ANNUAL GATHERINGS. THIS DECISION HAS PERPLEXED A FEW AND INCONVENIENCED THOUSANDS. I APOLOGIZE FOR THAT.

BUT IT'S FITTING AND PROPER THAT WE SHOULD DO THIS...BECAUSE NRA MEMBERS ARE, ABOVE ALL, AMERICANS. THAT MEANS WHATEVER OUR DIFFERENCES, WE ARE RESPECTFUL OF ONE ANOTHER AND WE STAND UNITED, ESPECIALLY IN ADVERSITY.

WELLINGTON WEBB, THE MAYOR OF DENVER, SENT ME A MESSAGE: "DON'T COME HERE. WE DON'T WANT YOU HERE."

I SAY TO THE MAYOR, "I VOLUNTEERED FOR THE WAR THEY WANTED ME TO ATTEND WHEN I WAS 18 YEARS OLD. SINCE THEN, I'VE RUN SMALL ERRANDS FOR MY COUNTRY FROM NIGERIA TO VIETNAM. I KNOW MANY OF YOU COULD SAY THE SAME. BUT THE MAYOR SAID, "DON'T COME."

I'M SORRY FOR THAT. I'M SORRY FOR THE NEWSPAPER ADS SAYING THE SAME THING. "DON'T COME HERE." THIS IS OUR COUNTRY. AS AMERICANS WE ARE FREE TO TRAVEL WHEREVER WE WISH IN OUR BROAD LAND.

THEY SAY WE'LL CREATE A MEDIA DISTRACTION. BUT WE WERE PRECEDED HERE BY HUNDREDS OF INTRUSIVE NEWS CREWS.

THEY SAY WE'LL CREATE POLITICAL DISTRACTION. BUT IT HAS NOT BEEN THE NRA PRESSING FOR POLITICAL ADVANTAGE, CALLING PRESS CONFERENCES TO PROPOSE VAST PACKAGES OF NEW LEGISLATION.

THEY SAY, "DON'T COME HERE." I GUESS WHAT SADDENS ME MOST IS HOW IT SUGGESTS COMPLICITY. IT IMPLIES THAT YOU AND I AND EIGHTY MILLION HONEST GUN OWNERS ARE SOMEHOW TO BLAME, THAT WE DON'T CARE AS MUCH AS THEY, OR THAT WE DON'T DESERVE

TO BE AS SHOCKED AND HORRIFIED AS EVERY OTHER SOUL IN AMERICA MOURNING FOR THE PEOPLE OF LITTLETON.

"DON'T COME HERE." THAT'S OFFENSIVE. IT'S ALSO ABSURD, BECAUSE WE LIVE HERE. THERE ARE THOUSANDS OF NRA MEMBERS IN DENVER AND TENS UPON TENS OF THOUSANDS IN THE STATE OF COLORADO.

NRA MEMBERS LABOR IN DENVER'S FACTORIES, POPULATE DENVER'S FACULTIES, RUN DENVER CORPORATIONS, PLAY ON COLORADO SPORTS TEAMS, WORK IN MEDIA ACROSS THE FRONT RANGE, PARENT AND TEACH AND COACH DENVER'S CHILDREN, ATTEND DENVER'S CHURCHES, AND PROUDLY REPRESENT DENVER IN UNIFORM ON THE WORLD'S OCEANS AND IN THE SKIES OVER KOSOVO AT THIS VERY MOMENT.

NRA MEMBERS ARE IN CITY HALL, FORT CARSON, NORAD, THE AIR FORCE ACADEMY AND THE OLYMPIC TRAINING CENTER. AND YES, NRA MEMBERS ARE SURELY AMONG THE POLICE AND FIRE AND SWAT TEAM HEROES WHO RISKED THEIR LIVES TO RESCUE THE STUDENTS OF COLUMBINE FROM EVIL, MINDLESS EXECUTIONERS.

"DON'T COME HERE"? WE ARE ALREADY HERE. THIS COMMUNITY IS OUR HOME. EVERY COMMUNITY IN AMERICA IS OUR HOME. WE ARE A 128-YEAR-OLD FIXTURE OF MAINSTREAM AMERICA. THE SECOND AMENDMENT ETHIC OF LAWFUL, RESPONSIBLE FIREARM OWNERSHIP SPANS THE BROADEST CROSS-SECTION OF AMERICAN LIFE IMAGINABLE.

SO WE HAVE THE SAME RIGHT AS ALL OTHER CITIZENS TO BE HERE... TO HELP SHOULDER THE GRIEF...TO SHARE OUR SORROW...AND TO OFFER OUR RESPECTFUL, REASONED VOICE TO THE NATIONAL DISCOURSE THAT HAS ERUPTED AROUND THIS TRAGEDY.

ONE MORE THING. OUR WORDS AND OUR BEHAVIOR WILL BE SCRU-TINIZED MORE THAN EVER THIS MORNING. THOSE WHO ARE HOSTILE TOWARD US WILL LIE IN WAIT TO SEIZE ON A SOUND BITE OUT OF CONTEXT, EVER SEARCHING FOR AN EMBARRASSING MOMENT TO RIDICULE US. SO LET US BE MINDFUL...THE EYES OF THE NATION ARE UPON US TODAY.

(the required business meeting dealing with necessary affairs of the Association was then conducted)

CLOSING REMARKS

I HAVE BEEN ADVISED NOT TO BE HERE, NOT TO SPEAK TO YOU HERE. IT'S NOT THE FIRST TIME.

IN 1963 I MARCHED ON WASHINGTON WITH DR. MARTIN LUTHER KING, LONG BEFORE HOLLYWOOD FOUND CIVIL RIGHTS FASHIONABLE. MY ASSOCIATES ADVISED ME NOT TO GO. THEY SAID IT WOULD BE UNPOPULAR AND MAYBE DANGEROUS.

THIRTY-SIX YEARS LATER MY ASSOCIATES ADVISED ME NOT TO COME TO DENVER. THEY SAID IT WOULD BE UNPOPULAR AND MAYBE DANGEROUS. BUT I AM HERE. LET ME TELL YOU WHY.

I SEE OUR COUNTRY TEETERING ON THE EDGE OF AN ABYSS. AT ITS BOTTOM BREWS THE SIMMERING BILE OF DEEP, DARK HATRED. HATRED THAT'S DIVIDING OUR COUNTRY POLITICALLY, RACIALLY, ECONOMICALLY, GEOGRAPHICALLY, IN EVERY WAY.

WHETHER IT'S POLITICAL VENDETTAS, SPORTS BRAWLS, CORPORATE TAKEOVERS, OR HIGH SCHOOL GANGS AND CLIQUES, THE AMERICAN COMPETITIVE ETHIC HAS CHANGED FROM "LET'S BEAT THE OTHER GUY" TO "LET'S DESTROY THE OTHER GUY." TOO MANY ARE TOO WILLING TO STIGMATIZE AND DEMONIZE OTHERS FOR POLITICAL ADVANTAGE, MONEY OR RATINGS.

THE VILIFICATION IS SAVAGE. THIS WEEK, REP. JOHN CONYERS SLANDERED THREE MILLION AMERICANS WHEN HE CALLED THE NRA "MERCHANTS OF DEATH" ON NATIONAL TELEVISION, AS THE FIRST LADY NODDED IN AGREEMENT.

A HIDEOUS EDITORIAL CARTOON BY MIKE PETERS RAN NATIONALLY, DEPICTING CHILDREN'S DEAD BODIES SPRAWLED OUT TO SPELL N-R-A.

THE COUNTLESS REQUESTS WE'VE RECEIVED FOR MEDIA APPEARANCES ARE IN FACT SUMMONS TO PUBLIC FLOGGINGS, WHERE THOSE WHO HATE FIREARMS WILL PREDICTABLY DON THE WHITE HAT AND HAND US THE BLACK.

THIS HARVEST OF HATRED IS THEN SOLD AS NEWS, AS ENTERTAINMENT, AS GOVERNMENT POLICY. SUCH HATEFUL, DIVISIVE FORCES ARE LEADING US TO ONE AWFUL END: AMERICA'S OWN FORM OF BALKANIZATION. A WEAKENED COUNTRY OF RABID FACTIONS, EACH LESS FREE, AND UNITED ONLY BY HATRED OF ONE ANOTHER.

IN THE PAST TEN DAYS WE'VE SEEN THESE BRUTAL BLOWS ATTEMPT-

ING TO FRACTURE AMERICA INTO TWO SUCH CAMPS. ONE CAMP WOULD BE THE MAJORITY – PEOPLE WHO BELIEVE OUR FOUNDERS GUARANTEED OUR SECURITY WITH THE RIGHT TO DEFEND OURSELVES, OUR FAMILIES AND OUR COUNTRY. THE OTHER CAMP WOULD BE A LARGE MINORITY – PEOPLE WHO BELIEVE THAT WE WILL BUY SECURITY IF WE WILL JUST SURRENDER THESE FREEDOMS.

THIS DEBATE WOULD BE ACCURATELY DESCRIBED AS THOSE WHO BELIEVE IN THE SECOND AMENDMENT, VERSUS THOSE WHO DON'T. BUT INSTEAD IT IS SPUN AS THOSE WHO BELIEVE IN MURDER, VERSUS THOSE WHO DON'T.

A STRUGGLE BETWEEN THE RECKLESS AND THE PRUDENT, BETWEEN THE DIM-WITTED AND THE ENLIGHTENED, BETWEEN THE ARCHAIC AND THE PROGRESSIVE, BETWEEN INFERIOR CITIZENS AND ELITISTS WHO KNOW WHAT'S GOOD FOR SOCIETY.

BUT WE'RE NOT THE RUSTIC, RECKLESS RADICALS THEY WISH FOR. NO, THE NRA SPANS THE BROADEST RANGE OF AMERICAN DEMOGRAPHY IMAGINABLE. WE DEFY STEREOTYPE, EXCEPT FOR LOVE OF COUNTRY. LOOK IN YOUR MIRROR, YOUR SHOPPING MALL, YOUR CHURCH OR GROCERY STORE. THAT'S US. MILLIONS OF ORDINARY PEOPLE AND EXTRAORDINARY PEOPLE – WAR HEROES, SPORTS IDOLS, SEVERAL U.S. PRESIDENTS AND YES, MOVIE STARS.

BUT THE SCREECHING HYPERBOLE LEVELED AT GUN OWNERS HAS MADE THESE TWO CAMPS SO WARY OF EACH OTHER, SO HOSTILE AND CONFRONTATIONAL AND DISRESPECTFUL, THAT TOO MANY ON BOTH SIDES HAVE FORGOTTEN THAT WE ARE, FIRST, AMERICANS.

I AM ASKING ALL OF US, ON BOTH SIDES, TO TAKE ONE STEP BACK FROM THE EDGE OF THAT CLIFF. THEN ANOTHER STEP AND ANOTHER, HOWEVER MANY IT TAKES TO GET BACK TO THAT PLACE WHERE WE'RE ALL AMERICANS AGAIN...DIFFERENT, IMPERFECT, DIVERSE – BUT ONE NATION...INDIVISIBLE.

THIS CYCLE OF TRAGEDY-DRIVEN HATRED MUST STOP. BECAUSE SO MUCH MORE CONNECTS US THAN DIVIDES US. AND BECAUSE TRAGEDY HAS BEEN AND WILL ALWAYS BE WITH US.

SOMEWHERE RIGHT NOW, EVIL PEOPLE ARE SCHEMING EVIL THINGS. ALL OF US WILL DO EVERY MEANINGFUL THING WE CAN DO TO PREVENT IT. BUT EACH HORRIBLE ACT CAN'T BECOME AN AXE FOR OPPORTUNISTS TO CLEAVE THE VERY BILL OF RIGHTS THAT BINDS US.

AMERICA MUST STOP THIS PREDICTABLE PATTERN OF REACTION. WHEN AN ISOLATED, TERRIBLE EVENT OCCURS, OUR PHONES RING, DEMANDING THAT THE NRA EXPLAIN THE INEXPLICABLE.

WHY US? BECAUSE THEIR STORY NEEDS A VILLAIN. THEY WANT US TO PLAY THE HEAVY IN THEIR DRAMA OF PACKAGED GRIEF, TO PROVIDE RIVETING PROGRAMMING TO RUN BETWEEN COMMERCIALS FOR CARS AND CAT FOOD.

THE DIRTY SECRET OF THIS DAY AND AGE IS THAT POLITICAL GAIN AND MEDIA RATINGS ALL TOO OFTEN BLOOM UPON FRESH GRAVES.

I REMEMBER A BETTER DAY, WHEN NO ONE DARED POLITICIZE OR PROFITEER ON TRAUMA. WE KEPT A RESPECTFUL DISTANCE THEN, AS NRA HAS TRIED TO DO NOW. SIMPLY BEING SILENT IS SO OFTEN THE RIGHT THING TO DO.

BUT TODAY, CARNAGE COMES WITH A CATCHY TITLE, SPLASHY GRAPHICS, REGULAR PROMOS, AND A REACTIONARY PACKAGE OF LEG-ISLATION. REPORTERS PERCH LIKE VULTURES ON THE BALCONIES OF HOTELS FOR A HUNDRED MILES AROUND. CAMERAS JOCKEY FOR SHOCKING ANGLES, AS NEWS ANCHORS RACE TO DRENCH THEIR MICROPHONES IN THE TEARS OF VICTIMS.

INJURY, SHOCK, GRIEF AND DESPAIR SHOULDN'T BE "BROUGHT TO YOU BY SPONSORS." THAT'S PORNOGRAPHY. IT TRIVIALIZES THE TRAGEDY, IT ABUSES VULNERABLE PEOPLE, AND MAYBE WORST OF ALL, IT MAKES THE UNSPEAKABLE SEEM COMMONPLACE.

AND WE'RE OFTEN CAST AS THE VILLAIN. THAT IS NOT OUR ROLE IN AMERICAN SOCIETY, AND WE WILL NOT BE FORCED TO PLAY IT. OUR MISSION IS TO REMAIN A STEADY BEACON OF STRENGTH AND SUPPORT FOR THE SECOND AMENDMENT, EVEN IF IT HAS NO OTHER FRIEND ON THE PLANET. WE CANNOT LET TRAGEDY LAY WASTE TO THE MOST RARE AND HARD-WON HUMAN RIGHT IN HISTORY.

A NATION CANNOT GAIN SAFETY BY GIVING UP FREEDOM. THIS TRUTH IS OLDER THAN OUR COUNTRY. THOSE WHO WOULD GIVE UP ESSENTIAL LIBERTY, TO PURCHASE A LITTLE TEMPORARY SAFETY, DESERVE NEITHER LIBERTY NOR SAFETY. BEN FRANKLIN SAID THAT.

IF YOU LIKE YOUR FREEDOMS OF SPEECH AND OF RELIGION, FREEDOM FROM SEARCH AND SEIZURE, FREEDOM OF THE PRESS AND OF PRIVACY, TO ASSEMBLE AND TO REDRESS GRIEVANCES, THEN YOU'D BETTER GIVE THEM THAT ETERNAL BODYGUARD CALLED THE SECOND

AMENDMENT. THE INDIVIDUAL RIGHT TO BEAR ARMS IS FREEDOM'S INSURANCE POLICY, NOT JUST FOR YOUR CHILDREN BUT FOR INFINITE GENERATIONS TO COME.

THAT IS ITS SINGULAR, SACRED BEAUTY, AND WHY WE PRESERVE IT SO FIERCELY. NO, IT IS NOT A RIGHT WITHOUT RATIONAL RESTRICTIONS. AND IT'S NOT FOR EVERYONE. ONLY THE LAW-ABIDING MAJORITY OF SOCIETY DESERVES THE SECOND AMENDMENT. ABUSE IT ONCE AND LOSE IT FOREVER. THAT'S THE LAW.

BUT REMARKABLY, THE NRA IS FAR MORE EAGER TO PROSECUTE GUN ABUSERS THAN ARE THOSE WHO OPPOSE GUN OWNERSHIP ALTO-GETHER...AS IF THE TOOL COULD BE MORE EVIL THAN THE EVILDOER.

THE NRA ALSO SPENDS MORE AND WORKS HARDER THAN ANYBODY IN AMERICA TO PROMOTE SAFE, RESPONSIBLE USE OF FIREARMS. FROM 38,000 CERTIFIED INSTRUCTORS TRAINING MILLIONS OF POLICE, HUNTERS, WOMEN AND YOUTH...TO 500 LAW ENFORCEMENT AGENCIES PROMOTING OUR EDDIE EAGLE GUN SAFETY PROGRAM DIS-TRIBUTED TO ELEVEN MILLION KIDS AND COUNTING.

BUT OUR ESSENTIAL REASON FOR BEING IS THIS. AS LONG AS THERE IS A SECOND AMENDMENT, EVIL CAN NEVER CONQUER US. TYRANNY, IN ANY FORM, CAN NEVER FIND FOOTING WITHIN A SOCIETY OF LAW-ABIDING, ARMED, ETHICAL PEOPLE.

THE MAJESTY OF THE SECOND AMENDMENT, THAT OUR FOUNDERS SO DIVINELY CAPTURED AND CRAFTED INTO YOUR BIRTHRIGHT, GUARANTEES THAT NO GOVERNMENT DESPOT, NO RENEGADE FACTION OF ARMED FORCES, NO ROVING GANGS OF CRIMINALS, NO BREAKDOWN OF LAW AND ORDER, NO MASSIVE ANARCHY, NO FORCE OF EVIL OR CRIME OR OPPRESSION FROM WITHIN OR FROM WITHOUT, CAN EVER ROB YOU OF THE LIBERTIES THAT DEFINE YOUR AMERICANISM.

AND WHEN THEY ASK, "SO INDEED YOU WOULD BEAR ARMS AGAINST GOVERNMENT TYRANNY?"...THE ANSWER IS, "NO. THAT COULD NEVER HAPPEN, PRECISELY BECAUSE WE HAVE THE SECOND AMENDMENT."

LET ME BE ABSOLUTELY CLEAR. THE FOUNDING FATHERS GUARAN-TEED THIS FREEDOM BECAUSE THEY KNEW NO TYRANNY CAN EVER ARISE AMONG A PEOPLE ENDOWED WITH THE RIGHT TO KEEP AND BEAR ARMS. THAT'S WHY YOU AND YOUR DESCENDANTS NEED NEVER

FEAR FASCISM, STATE-RUN FAITH, REFUGEE CAMPS, BRAINWASHING, ETHNIC CLEANSING, OR ESPECIALLY, SUBMISSION TO THE WANTON WILL OF CRIMINALS.

THE SECOND AMENDMENT. THERE CAN BE NO MORE PRECIOUS INHERITANCE. THAT'S WHAT THE NRA PRESERVES.

NOW, IF YOU DISAGREE, THAT'S YOUR RIGHT AND I RESPECT THAT. BUT WE WILL NOT RELINQUISH IT OR BE SILENCED ABOUT IT, OR BE TOLD, "DO NOT COME HERE. YOU ARE UNWELCOME IN YOUR OWN LAND."

LET'S GO FROM THIS PLACE RENEWED IN SPIRIT AND DEDICATED AGAINST HATRED. WE HAVE WORK TO DO, HEARTS TO HEAL, EVIL TO DEFEAT, AND A COUNTRY TO UNITE. WE MAY HAVE DIFFERENCES, YES. AND WE WILL AGAIN SUFFER TRAGEDY ALMOST BEYOND DESCRIPTION. BUT WHEN THE SUN SETS ON DENVER TONIGHT AND FOREVERMORE, LET IT ALWAYS SET ON WE, THE PEOPLE...SECURE IN OUR LAND OF THE FREE AND HOME OF THE BRAVE. I, FOR ONE, PLAN TO DO MY PART.

THANK YOU.

☆ ☆ ☆

REMARKS BEFORE THE
YOUNG REPUBLICANS ASSOCIATION CONVENTION

June 24, 1999 Cincinnati, OH

"Political Disobedience"

I'LL ADMIT IT TO YOU NOW: ALTHOUGH A LOT OF AMERICANS THINK OF ME AS "MR. CONSERVATIVE" OR SOME KIND OF "MOSES OF THE REPUBLICAN PARTY," I WASN'T ALWAYS A REPUBLICAN OR, FOR THAT MATTER, WHAT PEOPLE AT THE TIME WOULD HAVE CALLED A "CONSERVATIVE." SOME WOULD HAVE CALLED ME "LIBERAL" – BUT THE

MEANING OF THAT WORD HAS CHANGED PROFOUNDLY SINCE THEN.

I'VE COVERED MUCH POLITICAL GROUND IN MY 75 YEARS, AND IN THOSE TRAVELS I'VE SEEN A LOT. BUT NEVER HAVE I SEEN A POLITICAL ENVIRONMENT SO TOXIC, SO INFLAMED, SO DEVOID OF THE FRESH AIR OF OPEN DEBATE, AS I SEE IN AMERICA TODAY.

AND I'VE COME TO REALIZE OUR NATION IS ENGAGED IN A GREAT CULTURAL WAR...A WAR BETWEEN THE CYNICAL AND THE SINCERE... BETWEEN THE PRINCIPLED AND THE DUPLICITOUS. IT'S A WAR WAGED WITH INTOLERANCE, DISHONESTY, INTELLECTUAL TYRANNY AND HATRED...A CONFLICT THAT COULD LEAD TO ACTUAL TYRANNY THE LIKES OF WHICH OUR YOUNG NATION, THANK GOD, HAS NEVER ENDURED. AND IT'S A WAR YOUR GENERATION MUST FIGHT OR LOSE. SO YOU'D BETTER KNOW WHAT YOU'RE UP AGAINST.

I KNOW I DON'T HAVE TO TELL YOU SOMETHING IS TERRIBLY WRONG IN OUR SOCIETY TODAY.

IN HIS BOOK *THE END OF SANITY*, MARTIN GROSS SAYS "BLATANTLY IRRATIONAL BEHAVIOR IS RAPIDLY BEING ESTABLISHED AS THE NORM IN ALMOST EVERY AREA OF HUMAN ENDEAVOR. THERE SEEM TO BE NEW CUSTOMS, NEW RULES, NEW ANTI-INTELLECTUAL THEORIES REGULARLY FOISTED ON US FROM EVERY DIRECTION. UNDERNEATH, THE NATION IS ROILING. AMERICANS KNOW SOMETHING WITHOUT A NAME IS UNDERMINING THE NATION, TURNING THE MIND MUSHY WHEN IT COMES TO SEPARATING TRUTH FROM FALSEHOOD AND RIGHT FROM WRONG. AND THEY DON'T LIKE IT."

I BELIEVE THAT IN YOUR HEART YOU ALREADY KNOW SOMETHING IS PROFOUNDLY WRONG. WHEN BARTENDERS ARE RESPONSIBLE FOR THE ACTS OF DRUNKEN DRIVERS, WHEN WOMEN ARE TO BLAME FOR RAPISTS' ATTACKS, WHEN GUN MAKERS ARE RESPONSIBLE FOR CRIMINALS' ACTS, AND NOBODY IS RESPONSIBLE FOR O.J. SIMPSON'S ACTS, SOMETHING IS RADICALLY WRONG.

AN INSIDIOUS FORM OF DISHONESTY AND FALSE THINKING IS PERMEATING OUR CULTURE. IN POLITICS, IN THE PRESS, IN EVERY INSTITUTION OF THE AMERICAN EXPERIENCE, LIES ARE BEING ACCEPTED AS THE LEGITIMATE CURRENCY OF DEBATE.

SO, WE HAVE AN AMERICAN PRESIDENT WHO DIDN'T INHALE, WHO "NEVER HAD SEXUAL RELATIONS WITH THAT WOMAN," AND WHO DOESN'T KNOW WHAT "IS" IS.

WE HAVE A VICE PRESIDENT WHO LEARNS FAST...SO FAST INDEED THAT HE INVENTED THE INTERNET – AT THE RIPE OLD AGE OF 12. JUST LAST WEEK, VICE PRESIDENT GORE CLAIMED, FALSELY, THAT CHILDREN "CAN WALK INTO ANY GUN SHOP, ANY PAWN SHOP, ANY GUN SHOW, ANYWHERE IN AMERICA AND BUY A HANDGUN."

NOW I DON'T KNOW WHAT VICE PRESIDENT GORE WASN'T INHALING, BECAUSE THE FACT IS, IT'S BEEN ILLEGAL FOR ANYONE UNDER THE AGE OF 21 TO GO INTO A GUN STORE AND BUY A HANDGUN SINCE 1968. BUT I SUPPOSE THAT IN 1968, AL GORE WAS TOO BUSY INVENTING THE INTERNET TO KNOW THE CURRENT LAW!

DECEPTION, LYING, DISHONESTY AND CHEATING ARE NOW EPIDEMIC IN AMERICA. WHETHER IT'S A 9TH-GRADE GEOGRAPHY TEST, OR A DRIVER'S EXAM, OR SATS, JOB TESTS, TERM PAPERS OR RECRUITMENT EXAMS – OR BEFORE A GRAND JURY – CHEATING IS RAMPANT. THREE OUT OF FOUR COLLEGE STUDENTS NOW ADMIT TO CHEATING ON TESTS.

MEANWHILE, MANY IN POLITICS AND THE PRESS HAVE ADOPTED THAT SAME DUPLICITY IN THEIR WORDS AND DEEDS. AND THE ROUTINE OF THEIR STAGE-SHOW PRODUCTIONS IS SO PREDICTABLE THAT IT'S BECOME A CLICHÉ. IN A CLASSIC RENDITION OF THE QUICK BAIT-AND-SWITCH, POLITICIANS FIND NON-PROBLEMS TO SOLVE WITH THEIR NON-SOLUTIONS. THEIR MEDIA CHEERLEADERS WORK THE CROWD, REPEATING THE LIES AS IF RECITING A SCHOOL "FIGHT" SONG.

FOR EXAMPLE, GUN CONTROL HAS GOTTEN OBSESSIVE TOP MEDIA BILLING FOR WEEKS AS MANY NEWSPAPERS, NETWORKS AND SELF-SERVING POLITICIANS PUSHED NEW ANTI-GUN LAWS IN THE WAKE OF THE TRAGEDY AT COLUMBINE HIGH SCHOOL. FORTUNATELY, LAST WEEK, MANY MEMBERS OF THE HOUSE HAD THE INTEGRITY TO CROSS PARTY LINES, REJECT THEIR PRESIDENT'S AGENDA AND DEFEND SECOND AMENDMENT FREEDOM.

BUT WHAT'S SO DISHEARTENING ABOUT ALL THIS IS THAT, EVEN AS THE AUTHORS OF THIS LEGISLATION WERE PUSHING IT ON THE FLOOR OF THE CONGRESS, THEY ADMITTED THAT NONE OF IT COULD HAVE PREVENTED THE KILLINGS IN LITTLETON. WORSE, NOW THAT THE LEGISLATION HAS BEEN DEFEATED, THE MEDIA WILL CLAIM, BY AND LARGE, THAT AMERICA'S SCHOOLS ARE MORE DANGEROUS AS A RESULT. AND TOO MANY OF THE AMERICAN PEOPLE WILL BUY INTO THE LIE.

THE CLAIM THAT THE BRADY LAW HAS TURNED AWAY 400,000 PROHIBITED PERSONS, SUCH AS FELONS, MAKES EVERYONE FEEL SAFER. BUT WAIT A MINUTE. THOSE CRIMINALS CAN GO GET GUNS ANYWHERE. WHAT MATTERS TO YOU IS HOW MANY OF THOSE 400,000 WERE ARRESTED ON THE SPOT AND PROSECUTED FOR THE FEDERAL TEN-YEAR FELONY OF TRYING TO BUY A GUN? THE ANSWER – NOT ONE.

IT'S MADE-FOR-TV LAWMAKING AT ITS BEST: SCRIPTING AND SELLING NEW LAWS BASED ON POLLS AND FOCUS GROUPS WITH ABSOLUTELY NO INTENTION OF ENFORCING ANY OF THEM. IT'S ALL JUST WORDS, WITH NO ACTION TO BACK IT UP.

MEANWHILE, GETTING LITTLE MEDIA BILLING IF ANY, IS NO LESS THAN THE COLOSSAL LARCENY OF OUR COUNTRY'S NATIONAL SECURITY. ALL OF OUR NUCLEAR SECRETS WERE SHOPLIFTED OUT THE BACK DOOR BY THE WORLD'S BIGGEST BULLY. THE CONSEQUENCES ARE UNIMAGINABLE. BUT THEY SAY, "OH, LET'S JUST MOVE ON."

SO HERE WE ARE...THE STATE-BEHOLDEN MEDIA TELLING US OUR SCHOOLS ARE SAFER WHEN THEY'RE NOT, TELLING US THE BRADY LAW IS MAKING US SAFER WHEN IT'S NOT, AND ALL BUT IGNORING DEVASTATING CHINESE ESPIONAGE. SO WE SWITCH OVER TO LETTERMAN OR LENO AND FALL ASLEEP THINKING THE WORLD'S A SAFER PLACE – WHEN IT'S MORE UNSTABLE THAN EVER IN OUR LIFETIMES.

YET WHEN SOMEONE STANDS UP TO CORRECT THE LIES, OR REVEAL THE TRUTH, THEY'RE ROUTINELY SHOUTED DOWN OR SHUT OUT OF THE DEBATE.

OVER THE YEARS, WHEN VARIOUS ANTI-GUN BILLS HAVE BEEN DEBATED IN CONGRESS, AND THE NATIONAL-MEDIA-POLITICAL-COMPLEX WAS PUSHING THEM THROUGH WITH ALL ITS MIGHT, THE NRA HAS BEEN ROUTINELY, REPEATEDLY DENIED A PLACE IN THE POLITICAL DEBATE. WHEN WE TRIED TO GET OUR POINTS ACROSS TO THE NEWSPAPERS OR NETWORKS, OUR WORDS WERE EDITED DOWN TO A SOUND BITE OR TWO OF MEANINGLESS FLUFF. AND WHEN WE TRIED TO BUY A PLACE AT THE TABLE THROUGH COMMERCIALS OR ADS THAT EXPLAIN OUR SIDE, WE WERE OFTEN DENIED AIRTIME OR COLUMN SPACE AT ANY TIME FOR ANY PRICE.

JUST WEEKS AGO, WHEN PRESIDENT CLINTON CONVENED A "JUVENILE VIOLENCE SUMMIT" AT THE WHITE HOUSE IN THE WAKE OF THE COLUMBINE KILLINGS, HE INVITED ENTERTAINMENT

EXECUTIVES, CLERGY, VIDEO GAME MANUFACTURERS AND GUN MAKERS — YET HE PUBLICLY REJECTED AND HUMILIATED THE NRA BY SPECIFICALLY EXCLUDING US FROM PARTICIPATING IN DISCUSSIONS.

THIS SAME SUPPRESSION OF EVIDENCE IS GOING ON THROUGHOUT OUR SOCIETY. RIGHT NOW AT MORE THAN ONE MAJOR UNIVERSITY, SECOND AMENDMENT SCHOLARS AND RESEARCHERS ARE BEING TOLD TO SHUT UP ABOUT THEIR FINDINGS OR THEY'LL LOSE THEIR JOBS. WHY? BECAUSE THEIR RESEARCH FINDINGS WOULD UNDERMINE BIG-CITY MAYORS' PENDING LAWSUITS THAT SEEK TO EXTORT HUNDREDS OF MILLIONS OF DOLLARS FROM FIREARM MANUFACTURERS.

NOW, MANY OF MY EXAMPLES CONCERN THE ISSUE OF FIREARMS, BUT THIS ISN'T JUST ABOUT GUNS. IF YOUR VIEWS ON ANY ISSUE AREN'T "POLITICALLY CORRECT" TO OUR CULTURAL ELITES, YOU'D BETTER JUST SIT DOWN, SHUT UP, AND GET OUT OF THE WAY — FAST. I KNOW — I'VE SPENT MY SHARE OF TIME IN THE CROSSHAIRS.

FOR EXAMPLE, I MARCHED FOR CIVIL RIGHTS WITH DR. KING IN 1963 — LONG BEFORE HOLLYWOOD FOUND IT FASHIONABLE. BUT WHEN I TOLD AN AUDIENCE LAST YEAR THAT WHITE PRIDE IS JUST AS VALID AS BLACK PRIDE OR RED PRIDE OR ANYONE ELSE'S PRIDE, THEY CALLED ME A RACIST.

I'VE WORKED WITH BRILLIANTLY TALENTED HOMOSEXUALS ALL MY LIFE. BUT WHEN I TOLD AN AUDIENCE THAT GAY RIGHTS SHOULD EXTEND NO FURTHER THAN YOUR RIGHTS OR MY RIGHTS, I WAS CALLED A HOMOPHOBE.

I SERVED IN WORLD WAR II AGAINST THE AXIS POWERS. BUT DURING A SPEECH, WHEN I DREW AN ANALOGY BETWEEN SINGLING OUT INNOCENT JEWS AND SINGLING OUT INNOCENT GUN OWNERS, I WAS CALLED AN ANTI-SEMITE.

EVERYONE I KNOW KNOWS I WOULD NEVER RAISE A CLOSED FIST AGAINST MY COUNTRY. BUT WHEN I ASKED AN AUDIENCE TO OPPOSE THIS CULTURAL PERSECUTION, I WAS COMPARED TO TIMOTHY MCVEIGH.

FROM *TIME* MAGAZINE TO FRIENDS AND COLLEAGUES, THEY'RE ESSENTIALLY SAYING, "CHUCK, HOW DARE YOU SPEAK YOUR MIND. YOU ARE USING LANGUAGE NOT AUTHORIZED FOR PUBLIC CONSUMPTION!"

BUT I AM NOT AFRAID. IF AMERICANS BELIEVED IN POLITICAL CORRECTNESS, WE'D STILL BE KING GEORGE'S BOYS – SUBJECTS BOUND TO THE BRITISH CROWN.

UNFORTUNATELY, THE COLLUSION OF DECEPTION BETWEEN SO MANY IN POLITICS AND THE PRESS HAS GROWN SO PERVASIVE AND SO PROFOUND THAT OUR NATIONAL MEDIA ARE BEGINNING TO RESEMBLE THE STATE-MANAGED PROPAGANDA MACHINERY THAT FUELED TYRANNY ELSEWHERE THIS CENTURY.

MAKE NO MISTAKE: WE'RE ALMOST THERE. POLITICAL CORRECTNESS TELLS US WHAT TO THINK, SO THE POLLS TELL THE PRESS WHAT TO SAY IN ORDER TO REFLECT WHAT WE THINK, SO WE'LL FEEL NORMAL WHEN WE'RE WATCHING TV BECAUSE WE BELIEVE WHAT WE'RE BEING TOLD BECAUSE IT'S WHAT WE ASKED THEM TO TELL US.

THIS IS CLINTON'S LEGACY TO AMERICAN CULTURE. LEADERSHIP BY LOOKING IN MIRRORS. POLL-PLUG-'N-PLAY PRETENDING. CLOSED-CIRCUIT CONFIRMATION OF SELF-AFFIRMING, SELF-GRATIFYING, SELF-DELUSION. AND AN AUDIENCE THAT PLAYS ALONG.

THE CLINTON-GORE WHITE HOUSE RUNS THE SHIP OF STATE LIKE A CAREFULLY CHOREOGRAPHED, PAINSTAKINGLY PLOTTED MOVIE SCRIPT. AND ALL THE BIT PLAYERS ARE THERE: CLINTON AND GORE ARE THE CONQUERING HEROES. AND WHOEVER HAPPENS TO OPPOSE THEM ON ANY PARTICULAR DAY, IS CHARACTERIZED AS "EXTREME, ON THE FRINGES, OUT OF TOUCH WITH THE AMERICAN PEOPLE – OR PART OF A VAST RIGHT-WING ANTI-CLINTON CONSPIRACY." THIS ALL WOULD BE LAUGHABLE IF IT WEREN'T SO OFTEN EFFECTIVE, AND IF THE PRESS DIDN'T PARROT IT IN EVERY STORY THEY WROTE.

LET ME GIVE YOU AN EXAMPLE: IF YOU READ NEARLY ANY MAJOR NEWSPAPER OVER THE PAST FEW WEEKS, YOU WOULD HAVE THOUGHT CONGRESS WAS DEBATING WHETHER OR NOT TO OUTLAW THE NRA. IN THE HEADLINES, THE SOUND BITES, AND THROUGHOUT THE BODY OF EVERY STORY, THE NRA WAS MORE PROMINENT THAN THE POLICIES AND POSITIONS IN QUESTION.

THE REASON FOR THIS IS THAT THEY NEED A DEMON. AS ANY GOOD PROPAGANDIST KNOWS, THE BEST WAY TO DISCREDIT AN IDEA IS TO PERSONIFY IT IN AN INDIVIDUAL, THEN SOW HATRED AGAINST THAT INDIVIDUAL.

SARAH BRADY, THE HEAD OF HANDGUN CONTROL INCORPORATED, ENDLESSLY APPEALS FOR "COMMON SENSE" GUN LAWS. WHO COULDN'T BE FOR "COMMON SENSE"? THE UNDERLYING, NOT-SO-SUBTLE MESSAGE IS THAT, IF YOU OPPOSE THEIR "COMMON SENSE" GUN BANS, YOU NOT ONLY DON'T HAVE COMMON SENSE – YOU'RE ALSO SOMEHOW ALLIED WITH EVIL, AND AS SUCH, SUBJECT TO SOCIETAL HATRED.

A RECENT EPISODE OF THE "ROSIE O'DONNELL SHOW" SERVES AS A PERFECT EXAMPLE. ACTOR AND NRA MEMBER TOM SELLECK AGREED TO APPEAR ON THE SHOW TO PROMOTE HIS NEW MOVIE. BUT ONCE HE WAS ON STAGE AND THE CAMERAS WERE ROLLING, ROSIE ATTACKED HIM FOR PROMOTING THE NRA, AS IF HE OR THE NRA WERE TO BLAME FOR THE COLUMBINE HIGH SCHOOL KILLINGS.

YET WHILE TOM SELLECK VOLUNTEERED HIS TIME AND EFFORT TO HELP PROMOTE THE NRA – AND BORE THE BRUNT OF ATTACKS FROM ANTI-GUN ZEALOTS LIKE ROSIE O'DONNELL – ROSIE CASHED IN ON HER ENDORSEMENT OF K-MART, THE LARGEST FIREARM RETAILER IN AMERICA. UNFORTUNATELY, SOME DON'T SEE THAT AS HYPOCRISY.

NOW, AT THE BEGINNING OF MY SPEECH, I SAID THAT THE MEANING OF "LIBERAL" HAS CHANGED – AND IT HAS. LIBERAL USED TO MEAN DISCUSSING ISSUES OBJECTIVELY, ON THEIR OWN MERITS, WITH INTELLECTUAL HONESTY AND – ABOVE ALL – AN OPENNESS TO ANY VIEWPOINT. BUT LIBERALS LIKE O'DONNELL TODAY AREN'T LIBERAL – THEY'RE MILITANT. AND THEIR INTOLERANT DEMANDS FOR "POLITICALLY CORRECTED," CENSORED SPEECH PRODUCE ONLY HYPOCRISY AND RIDICULOUS REVISIONS OF HISTORY. GET THIS: RIGHT AFTER ATTACKING TOM SELLECK, O'DONNELL REPORTEDLY TOLD THE CAST OF ANNIE GET YOUR GUN TO REWRITE A 53-YEAR-OLD SONG FROM THE MUSICAL BEFORE PERFORMING IT ON HER SHOW. ACCORDING TO CAST MEMBERS, O'DONNELL WANTED TO REMOVE THE WORDS "I CAN SHOOT A PARTRIDGE WITH A SINGLE CARTRIDGE" BECAUSE OF HER HATRED FOR FIREARMS.

IF ROSIE HAD HER WAY, WE'D HAVE TO REMOVE "THE ROCKETS' RED GLARE, THE BOMBS BURSTING IN AIR" FROM THE STAR SPANGLED BANNER. WHILE WE'RE AT IT, LET'S REMOVE THE ARROWS FROM THE EAGLE'S TALONS IN THE GREAT SEAL OF THE UNITED STATES. AFTER ALL, IN O'DONNELL'S ROSY VIEW OF THE WORLD, THE MERE MENTION OF WEAPON-RELATED WORDS CAN CONJURE EVIL SPIRITS.

YET IN THIS SAME CLIMATE, WHERE "FIREARM" IS SUDDENLY A VERBOTEN WORD, HATE SPEECH AGAINST GUN OWNERS IS NOW NOT JUST ACCEPTED, BUT ENCOURAGED AS A CATALYST FOR POSITIVE SOCIAL CHANGE. PERSONAL ATTACKS, NAME-CALLING, CHARACTER ASSASSINATION AND EVEN REAL ASSASSINATION ARE APPARENTLY NOW ACCEPTABLE TO THESE "LIBERAL" FREE-THINKERS.

I KNOW. SOON AFTER THE LITTLETON MASSACRE, SINGER LORNA LUFT WROTE TO ME AND SAID, "I HOPE YOU'RE HAPPY NOW." WORSE, SOON AFTER ROSIE'S ATTACKS ON TOM SELLECK, INFLUEN-TIAL FILMMAKER SPIKE LEE TOLD THE *NEW YORK POST* THAT THE SOLUTION TO VIOLENCE IN AMERICA WAS TO DISBAND THE NRA. ASKED ABOUT ME AND MY ROLE AS PRESIDENT OF THE ASSOCIATION, LEE REPORTEDLY SAID, "SHOOT HIM WITH A .44 CALIBER BULLDOG."

NOW, I DON'T MEAN TO MAKE MORE OF THIS THAN IT IS, BUT IMAG-INE IF THE SHOE WERE ON THE OTHER FOOT. IF I HAD SAID THE SAME THING OR ANYTHING EVEN REMOTELY RESEMBLING IT ABOUT SPIKE LEE, THE BACKLASH FROM OUR POLITICAL POLICE WOULD HAVE BEEN DEAFENING. BUT BECAUSE I BELONG TO A GROUP WHOM IT'S CUL-TURALLY CORRECT TO HATE, NO ONE UTTERS A WORD ABOUT THIS INFLAMMATORY AND HATEFUL SPEECH.

NOW: WHAT'S THE ANSWER FOR ALL OF THIS? HOW CAN WE STOP THE SLIDE INTO TOTAL INTELLECTUAL TYRANNY AND THE EXTINCTION OF DEBATE?

THE ANSWER'S BEEN HERE ALL ALONG. I LEARNED IT 36 YEARS AGO, ON THE STEPS OF THE LINCOLN MEMORIAL IN WASHINGTON, D.C., STANDING WITH DR. MARTIN LUTHER KING AND TWO HUNDRED THOUSAND PEOPLE.

YOU SIMPLY...DISOBEY. PEACEABLY, YES. RESPECTFULLY, OF COURSE. NONVIOLENTLY, ABSOLUTELY. BUT WHEN TOLD HOW TO THINK OR WHAT TO SAY OR HOW TO BEHAVE, WE DON'T. WE DISOBEY SOCIAL PROTOCOL THAT STIFLES AND STIGMATIZES PERSONAL FREEDOM.

I LEARNED THE AWESOME POWER OF DISOBEDIENCE FROM DR.KING... WHO LEARNED IT FROM GANDHI, AND THOREAU, AND JESUS, AND EVERY OTHER GREAT MAN WHO LED THOSE IN THE RIGHT AGAINST THOSE WITH THE MIGHT.

DISOBEDIENCE IS IN OUR DNA. WE FEEL INNATE KINSHIP WITH THAT DISOBEDIENT SPIRIT THAT TOSSED TEA INTO BOSTON HARBOR, THAT

SENT THOREAU TO JAIL, THAT REFUSED TO SIT IN THE BACK OF THE BUS, THAT PROTESTED A DISHONESTLY-THOUGHT WAR IN VIET NAM.

IN THAT SAME SPIRIT, I AM ASKING YOU TO DISAVOW CULTURAL CORRECTNESS, REJECT THE LIES, DENOUNCE THE HATRED FOR EXACTLY WHAT IT IS, AND REFUSE TO BE SILENCED BY THOSE WHO WOULD EXTINGUISH ALL DEBATE IN THIS COUNTRY.

BUT BE CAREFUL...IT HURTS. DISOBEDIENCE DEMANDS THAT YOU PUT YOURSELF AT RISK. DR. KING STOOD ON LOTS OF BALCONIES.

YOU MUST BE WILLING TO BE HUMILIATED...TO ENDURE THE MODERN-DAY EQUIVALENT OF THE POLICE DOGS AT MONTGOMERY AND THE WATER CANNONS AT SELMA. YOU MUST BE WILLING TO EXPERIENCE DISCOMFORT. YOU MUST BE WILLING TO ACT, NOT JUST TALK.

WHEN POLITICIANS AND THE PRESS FEED YOU LIES AND DECEIT, EXPOSE THEM AND EMBARRASS THEM WITH THE WHITE-HOT LIGHT OF THE TRUTH.

WHEN YOUR CITY SUES THE FIREARM INDUSTRY BECAUSE IT REFUSES TO CONTROL CRIMINALS...JAM EVERY SWITCHBOARD IN THE MAYOR'S AND DISTRICT ATTORNEY'S OFFICES.

WHEN SOMEONE YOU ELECTED IS SEDUCED BY POLITICAL POWER AND BETRAYS YOU...EXPOSE THEM, PETITION THEM, OUST THEM, BANISH THEM.

WHEN THE POLITICAL ELITES TRY TO SILENCE OR EXCLUDE YOU, STAND LOUD AND PROUD WITH CONFIDENCE IN YOUR VIEWS...AND SOONER THAN YOU KNOW IT, OTHERS WILL FOLLOW IN FORCE.

SO THAT THIS NATION MAY LONG ENDURE, I URGE YOU TO FOLLOW IN THE HALLOWED FOOTSTEPS OF THE GREAT DISOBEDIENCES OF HISTORY THAT FREED EXILES, FOUNDED RELIGIONS, DEFEATED TYRANTS, AND YES, IN THE HANDS OF AN AROUSED RABBLE IN ARMS AND A FEW GREAT MEN, BY GOD'S GRACE, BUILT THIS COUNTRY.

IF DR. KING WERE HERE, I THINK HE WOULD AGREE.

THANK YOU.

REMARKS AT PENN STATE UNIVERSITY

September 21, 1999 State College, PA

"Freshmen, Fads and Freedom"

IN THIS BUSINESS OF BEING SOMEONE YOU'RE NOT, MY "PEOPLE" HAVE INCLUDED KINGS, PRESIDENTS, PROPHETS, CRUSADERS. PLUS A COWBOY OR TWO, EVEN SOME SAINTS. BUT WHEN THOSE STAGE LIGHTS DIM YOU GOTTA GO BACK TO THE REAL WORLD, THE SAME WAY EVERYBODY ELSE DOES.

LIKE ANYONE WHO ACTUALLY EARNS A LIVING UNDER THE SPOT-LIGHTS, I LEARNED FROM THE ARTISTS THAT CAME BEFORE ME. THE RECIPE FOR GOOD ACTING IS A PINCH OF MOTIVATION AND A POUND OF HARD WORK. I THINK YOU'LL FIND THAT TO BE TRUE IN ANY OCCUPATION. THE STAGE MAY SEEM GLAMOROUS WHEN YOU VIEW THE FINISHED PRODUCT, BUT IN FACT WHAT WE DO IS THE PRODUCT OF SEEMINGLY ENDLESS DAYS THAT START AT 5 A.M. AND END IN EXHAUSTION.

REMEMBER THAT WHEN YOU CRAM FOR YOUR NEXT EXAM. I DON'T CARE IF YOU'RE BRAD PITT OR SHARON STONE OR AN ACCOUNTING MAJOR AT PENN STATE. YOU ONLY REAP REWARDS IF YOU'RE WILLING TO WORK HARD AT IT. GET USED TO THAT IDEA, EVEN IF YOU TAKE NOTHING ELSE WITH YOU FROM YOUR YEARS IN COLLEGE. TALENT MAY EARN YOU A SPOT AT THE STARTING GATE, BUT TENACITY CARRIES YOU THROUGH TO THE FINISH LINE.

I WORKED IN A CHICAGO STEEL MILL WHILE I LEARNED MY CRAFT. SOME OF THE BEST IN THE BUSINESS ALMOST STARVED TO DEATH, WAITING FOR A BREAK. BUT YOU'VE GOTTA LOVE THE FACT THAT WE LIVE IN A COUNTRY WHERE HOPE REMAINS IN THE SCRIPT BY CONSTI-TUTIONAL DECREE – NO MATTER IF YOU'RE BLACK, WHITE, HISPANIC, RICH OR POOR, BACK EAST, OUT WEST, OR RIGHT HERE IN THE GREEN HILLS OF PENNSYLVANIA.

THE GREAT MIRACLE OF OUR NATION IS THAT TODAY, SOME 70 YEARS AFTER I WAS BORN AND SOME TWO AND ONE QUARTER CENTURIES AFTER THE DECLARATION OF INDEPENDENCE, WE STILL ENJOY THE LIBERTY THAT ALLOWS US AN UNLIMITED ARRAY OF CHOICES.

FREEDOM IS SO AVAILABLE IN AMERICA THAT WE EVEN INDULGE OURSELVES IN THE LUXURY OF TAKING IT FOR GRANTED.

THAT SCARES ME A LITTLE, BECAUSE MY LIFE INCLUDES THE GREAT DEPRESSION, WORLD WAR II, THE COLD WAR, THE THREAT OF ATOMIC HOLOCAUST. DURING EACH OF THESE HISTORIC EPISODES WE WONDERED IF WE'D EVEN HAVE A COUNTRY LEFT, MUCH LESS A BILL OF RIGHTS AND A CONSTITUTION.

ALL THESE WERE NATIONAL CRISES OF THE FIRST ORDER, AND THEY LEFT AN IMPRINT ON MY WAY OF THINKING. YET AT THE SAME TIME I MUST ALSO REMEMBER THAT MANY OF YOU WEREN'T EVEN ALIVE IN THE 1970S, CAN'T RECALL THE REAGAN PRESIDENCY, WERE STILL IN GRADE SCHOOL DURING THE GULF WAR, NEVER KNEW LIFE PRIOR TO AIDS, HAVE NO IDEA OF THE MAGNITUDE OF THE TRAGEDY OF TIANAMEN SQUARE AND NEVER HAD TO CARRY A SPECIAL TOOL TO POP THE METAL CAPS OFF YOUR BEER BOTTLES.

SO WHAT DO WE HAVE IN COMMON, YOUR GENERATION AND MINE? NO WARS. NOT MUCH CIVIL UNREST TO SPEAK OF. CERTAINLY NOT MUSIC OR FASHION. WHAT WE DO HAVE CAN BE SUMMED UP IN TWO VERY MEANINGFUL WORDS: AN ABSOLUTELY UNIQUE HERITAGE, AND TRADITION.

NOW THOSE TWO WORDS CAN MEAN A LOT OF THINGS. MAYBE FOR YOU IT'S THE WINNING WAYS OF THE NITTANY LIONS. IF YOU'RE SEARCHING FOR A LIVING ICON OF GREAT AMERICAN HERITAGE, LOOK NO FARTHER THAN JOE PATERNO. JOE STANDS FOR SOMETHING GOOD THAT GOES WAY BACK, AND THAT'S WHAT I MEAN BY TRADITION. IN AMERICA WE HAVE TRADITIONS THAT RANGE FROM SPORTS TO DEFENDING THE RIGHTS OF THE DOWNTRODDEN TO WRITING GREAT LITERATURE. ACTUALLY THAT'S WHAT COLLEGE IS ALL ABOUT: DISCOVERING HOW YOU FIT INTO THE GRAND SCHEME OF THINGS, AND THEN DECIDING HOW YOU PLAN TO MAKE YOUR CONTRIBUTION.

IT ALL BEGINS WITH THIS GREAT HOUSE YOU SHARE, THE ONE YOU CALL PENN STATE UNIVERSITY. WHEN YOU COME TO THIS COLLEGE YOU ACCEPT ITS HISTORY AND ITS GHOSTS, ITS LEGENDS AND ITS TRADITIONS. YOU BECOME A PART OF THE FAMILY OF THIS PLACE, AND EACH AND EVERY ONE OF YOU LEAVE SOMETHING OF YOUR-SELVES BEHIND TO NOURISH THE HEARTS AND MINDS OF SOME OTHER CLASS IN SOME OTHER GENERATION.

Now let's make sure we get the semantics straight. There are fads, like swallowing goldfish. Fads are fleeting, while tradition is as solid as the cornerstone in the administration building.

You chose Penn State to become your Alma Mater because it is a school with a strong heritage, an institution steeped in tradition. The rules were strict and the curriculum tough, but it beat the hell out of second best. You chose this great academic house as your own because it had stature.

That's the way my generation felt about our country. It was a place of great heritage and tradition, a place that made it easy to be a patriot. Mostly what we felt, growing up and coming of age in America, was just plain lucky. Before this turns into a Fourth of July speech, let me stress that my generation's hearts swelled at the prospects of being an American. Yet at the same time we weren't blind to the nation's flaws. To our credit, we did what we could to fix them.

In the 1960s a black American in the South had fewer rights than some of the privileged pets that now stay in the same hotels I do. Think about it: 40 years ago many black human beings couldn't eat or rest in a public place, or get the care and respect that today is commonplace for your average poodle.

Then like the saint he was, a man known as Dr. Martin Luther King stepped forward to lead his people out of this terrible bondage. Marching with Dr. King were white students, nuns, ministers of all races and yes, one actor with you tonight who decided that the Constitution and the liberties it guaranteed meant more than a role with a major studio.

You have to remember that at that time, black Americans couldn't even work as stage hands in Hollywood. It may not seem like much today, but those of us who marched with Dr. King were truly afraid of what might happen to us, both personally and professionally.

THERE WERE VICIOUS DOGS, AND GOON COPS AND THEIR BEATINGS, AND DARK, LONELY ROADS THAT SEEMED TO DISAPPEAR INTO AN ONGOING NIGHTMARE. YOUNG PEOPLE OF BOTH RACES DIED OUT THERE UNDER THE MOSS-DRAPED BOUGHS OF WHAT WAS THEN A BITTER LAND. BUT WE BELIEVED IN OUR HEARTS THAT THE HERITAGE AND TRADITIONS OF AMERICA'S FOUNDING FATHERS MUST BE MAINTAINED. THE CONSTITUTION, AS WE READ IT, REMAINED COLORBLIND. WE MARCHED TO SET OUR GREAT HOUSE IN ORDER.

TODAY, LESS THAN A HALF CENTURY LATER, THE FRUITS OF OUR LABOR ARE SELF-EVIDENT. BLACK STUDENTS, BLACK PROFESSORS, BLACK CONGRESSMEN, BLACK MAYORS, A BLACK CHIEF OF STAFF FOR OUR MILITARY. MY OWN PROFESSION IS POPULATED BY MEN AND WOMEN OF COLOR WHO ACT, DIRECT, STAR IN EVERY CONCEIVABLE ASPECT OF THE ENTERTAINMENT INDUSTRY. BEFORE WE MARCHED, SOME COULDN'T EVEN FIND A SEAT IN A MOTION PICTURE THEATER.

BUT THE TIMES CHANGE, AND MEMORIES DIM. NOT LONG AGO A POPULAR YOUNG DIRECTOR NAMED SPIKE LEE RIDICULED MY WORK IN BEHALF OF THE SECOND AMENDMENT TO THE CONSTITUTION, THE AMENDMENT THAT GUARANTEES YOUR RIGHT TO KEEP AND BEAR ARMS. SPIKE SAID I SHOULD BE SHOT FOR MY BELIEFS. AND I WANTED TO SAY TO HIM, "SPIKE, YOU WERE STILL IN DIAPERS WHEN I WAS HELPING PAVE THE WAY INTO HOLLYWOOD FOR BLACK DIRECTORS."

HOW EASILY WE FORGET WHEN TIMES ARE GOOD. BUT THAT'S WHAT HAPPENS WHEN THE CULTURAL WHIMS OF THE MOMENT SUPERSEDE OUR FREE HERITAGE AND THE STRENGTH OF SOLID TRADITION.

I'D LIKE TO REMIND SPIKE LEE THAT AFTER THE CIVIL WAR, THE FIRST THING THAT CARPETBAGGER GOVERNMENTS SOUGHT WERE LAWS THAT KEPT NEWLY FREED SLAVES FROM GETTING THEIR HANDS ON FIREARMS. GUNS MADE THE BLACK MAN EQUAL, LETHALLY SO. NO RACE-HATING CRACKER IN HIS RIGHT MIND WANTED A FREE BLACK MAN WITH A GUN AROUND. YOU CAN'T BEAT, BULLY OR LYNCH AN ARMED CITIZEN.

THANK GOD OUR COURTS OVERTURNED THESE LAWS THAT DENIED SECOND AMENDMENT RIGHTS FOR MINORITY CITIZENS. LATER IT WOULD BE IMMIGRANT IRISH AND ITALIANS – ANY GROUP THE CULTURAL ELITE FELT OBLIGED TO DELEGATE TO SECOND CLASS CITIZENRY.

So when today's cultural reformers say we have no legal precedent for upholding the Second Amendment, I say they should do their homework. And when they say the Constitution's framers never made it clear that the Second Amendment is an individual right, I say listen to this:

"No free man shall ever be debarred the use of arms." That's Thomas Jefferson talking.

"The Constitution preserves the advantage of being armed, which Americans possess over the people of almost every other nation where the governments are afraid to trust the people with arms." That's James Madison.

More? How about these words from Samuel Adams: "The Constitution shall never be construed to prevent the people of the United States who are peaceable citizens from keeping their own arms."

Or this, one of my most eloquent favorites from Thomas Paine: "Arms keep the invader and plunderer in awe, and preserve order in the world as well as property. Horrid mischief would ensue were the law abiding deprived the use of them."

So, while I dedicate much of my time and energy to the preservation of our Bill of Rights, I cannot and will not exclude the Second Amendment, our right to keep and bear arms, from among them. In fact, I have been fortunate to be asked to serve as President of the National Rifle Association of America, which granted me a forum. Of course I have also endured some rather scathing abuse, having been called everything from ridiculous to duped to a brain-injured, senile, crazy old man.

On the other hand, coming from today's media, that could be construed as a compliment.

As for senile, here I am. You reach your own conclusions. And do me one other favor. When it comes to ascertaining the viability of your constitutionally protected rights, reach your own conclusions there, too, rather than allowing NBC or CBS or Time Warner or Bill Clinton to do it for you.

LAWRENCE TRIBE, A HARVARD LAW PROFESSOR AND MAYBE TODAY'S MOST INFLUENTIAL CONSTITUTIONAL SCHOLAR, HAS BEEN THE DARLING OF THE CONTEMPORARY LEFT – UNTIL, THAT IS, THE FIRST VOLUME OF HIS REVISED AMERICAN CONSTITUTIONAL LAW RE-EXAMINED THE RIGHT TO KEEP AND BEAR ARMS AND ELEVATED ITS STATURE. WHEN TRIBE ASSERTED THAT THE RIGHT TO BEAR ARMS WAS CONCEIVED AS AN IMPORTANT POLITICAL RIGHT AND SHOULD NEVER BE DISMISSED AS TOTALLY IRRELEVANT, TODAY'S GUN-HATING CULTURAL ELITE SUFFERED PSYCHOLOGICAL SEIZURES.

TRIBE'S FURTHER CONTENTION THAT THE FEDERAL GOVERNMENT MAY NOT DISARM INDIVIDUAL CITIZENS WITHOUT SOME UNUSUALLY STRONG JUSTIFICATION EARNED HIM STACKS OF HATE MAIL FROM INCENSED LIBERALS WHO LOVED THE WAY THE SCHOLAR VIEWED THE CONSTITUTION…AS LONG AS IT FELL IN LINE WITH THEIR CULTURAL EXPECTATIONS.

AS ENGLAND, AUSTRALIA AND CANADA DISARM THEIR PEOPLE, CRIMINAL ASSAULTS AND HOME INVASIONS SOAR. AND WHEN YOU LOOK AROUND AMERICA, THE PLACES WITH THE TOUGHEST FIREARM RESTRICTIONS – WASHINGTON, D.C., FOR EXAMPLE – ROUTINELY HAVE THE HIGHEST VIOLENT CRIME RATES IN THE NATION.

BUT ENOUGH ABOUT GUNS. YOU KNOW MY VIEWS, AND YOU'RE PROBABLY IN THE PROCESS OF FORMING YOURS. AT THE BOTTOM LINE, GUN OWNERSHIP IS A RIGHT. AND THE RIGHT, WHEN YOU EXAMINE IT CLOSELY, IS PROTECTED BY A VERY CLEAR AND MEANING-FUL CONSTITUTIONAL REASON.

IN THE YEARS AHEAD YOU WILL BE UNDER EVEN MORE PRESSURE TO MAKE AGELESS RIGHTS AND TRADITIONS CONFORM TO CULTURAL BIAS AND CONSTRAINTS. MY GENERATION WILL BE GONE THEN, AND YOU'LL FEEL THE WEIGHTY YOKE OF THIS AGELESS BURDEN. IT CAN BE HARD WORK, STANDING UP FOR WHAT YOU BELIEVE IN. I COULD BE MORE COMFORTABLE SITTING AT HOME, POLISHING MY OSCAR AND PLAYING WITH MY GRANDCHILDREN. YET I CHOOSE OF MY OWN FREE WILL TO ENGAGE IN THIS DEBATE. HOW ELSE CAN LIBERTY'S TORCH MARCH FORWARD?

I BELIEVE OUR GREAT HOUSE WILL ENDURE AS LONG AS WE RESPECT THE RULES, AND RETAIN ITS CHARITABLE AND DIGNIFIED ORDER. THE BLUEPRINT IS CLEAR, AND IT'S CALLED THE BILL OF RIGHTS. DON'T

LOSE TRACK OF IT, DON'T BE SEDUCED BY ANY FASHION OF THE MOMENT THAT SEEKS TO SUPERSEDE IT.

THIS NOTION OF INDIVIDUAL FREEDOM IS AS OLD AS PLATO AND PLINY, AS RECENT AS JEFFERSON AND LINCOLN, ROOSEVELT AND REAGAN. CULTURE IS MALLEABLE AS CLAY. FADS ARE FICKLE. POLITICAL CORRECTNESS IS CAPRICIOUS. BUT YOUR PRECIOUS HERITAGE OF FREEDOM, MY YOUNG FRIENDS, WILL TAKE HALF YOUR LIFETIME TO COMPREHEND.

OVER THE YEARS I COLLECTED NOTES ABOUT WHAT EXTRAORDINARY AMERICANS HAVE SAID ABOUT AMERICA. ONE DAY I FITTED THEM TOGETHER INTO A SINGLE PARAGRAPH WITH AN EASE THAT STUNNED ME. THESE WORDS FROM DIFFERENT MEN SEEMED TO SPEAK TO US WITH THE SAME VOICE FROM ACROSS THE AGES. LISTEN TO THESE WORDS OF MARTIN LUTHER KING, JR., F. SCOTT FITZGERALD, TOM PAINE, SAMUEL ELIOT MORISON, WILLIAM FAULKNER AND ABRAHAM LINCOLN.

"I HAVE A DREAM. I REFUSE TO ACCEPT THE END OF MAN. I BELIEVE HE WILL ENDURE. HE WILL PREVAIL. MAN IS IMMORTAL, NOT BECAUSE, ALONE AMONG GOD'S CREATURES, HE HAS A VOICE, BUT BECAUSE HE HAS A SOUL...A SPIRIT, CAPABLE OF COMPASSION...AND SACRIFICE...AND ENDURANCE.

"ABOUT AMERICA, AND AMERICANS, THIS IS PARTICULARLY TRUE. IT IS A FABULOUS COUNTRY, THE ONLY FABULOUS COUNTRY...WHERE MIRACLES NOT ONLY HAPPEN, THEY HAPPEN ALL THE TIME.

"AS A NATION WE HAVE, PERHAPS UNIQUELY, A SPECIAL WILLINGNESS OF THE HEART...A BLITHE FEARLESSNESS...A SIMPLE YEARNING FOR RIGHTEOUSNESS AND JUSTICE THAT IGNITED IN OUR REVOLUTION A FLAME OF FREEDOM THAT CANNOT BE STAMPED OUT. THAT IS THE LIVING, FRUITFUL SPIRIT OF THIS COUNTRY.

"THESE ARE THE TIMES THAT TRY MEN'S SOULS. THE SUNSHINE PATRIOT AND SUMMER SOLDIER WILL IN THIS CRISIS SHRINK FROM SERVICE. BUT HE THAT STANDS AND SERVES HIS COUNTRY NOW WILL EARN THE THANKS OF MAN AND WOMAN.

"WE MUST BIND UP THE NATION'S WOUNDS. WITH FIRMNESS IN THE RIGHT AS GOD GIVES US TO SEE RIGHT, LET US FINISH THE WORK WE ARE IN."

I BELIEVE THAT SAYS IT ALL. THANKS. IT'S BEEN A PLEASURE.

THANK YOU.

AN INTRODUCTION OF SIR CASPAR WEINBERGER AT THE U.S. ARMY WAR COLLEGE

November 4, 1999 Harrisburg, PA

AS THE THIRD MILLENNIUM RUSHES TOWARD US, AND EVERYONE TRIES TO MAKE SPECIAL SENSE OF AN OTHERWISE COMMON TICK OF THE CLOCK, WE'RE ALL REFLECTING ON HOW WE GOT HERE.

I'VE NOTICED THERE ARE LOTS OF DOCUMENTARIES ABOUT "TOP NEWS OF THE DECADE" AND "THE CENTURY'S TOP 100 PEOPLE" AND EVEN "THE BEST OF THE MILLENNIUM." I WATCHED ONE ON THE A&E CHANNEL CALLED THE "100 MOST INFLUENTIAL PEOPLE OF THE LAST THOUSAND YEARS." OF COURSE, THERE WERE PLENTY OF YOUR NAPOLEONS AND FRANKLINS AND ELVISES. BUT I WAS STRUCK BY HOW MANY OF THEM WERE NOT HOUSEHOLD NAMES. MANY WERE PEOPLE WHO DIDN'T MAKE ADVANCEMENTS, BUT WHO MADE THE ADVANCEMENTS OF OTHERS POSSIBLE.

FOR EXAMPLE, FOR THE NUMBER ONE SLOT AS THE MOST INFLUENTIAL PERSON OF THE PAST THOUSAND YEARS, A&E PICKED AN UNREMARKABLE GERMAN PRINTER NAMED JOHANN GUTENBERG. NOT BECAUSE HE INVENTED THE PRINTING PRESS (HE DIDN'T – THE CHINESE DID THAT) OR BECAUSE HE EVER WROTE ONE SINGLE MEMORABLE WORD.

NO, JOHANN GUTENBERG INVENTED A MOVABLE-TYPE PRINTING PROCESS THAT MADE VAST PRODUCTION OF AFFORDABLE PRINTED MATERIAL POSSIBLE FOR THE MASSES. AND THUS, IDEAS WERE SPREAD, AND EUROPE WAS AWAKENED FROM THE DARK AGES...GALILEO COULD BE READ BY ISAAC NEWTON; ISAAC NEWTON COULD BE READ BY ALBERT EINSTEIN; AND ALBERT EINSTEIN COULD CHANGE THE WORLD. GUTENBERG WAS A MAN WHOSE UNSEEN HAND, AND UNSUNG GENIUS, GAVE A NEW AND BETTER LIFE TO ALL MANKIND.

I BELIEVE THAT CAREFUL OBSERVERS WILL SOMEDAY BESTOW A SIMILAR LEVEL OF FAR-REACHING, UNFORESEEABLE BENEVOLENCE ON THE MAN WE'RE HERE TO HONOR TONIGHT.

BY CONVENTIONAL TERMS, CAP WEINBERGER HAS AN IMPRESSIVE RÉSUMÉ. GRADUATED MAGNA CUM LAUDE AT HARVARD COLLEGE.

SERVED IN THE PACIFIC THEATER AND LATER WITH GENERAL MACARTHUR'S INTELLIGENCE STAFF. HE MADE A FINE LAWYER, AN EFFECTIVE CALIFORNIA LEGISLATOR, A FEDERAL TRADE COMMISSIONER, AND SECRETARY OF HEALTH, EDUCATION AND WELFARE.

I HOPE YOU AND HE WILL FORGIVE ME IF I SKIP HIS VERY LONG LIST OF CREDENTIALS, BUSINESS ACHIEVEMENTS, CIVIC CHAIRS, AWARDS, MEDALS, HONORS, TITLES, AND EVEN HIS KNIGHTHOOD. BECAUSE IT WAS AS SECRETARY OF DEFENSE THAT CAP WEINBERGER, THE MASTERMIND OF RONALD REAGAN'S DEFENSE TEAM, QUIETLY ORCHESTRATED NO LESS THAN THE SECURITY OF THE WESTERN HEMISPHERE.

DESPITE VICIOUS PUBLIC RIDICULE AND POLITICAL SUBTERFUGE, IT WAS CAP WEINBERGER'S PEACE-THROUGH-STRENGTH VISION THAT EMASCULATED COMMUNIST AGGRESSION, EXORCISED THE EVIL EMPIRE, PULLED THE CORNERSTONE THAT COLLAPSED THE BERLIN WALL AND ENDED THE TERRIBLE PERILS OF THE COLD WAR.

CAP WEINBERGER'S LEGACY LIES IN ALL THE HORRORS THAT HAVEN'T HAPPENED. THE WARS NOT DECLARED, THE BLOOD NOT SHED, AND THE THOUSANDS OF BOY SOLDIERS WHO AREN'T DEAD.

HIS GIFT IS THE MILLIONS OF SONS AND DAUGHTERS WHO DIDN'T LOSE EYES OR LIMBS OR SANITY TO BATTLE. THE SOILS AND WATERS AND SKIES THAT AREN'T CONTAMINATED WITH RADIOACTIVE FALL-OUT. THE VULNERABLE COUNTRIES THAT DON'T SQUANDER MONEY AND BODIES FIGHTING COMMUNIST EXPANSION. THE GENERATIONS OF CHILDREN WHO AREN'T TRAUMATIZED BY BOMB DRILLS AT SCHOOL, AND THE MILLIONS OF PARENTS WHO DON'T LIE AWAKE IN FEAR OF INSTANT INCINERATION BY A MUSHROOM CLOUD.

THEY ARE THE MILLIONS UPON MILLIONS OF HEALTHY, LIVING, LEARNING BEINGS WHOSE LIVES WILL SOMEDAY LEAD TO AN END TO HUNGER, A CURE FOR CANCER AND HEART DISEASE, CLEAN RENEWABLE ENERGY, AN UNDERSTANDING OF THE BRAIN AND THE UNIVERSE, UNIMAGINABLE TECHNOLOGIES, AND JUST MAYBE, MORE PEACE ON EARTH.

IT'S FITTING THAT THE WAR COLLEGE HONOR THE MAN WHO DETERRED IT, BECAUSE I KNOW MANKIND WILL.

LADIES AND GENTLEMEN, SIR CASPAR WEINBERGER.

REMARKS BEFORE THE
BLANCHARD INVESTMENT GROUP

November 5, 1999 New Orleans, LA

"Invest in Freedom"

THANK YOU FOR THE KIND INTRODUCTION, AND FOR THE OPPORTU-
NITY TO BE WITH YOU HERE IN NEW ORLEANS...AN AMERICAN
ORIGINAL. THIS CITY HAS A STYLE ALL ITS OWN, AND YOU JUST
GOTTA LOVE IT. AN OLD-FASHIONED HELPING OF FRENCH ARISTOC-
RACY WITH SOME CAJUN SEASONING STIRRED IN JUST TO ADD A
LITTLE SPICE.

YOU CAN'T OVERLOOK THE INFLUENCE OF THE ANTEBELLUM SOUTH,
OR THE REMARKABLE CONTRIBUTIONS THIS CITY HAS MADE TO ART,
MUSIC AND OUR UNIQUE, MULTI-FACETED, AMERICAN CULTURE. A
FEW NOTES OF DIXIELAND JAZZ DOWN IN THE QUARTER IS ENOUGH
TO MAKE A YOUNG MAN'S HEART BEAT FASTER AND AN OLD MAN'S
HEART BEAT YOUNGER.

SO TONIGHT LET'S CELEBRATE BEING SPECIAL, BOTH THE SPECIAL
FLAVOR OF THIS ONE-OF-A-KIND CITY AND THE SPECIAL FREEDOMS
ENJOYED BY OUR ONE-OF-A-KIND NATION. ONE OF THE BIGGEST
REASONS OUR NATION IS ONE OF A KIND IS BECAUSE OF PEOPLE LIKE
YOU...THE INVESTORS OF OUR COUNTRY, WHO PROVIDE THE FUEL
THAT DRIVES THE MOST POWERFUL AND PRODUCTIVE ECONOMIC
ENGINE IN THE WORLD.

FROM MEDICINES TO TECHNOLOGY TO THE SMOKESTACKS OF INDUS-
TRY, THANKS TO YOU, OUR ECONOMY DELIVERS THE BEST PRODUCTS
AND SERVICES FOR MORE PEOPLE, FASTER AND MORE EFFICIENTLY
THAN ANY CIVILIZATION IN HISTORY. YOU PUT UP THE MONEY. YOU
TOLERATE THE RISKS. YOU HAVE TO LIVE WITH THE LOSSES. AND YOU
DESERVE TO REAP THE REWARDS.

WELL, I SUBMIT TO YOU TODAY THAT, JUST AS YOU MONITOR AND
TRACK YOUR INVESTMENTS, YOU ALSO NEED TO SAFEGUARD YOUR
FREEDOMS. IF YOU DON'T PREVENT THE EROSION OF YOUR RIGHTS AS
VIGILANTLY AS YOU PREVENT THE EROSION OF YOUR INVESTMENTS,

YOU STAND TO LOSE BOTH. BECAUSE WHETHER YOU KNOW IT OR NOT, YOUR LIBERTIES TODAY ARE BEING LOST.

RIGHT NOW, THROUGHOUT OUR SOCIETY, A WHOLESALE REJECTION OF PERSONAL RESPONSIBILITY IS TAKING PLACE, AND IT'S COSTING YOU THE VERY FREEDOMS AND OPPORTUNITIES THAT HAVE ALLOWED OUR ECONOMY TO THRIVE. NO ONE WANTS TO BE HELD ACCOUNTABLE FOR THEIR ACTIONS ANYMORE. AND NO ONE EXPECTS ANYONE TO BE HELD ACCOUNTABLE ANYMORE.

DRUNKEN DRIVERS BLAME BARTENDERS. RAPISTS BLAME VICTIMS. CRIMINALS BLAME SOCIETY. AND GOVERNMENT BLAMES GUNS.

WHY IS IT THAT, OUT OF 250,000 CRIMINALS WHO COMMITTED A FEDERAL FELONY BY TRYING TO BUY A GUN UNDER THE BRADY LAW, THE CLINTON ADMINISTRATION DIDN'T PROSECUTE EVEN ONE IN THREE STRAIGHT YEARS? WHY IS IT THAT IN RICHMOND, VIRGINIA, THEY'VE CUT MURDER RATES BY ALMOST HALF, JUST BY ENFORCING EXISTING LAWS – BUT 90 MILES AWAY, IN THE NATION'S MURDER CAPITAL OF WASHINGTON, D.C., ARMED, VIOLENT FELONS ARE ROUTINELY FREED TO THE STREETS TO MURDER AGAIN?

HOW CAN PRESIDENT CLINTON INSIST THAT WHAT WE NEED ARE MORE ANTI-GUN LAWS WHEN FEDERAL GUN PROSECUTIONS UNDER HIS WATCH HAVE BEEN CUT BY NEARLY HALF? THE ANSWER IS SIMPLE: GOVERNMENTS ENCOURAGE IRRESPONSIBLE BEHAVIOR AS RELENTLESSLY AS POLITICIANS SEEK PROBLEMS TO SOLVE. AND THE MORE THAT CITIZENS DEMAND FROM GOVERNMENT, THE MORE THE GOVERNMENT DENIES THEM. NO ONE ACCEPTS RESPONSIBILITY, NO ONE GETS "TAKEN CARE OF," AND WE ALL HAVE TO PAY THE PRICE.

IT'S TIME TO PUT AN END TO THIS DISHONEST CHARADE.

WHEN CIGARETTE MAKERS ARE HELD RESPONSIBLE FOR SMOKERS' ACTIONS…AND GUN MAKERS ARE HELD RESPONSIBLE FOR KILLERS' ACTIONS…AND NO ONE IS HELD RESPONSIBLE FOR O.J.'S ACTIONS…WELL, THAT'S WHEN THE SOLUTION IS MORE DANGEROUS THAN THE PROBLEM.

WHEN NANNIES REPLACE MORALS, WHEN VICE DISPLACES VIRTUE, AND WHEN WE CAN'T AGREE OF WHAT "IS" IS ANYMORE, WE'VE LOST A LOT. AND THE STATE HAS TAKEN IT OVER. JUST LOOK AT HOW FAR WE'VE COME. AS JAMES BOVARD POINTED OUT IN HIS BOOK *LOST*

RIGHTS, AMERICANS TODAY MUST OBEY 30 TIMES AS MANY LAWS AS AT THE TURN OF THE CENTURY.

UNDER IRS REGULATIONS AND ASSET-FORFEITURE LAWS, YOU'RE GUILTY UNTIL PROVEN INNOCENT. GOVERNMENT AUTHORITIES HAVE SEIZED THE PROPERTY OF HUNDREDS OF THOUSANDS OF AMERICANS, OFTEN WITH NO MORE PROOF OF A CRIMINAL OFFENSE THAN THE BASELESS CLAIMS OF SOME ANONYMOUS INFORMANT.

YOU HAVE A RIGHT TO PRIVATE PROPERTY. THAT IS, UNLESS GOVERN-MENT OFFICIALS DISCOVER THAT YOUR LAND CONTAINS A WETLAND. OR YOUR HOUSE CONTAINS LEAD-BASED PAINT. OR YOUR YARD CON-TAINS TOO MANY BROKEN-DOWN CARS. OR YOUR WALLET CONTAINS TOO MUCH CASH FOR YOU TO BE ENGAGED IN LEGITIMATE BUSINESS.

FROM THE EEOC TO THE FDA, EPA AND IRS, FROM HUD TO OSHA TO RICO AND BEYOND, AN ARMY OF FEDERAL TAX COLLEC-TORS, REGULATORS AND BUREAUCRATIC BUSYBODIES IS WORKING AROUND THE CLOCK, ON YOUR DIME, TO DEPRIVE YOU OF YOUR MONEY, YOUR PROPERTY AND YOUR LIBERTY – AND TO FRIGHTEN YOU FROM TRYING TO DO ANYTHING ABOUT IT.

THEY'RE BURYING THE MOST PRODUCTIVE MEMBERS OF SOCIETY UNDER AN AVALANCHE OF REGULATION. EVERYTHING IS SUBJECT TO SOME RULE OR OBSCURE GUIDELINE. *THE FEDERAL REGISTER* – UNCLE SAM'S OFFICIAL COMPENDIUM OF REGULATIONS, RULES, LEGAL NOTICES, AND BUREAUCRATIC MUMBO JUMBO – HAS GROWN TO OVER 68,000 PAGES UNDER PRESIDENT CLINTON. SIXTY-EIGHT-THOUSAND PAGES, 132 REAMS OF PAPER.

HIS AGENCIES HAVE ADDED OVER 21,000 FINAL RULES OVER THE PAST FIVE YEARS. THEY'VE DEPLOYED 128,000 FEDERAL BUREAUCRATS TO ENCODE AND ENFORCE THEM. ENFORCEMENT ALONE GOBBLES UP NEARLY $18 BILLION EACH YEAR. BUT THAT'S JUST THE BEGINNING. BECAUSE IT COSTS YOU A LOT MORE – IN LOST OPPORTUNITIES, REDUCED PRODUCTIVITY, PAPERWORK, COMPLIANCE COSTS AND PLAIN OLD AGGRAVATION.

WHEN YOU CAN'T DEVELOP YOUR LAND BECAUSE SOME BUREAUCRAT SAYS AN ENDANGERED WATERBUG LIVES IN ITS MUD PUDDLES…WHEN YOU WIPE OUT YOUR SAVINGS TO PAY LAWYERS BECAUSE YOU DON'T EMPLOY THE RIGHT RACES OR GENDERS IN THE PROPER PROPOR-TIONS…WHEN PAPERWORK CROWDS OUT PRODUCTION AS THE MAIN BUSINESS OF INDUSTRY…THE ECONOMY CEASES TO WORK.

IF YOU TOTAL UP THE COSTS OF COMPLYING WITH ALL THESE REGULA-
TIONS, AS ONE GROUP DID, YOU'LL SEE IT COSTS ABOUT $737 BILLION
A YEAR. AM I THE ONLY ONE WHO FINDS IT ODD THAT THAT FIGURE
EXACTLY MATCHES INDIVIDUAL INCOME TAXES COLLECTED IN 1996?

LET ME GET THIS STRAIGHT. THE MONEY WE PAY GOVERNMENT TO
REGULATE AND PROTECT US ENDS UP COSTING US TWICE AS MUCH TO
COMPLY...SO WE CAN CONTINUE TO MAKE MONEY TO PAY MORE
TAXES TO HIRE MORE REGULATORS TO IMPOSE MORE RULES...WHOA,
THAT'LL MAKE YOU DIZZY.

AND IT SHOULD. IF YOU'VE GOT A WIFE AND TWO KIDS, THOSE REGU-
LATORY COSTS CUT OUT ABOUT 20 PERCENT OF YOUR AFTER-TAX
BUDGET. NO EXPENSE EXCEPT HOUSING EATS UP MORE. AND THAT'S
JUST REGULATION. YOU'VE STILL GOT TO PAY FOR IT WITH YOUR TAXES.

IN 1948, WHEN I WAS JUST BEGINNING MY FAMILY AND CAREER, FED-
ERAL USED ABOUT 3% OF THE TYPICAL FAMILY'S INCOME. TODAY,
FEDERAL TAXES EAT UP NEARLY 25 PERCENT.

WHY? MAYBE BECAUSE SINCE THEN, THOSE BUSY BEES IN
WASHINGTON HAVE CREATED OVER 1,000 NEW SUBSIDY PROGRAMS
ON EVERYTHING FROM MEDICAL CARE TO STATE-SPONSORED "ART"
MADE FROM HUMAN URINE OR ELEPHANT DUNG. WELL...I GUESS
YOU GET WHAT YOU PAY FOR. BUT WE'RE THROWING GOOD MONEY
AFTER BAD.

DON'T GET ME WRONG: SOCIETY NEEDS A SAFETY NET, AND THERE
ARE THINGS WE ALL HAVE TO AGREE TO PAY FOR.

BUT IN 1904, WHEN JUSTICE HOLMES SAID THAT TAXES WERE THE
PRICE WE PAY FOR A CIVILIZED SOCIETY, TAXES TOTALED $340
PER PERSON IN MODERN-DAY DOLLARS. NOW THEY'RE $10,000 PER
PERSON, ACCORDING TO THE TAX FOUNDATION.

INTERESTING. IN OTHER WORDS, WE'RE PAYING 30 TIMES AS MUCH IN
TAXES TO OBEY 30 TIMES AS MANY LAWS AS WE DID AT THE TURN OF
THE CENTURY? I DON'T KNOW ABOUT YOU, BUT TO ME THAT
SOUNDS LIKE A BAD INVESTMENT. AND WHEN YOU ADD THE COSTS
OF THE TWO – TAXATION AND REGULATION – YOU REALLY BEGIN TO
SEE RED. ACCORDING TO AMERICANS FOR TAX REFORM, THE AVER-
AGE AMERICAN DIDN'T FINISH PAYING FOR TAXES AND REGULATION
UNTIL JUNE 25TH.

AMAZING.

IMAGINE TELLING JEFFERSON OR ADAMS OR ANY OF THE FRAMERS THAT CITIZENS TODAY HAVE TO WORK HALF THE YEAR JUST TO PAY FOR GOVERNMENT. IMAGINE THE LOOK ON BENJAMIN FRANKLIN'S FACE IF YOU ATTEMPTED TO DESCRIBE TO HIM WHAT "AFFIRMATIVE ACTION" MEANS. TRY EXPLAINING TO GEORGE WASHINGTON, THE MAN WHO TURNED DOWN OFFERS TO BE KING, THAT MODERN AMERICAN GOVERNMENT YEARNS TO BE ANOTHER BLOATED MONARCHY. IMAGINE TELLING THEM WHAT KIND OF LAWS THEY PUSH TO "PROTECT" US.

GUN BANS THAT DO NOTHING BUT DENY LAW-ABIDING CITIZENS THE RIGHT TO SELF-DEFENSE.

QUOTA SYSTEMS THAT SACRIFICE EQUAL OPPORTUNITY FOR EQUAL RESULTS.

CAMPAIGN FINANCE LAWS THAT DENY ORDINARY CITIZENS POLITICAL SPEECH.

AND MORE TAXES AND REGULATIONS TO KEEP THE WHOLE MERRY-GO-ROUND GOING.

I JOKE – BUT IT'S NOT FUNNY. BETWEEN TAXATION, REGULATION, LEGISLATION AND COERCION, WHEN YOU SEE HOW THIS WHOLE PROCESS TAKES ON A MOMENTUM OF ITS OWN – LIKE THE WIND A WILDFIRE WHIPS UP AS IT FEEDS ITSELF – YOU SEE HOW DANGEROUS TO OUR FREEDOMS IT REALLY IS.

IT'S NOT A CHANCE EVENT. IT'S A CAREFULLY CONSIDERED, WELL EXECUTED ATTEMPT TO REVERSE THE BALANCE OF POWER AWAY FROM THE LOCAL AND DIRECTLY TO THE FEDERAL. AND IT IS WORKING. BUT IT CAN BE STOPPED. HOW? LET ME TELL YOU A STORY TO ILLUSTRATE.

IN 1963, I MARCHED WITH DR. MARTIN LUTHER KING ON WASHINGTON. AT THE TIME, CIVIL RIGHTS WASN'T YET A FASHIONABLE ISSUE. BUT TOGETHER, A FEW COMMITTED, LIKE-MINDED PEOPLE ALL PUSHED IN THE SAME DIRECTION AND REFUSED TO SIT AT THE BACK OF THE BUS – AND THEY WERE ABLE TO CHANGE THE LAWS OF THE LAND.

CHANCES ARE YOU'VE SEEN THAT SAME PHENOMENON IN YOUR OWN BUSINESS DEALINGS. TIME AND TIME AGAIN, WHEN A SMALL NUMBER OF PEOPLE GET TOGETHER TO FOCUS THEIR EFFORTS, THEY CAN EASILY OUTDO A MUCH LARGER, INDIFFERENT, LUMBERING FORCE. INVARIABLY, THE FIGHT GOES TO THE FEW AND THE QUICK. AND THE

PEOPLE I SEE IN THIS ROOM DEFINE THAT.

WHEN YOU PUT UP THE MONEY, TAKE THE RISKS, AND BANKROLL THE DYNAMO THAT DRIVES THIS ECONOMY – THAT TAKES GUTS. ALL A BUREAUCRAT NEEDS IS A GUT. BUREAUCRACIES AREN'T BRAVE – THE PEOPLE WHO TAKE AWAY OUR RIGHTS ARE COWARDS. IT'S WHAT YOU DO THAT TAKES COURAGE AND WHAT YOU DO THAT WORKS.

SO I URGE YOU: GO OUT THERE AND DEVOTE THE SAME ENERGY AND VISION TO PROTECTING YOUR FREEDOMS AS PROTECTING YOUR INTERESTS. GIVE THE SAME CARE AND ATTENTION YOU GIVE YOUR INVESTMENTS TO THE LIBERTIES THAT MAKE THOSE INVESTMENTS POSSIBLE. REVEL IN YOUR VICTORIES. CLAIM CREDIT FOR YOUR ACCOMPLISHMENTS. AND DON'T BE ASHAMED TO CLAIM WHAT'S YOURS.

YOU ARE THE GOVERNMENT AND YOU CAN CHANGE IT. SO GO OUT AND DO IT.

THANK YOU VERY MUCH.

REMARKS BEFORE THE
BUILDING INDUSTRY ASSOCIATION OF WASHINGTON

October 28, 1999 Seattle, WA

"Fight the Good Fight"

THANK YOU FOR THE KIND WORDS AND WARM WELCOME.

GOOD TO BE HERE IN THE LAND OF GREEN, WITHOUT THE BIG WATER BILL. I GREW UP IN MICHIGAN, SO I UNDERSTAND THE PRINCIPLE OF WATER FALLING NATURALLY FROM THE SKY. AS A SOUTHERN CALIFORNIAN, I SPEND A LOT OF TIME EXPLAINING IT TO MY NEIGHBORS.

WE MAY NOT SHARE WEATHER SYSTEMS, BUT ALL OF US UP AND DOWN THIS GREAT WEST COAST DO SHARE SOMETHING IN COMMON. WE LIVE WHERE LOTS OF OTHER PEOPLE WANT TO.

AND IT'S BEEN THAT WAY SINCE BACK BEFORE THE MID-1800S, WHEN SETTLERS, MINERS, INVESTORS AND RAILROAD MEN GOT THE ITCH TO TRAVEL ACROSS THE STARK MIDRIFF OF OUR NATION TO REACH AMERICA'S LAND OF MILK AND HONEY. SO THEY SET OUT FOR THE PROMISED LAND, OUR ANCESTORS DID, ON THE GREAT WILDERNESS PATHWAYS: THE OREGON AND THE CALIFORNIA TRAILS. FACING WEATHER, DISEASE, INDIANS – HARDSHIPS YOU AND I CAN'T EVEN IMAGINE.

THEY DIDN'T NEED ME ALONG TO PART THE RED SEA. BUT THEY DID CROSS A FEW RED RIVERS. AND AT TIMES, BEING A ROMANTIC WITH AN ACTIVE IMAGINATION, I ENVY THEM AND THEIR ADVENTURES. AND WHO KNOWS? MAYBE I'LL MAKE IT YET. I'M FEELING GREAT, AND THERE JUST MIGHT BE A WAGONMASTER ROLE RIGHT FOR ME.

I KNOW A LOT OF YOU THINK THAT ACTORS LIVE IN LA LA LAND. BUT IN TRUTH, WHAT WE DO IS A WHOLE LOT LIKE WHAT YOU DO – WE WORK TOO MANY DAYS FILLED WITH TOO MANY HOURS.

IT'S JUST A CRAFT, LIKE BUILDING HOMES OR DEVELOPING SUBURBS. IT MAY SEEM MORE GLAMOROUS, BUT BELIEVE ME, THAT'S NOT THE WORD FOR IT. NOT AT FIVE IN THE MORNING, ENDURING HOURS OF MAKEUP THAT WON'T GET SCRUBBED OFF UNTIL SOMEWHERE AROUND MIDNIGHT. AND EVEN WHEN SOMETHING AS EXCITING AS A CECIL B. DEMILLE CHARIOT RACE IS IN THE CAN, SOMEONE HAS TO CLEAN UP AFTER THE HORSES.

WHAT I'M GETTING AT IS THIS: THERE'S A LOT OF…WELL, HORSE APPLES…IN ANY LINE OF WORK. AND WE ALL HAVE TO WADE THROUGH IT. EVEN SO, SOMETIMES IT SEEMS THAT THE HIGHER YOU STEP, THE HIGHER THEY PILE IT. I'VE FOUND THAT OUT THE HARD WAY…BOTH IN HOLLYWOOD AND IN MY VOLUNTEER WORK FOR THE NATIONAL RIFLE ASSOCIATION.

I BECAME PRESIDENT OF THE NRA BECAUSE I BELIEVED THE BILL OF RIGHTS – ALL OF IT – WAS IN NEED OF SOME HIGH-PROFILE DEFENDERS.

I'M A VERY FORTUNATE MAN. MY COUNTRY HAS BEEN GOOD TO ME, AND I'M GLAD I CAN GIVE SOMETHING BACK. BUT LET ME TELL YOU…THE GIFT HASN'T ALWAYS BEEN APPRECIATED, NOR HAS THE

ACT OF GIVING ALWAYS BEEN EASY. IF I'D BEEN SEEKING ADORATION, IT WOULD HAVE BEEN MUCH EASIER FOR ME TO JUMP ON SOME MORE POLITICALLY CORRECT BANDWAGON.

DON'T GET ME WRONG. I'M NOT A FLAMBOYANT, CRUSADING REFORMER. BUT I'VE ALWAYS FELT THAT A MAN MUST SPEAK HIS MIND AND ACT ON HIS PRINCIPLES IF HE'S GONNA RESPECT THAT FACE IN THE MIRROR.

I FELT THAT WAY WHEN I MARCHED WITH DR. MARTIN LUTHER KING BACK IN THE SIXTIES. AT THAT TIME A BLACK MAN IN HOLLYWOOD COULDN'T EVEN GET A JOB AS A STAGEHAND. BLACK PEOPLE SIMPLY WEREN'T WELCOME AROUND THE STUDIOS. AND I MIGHT ADD THAT AT THAT TIME, WHITE ACTORS WHO MARCHED FOR A BLACK MAN'S CIVIL RIGHTS WEREN'T EXACTLY POPULAR.

TODAY SOME OF THE MOST GIFTED PEOPLE IN OUR INDUSTRY ARE BLACK. AND I'M PROUD OF THAT, BECAUSE I FEEL I HAD A PART IN MAKING IT HAPPEN. SO...I WAS A LITTLE BIT SURPRISED A FEW WEEKS BACK WHEN A YOUNG BLACK DIRECTOR OF SOME RENOWN SAID I SHOULD BE SHOT FOR MY VIEWS CONCERNING THE SECOND AMENDMENT. SPIKE LEE – A GIFTED YOUNG FELLOW WITH A MOUTH THAT TENDS TO RUN AWAY WITH HIS BRAIN – SAID I SHOULD TAKE A BULLET FOR PRESERVING THE RIGHT TO KEEP AND BEAR ARMS.

I'M SURE SPIKE WOULD BE EMBARRASSED TO KNOW HOW MUCH HIS WORDS SOUNDED LIKE SOME OF THOSE REDNECK GOONS WHO PASSED FOR SHERIFF'S DEPUTIES BACK IN SELMA IN '63.

THE RIGHT TO KEEP AND BEAR ARMS IS ONE OF THE WAYS WE DEFINE INDIVIDUAL LIBERTY IN A FREE SOCIETY. IT GUARANTEES THAT YOU AND I HAVE EQUAL STATURE WITH GOVERNMENT, MILITARY, POLICE, AND CRIMINALS. IN FACT, I BELIEVE THE RIGHT TO KEEP AND BEAR ARMS IS THE FIRST AMONG EQUALS; IT'S THE ONE RIGHT THAT MAKES ALL OTHER RIGHTS POSSIBLE.

BUT THEY'RE ALL ESSENTIAL. TAKE THE RIGHT OF FREE SPEECH, FOR EXAMPLE. IT'S WORKING RIGHT UP HERE BEFORE YOUR VERY EYES. I CONTINUE CHALLENGING THE PRESS AT EVERY OPPORTUNITY, WHICH IN TURN WILL CALL ME A SENILE OLD MAN SOMEWHERE IN AMERICA BEFORE THE DAY IS OVER.

OR FREEDOM OF RELIGION. YOUR GOD MAY NOT BE QUITE THE SAME AS MY GOD, BUT BY GOD I'LL FIGHT TO DEFEND YOUR RIGHT TO

WORSHIP. OR THE FIFTH AMENDMENT, PREVENTING THE TAKING OF PRIVATE PROPERTY FOR PUBLIC USE. FEW THINGS ARE MORE PRECIOUS TO FREE MEN AROUND THE WORLD THAN THE RIGHT TO OWN PROPERTY. TO WORK IT, BUILD IT, BUY IT, SELL IT.

AS LONG AS YOU DON'T IMPERIL YOUR FELLOW MAN, THERE'S NO REASON FOR THE HEAVY HAND OF GOVERNMENT TO INTERFERE WITH THIS FREE PROCESS. AFTER ALL, THAT'S WHY WE DUMPED WHOLE LOT OF TEA – AND A KING – OVERBOARD MORE THAN TWO HUNDRED YEARS AGO.

BUT AS THE YEARS GO BY, WE GET COMPLACENT WITH OUR FREEDOMS. AND BEFORE YOU KNOW IT, THERE'S A PERMIT FOR THIS AND A LICENSE FOR THAT, A FEDERAL INSPECTOR AT THE FRONT DOOR, AN IRS AGENT SNEAKING ROUND THE BACK DOOR AND SOMEBODY FROM THE EPA STUCK IN THE CHIMNEY.

I'M AWARE OF YOUR PROBLEM CONCERNING SALMON AND ITS SUDDEN APPEARANCE ON THE ENDANGERED SPECIES LIST. THIS IS WHAT HAPPENS WHEN WE ASSUME GOVERNMENT WILL LEAVE OUR RIGHTS ALONE, AND WE AWAKE ONE MORNING TO FACE A FULL-BLOWN FEDERALLY MANDATED EPIDEMIC.

THE NRA KNOWS THAT IF YOU TURN THE OTHER CHEEK AND ALLOW THE GOVERNMENT TO REGISTER A HANDGUN HERE AND CONFISCATE A SEMI-AUTO RIFLE THERE, BEFORE LONG THE GOVERNMENT WILL SUPERSEDE THE WILL OF THE PEOPLE AND SIMPLY TAKE WHAT IT WANTS TO. AND THAT'S EXACTLY WHAT HAPPENED RECENTLY IN ENGLAND AND AUSTRALIA.

NOW IT SEEMS THE ENDANGERED SPECIES LIST HAS BECOME A WEAPON WIELDED BY BULLYING AUTHORITIES, RATHER THAN A SIMPLE TOOL TO SAVE WILDLIFE IN JEOPARDY. AND WHAT'S REALLY ENDAN-GERED NOW IS AFFORDABLE HOUSING FOR WASHINGTON STATE FAMILIES. AND MY DICTIONARY SAYS FAMILIES COME BEFORE FISHES.

I'VE HEARD SOME OF THE HORROR STORIES. PROPERTY OWNERS WHO CAN'T DEVELOP, REFURBISH OR MAXIMIZE THE VALUE OF THEIR HOLD-INGS BECAUSE SOME BUREAUCRAT PREFERS TO MAXIMIZE HIS OR HER SELF-IMPORTANCE.

NOR DO I THINK ANYONE IN THIS ROOM HAS ANYTHING PERSONAL AGAINST SALMON. IT'S A GRAND FISH, A CREATURE THAT PREFERS TO

SPAWN IN SOME OF THE WORLD'S MOST BEAUTIFUL PLACES. BUT THESE PLACES ALSO HAPPEN TO BE PEOPLE PLACES. WE CAN'T JUST MOVE EVERYONE OUT AND MOVE THE CLOCK BACK SEVERAL CENTURIES. SO WHAT CAN WE DO? LET'S START WITH EXERCISING A LITTLE COMMON SENSE.

THERE ARE THINGS THAT CAN BE DONE TO HELP ENDANGERED SPECIES. AND IF THE SCIENCE WAS GOOD AND THE PROCESS DIDN'T CREATE REAMS OF RED TAPE THAT LEFT LOCAL ECONOMIES HAMSTRUNG, I IMAGINE WE'D ALL RAISE OUR VOICES IN A HEARTY CHEER FOR THE SALMON.

BUT IF THE SCIENCE ISN'T CLEARLY THOUGHT THROUGH, AND PROPERTY VALUES DECLINE, AND TRANSPORTATION PROJECTS STALL, AND THE GOVERNMENT CANCELS EVEN MINOR CONSTRUCTION BECAUSE IT MIGHT AFFECT A PERHAPS ENDANGERED SPECIES...WELL, THEN YOU'VE GOT A PROBLEM. IT'S A PROBLEM OF TOO MUCH POWER UP THERE, WHERE GOVERNMENT RESIDES, AND NOT ENOUGH POWER DOWN HERE, WHERE YOU AND I DWELL. DOWN HERE, SO TO SPEAK, WITH THE FISHES.

IT'S A PROBLEM THAT WASN'T MEANT TO BE A PROBLEM. THE FOUNDING FATHERS DIDN'T INTEND FOR THE GOVERNMENT TO GROW SO LARGE AND DICTATORIAL. BUT OVER THE GENERATIONS WE LET THINGS SLIDE, AND IT JUST SORT OF HAPPENED.

SO HOW DO WE GET OUR RIGHTS BACK? OUR INDIVIDUAL RIGHTS, FIRST AND FOREMOST – OUR RIGHT TO OWN, BUY, SELL AND BUILD PROPERTY; OUR RIGHT TO MAKE COMMON SENSE DECISIONS CONCERNING OUR EXPANSION OR REDUCTION; OUR RIGHT TO CUT THE CRAP OUT OF THE EQUATION.

IN A GOVERNMENT FOR AND BY THE PEOPLE, YOU'VE GOT A RIGHT TO RAISE A RUCKUS. YOU'VE GOT A RIGHT TO GO BEFORE THE NATIONAL MARINE FISHERIES SERVICE AND MAKE IT CLEAR THAT ALL THESE MORATORIUMS ON BUILDING AND HIGHWAY DIVERSIONS AND ELABORATE STREAM BYPASS PROJECTS AREN'T GONNA DO A THING TO RESCUE DWINDLING SALMON NUMBERS...NOT AS LONG AS MILES OF NETS ARE STRETCHED ACROSS EVERY CONCEIVABLE INLET. IF WE WANT TO SAVE THE FISH, LET'S QUIT CATCHING SO MANY OF THEM, FOR GOD'S SAKE.

MAKES PERFECTLY GOOD SENSE TO ME. BUT NOT TO A GOVERNMENT THAT'S SO HIDEBOUND AND JADED THAT IT NOT ONLY FORCES

EXPENSIVE POLLYANNA MANDATES UPON THE VARIOUS STATES, BUT IT ALSO DEMANDS THAT HARDWORKING CITIZENS PAY FOR THEM. STRANGE HOW A GOVERNMENT CAN FORCE RESTRICTIONS UPON YOU THAT CUT YOUR INCOME, THEN RAISE YOUR TAXES TO PAY FOR IT. MY FRIENDS, ANY GOVERNMENT THAT DOES THAT IS NOT THE GOVERNMENT OF JEFFERSON, OR MADISON, OR LINCOLN.

THAT'S A BILL CLINTON GOVERNMENT, AND IT WILL GO DOWN IN HISTORY...PROBABLY IN A PLAIN BROWN WRAPPER. NEVER IN THE HISTORY OF THE UNITED STATES HAS THERE BEEN ANYONE SO ADEPT AT POLITICAL SLEIGHT OF HAND. AND THE CABINET OFFICIALS THAT DO HIS DIRTY WORK ARE CUT FROM THE SAME COARSE CLOTH AS BILL CLINTON.

AND HE SUCCEEDS BECAUSE WE DON'T STOP HIM. WE, THE PEOPLE, DON'T VOTE ENOUGH; WE DON'T ORGANIZE ENOUGH TO FIGHT AGAINST POLICIES THAT ATTACK OUR HERITAGE; WE DON'T WRITE ENOUGH LETTERS; WE DON'T CARRY PLACARDS; WE DON'T MARCH. SO IN RETURN WE GET UNFUNDED MANDATES, RIDICULOUSLY DEVALUED PROPERTY RIGHTS, AND A FAT FEDERAL GOVERNMENT THAT UNDERMINES YOUR ECONOMIC STABILITY...ALL IN HOPES THAT BILLIONS OF DOLLARS WORTH OF LAVISH PROJECTS MAY HELP SALMON.

WHAT WOULD HELP MORE THAN ANYTHING IS SOME PLAIN, OLD, HONEST ACCOUNTABILITY. BUT YOU AIN'T GONNA GET IT UNTIL YOU DEMAND IT. SO IF YOU VALUE THE THINGS YOU'VE WORKED FOR, START DEMANDING. DO WHATEVER IT TAKES TO GET YOUR RIGHTS BACK, YOUR BUSINESS BACK, YOUR HAND-BUILT DREAMS BACK. DO IT BECAUSE YOUR FAMILIES' MORTGAGES SHOULDN'T HAVE TO PAY FOR FISH BEING HAULED OUT OF NETS BY THE TRUCKLOAD.

IN THE OTHER WASHINGTON, ELECTED OFFICIALS KNOW THAT WHENEVER A GUN-HATER'S BILL APPEARS ON THE HILL, ITS SUPPORT-ERS ARE GONNA GET A BASHING. THE NRA WILL DESCEND UPON THEM LIKE STINK ON...WELL, ON A HORSE APPLE. WE DO IT BECAUSE WE CARE, WE'RE COMMITTED, WE'VE GOT THE NUMBERS, AND FREEDOM IS COUNTING ON US.

SO IF YOU WANT SENSIBLE, SCIENTIFIC PROGRESS IN RESTORING SALMON TO THIS WASHINGTON'S WATERS, I'D SUGGEST YOU ORGAN-IZE, RAISE SOME CASH AND GATHER SOME NUMBERS. GENERALLY MOST PROBLEMS WITH WILDLIFE AND THE ENVIRONMENT CAN BE

WORKED OUT AS LONG AS SOMEBODY SLAMS THE DOOR ON GOVERN-
MENT BULLYING. IT'S NOT AN ALIEN CONCEPT TO WANT PROGRESS,
DECENT FISHING AND CLEAN WATERS.

BUT YOU'VE GOT TO FIGHT. GIVE IN NOW, AND SOME DAY YOUR
VERY OWN GOVERNMENT WILL BE MOVING YOU OUT OF YOUR VERY
OWN HOMES WHENEVER THE SALMON SPAWN LOOKS A LITTLE
TEPID. DON'T LET A BLOATED BUREAUCRACY CONTINUE TO WALLOW
IN ITS OWN SELF-INDULGENCE, AND IN DOING SO, DIMINISH THE
TORCH OF LIBERTY.

IN THE WORDS OF THE POET DYLAN THOMAS, "DO NOT GO GENTLE
INTO THAT GOOD NIGHT...FIGHT, FIGHT AGAINST THE DYING OF THE
LIGHT."

THANK YOU.

REMARKS BEFORE THE
GOLDWATER INSTITUTE ANNUAL AWARD DINNER

November 19, 1999 Phoenix, AZ

IT'S SOMEWHAT IRONIC THAT WE SHOULD COME HERE TODAY TO
ADVOCATE THE IDEAS OF BARRY GOLDWATER, BECAUSE THE FACT IS,
THOSE IDEAS HAVE DONE JUST FINE ON THEIR OWN.

IN 1964, SOME CALLED GOLDWATER A "RIGHT-WING REACTIONARY"
AND CALLED HIS IDEAS "EXTREME," BUT TODAY, IF ANYTHING, THEY'RE
NOT EX-TREME...THEY'RE MAIN-STREAM. GOLDWATER'S VISION HAS
BEEN VINDICATED BY REPUBLICANS, DEMOCRATS, INDEPENDENTS,
REFORMERS AND POLITICIANS OF EVERY STRIPE, AROUND THE WORLD.

FROM WASHINGTON TO MOSCOW TO BEIJING AND BEYOND, FREE
MARKETS, FREE TRADE, INDIVIDUAL FREEDOM AND DEMOCRACY ARE
CIRCLING THE GLOBE WITH THE SPEED OF A FIBER-OPTIC RING. AND
THE REASON IS SIMPLE: IT'S NATURAL. ONLY A SYSTEM THAT

EMBRACES HUMAN NATURE CAN SURVIVE. THE ONLY SYSTEM THAT WORKS IS ONE THAT AFFORDS THE OPPORTUNITY TO EXCEL...ALLOWS INDIVIDUALS TO ADVANCE...AND REWARDS HARD WORK. ANYTHING ELSE IS A FRAUD...AND ULTIMATELY, A FAILURE.

GOLDWATER HAD THE GUTS TO SAY IT WHEN THE CONVENTIONAL WISDOM WAS THAT WE ALL OUGHT TO LIVE IN SOME GRAY, GREAT SOCIETY OF FEDERALLY ENFORCED SAMENESS WHERE THE COST OF NO ONE FALLING BEHIND WAS THAT NO ONE COULD GET AHEAD. AND GOLDWATER SAW WHICH WAY THE TIDE WAS MOVING.

HE SAID "I BELIEVE THE COMMUNISM WHICH BOASTS IT WILL BURY US WILL INSTEAD GIVE WAY TO THE FORCES OF FREEDOM." THAT WAS IN 1964.

"EXTREME?" SOUNDS TO ME LIKE THE CHEERS OF THE WORLD IN 1989, WHEN A CONCRETE MONSTROSITY CRUMBLED IN BERLIN. OR 1991, WHEN A BRONZE STATUE OF LENIN WAS HOISTED OFF ITS THRONE IN A PLACE THAT USED TO BE CALLED "LENINGRAD."

IN 1964, GOLDWATER SAID, "I CAN SEE A DAY WHEN ALL THE AMERICAS, NORTH AND SOUTH, WILL BE LINKED IN A MIGHTY SYSTEM IN WHICH THE ERRORS AND MISUNDERSTANDINGS OF THE PAST WILL BE SUBMERGED, ONE BY ONE, IN A RISING TIDE OF PROSPERITY AND INTERDEPENDENCE."

"RIGHT-WING REACTIONARY?" SOUNDS TO ME LIKE BILL CLINTON WHEN HE SIGNED THE NORTH AMERICAN FREE TRADE AGREEMENT!

IN 1964, GOLDWATER SAID, "A GOVERNMENT BIG ENOUGH TO GIVE YOU ALL YOU WANT IS BIG ENOUGH TO TAKE IT ALL."

BUT AGAIN, "MISTER REPUBLICAN" IN 1964 SOUNDS LIKE PRESIDENT CLINTON OR THE DEMOCRATIC LEADERSHIP COUNCIL IN 1996, WHEN THEY TRIED TO STEAL THE REPUBLICANS' THUNDER, CLAIMING "THE ERA OF BIG GOVERNMENT IS OVER." THE REASON THEY'VE TRIED TO STEAL THOSE IDEAS IS BECAUSE THEY WORK.

FREE TRADE...OPEN MARKETS...PROFIT-DRIVEN RESEARCH AND DEVELOPMENT AND GOOD, OLD-FASHIONED, CREATIVE INGENUITY ALL FOCUSED ON BUILDING THE AMERICAN DREAM. THEY'RE ALL PRINCIPLES THAT HARNESS HUMAN NATURE. IF BENJAMIN FRANKLIN HAD WRITTEN THOSE SPEECHES FOR GOLDWATER, HE WOULD HAVE CALLED THEM "SELF-EVIDENT IDEALS" – AND HE WOULD HAVE BEEN

RIGHT. THEY EXERT THEMSELVES AS A NATURAL ASPECT OF THE EXPERIENCE OF BEING HUMAN.

SOMETIMES, IT TAKES BARRY GOLDWATER'S BRAND OF FIREBRAND HONESTY AND DAUNTLESS DEDICATION TO PERSONAL BELIEFS TO GET PEOPLE TO SEE THE LIGHT. I KNOW THAT'S WHAT CONVINCED ME.

IN 1964, AFTER I HAD MARCHED WITH DR. MARTIN LUTHER KING IN WASHINGTON, IT SEEMED TO ME THAT PRESIDENT JOHNSON WAS THE BEST MAN SUITED TO CARRY OUT JACK KENNEDY'S AGENDA, WHICH I HAD EARLIER SUPPORTED.

THE DEMOCRATS WANTED TO INCLUDE ME IN PRESIDENT JOHNSON'S CAMPAIGN. BUT I WAS SHOOTING A MOVIE IN NORTHERN CALIFORNIA AT THE TIME, SO I WASN'T ABLE TO HELP. BEFORE AND AFTER EACH DAY'S FILMING, I HAD A LONG COMMUTE ON WHICH I PASSED A CAMPAIGN BILLBOARD FOR MR. GOLDWATER. IT FEATURED HIS PORTRAIT AND SEVEN WORDS: "IN YOUR HEART, YOU KNOW HE'S RIGHT." IT MADE ME UNEASY TO DRIVE BY THAT BILLBOARD EVERY DAY, AND I'D TRY NOT TO LOOK, OR AT LEAST NOT THINK ABOUT IT: "IN YOUR HEART, YOU KNOW HE'S RIGHT."

BUT ONE MORNING, I EXPERIENCED A TRUE REVELATION, ALMOST AN EPIPHANY, LIKE ST. PAUL ON THE ROAD TO DAMASCUS. I LOOKED AT THAT PHOTOGRAPH OF GOLDWATER, AND SAID SOFTLY, "SON OF A BITCH...HE IS RIGHT!" AND I KNEW HE WAS.

NOW THE WORLD KNOWS "MISTER REPUBLICAN" WAS RIGHT. AND WE'RE ALL BETTER OFF FOR HAVING WITNESSED HIS HEAT AND HIS LIGHT. GOD BLESS HIM.

THANK YOU VERY MUCH.

REMARKS UPON THE OPENING SESSION OF THE ARIZONA STATE LEGISLATURE

January 8, 2000 Phoenix, AZ

LADIES AND GENTLEMEN OF THE LEGISLATURE, THANK YOU FOR HAVING ME. IT'S TEMPTING TO TROT OUT POMPOUS SUPERLATIVES ABOUT THIS, THE OPENING DAY OF THE FIRST LEGISLATIVE SESSION OF THE FIRST YEAR OF THE FIRST DECADE OF THE 21ST CENTURY IN THE THIRD MILLENNIUM AND SO ON.

BUT THE TRUTH IS, IT'S JUST THE FIRST DAY OF THE SECOND REGULAR SESSION OF THE 44TH LEGISLATURE...ANOTHER DAY IN WHAT'LL BECOME SEAMLESS WEEKS OF GENERALLY SELFLESS PATRIOTS DOING THE GENERALLY THANKLESS JOB OF MANAGING THE PEOPLE'S BUSINESS. THAT'S THE NATURE OF PUBLIC SERVICE. I COMMEND YOU FOR IT.

YOU ARE HERE BECAUSE YOU WANT TO LEAVE THE FUTURE BETTER THAN YOU FIND THE PRESENT. YOU WANT TO MAKE BETTER HISTORY. THAT'S A NOBLE THING. TO THAT END, I WISH FOR YOU THE COURAGE TO BE UNPOPULAR.

HAVING PORTRAYED DOZENS OF HISTORIC PEOPLE – AND HAVING LIVED A FEW YEARS MYSELF – I CAN TELL YOU THIS: POPULARITY IS HISTORY'S POCKET CHANGE. COURAGE IS THE TRUE CURRENCY OF HISTORY.

I KNOW, BECAUSE I'VE WATCHED IT HAPPEN. IN 1963, MARTIN LUTHER KING WAS PLANNING A MASSIVE MARCH ON WASHINGTON, D.C. BUT IN ALL OF HOLLYWOOD, AN EMBARRASSINGLY SMALL GROUP OF US WERE WILLING TO MARCH WITH HIM. CIVIL RIGHTS WASN'T FASHIONABLE IN THOSE DAYS. FOR A FAMOUS FACE, MARCHING WITH DR. KING COULD END YOUR CAREER – MAYBE YOUR LIFE.

BUT WE MARCHED ANYWAY. I'M NOT SAYING IT WAS A COURAGEOUS THING FOR ME TO DO. I'M SAYING IT WAS THE RIGHT THING FOR ME TO DO, EVEN THOUGH IT WAS UNPOPULAR – AS ARE SOME CAUSES I FIGHT FOR TODAY.

TODAY I WISH FOR YOU COURAGE TO MAKE YOUR OWN MARCH... COURAGE TO TAKE THE UPHILL ROAD, THE ROAD THAT DOES NOT YIELD TO POLITICAL CORRECTNESS, THE ROAD OFTEN LINED WITH

WATER CANNONS AND POLICE DOGS, CRITICISM, RIDICULE, SNARLING REPORTERS AND HATE MAIL.

IF YOU NEED A GUIDEPOST, PLEASE MAKE IT THE BILL OF RIGHTS – THOSE SACRED PERSONAL FREEDOMS GRANTED NOT BY GOVERNMENT BUT BY GOD. THEY'RE NOT YOURS TO TAKE AWAY – THEY'RE YOURS TO GUARANTEE. THAT'S YOUR JOB.

ONE MORE THING ABOUT THE BILL OF RIGHTS. PLEASE KEEP FAITH IN ITS PURITY. THOSE WHO SAY IT NEEDS EDITING MUST ADMIT AMERICANS ARE NO LONGER WORTHY OF ITS BLESSINGS. THOSE WHO SAY IT'S ARCHAIC MUST ADMIT THIS COUNTRY CAN'T LIVE UP TO ITS FOUNDERS' DREAMS. THOSE WHO SAY THEY KNOW BETTER, LET THEM GO INVENT A COUNTRY OF THEIR OWN. MEANWHILE, DEMAND THAT THEY LEAVE THE BILL OF RIGHTS ALONE.

I WISH FOR YOU THE COURAGE TO DEFY POLITICAL THEATER. WE, THE PEOPLE, HAVE BECOME A WILLING AUDIENCE TO MADE-FOR-TV LAWMAKING, WATCHING NATIONAL POLICY UNFOLD LIKE A SCRIPTED STORY LINE – BECAUSE IT IS.

YOU ARE HEIRS TO A GOVERNING MACHINE THAT CHURNS OUT POLL-TESTED, PACKAGED POLICY WITH POLITICALLY CORRECT LABELLING, AND A MEDIA ALL TOO WILLING TO MARKET IT FOR FREE. WHATEVER SHADE MATCHES THE NATIONAL MOOD RING BECOMES LAW OF THE LAND. OUR FOUNDING FATHERS WOULD HARDLY RECOGNIZE THIS FEDERAL SPECTACLE OF POSTURING, SCRIPTING AND STAGING.

I WISH FOR YOU THE COURAGE TO CALL IT WHAT IT IS: POLITICAL CORRECTNESS IS JUST TYRANNY WITH MANNERS.

LET'S FACE IT: WHO HERE CAN SAY WHAT YOU REALLY BELIEVE? WHO HERE DOESN'T EDIT YOUR WORDS AND CLEANSE YOUR THOUGHTS TO MOLLIFY THE REACTIONARIES? WHOSE ZEAL AND FERVOR AND PASSION FOR GREATNESS ISN'T STRAITJACKETED BY BUREAUCRACY? IT SCARES ME TO DEATH, AND SHOULD SCARE YOU TOO, THAT THE TYRANNY OF POLITICAL CORRECTNESS NOW RULES THE HALLS OF GOVERNANCE.

YOU ARE THE BEST, THE BRIGHTEST, THE ONES CHOSEN TO LEAD YOUR PEOPLE. BUT IF YOU SUBMIT TO THE CHOKEHOLD OF POLITICAL CORRECTNESS, YOU AND YOUR COUNTERPARTS IN STATE HOUSES ACROSS THE LAND WILL BE THE MOST SOCIALLY CONFORMED AND

POLITICALLY SILENCED LEGISLATORS SINCE CONCORD BRIDGE. AND THAT'S COWARDICE.

SO I WISH FOR YOU FEARLESSNESS...TO REPLACE SHOWMANSHIP WITH LEADERSHIP...TO REPLACE CORRECTNESS WITH COURAGE.

EARLIER I INVOKED THE NAME OF DR. KING. I WANT TO CLOSE BY INVOKING HIS PRAYER, FROM A FREEDOM RALLY SPEECH IN 1957:

> O GOD, GIVE US LEADERS...
> LEADERS WHOM THE LUST OF OFFICE CANNOT KILL;
> LEADERS WHOM THE SPOILS OF LIFE CANNOT BUY;
> LEADERS WHO POSSESS OPINIONS AND WILL;
> LEADERS WHO WILL NOT LIE;
> LEADERS WHO CAN STAND BEFORE A DEMAGOGUE AND DAMN HIS TREACHEROUS FLATTERIES WITHOUT WINKING.
> TALL LEADERS, SUN-CROWNED, WHO LIVE ABOVE THE FOG IN PUBLIC DUTY AND IN PRIVATE THINKING.
> AMEN, AND THANK YOU.

NOW, LET'S ALL GET TO WORK.

REMARKS AT BRANDEIS UNIVERSITY

March 28, 2000 Waltham, MA

"Free Thought and Freedom"

THANK YOU FOR THE TENACITY YOU'VE SHOWN IN HAVING ME HERE. I KNOW THE UNIVERSITY GAVE YOU THE FINANCIAL AND LOGISTICAL BURDEN OF MY VISIT HERE, AND I APPRECIATE WHAT YOU'VE DONE AGAINST THOSE HEAVY ODDS. SO FOR ME, PLEASE GIVE YOURSELVES A BIG ROUND OF APPLAUSE.

I REMEMBER MY SON, WHEN HE WAS FIVE, EXPLAINING TO HIS KINDER-GARTEN CLASS WHAT HIS FATHER DID FOR A LIVING. "MY DADDY," HE

SAID, "PRETENDS TO BE PEOPLE." FORTUNATELY THERE'VE BEEN QUITE
A FEW OF THEM. THERE WERE PROPHETS FROM THE OLD AND NEW
TESTAMENTS, A COUPLE OF CHRISTIAN SAINTS, GENERALS OF
VARIOUS NATIONALITIES AND DIFFERENT CENTURIES, SEVERAL KINGS,
THREE AMERICAN PRESIDENTS, A FRENCH CARDINAL AND A COUPLE
OF GENIUSES, INCLUDING MICHELANGELO.

IT'S BEEN MY GOOD FORTUNE TO EXPLORE SEVERAL GREAT MEN WHO
HAVE MADE A DIFFERENCE…RISEN ABOVE THE ORDINARY TO CHANGE
THE COURSE OF HUMAN EVENTS. SO AS I PONDERED OUR VISIT
TONIGHT IT STRUCK ME: IF MY CREATOR GAVE ME THE GIFT TO
CONNECT YOU WITH THE HEARTS AND MINDS OF THESE GREAT MEN,
THEN I SHOULD USE THAT SAME GIFT TO RECONNECT YOU WITH
SOMETHING EVEN MORE IMPORTANT: YOUR OWN SENSE OF INDIVID-
UAL PURPOSE.

WHEN HE DEDICATED THE MEMORIAL AT GETTYSBURG, ABRAHAM
LINCOLN SAID THIS ABOUT THOSE TROUBLED TIMES: "WE ARE
NOW ENGAGED IN A GREAT CIVIL WAR, TESTING WHETHER THIS
NATION OR ANY NATION SO CONCEIVED AND SO DEDICATED CAN
LONG ENDURE." IN MANY WAYS, THOSE WORDS RING TRUE AGAIN. I
BELIEVE THAT TODAY, RIGHT HERE AND NOW, WE ARE AGAIN
ENGAGED IN A GREAT CIVIL WAR. AND THIS CAMPUS IS ONE OF MANY
BATTLEGROUNDS.

THE WAR I'M REFERRING TO IS CULTURAL RATHER THAN MILITARY,
BUT THERE'S SOMETHING VERY VITAL AT STAKE. TODAY THE BATTLE
IS FOR YOUR HEARTS AND MINDS, FOR THE FREEDOM TO THINK THE
WAY YOU CHOOSE TO THINK, TO FOLLOW THAT MORAL COMPASS
THAT POINTS TO WHAT'S RIGHT.

LET ME OFFER AN EXAMPLE. A COUPLE OF YEARS AGO I WAS SWORN
IN AS PRESIDENT OF THE NATIONAL RIFLE ASSOCIATION. I BELIEVE
STRONGLY IN THE BILL OF RIGHTS AND ITS SECOND AMENDMENT
PROVISION TO KEEP AND BEAR ARMS AS ONE OF THOSE RIGHTS. I FELT
I COULD MAKE A DIFFERENCE – THAT IT WAS THE RIGHT THING TO
DO. AND THAT'S WHEN THE BOMBSHELLS OF THE CULTURAL WAR
BEGAN TO BLOW UP ALL AROUND ME. TO SOME, I WENT STRAIGHT
FROM MOSES TO THE DEVIL. TO SOME, I FELL FROM CELLULOID SAINT
TO CULTURAL SINNER, BECAUSE I FELT OBLIGATED TO DEFEND AN
INDIVIDUAL FREEDOM OUR CONSTITUTION PROTECTS.

AT FIRST I THOUGHT THE ISSUE WAS JUST ABOUT GUNS. SHOULD LAW-ABIDING CITIZENS BE ABLE TO OWN THEM, AS THE FOUNDING FATHERS MANDATED, OR SHOULD A BIG BROTHER GOVERNMENT BE ALLOWED TO DISMANTLE THE BILL OF RIGHTS? SEEMS SIMPLE ENOUGH, RIGHT?

WELL, SINCE THEN I'VE LEARNED THAT THE GUN DEBATE IS A LOT MORE COMPLICATED. WHAT I CONFRONTED WHEN I BECAME PRESIDENT OF THE NRA WAS AN OVERWHELMING ORWELLIAN TYRANNY SWEEPING THIS COUNTRY, A FANATIC FERVOR OF POLITICALLY CORRECT THOUGHT AND LANGUAGE.

ZEALOTRY IS NOT A PRETTY SIGHT. IT'S UGLY IN THE STREETS OF TEL AVIV, WHERE MISGUIDED YOUNG MEN STRAP BOMBS TO THEIR BODIES AND SHATTER NOT ONLY MORTAR AND STEEL, BUT ALSO THE LIVES OF THE INNOCENT. WE USED TO THINK WE WERE ABOVE ALL THAT. THEN A FEDERAL BUILDING IN OKLAHOMA CITY EXPLODED, AND WE REALIZED THAT THE VERY SAME UGLINESS CAN SMOLDER AMONG US.

MORE AND MORE WE ARE FUELED BY ANGER, A FURY FED BY THOSE WHO PROFIT FROM IT. DEMOCRATS HATE REPUBLICANS. GAYS HATE STRAIGHTS. WOMEN HATE MEN. LIBERALS HATE CONSERVATIVES. VEGETARIANS HATE MEAT EATERS. GUN BANNERS HATE GUN OWNERS.

POLITICIANS, THE MEDIA, EVEN THE ENTERTAINMENT INDUSTRY IS KEENLY AWARE THAT HEATED CONTROVERSY WINS VOTES, SNARES RATINGS AND KEEPS THE BOX OFFICE HUMMING. THEY ARE EXPERTS AT DANGLING THE BAIT, AND AMERICANS ARE EAGER TO RISE TO IT. OUR CULTURE HAS REPLACED THE BLOODY ARENA FIGHTS OF ANCIENT ROME WITH STAGE FIGHTS ON TV WITH SALLY, RICKI, JERRY, JENNY AND ROSIE. FEAR OF IDEAS CREATES MORE DIVISIONS. AS A RESULT, WE ARE BECOMING INCREASINGLY FRAGMENTED AS A PEOPLE. OUR ONE NATION, UNDER GOD, WITH LIBERTY AND JUSTICE FOR ALL NOW SEEMS MORE LIKE THE FRACTURED STREETS OF BEIRUT, ECHOING WITH ANGER.

BACK IN THE MIDST OF ANOTHER TROUBLED ERA, AS A YOUNG ACTOR, I DID SOMETHING THAT WAS DEFINITELY NOT FASHIONABLE IN HOLLYWOOD. I MARCHED WITH DR. MARTIN LUTHER KING IN 1963 LONG BEFORE IT BECAME FASHIONABLE IN THAT STRANGE CITY. IT COULD HAVE COST ME MY CAREER.

THAT WAS A TIME WHEN A BLACK AMERICAN COULDN'T EVEN GET A JOB AS A UNION STAGE HAND. THOSE OF US IN THE CIVIL RIGHTS MOVEMENT BATTLED THE STUDIOS OVER THIS BLATANT DISCRIMINATION, AND WE WON. NOW BLACK ACTORS AND DIRECTORS ARE AMONG THE BEST IN OUR BUSINESS. I'M PROUD THAT SOME OF US HELPED OPEN THOSE DOORS. TWO YEARS LATER, AS PRESIDENT OF THE SCREEN ACTORS GUILD, I WALKED BEHIND DR. KING, LEADING THE ARTS CONTINGENT IN HIS MARCH ON WASHINGTON. THAT WAS A PROUD DAY.

NOW, FAST FORWARD 35 YEARS. I RECENTLY TOLD AN AUDIENCE THAT I FELT THAT WHITE PRIDE IS JUST AS VALID AS BLACK PRIDE OR RED PRIDE OR WHATEVER COLOR PRIDE YOU PREFER. FOR THOSE WORDS, I WAS CALLED A RACIST.

I'VE WORKED WITH BRILLIANTLY TALENTED HOMOSEXUALS ALL MY LIFE. BUT WHEN I TOLD ANOTHER AUDIENCE THAT GAY RIGHTS SHOULD BE GIVEN NO GREATER CONSIDERATION THAN YOUR RIGHTS OR MY RIGHTS, I WAS CALLED A HOMOPHOBE.

I SERVED IN WORLD WAR II, AND IF YOU SAW *SAVING PRIVATE RYAN*, YOU HAVE SOME INSIGHT INTO WHAT A SAVAGE CONFLICT THAT WAS. BUT WHEN I TOLD AN AUDIENCE THAT I THOUGHT LAW-ABIDING GUN OWNERS WERE BEING SINGLED OUT FOR CULTURAL STEREOTYPING MUCH LIKE JEWS WERE UNDER THE AXIS POWERS, I WAS BRANDED AN ANTI-SEMITE.

I LOVE THIS COUNTRY WITH ALL MY HEART. BUT WHEN I CHALLENGED AN AUDIENCE TO RESIST CULTURAL PERSECUTION, I WAS COMPARED TO TIMOTHY MCVEIGH!

AFTER A COUPLE OF YEARS WITH THE CULTURALLY CORRECT CROSSHAIRS TRAINED ON MY CHEST, I MUST ADMIT IT WAS A WHOLE LOT EASIER BEING MOSES. BUT I CAN SAY THIS: GET INVOLVED WITH A POLITICALLY UNPOPULAR CAUSE AND YOU'LL QUICKLY FIND OUT WHO YOUR FRIENDS ARE. I'VE BEEN BLASTED FROM TIME MAGAZINE TO THE WASHINGTON POST TO THE TODAY SHOW TO THE GUY DOWN THE STREET. THEY SAY, "THAT'S ENOUGH, CHUCK. IT MAY BE YOUR OPINION, BUT IT'S NOT LANGUAGE AUTHORIZED FOR PUBLIC CONSUMPTION."

WELL, IF WE'D BEEN ENAMORED WITH POLITICAL CORRECTNESS, WE'D STILL BE KING GEORGE'S BOYS.

1776 WASN'T ALL THAT LONG AGO, AND WE'VE GOT PLENTY OF GOOD GENES LEFT TO FIRE OUR PASSION FOR FREEDOM.

IN HIS BOOK, *THE END OF SANITY*, MARTIN GROSS WRITES THAT "BLATANTLY IRRATIONAL BEHAVIOR IS RAPIDLY BEING ESTABLISHED AS THE NORM IN ALMOST EVERY AREA OF HUMAN ENDEAVOR. THERE SEEM TO BE NEW CUSTOMS, NEW RULES, NEW ANTI-INTELLECTUAL THEORIES REGULARLY FOISTED ON US FROM EVERY DIRECTION..."

"UNDERNEATH, THE NATION IS ROILING. AMERICANS KNOW SOME-THING WITHOUT A NAME IS UNDERMINING THE NATION, TURNING THE MIND MUSHY WHEN IT COMES TO SEPARATING TRUTH FROM FALSEHOOD AND RIGHT FROM WRONG...AND THEY DON'T LIKE IT."

LET'S STROLL AROUND YOUR OWN CAMPUS JUST FOR A MINUTE AND SEE IF WE CAN FIND A FEW EXAMPLES. ONE THAT COMES TO MIND IS FREEDOM MAGAZINE. LAST YEAR, I'M TOLD, FUNDING FOR THIS CON-SERVATIVE CAMPUS PUBLICATION WAS CUT OUT ENTIRELY BECAUSE MEMBERS OF THE STUDENT SENATE DIDN'T CARE FOR ITS MESSAGE. DIDN'T CARE FOR ITS MESSAGE?

NOW, I DON'T KNOW IF THE PHILOSOPHY EXPRESSED ON THOSE PAGES WAS RIGHT OR WRONG. BUT IT DESERVES TO BE HEARD, DON'T YOU THINK? ISN'T THAT WHAT COLLEGE IS ALL ABOUT? EXAMINING A DIVERSITY OF IDEAS BEFORE YOU DRAW CONCLUSIONS?

I'VE ALSO BEEN TOLD THAT HERE ON CAMPUS, THERE'S A PUSH FOR MORE AFFIRMATIVE ACTION IN THE ADMISSIONS PROCESS. WELL, I'M FOR AFFIRMATIVE ACTION. I BELIEVE IT STARTS IN GRAMMAR SCHOOL, SURVIVES THE GROWING PAINS OF HIGH SCHOOL, AND REACHES FRUITION DURING COLLEGE ENTRANCE EXAMS.

AND I ALSO BELIEVE IT SHOULD BE COLOR-BLIND. I'VE FOUGHT AGAINST RACISM ALL MY LIFE. SO WHY WOULD I TOLERATE RACISM IN REVERSE? SKIN-COLOR LITMUS TESTS HEARKEN BACK TO CARPET-BAGGERS AND RECONSTRUCTION. I BELIEVE IN LEVEL PLAYING FIELDS AND THE EQUALITY THAT COMES WITH ACCOMPLISHMENT. ONE STANDARD FOR ALL, NO MORE AND NO LESS.

BUT WE HAVE TO BE CAREFUL HERE, BECAUSE TELLING US WHAT TO THINK HAS EVOLVED INTO TELLING US WHAT TO SAY. SO TELLING US WHAT TO DO CAN'T BE VERY FAR AWAY.

I ARGUE PASSIONATELY FOR THE FREEDOM TO KEEP AN OPEN MIND, BECAUSE IN AUDIENCES LIKE THIS ONE I SENSE AND SEE AMERICA'S

BEST AND BRIGHTEST. BRANDEIS REMAINS A FERTILE CRADLE OF AMERICAN ACADEMIA, AND EACH OF YOU ARE THE BEST HOPE WE HAVE FOR A PRODUCTIVE, LIVABLE, SPIRITUAL FUTURE.

BUT I SUBMIT THAT YOU, AND YOUR COUNTERPARTS IN COLLEGES FROM COAST TO COAST, ALSO APPEAR TO BE THE MOST SOCIALLY CONFORMED AND POLITICALLY SILENCED GENERATION SINCE CONCORD BRIDGE. AND AS LONG AS YOU SHRUG YOUR SHOULDERS AND ABIDE IT, THEN BY THE STANDARDS OF YOUR GRANDFATHERS, YOU ARE CULTURAL COWARDS.

IF YOU TALK ABOUT RACE, IT DOESN'T MAKE YOU A RACIST. IF YOU SEE DISTINCTIONS BETWEEN THE GENDERS, IT DOESN'T MAKE YOU A SEXIST. IF YOU THINK CRITICALLY ABOUT A GIVEN DENOMINATION, IT DOESN'T MAKE YOU ANTI-RELIGION. IF YOU ACCEPT HOMOSEXUALITY BUT DON'T CELEBRATE IT, IT DOESN'T MAKE YOU A HOMOPHOBE.

A FREE PEOPLE CAN USE A NEW REVOLUTION EVERY DAY, AND I CHALLENGE YOU TO RESIST THE DOGMA OF CULTURAL AND SOCIAL STEREOTYPING. DON'T LET AMERICA'S UNIVERSITIES SERVE AS INCUBATORS FOR A RAMPANT EPIDEMIC OF THIS NEW BRAND OF MCCARTHYISM. STAND UP, SPEAK OUT, FOLLOW YOUR HEART, EVEN IF IT GOES AGAINST THE CONVENTIONAL GRAIN. TAKE HEART IN THE FACT THAT OTHERS HAVE WALKED THAT SAME PATH. JESUS. JOAN OF ARC. GANDHI. JEFFERSON. LINCOLN. MARTIN LUTHER KING. SUSAN B. ANTHONY.

I THINK THE GERM OF DISOBEDIENCE IS IN OUR DNA. WHO HERE DOESN'T FEEL A CERTAIN KINSHIP WITH THE REBELLIOUS SPIRIT THAT TOSSED THAT TEA INTO BOSTON HARBOR? IT'S THE SAME SPIRIT THAT SENT THOREAU TO JAIL, THAT REFUSED TO SIT IN THE BACK OF THE BUS, THAT FILLED OUR STREETS WITH VIETNAM WAR PROTESTORS. BUT LET ME WARN YOU – IT AIN'T EASY. DR. KING STOOD ON A LOT OF BALCONIES. THE POLICE DOGS IN MONTGOMERY WERE VICIOUS. THE WATER CANNONS IN SELMA WERE PAINFUL. MODERN VERSIONS OF THE SAME WEAPONS OF OPPRESSION EXIST TODAY.

JUST A FEW WEEKS AGO MY GOOD FRIEND WAYNE LAPIERRE, HEAD OF THE NATIONAL RIFLE ASSOCIATION, SPOKE CANDIDLY ON NATIONAL TELEVISION ABOUT THE PRESIDENT'S GUN POLICIES. IN RETURN, HE WAS PERSONALLY AND PROFESSIONALLY CRUCIFIED FOR DARING TO SPEAK HIS MIND.

DURING THE PAST EIGHT YEARS, PRESIDENT CLINTON HAS FOUGHT HARD FOR EVERY KIND OF FIREARM RESTRICTION IMAGINABLE. YET AT THE SAME TIME HE HAS, AS A MATTER OF POLICY, REFUSED TO VIGOROUSLY ENFORCE FEDERAL GUN LAWS ALREADY ON THE BOOKS.

WAYNE SAID THAT PROSECUTING FELONS WITH FIREARMS IS THE ONLY PROVEN POLICY THAT HAS CUT GUN MURDERS – BY HALF! HE WATCHED IT WORK IN RICHMOND, VIRGINIA, UNDER A PROGRAM CALLED PROJECT EXILE. EVERY FELON CAUGHT WITH A FIREARM THERE SERVES A MANDATORY FIVE YEARS IN PRISON. NO PLEA BARGAIN, NO DEAL. BELIEVE ME, NOT MANY FELONS CARRY FIREARMS IN RICHMOND ANY MORE.

THE NRA HELPED FUND THAT PROJECT WHEN THE CLINTON ADMINISTRATION WOULDN'T. SO I THINK WAYNE LAPIERRE SPOKE THE SIMPLE TRUTH WHEN HE SAID THE PRESIDENT SEEMED WILLING TO ACCEPT A CERTAIN AMOUNT OF FIREARM-RELATED VIOLENCE, BECAUSE ENFORCEMENT INTERFERED WITH HIS PERSONAL ANTI-GUN AGENDA. THE WORDS WERE NO MORE OUT OF WAYNE'S MOUTH WHEN THE MEDIA ERUPTED. FOR TWO SOLID WEEKS HE WAS DEMONIZED, SCORNED, VILIFIED.

BUT DURING THOSE SAME TWO WEEKS, THE MEDIA WAS FAR MORE INTERESTED IN REPORTING WHAT WAYNE SAID THAN INVESTIGATING WHAT CLINTON DID, OR FAILED TO DO. IN FACT, THE PRESIDENT HAS BEEN MISERABLY LAX IN ENFORCING FEDERAL GUN LAWS. BUT IT WAS EASIER TO CONDEMN A GOOD MAN FOR MAKING A POLITICALLY INCORRECT STATEMENT THAN IT WAS TO DIG OUT THE FACTS AND EXONERATE A VICTIM OF CULTURAL WARFARE.

TO ME, POLITICAL CORRECTNESS IS JUST TYRANNY WITH MANNERS. THE SPECTACLE OF WAYNE LAPIERRE'S MEDIA CRUCIFIXION APPALLED ME. YET AT THE SAME TIME IT STIFFENED MY DETERMINATION TO SPEAK OUT EVEN LOUDER, WITH ALL THE BREATH I HAVE, ABOUT THIS CULTURAL CANCER THAT IS EATING AWAY AT OUR SOCIETY.

SO IN CLOSING, LET ME CHALLENGE THOSE GOOD YOUNG MINDS OF YOURS. DARE TO CONSIDER BOTH SIDES OF ANY ISSUE. AND FIND THE COURAGE TO QUESTION AUTHORITY.

DON'T ALWAYS BELIEVE EVERYTHING YOU HEAR FROM A BILL CLINTON, OR A DAN RATHER, A GEORGE W. BUSH OR AN AL GORE. DIG DEEPER THAN THE HEADLINES OR THE STUMP SPEECHES OR THE

TELEVISION NEWS. DON'T TRUST ANY OF US – NOT A MICHAEL JORDAN, OR A DENNIS MILLER, NOT EVEN CHARLTON HESTON. BECAUSE WE ALL HAVE OUR PREJUDICES, AND IT'S YOUR JOB TO SORT THROUGH ALL THE RHETORIC, WEIGH AND MEASURE EACH WORD, AND DECIDE ON YOUR OWN.

AND THEN, JUST AS I FELT COMPELLED TO STAND WITH DR. KING, YOU'LL FIND YOURSELF COMPELLED TO ACT, TOO. WHEN A FATHER-LESS KID IN A CRACKHOUSE FINDS A STOLEN GUN AND SHOOTS A SCHOOLMATE, STAND UP AND SAY GIVING DRUG DEALERS TRIGGER-LOCKS ISN'T A SOLUTION.

WHEN A MUGGER SUES HIS ELDERLY VICTIM FOR DEFENDING HERSELF, JAM THE SWITCHBOARD AT THE DISTRICT ATTORNEY'S OFFICE AND RAISE THE ROOF WITH YOUR OUTRAGE.

OR WHEN YOUR UNIVERSITY IS PRESSURED TO LOWER STANDARDS UNTIL 80% OF THE STUDENTS GRADUATE WITH HONORS, CHOKE THE HALLS OF THE BOARD OF REGENTS IN A UNIFIED SHOW OF DISGRUNTLED FORCE.

WHEN AN EIGHT-YEAR-OLD BOY PECKS A GIRL'S CHEEK ON A PLAY-GROUND AND GETS HAULED INTO COURT FOR SEXUAL HARASSMENT, DESCEND ON THAT SCHOOL LIKE AVENGING ANGELS…UNTIL SOME-ONE IN CHARGE EXERCISES COMMON SENSE.

AND WHEN SOMEONE YOU'VE ELECTED IS SEDUCED BY THE POWER OF THE OFFICE AND BETRAYS YOU, MUSTER THE COLLECTIVE WILL TO BANISH THEM FROM PUBLIC LIFE.

BECAUSE UNLESS YOU DO THESE THINGS, FREEDOM AS WE HAVE KNOWN IT CANNOT ENDURE.

SO I CHALLENGE YOU TO TAKE UP THE TORCH THAT FREED EXILES, FOUNDED RELIGIONS, DEFEATED TYRANTS AND PROVOKED AN ARMED AND ROUSED RABBLE TO BREAK OUT OF BONDAGE AND BUILD THIS COUNTRY.

THERE IS STILL SOME OF THEM IN ALL OF US. SO DON'T GIVE UP JUST YET. WE'RE NOT QUITE FINISHED WITH THEIR REVOLUTION.

THANK YOU.

REMARKS BEFORE THE BRITISH COLUMBIA WILDLIFE FEDERATION

March 11, 2000 Prince George, British Columbia, Canada

LET ME BEGIN BY SAYING THAT I'M A LITTLE ENVIOUS OF YOU AND YOUR FEDERATION OF HUNTERS, FISHERMEN AND CONSERVATIONISTS. SURELY IF YOUR CANADIAN HEARTS PUMP REAL RED BLOOD, THEN THIS BEAUTIFUL PROVINCE OF YOURS, THIS BRITISH COLUMBIA, MUST SEEM AN EDEN.

IF I WERE A YOUNGER MAN, THIS SPLENDID REMINDER OF A WILDER, MORE REGAL NORTH AMERICA WOULD CERTAINLY TEMPT ME WITH ITS NATURAL BOUNTY. AS THE PRESSURES OF DAILY LIFE WEIGH DOWN UPON US, MORE AND MORE AMERICANS LONG FOR THE SOLACE OF JUST SUCH A LAST GREAT PLACE.

WE, TOO, HAVE LOOKED TO THE WEST AND FOUND RENEWAL ALONG OUR UNTRAMMELED COASTS, AND IN THE CLOUD-PIERCING MAJESTY OF OUR NORTHWESTERN ROCKIES. WE MAKE PILGRIMAGE THERE FOR THE GIFT OF GOOD LAND THAT CAN HEAL A SICK SPIRIT AND LIFT A HEAVY HEART. AND YOU, MY BRITISH COLUMBIA FRIENDS, HAVE BEEN BLESSED WITH THE GIFT OF A VERY GOOD LAND INDEED.

I KNOW ALL ABOUT BEING BLESSED, BECAUSE I'VE PLAYED SEVERAL SAINTS, PRESIDENTS, KINGS AND GENIUSES, AND PARTED THE RED SEA IN ONE PICTURE. EVEN TODAY, THE PRESIDENT OF THE UNITED STATES REFERS TO ME AS MOSES. BUT NOT WITH MUCH REVERENCE, I'M AFRAID.

OUR PRESIDENT AND I TEND TO DISAGREE QUITE OPENLY ABOUT A CONSTITUTIONALLY PROTECTED RIGHT I CHERISH AND HE DETESTS – THE RIGHT TO KEEP AND BEAR ARMS. WHEN I BECAME PRESIDENT OF THE NATIONAL RIFLE ASSOCIATION, I FELL OUT OF POLITICAL FAVOR WITH HIM. BUT THEN, IT WASN'T REALLY MUCH OF A FALL, ALL THINGS CONSIDERED. OUR ADMINISTRATION HAD ALREADY HIT BOTTOM.

GUN RIGHTS ARE AT THE CENTER OF A GREAT POLITICAL DEBATE IN AMERICA RIGHT NOW, JUST AS THEY ARE IN CANADA. WHEN I ENTERED THE FRAY, I WENT FROM CELLULOID SAINT TO CULTURAL SINNER. I GET PICKETED AT COLLEGE SPEAKING ENGAGEMENTS AND,

ACCORDING TO THE NRA'S POLITICAL ENEMIES, I'M SOME SORT OF GREAT SATAN. THAT'S THE KIND OF HEATED EMOTION THE DEBATE OVER GUN OWNERSHIP CAN BRING ABOUT. BUT AS I TELL MY COLLEAGUES, THE GUN ITSELF IS JUST A SYMBOL. IT'S INDIVIDUAL FREEDOM WE'RE FIGHTING FOR. A THOUSAND YEARS AGO YOU COULD HAVE SUBSTITUTED A SWORD OR A LONG BOW AND HAD THE VERY SAME ARGUMENT.

I'M SURE THAT FOR THE MEMBERS OF THE BRITISH COLUMBIA WILDLIFE FEDERATION, FIREARMS ARE BOTH TOOL AND SYMBOL. IT WAS THE SAME FOR ME, GROWING UP IN AMERICA'S NORTH WOODS. THAT'S WHY I CAN SPEAK OF THESE THINGS FROM EXPERIENCE, NOT JUST A SCRIPT. YOU AND I HAVE A LOT IN COMMON.

TODAY I MAKE MY HOME IN SOUTHERN CALIFORNIA. BUT THE NORTHERN MICHIGAN OF MY BOYHOOD IS STILL IN MY BLOOD. THE DARK WOODS, THE SMELL OF A CAMPFIRE, THE BARK OF A RIFLE, THE BAYING OF HOUNDS, THE WAY A TROUT RISES TO A DRY FLY. IT'S BEEN A NUMBER OF YEARS SINCE THAT WAS MY LIFE. BUT BEING HERE WITH YOU TODAY REMINDS ME OF THE GOOD TIMES, THE TREASURED TIMES. TIME SPENT AFIELD WITH A DOG, A GUN AND THE UNFETTERED FREEDOM TO BE PART OF GOD'S GREEN EARTH.

I MAY NOT DO THAT MUCH ANYMORE, BUT I STILL CHERISH IT. IT IS A PART OF MY HERITAGE, PART OF A GRAND AND WONDERFUL TRADITION. THE RIGHT – MAYBE A BETTER WORD WOULD BE THE NEED – TO HUNT, FISH AND BE OUTDOORS IS STILL FIERCELY DEFENDED IN THE WOODLANDS OF MY YOUTH, JUST AS IT IS HERE IN CANADA.

AS WELL IT SHOULD BE. BECAUSE I BELIEVE THAT FREEDOM IS A NORTH AMERICAN LEGACY. AFTER ALL, YOU AND WE REMAIN BASICALLY THE SAME PEOPLE SHARING A COMMON HISTORY, SEPARATED ONLY BY A MOSTLY IMAGINARY POLITICAL LINE THAT DOES VERY LITTLE TO DIVIDE OUR UNIQUELY LINKED HERITAGE AND SHARED BLOOD.

WE ARE NORTH AMERICANS BY BIRTH, ON EITHER SIDE OF THE LINE. THE REST IS JUST SURVEY STAKES AND POLITICS. OUR SHARED COASTS DON'T STOP AT THE BORDERLINE. THE ROCKY MOUNTAINS DON'T SUDDENLY DISAPPEAR WHERE SOMEONE ERECTED A BORDERLINE CHECKPOINT TO SCRUTINIZE CREDENTIALS OR SEARCH YOUR TRUNK FOR GUNS THAT CAME ABOARD DOWN IN THE STATES.

GEESE CROSS THE BORDER AT WILL. DEER MOVE BACK AND FORTH. SALMON RUSH INLAND FROM THE SAME OCEAN. THESE CREATURES THAT WE CHERISH AND WORK TO CONSERVE ARE NO RESPECTERS OF POLITICS. THEY PAY PRESIDENTS NO HEED, NOR PRIME MINISTERS.

BUT AT THE SAME TIME, POLITICS CAN CERTAINLY ERODE OUR COMMON HERITAGE AND TRADITIONS. IN AMERICA OUR MOST CHERISHED DOCUMENT, OUR CONSTITUTION'S BILL OF RIGHTS, HAS BEEN SINGLED OUT FOR SCORN BY THOSE WHO BELIEVE IT IS OUT OF DATE, OR SOMEHOW OUT OF SOCIAL ORDER. AMERICAN GUN HATERS WANT TO CULL CERTAIN FREEDOMS THEY VIEW WITH DISTASTE. HAD THEY HAD THEIR WAY, OUR RIGHT TO KEEP AND BEAR ARMS ALREADY WOULD HAVE SUFFERED A SAVAGE POLITICAL GUTTING. WERE IT NOT FOR THE CONVICTION OF AMERICA'S 80 MILLION GUN OWNERS AND THE GRITTY RESOLVE OF 3.5 MILLION NRA MEMBERS.

WE'VE FOUGHT IN LOCAL, STATE AND FEDERAL COURT, MUNICIPAL GOVERNMENTS, STATE LEGISLATURES, IN THE HALLS OF CONGRESS. WE'VE BATTLED IN PRINT AND IN THE MEDIA, GIVEN THE OPPORTUNITY. AND IF WE'RE NOT GIVEN THE OPPORTUNITY, WE JUST MAKE OUR OWN OPPORTUNITIES. SOMETIMES WE LOSE AN INCH AND GAIN A MILE. OTHER DAYS, IT'S VICE VERSA. BUT OVER THE LONG RUN WE'VE MANAGED TO BEAT BACK THE GUN HATERS AND RETAIN OUR RIGHT TO KEEP AND BEAR ARMS WITHOUT REGISTRATION AND WITHOUT CONFISCATION.

THAT'S NO EASY TASK. AS YOU'VE COME TO LEARN, RIGHT HERE IN CANADA. OUR COUNTRIES MIRROR EACH OTHER IN SO MANY WAYS. BUT NOW, WHILE WE STILL FIGHT TO PROTECT THIS MOST BASIC FREEDOM, YOUR GOVERNMENT FINDS IT CONVENIENT TO RUN ROUGHSHOD OVER YOUR GUN RIGHTS. C-68, I BELIEVE IT IS CALLED. MY FRIENDS, HOW DID THIS HAPPEN? I KNOW YOU FOUGHT BITTERLY, BUT IT WASN'T ENOUGH. IT WILL BE A SAD DAY ON JANUARY 1, 2003, WHEN EVERY GUN IN CANADA HAS TO BE REGISTERED WITH YOUR GOVERNMENT. WRITTEN OR UNWRITTEN, GUN OWNERSHIP IN A FREE NATION REMAINS AN INDIVIDUAL RIGHT. YOU MAY NOT BE ABSOLUTELY FREE WHEN YOU OWN A FIREARM. BUT I GUARANTEE YOU WILL NEVER BE FREE WHEN YOU CAN'T. THAT'S NOT WRITTEN, THAT'S GOD-GIVEN.

FIRST YOU GAVE IN ON HANDGUNS, THEN YOU COMPROMISED ON LONG GUNS. THEN CAME REGISTRATION. NEXT COMES CONFISCA-

TION. TRUST ME – THAT'S HISTORY'S PROVEN SEQUENCE OF EVENTS. AND THAT'S WHY, WITH EVERY PASSING DAY, MORE AND MORE CANADIANS NO LONGER TRUST THEIR GOVERNMENT. YOU KNOW YOUR REGISTRATION SCHEME IS UNWORKABLE, INEFFECTIVE AND OUTRAGEOUSLY EXPENSIVE. YOU KNOW YOU'LL SPEND SOME 700 MILLION DOLLARS ON THIS FARCE WHILE THE ROYAL CANADIAN MOUNTED POLICE BEGS FOR MONEY TO FIGHT ORGANIZED CRIME. THAT, MY FRIENDS AND NEIGHBORS, IS SACRILEGE.

IT'S ALWAYS THE SAME, NORTH OF THE BORDER OR SOUTH. LAW-ABIDING GUN OWNERS PAY THE PRICE FOR LAWBREAKERS WHO GO UNPUNISHED.

IN AMERICA, THE NRA HAS TOLD GUN OWNERS FOR YEARS WHAT WILL HAPPEN IF WE DROPPED OUR GUARD. NOW WE'VE GOT LIVING PROOF – WE JUST POINT IN YOUR DIRECTION. WE'VE SEEN WHAT TRANSPIRED IN ENGLAND, WHEN POLICE WENT DOWN THE REGISTRA-TION LIST AND CALLED IN ALL PRIVATELY OWNED GUNS. IT'S NOT A PRETTY SIGHT, IF FINE FIREARMS STIR FOND MEMORIES. BEAUTIFULLY CRAFTED SHOTGUNS, WORLD WAR I HEIRLOOMS, FAMILY KEEPSAKES. ALL WENT INTO THE PILE TO BE PULVERIZED LIKE RUBBISH AND HAULED AWAY AS SO MUCH SCRAP METAL.

IN AUSTRALIA, THE GUN BANS CAME AS A KNEE-JERK REACTION TO ONE ISOLATED TRAGEDY. BUT IN THE AFTERMATH, CRIME WITH GUNS WENT UP, NOT DOWN, AND THE BUREAUCRATS ARE DODGING HEATED QUES-TIONS FROM ANGRY CITIZENS. WHO WOULD HAVE THOUGHT THAT THESE NATIONS, ALLIES THAT FOUGHT SO HARD TO FREE THE PLANET FROM TYRANNY DURING WORLD WAR II, WOULD NOW DISAVOW THE MOST BASIC FREEDOMS WE SHED BLOOD TO PRESERVE?

I SERVED IN WORLD WAR II...I STILL HAVE MY MILITARY SIDEARM: A COLT .45. IT'S A FINE PIECE...WE SERVED TOGETHER TWO YEARS OVERSEAS. BUT UNDER YOUR NEW LAWS, THAT OLD PISTOL COULD WELL BE CONTRABAND. AND FOR OWNING IT, I COULD BE A CRIMINAL.

HERE IT COULD END UP ON A HANDGUN OWNER'S LIST, MAYBE CON-FISCATED AND DESTROYED. YOU KNOW, I DON'T THINK I COULD LET THAT HAPPEN. THAT GUN STANDS FOR SOMETHING. AND I WILL STAND FOR SOMETHING AS LONG AS I OWN IT. EVEN YOUR LAW ENFORCEMENT OFFICERS CALL THIS LATEST CANADIAN GUN SHAM A FINANCIAL, UNENFORCEABLE FRAUD. SO WHY IS YOUR GOVERNMENT DOING IT? BECAUSE THEY CAN.

EVEN WORSE, BECAUSE YOU LET THEM. LIKE MILLIONS OF AMERICANS ARE DOING NOW, YOU STOOD BY AND WATCHED WHILE ONE OF YOUR MOST BASIC FREEDOMS WAS CRUSHED UNDER THE BOOT HEEL OF AN INDIFFERENT BUREAUCRACY. NOW THAT IT'S DONE, YOU'RE ANGRY. AND YOU'RE LEARNING THAT GOVERNMENT LOVES TO MAKE LAWS, BUT LOATHES TO RESCIND THEM. FREEDOM SURRENDERED IS NEVER RESTORED.

AND IF YOU THINK THIS GUN GRAB WILL MAKE YOUR STREETS SAFER, GO TO YOUR PRISONS AND LISTEN TO WHAT THE CRIMINALS SAY. WE'VE GOT SOME OF THEM ON VIDEOTAPE. THEY'RE LAUGHING AT THIS LAW. ONE OF THEM PUT IT BLUNTLY. HE SAID, "CRIME WILL INCREASE. ALREADY HAS, IN FACT. WHAT DID YOU EXPECT?" HE LAUGHED. YOUR OFFICIALS CONDONE EARLY RELEASE OF VIOLENT CRIMINALS, YET WON'T BATTLE FOR TRUTH-IN-SENTENCING LAWS. SO YOU FILL YOUR STREETS WITH VIOLENT FELONS, AND TAKE GUNS AWAY FROM HONEST CITIZENS.

THAT'S AN ABSURD WAY TO SERVE JUSTICE, AND I HAVE STATISTICS TO PROVE IT. IN RICHMOND, VIRGINIA, WHEN LAWS AGAINST FELONS WITH FIREARMS WERE VIGOROUSLY ENFORCED, HOMICIDES FELL FROM 140 TO 34 IN A SINGLE YEAR. ARMED ROBBERIES DROPPED BY ONE THIRD. THE REASON WAS SIMPLE: ARMED CRIMINALS WERE ROUND-ED UP OFF THE STREET AND SENTENCED TO A MANDATORY FIVE YEARS IN PRISON. IF DRUGS WERE INVOLVED, ADD ON FIVE MORE YEARS. THAT'S THE KIND OF TOUGH JUSTICE BOTH OUR NATIONS NEED A LOT MORE OF. BUT IT TAKES COURAGEOUS LAWMAKERS AND LAW ENFORCERS TO DELIVER.

WHILE THUGS GO FREE AFTER SERVING ONLY A SIXTH OF THEIR SENTENCES, YOU'VE HAD HELICOPTERS AND SWAT TEAMS RAIDING LEGAL GUN DEALERSHIPS, ALL IN A HEADLINE-MAKING SHOW OF FORCE. CAN THIS BE THE CANADA OF OLD, CARVED OUT OF WILDER-NESS BY INDEPENDENT MEN AND WOMEN OF UNCOMMON VALOR?

AT THE NRA WE HAVE VIDEOTAPE OF WHAT HAPPENS TO CONFIS-CATED FIREARMS – FINE SHOTGUNS AND HUNTING RIFLES, SUCH AS MEMBERS OF THE BRITISH COLUMBIA WILDLIFE FEDERATION WOULD OWN AND MAY NEVER OWN AGAIN AFTER JANUARY 1, 2003. I WISH YOU COULD SEE HOW THE SPARKS FLY WHEN A GOVERNMENT SAW BLADE SLICES THROUGH THE BLUE STEEL OF A CUSTOM ENGRAVED DOUBLE GUN. OF COURSE YOU MAY LEARN ABOUT IT FIRSTHAND

WHEN YOUR SPORTING ARMS REGISTRATION LIST IS TURNED OVER TO THE LOCAL POLICE, AND A KNOCK AT THE DOOR TURNS INTO A MORAL AND ETHICAL NIGHTMARE.

SURE, YOU CAN HIDE THEM, BURY THEM, SIMPLY NOT COMPLY. BUT HOW ARE YOU GOING TO USE YOUR SPORTING ARMS, IF THEY'RE BURIED IN THE BARN? YOU MAY SALVAGE SOME OF YOUR PERSONAL PRIDE THAT WAY, BUT THE GOVERNMENT STILL WINS. THEY MAY NOT HAVE ACTUALLY TAKEN YOUR FIREARMS, BUT YOU CAN NO LONGER USE THEM.

BACK IN THE SIXTIES, AMERICAN GUN OWNERS WERE CAUGHT UNAWARE BY A DELUGE OF HARSH GUN LAWS THAT SURFACED IN THE MIDST OF A PERIOD OF CIVIL UNREST. FOR A HUNDRED YEARS UP UNTIL THAT TIME, THE NRA HAD BEEN MOSTLY A HUNTING, SHOOTING AND GUN SAFETY ORGANIZATION. BUT SUDDENLY, THINGS CHANGED. WE WERE FORCED TO ORGANIZE, LOBBY AND FIGHT. AND WE LEARNED TO WIN. IT TOOK A FEW YEARS, BUT WE WON BACK SOME OF WHAT WE'D LOST. SO LET ME CHALLENGE YOU TO DO THE SAME.

ORGANIZE, LEARN TO LOBBY AND FIGHT THE GOOD FIGHT. YOU CAN RECLAIM YOUR GOD-GIVEN RIGHTS, YOU CAN OVERCOME A CALLOUS, SELF-SERVING GOVERNMENT, YOU CAN PREVAIL IN BEHALF OF MILLIONS OF AVERAGE CITIZENS WHO HAVE DONE NOTHING WRONG EXCEPT EXPRESS THE DESIRE TO OWN A GUN FOR SPORT OR SELF-PROTECTION.

LET ME TELL YOU A STORY. NOT LONG AGO, PRESIDENT CLINTON SLAMMED THE DOOR SHUT ON AMERICAN FIREARM EXPORTS TO CANADA. THE CLINTON ADMINISTRATION HAD NOTICED A PRETTY LARGE INCREASE IN THIS YEAR'S REQUEST FOR IMPORT PERMITS. SOMETHING ILLEGAL MUST BE GOING ON UNDER THE TABLE. SOUNDED LIKE A LITTLE GUNRUNNING GOING ON NORTH OF THE BORDER. THAT WAS THE BIG NEWS HEADLINE.

BUT AFTER SOME DETECTIVE WORK, THE NRA DISCOVERED THAT YOUR LAW ENFORCEMENT COMMUNITY WAS PREPARING TO ORDER NEW GUNS FOR ITS OFFICERS. SO THE AGENCIES HAD TO MAKE APPLI-CATION FOR SEVERAL THOUSAND GUNS FROM SEVERAL DIFFERENT MANUFACTURERS, EVEN THOUGH ONLY ONE MANUFACTURER WOULD FILL THE FINAL ORDER. THAT PART WAS NOT REPORTED. BUT THAT'S HOW GOVERNMENT USES MEDIA TO TURN AN INNOCENT BUSINESS TRANSACTION INTO AN ANTI-GUN INTERNATIONAL INCIDENT. IF YOU LET THEM.

I THINK C-68 WAS YOUR GOVERNMENT'S CHOICE, NOT THE WILL OF THE PEOPLE. IN AMERICA WE'RE FIGHTING THE SAME RASH OF ANTI-GUN MADNESS THAT'S SWEEPING THROUGH YOUR COUNTRY. I THINK WE CAN HOLD OUR GROUND. AND MAYBE, JUST MAYBE, WE CAN HELP YOU GET SOME OF YOURS BACK IN THE PROCESS. AFTER ALL, WE'RE NOT THAT MUCH DIFFERENT, YOU AND I. WE CAN WATCH, AND SUPPORT, AND LEARN FROM EACH OTHER. WE SHARE A BORDER THAT'S MORE MYTH THAN FACT. AND WE SHARE A HERITAGE OF HUNTING, SHOOTING AND SELF-DEFENSE THAT DESERVES TO BE HONORED.

SO LET'S TEAR DOWN THE BARRIERS THAT ROB US OF OUR RIGHTS. TOGETHER IN SPIRIT WE CAN REMAIN TWO NATIONS CONCEIVED IN LIBERTY AND JUSTICE FOR ALL. I BORROWED THOSE WORDS FROM OUR DECLARATION OF INDEPENDENCE. BUT I THINK THEY FIT BRITISH COLUMBIA EQUALLY WELL.

THAT INVISIBLE BORDER DOESN'T MAKE YOU ONE MOLECULE LESS WORTHY OF LIBERTY THAN AN AMERICAN CITIZEN. WE'RE OF THE SAME STURDY PIONEER STOCK, CUT FROM THE SAME FRONTIER CLOTH. FREEDOM IS A NORTH AMERICAN LEGACY, AND OUR GOVERNMENTS HAD BETTER NEVER FORGET IT.

AND IF THEY DO, THANK GOD THERE WILL BE A BRITISH COLUMBIA WILDLIFE FEDERATION AND AN NRA AROUND TO GIVE THEM A NOT-SO-SUBTLE REMINDER.

THANK YOU.

REMARKS BEFORE THE 129TH ANNUAL MEETING OF MEMBERS OF THE NATIONAL RIFLE ASSOCIATION

May 20, 2000 Charlotte, NC

IT LOOKS LIKE I'M BACK FOR ONE MORE ENCORE. I'VE BEEN ASKED TO SERVE A THIRD TERM AS YOUR PRESIDENT. I DON'T THINK ANYONE'S DONE THAT BEFORE. BUT GEORGE WASHINGTON HUNG AROUND

UNTIL THE REVOLUTIONARY WAR WAS WON. ROOSEVELT HUNG AROUND UNTIL WORLD WAR II WAS WON. REAGAN HUNG AROUND UNTIL THE COLD WAR WAS WON. IF YOU WANT, I'LL HANG AROUND UNTIL WE WIN THIS ONE, TOO.

DO YOU FEEL THAT INCREDIBLE ENERGY IN THE AIR HERE TODAY? I'LL TELL YOU WHAT IT IS. IT'S THE FEELING YOU GET WHEN YOU'RE MAKING A DIFFERENCE IN THE FUTURE OF YOUR COUNTRY.

THAT WAS MY GOAL – TO MAKE A DIFFERENCE – WHEN I BECAME YOUR PRESIDENT TWO YEARS GO. SO I SET SOME LOFTY GOALS. I SAID I'D DO MY PART IF YOU'D DO YOURS. NOW, JUST TWO YEARS LATER, WE'VE ACCOMPLISHED THEM ALL. ALL EXCEPT ONE.

FIRST, I ASKED YOU TO REBUILD OUR NRA MEMBERSHIP, AND YOU HAVE. NOT BY JUST A FEW THOUSAND MEMBERS, BUT BY ONE MILLION MEMBERS.

SECOND, I ASKED YOU TO REBUILD OUR NRA WAR CHEST, AND YOU HAVE. I DON'T MEAN JUST IN DOLLARS, BUT IN SENSE. THE GOOD SENSE OF THE NRA LEADERSHIP YOU SEE HERE TODAY. YOUR LEADERS ARE QUALIFIED, COMPETENT, UNIFIED, AND BELIEVE ME, FEARLESS.

THIRD, I WANTED TO BRING THE NRA BACK TO THE TABLE OF MAINSTREAM POLITICAL DEBATE, AND WE HAVE. YOU SAW WAYNE ON THAT TAPE. I'D SAY WE'RE NOT JUST AT THE TABLE. WE'RE EATING THEIR LUNCH.

BUT MORE THAN ANYTHING ELSE, I ASKED YOU TO BELIEVE IN EACH OTHER AGAIN. TO BELIEVE THAT GUN OWNERSHIP IS AS WHOLESOME AS IT IS CONSTITUTIONAL. TO BELIEVE THAT AN NRA STICKER ON YOUR WINDSHIELD IS A SIGN OF PRIDE. TO BELIEVE THAT A KID WHO WANTS TO PLINK AT TIN CANS IS NOT A KID GONE WRONG. TO BELIEVE THAT THE GREAT FLAME OF FREEDOM OUR FOUNDING FATHERS IGNITED HAS NOT GROWN COLD.

I DECLARE THAT MISSION ACCOMPLISHED! I LOOK AROUND THIS GREAT HALL AND I SEE THE FIRE IS IN YOUR EYES, THE PRIDE IS IN YOUR HEARTS, AND THE COMMITMENT IS HERE IN YOUR PRESENCE TODAY. THE NRA IS BAAAAAACK.

ALL OF WHICH SPELLS VERY SERIOUS TROUBLE FOR A MAN NAMED GORE.

DID'JA SEE THAT GORE RALLY IN D.C. LAST WEEKEND? ONE OF THE MARCHERS SAID, "THE HANDS THAT ROCK THE CRADLE RULE THIS NATION." AND I THOUGHT, NO MADAM, THE HANDS THAT ROCK THE CRADLE RULE OUR FAMILIES AND GOVERNMENTS AND CORPORATIONS. THE HANDS THAT WROTE THE CONSTITUTION RULE THIS NATION.

ALL THE ANTI-GUN CELEBS CAME OUT TO MARCH. TIPPER GORE WAS THERE, ROSIE O'DONNELL WAS THERE (I LIKE TO CALL HER TOKYO ROSIE). A FINE ACTRESS, SUSAN SARANDON, WAS THERE AND SHOUTED WITH GREAT DIPLOMACY AND STATESWOMANSHIP, "WE MOMS ARE REALLY PISSED OFF!"

I MUST ASK, PISSED OFF ABOUT WHAT? IF IT'S CRIME, WHY AREN'T YOU PISSED OFF AT THE FAILURE OF THIS ADMINISTRATION TO PROSECUTE GUN-TOTING CRIMINALS?

IF IT'S ACCIDENTS, WHY AREN'T YOU PISSED OFF AT SWIMMING POOL OWNERS, OR STAIRWAY OWNERS, OR PICKUP OWNERS?

WHY AREN'T YOU PISSED OFF THAT GUN ACCIDENT PREVENTION PROGRAMS AREN'T IN EVERY ELEMENTARY CLASSROOM IN AMERICA?

AS A MATTER OF FACT, WHY AREN'T YOU PISSED OFF AT PARENTS WHO'RE OBLIVIOUS THAT THEIR KIDS ARE BUILDING BOMBS IN THEIR BEDROOMS?

WHY AREN'T YOU PISSED OFF THAT MR. GORE WANTS REGISTRATION AND LICENSING INSTEAD OF PARENTING AND PROSECUTION?

WHICH LEADS ME TO THAT ONE MISSION LEFT UNDONE: WINNING IN NOVEMBER. THAT'S WHY I'M STAYING ON FOR A THIRD TOUR OF DUTY.

TODAY I CHALLENGE YOU TO FIND YOUR THIRD TERM, AND SERVE IT. FIND YOUR EXTRA MILE, AND WALK IT.

ONLY YOU KNOW WHAT YOU CAN DO BETWEEN NOW AND THAT DECISIVE NOVEMBER DAY TO TURN THE TIDE OF THESE ELECTIONS IN FAVOR OF FREEDOM. I ASK YOU TO FIND IT AND FULFILL IT.

GO THE EXTRA DISTANCE, FIND THAT EXTRA MEMBER, WRITE THE EXTRA CHECK, KNOCK ON ONE MORE DOOR, WORK ONE MORE HOUR, MAKE ONE MORE CALL, CONVINCE ONE MORE FRIEND, TURN THE OTHER CHEEK IF YOU MUST, BUT FIND YOUR THIRD TERM AND SERVE IT.

THAT'S YOUR PART TO PLAY. WHAT MORE IMPORTANT ROLE CAN THERE BE...THAN TO BEQUEATH OUR FREEDOM TO THE NEXT GENERATION AS PURE AND INTACT AS IT WAS GIVEN TO US. AS MR. LINCOLN COMMANDED: "WITH FIRMNESS IN THE RIGHT, AS GOD GIVES US TO SEE THE RIGHT, LET US FINISH THE WORK WE ARE IN...AND THEN WE SHALL SAVE OUR COUNTRY."

EACH OF US IN HIS OWN WAY, PLUS ALL OF US IN OUR COLLECTIVE MILLIONS, MUST GIVE THAT EXTRA MEASURE THAT FREEDOM DEMANDS OF US.

LET ME TELL YOU WHAT I MEAN. UNTIL A FEW HOURS AGO I WAS FINISHING MY 80TH FILM IN VANCOUVER, CANADA. I WAS THERE BECAUSE I LOVE MY CRAFT, AND I LOVE TO FEED MY FAMILY.

SO YOU'LL FORGIVE ME IF I'M A LITTLE TIRED. I FLEW ALL NIGHT, ACROSS A CONTINENT AND THREE TIME ZONES, TO BE HERE WITH YOU. I'M HERE BECAUSE I LOVE MY COUNTRY, AND I LOVE THIS FREEDOM.

BUT IT WAS JUST THE MOST RECENT FLIGHT IN THOUSANDS OF FLIGHTS, THE MOST RECENT MILE ON THOUSANDS OF ROADS I'VE TRAVELLED IN MY TEN YEARS OF ACTIVE SERVICE TO THIS GREAT ASSOCIATION. IT'S BEEN A HELLUVA RIDE.

I REMEMBER A DECADE AGO AT MY FIRST ANNUAL MEETING IN ST. LOUIS. AFTER MY BANQUET REMARKS TO A PACKED HOUSE, THEY PRESENTED ME WITH A VERY SPECIAL GIFT. IT WAS A SPLENDID HAND-CRAFTED MUSKET. I ADMIT I WAS OVERCOME BY THE POWER OF ITS SIMPLE SYMBOLISM. I LOOKED AT THAT MUSKET, AND I THOUGHT OF ALL OF THE LIVES GIVEN FOR THAT FREEDOM. I THOUGHT OF ALL OF THE LIVES SAVED WITH THAT FREEDOM. IT DAWNED ON ME THAT THE DOORWAY TO ALL FREEDOMS IS FRAMED BY MUSKETS.

SO I LIFTED THAT MUSKET OVER MY HEAD FOR ALL TO SEE. AND AS FLASHBULBS POPPED AROUND THE ROOM, MY HEART AND A FEW TEARS SWELLED UP, AND I UTTERED FIVE UNSCRIPTED WORDS. WHEN I DID, THAT ROOM EXPLODED IN SUSTAINED APPLAUSE AND HOOTS AND SHOUTS THAT SEEMED TO LAST FOREVER.

IN THAT MOMENT, I BONDED WITH THIS GREAT ASSOCIATION. AND IN THOUSANDS OF MOMENTS SINCE, I'VE BEEN ASKED TO REPEAT THOSE FIVE WORDS IN AIRPORTS AND HOTELS AND RALLIES AND SPEECHES ACROSS THIS LAND.

IN YOUR OWN WAY, YOU HAVE ALREADY HEARD THEM. THAT'S WHY YOU'RE HERE.

EVERY TIME OUR COUNTRY STANDS IN THE PATH OF DANGER, AN INSTINCT SEEMS TO SUMMON HER FINEST FIRST – THOSE WHO TRULY UNDERSTAND HER. WHEN FREEDOM SHIVERS IN THE COLD SHADOW OF TRUE PERIL, IT'S ALWAYS THE PATRIOTS WHO FIRST HEAR THE CALL. WHEN LOSS OF LIBERTY IS LOOMING, AS IT IS NOW, THE SIREN SOUNDS FIRST IN THE HEARTS OF FREEDOM'S VANGUARD. THE SMOKE IN THE AIR OF OUR CONCORD BRIDGES AND PEARL HARBORS IS ALWAYS SMELLED FIRST BY THE FARMERS, WHO COME FROM THEIR SIMPLE HOMES TO FIND THE FIRE AND FIGHT.

BECAUSE THEY KNOW THAT SACRED STUFF RESIDES IN THAT WOODEN STOCK AND BLUED STEEL, SOMETHING THAT GIVES THE MOST COMMON MAN THE MOST UNCOMMON OF FREEDOMS. WHEN ORDINARY HANDS CAN POSSESS SUCH AN EXTRAORDINARY INSTRUMENT, THAT SYMBOLIZES THE FULL MEASURE OF HUMAN DIGNITY AND LIBERTY.

THAT'S WHY THOSE FIVE WORDS ISSUE AN IRRESISTIBLE CALL TO US ALL, AND WE MUSTER.

SO, AS WE SET OUT THIS YEAR TO DEFEAT THE DIVISIVE FORCES THAT WOULD TAKE FREEDOM AWAY, I WANT TO SAY THOSE WORDS AGAIN FOR EVERYONE WITHIN THE SOUND OF MY VOICE TO HEAR AND TO HEED, AND ESPECIALLY FOR YOU, MR. GORE:

(I LIFTED A MUSKET ABOVE MY HEAD)

FROM MY COLD DEAD HANDS!